MATCHES: A LIGHT BOOK

Praise for *Matches*

"The vision of history illuminating these pages is not the conventional one of progress, but the much more radical one of Rousseauism: a 'left-wing nostalgia' that performs a detour through the past—a world anterior to privilege and hypocrisy—with the aim not of restoring it, but of giving it a radically new form."

—Michael Löwy, *Le Monde diplomatique*

"There are books that have the ability to throw your whole life into question, but these are the terms of engagement.... In the weeks I spent reading *Matches* I was more jittery than usual, my mind constantly reeling. I felt like I was on the edge of something, though I could not tell what that might be. I am always behaving badly, but this was different. I wanted to quarrel, I needed to question everything. Books seemed to be ruining my life.... But I love changing my mind."

—Anna Zalokostas, *Full Stop*

"A truly thorough examination of *Matches: A Light Book* would map all the terrain and take an unusual form: a multi-week course containing lectures, slides, video, theatre, playtime, and interactivity. S.D. Chrostowska is a writer of importance, and with this work she has raised her own personal bar."

—Jeff Bursey, *Numéro Cinq*

"As in the writings of Nietzsche and Adorno, the targets of Chrostowska's illuminating arson are cultural: the art world, publishing, academia, popular media, political economy, and the various phenomena that are the warp and woof of our daily newsfeeds.... At more than 500 pages, Matches is an epic of the little form. Encyclopedic in its range and ambition, it includes nearly every variant on the aphorism attempted since the *Corpus Hippocraticum*. The book puts itself in dialogue with its most important practitioners as well as with today's thinkers."
    —Ryan Ruby, *Lapham's Quarterly*

"*Matches* poses its greatest challenge to academic criticism, demonstrating that intellectually rigorous issues can be addressed in an accessible way without diluting or oversimplifying those issues.... Certainly *Matches* demonstrates that an intelligent, informed critic can use the aphorism and the fragment to explore the most serious and substantive critical and philosophical subjects, providing sufficiently radiant illumination to guide us in our own consideration of these subjects. It is a very rewarding book, read either in sequence and in its entirety or in isolated selections, but...it is less a specific model of what criticism might become in the digital age than simply a challenge to seriously reflect on what Matthew Arnold called 'the function of criticism at the present time.'"
    —Daniel Green, *Los Angeles Review of Books*

Before you start to read this book,
take this moment to think about making a donation to punctum books, an independent non-profit press,

@ http://punctumbooks.com/about/

If you're reading the e-book, you can click on the image below to go directly to our donations site. Any amount, no matter the size, is appreciated and will help us to keep our ship of fools afloat. Contributions from dedicated readers will also help us to keep our commons open and to cultivate new work that can't find a welcoming port elsewhere. Our adventure is not possible without your support.

Vive la Open Access.

Fig. 1. Hieronymus Bosch, *Ship of Fools* (1490-1500)

MATCHES: A LIGHT BOOK
© 2015, 2019 S.D. Chrostowska

This work carries a Creative Commons BY-NC-SA 4.0
International license, which means that you are free to copy and redistribute the material in any medium or format, and you may also remix, transform and build upon the material, as long as you clearly attribute the work to the authors (but not in a way that suggests the authors or punctum endorses you and your work), you do not use this work for commercial gain in any form whatsoever, and that for any remixing and transformation, you distribute your rebuild under the same license.
http://creativecommons.org/licenses/by-nc-sa/4.0/

First edition 2015
Second edition published in 2019 by
punctum books
Earth, Milky Way
http://punctumbooks.com

A number of the pieces in this volume have previously appeared in *The Review of Contemporary Fiction*, *Convolution*, *3:AM*, *BOMB*, and *Off the Books*.

ISBN-13: 978-1-950192-21-2 (print)
ISBN-13: 978-1-950192-22-9 (ePDF)

DOI: 10.21983/P3.251.1.00

LCCN: 2019937768
Library of Congress Cataloging Data is available from the Library of Congress

Cover and interior images:
"Strike," design by Schneck & Zweigbergk, HAY.
With the striking surface moved from the side to the front, "Strike" matchboxes honour the activity of making a flame.
The common matchbox and book have long been used for advertising, including of literature: though rarely, they have borne poems, short fiction, and reproductions of book covers. Putting "Strike" matchboxes on the cover of this book seconds their tribute to flame-making and acknowledges the small and unlikely role matches have played in promoting books.

Cover and book design: Chris Piuma.

MATCHES
A LIGHT BOOK

S.D. CHROSTOWSKA

CONTENTS

xvii **Foreword: Infernal Unity** *by Alexander Kluge*

xxv **Proem**

1 **Book I**

Ethics of Reading · Ethics of Reading ·
Who Spits Farther · Called Literature ·
No Other Gods · Last Words · Burial Site ·
Unembarrassable · Broken Levees ·
The Good, the Bad, and the Beyond ·
Novel Experiments · Stranger than Fiction ·
Prise d'abyme · No Outstanding Work · Outpatients ·
Poetry of Genocide · Art / Barbarism · Under Attack ·
Page from the History of Cultural Warfare ·
Art, Alienation, Extinction · Down and Dirty ·
Scenes of Abduction · Coming Clean ·
Red Is the Colour of Attention · Ur-Colour ·
Art (Theory) Brut · Withdrawing ·
Et remotissima prope · *Marmi finti* ·
Unvarnished · It's Alive! · Virtual Promiscuity ·
This Will Kill That · Return of the Image ·
What Did You Do in the Theatre? ·
The Mask-Produced Spectator; or, Drowning in the Theatre ·
Fatal Attraction · *Pentimenti* · Great Passion ·
Instrument of Instruments · Eupsychian ·
Mirabile scriptu · Genius and Truth ·
The Making Of · Look No Further · Work of Exception ·
Stranger in One's Own Work · Abyss-Gazing ·
Little Pieces · Beasts for Kicks · Cannonball ·
Art Curation · Moratorium I · No Trespassing ·
Rubens in Furs · Fake Fires · Inscrutable Relation ·
Barbarogenesis · Perfect State · Letting Slide ·
Great Art Belonging to Everyone · De-Colonizing Art

Book II

No Outside · Proof (in the Recipe) · Dry Run ·
From the Thinking Hat · A Kind of Illusionism ·
Three Clear Thoughts · Impressions · The Clarity of Clouds ·
Found Ideas · Finish Your Thought! · Think for Yourself… ·
Overheard · Proverbial Philosophy · Robust Arguments ·
Tyranny of Knowledge · Take My Word for It ·
Philosophizing without a Hammer · Settling Ignorance ·
The Umbrella of Unknowing · Professing Ignorance ·
Smarter and Dumber · Can Speak, Will Travel · Mark My Words ·
Almost Being · Don't Imagine… · Think, Pig! ·
Thinking Thinking · New Line of Thought · The Thinking Head ·
Self-Inquisition · Phases of Power · One Leg in Paradise ·
False Analogues · Unconvinced · Humble Pie · Prison Yard ·
A Sublime Mind · Threaded · *Vita contemplativa* · Beheading Games ·
Scattered · Hoping for Queequeg? · Crime Is a Failure of Society ·
The Problem · How Playful! · *Bodenlos* · The Ineffable ·
Perish the Thought · Thinking in Tongues · *Sancta simplicitas* ·
Encyclops · Outline of a Shadow · Chicken Fence · Tripwire ·
Seeing the Light · Seek and Hide · *Merveille du jour* ·
Whose Time Has Not yet Come · On Time · *Punctum* ·
The Time Is Now · Time Out · House Arrest ·
Of "Saints" and "Miracles" of Reason · Furnished Rooms ·
Introspection · Sick · Family Business ·
Central Tenet of Modern Philosophy · Terms of Engagement ·
Notions · Babbling Brook · Not Taken Lightly · Freethinking ·
Casual Philosopher · Sides · Short Spam · *Caecigenus* ·
Pursuit of Ignorance · *Amor vincit?* · No Drinking at the Source ·
Critique as a Virtue · After Critique · Anchors and Switches ·
After Truth · Truth to Go · Gymnosophy · Consolation Prize ·
Modifications · Know Thyself · P4E (Philosophy for Embryos) ·
Peekaboo · Done In? · Brain-Machine · Ghost Machine ·
Sex Life of Tools · Criterion of Truth · The Beauty of Wildlife ·
Extremities · Family of Man · O Humanity! · A Deadly Presence ·
When Autumn Leaves · A Big If · A Mote in a Sunbeam ·
Keyhole · Crowded Fields · Memory Viewed · Fragility of Forgetting ·
Shaking the Tree of Knowledge · Changing Taxonomies ·
Go-Between · Fragments of a Hole · Mosaic · No Philosopher ·
Flypaper · The Flies · Most True · Small Talk · [Untitled]

Book III

The Impossible Handshake · *Verblendungszusammenhang* ·
Politics and Truth-Power · New in States · *Sua cuique persona* ·
What Words Could · Privacy Settings · Snowdown ·
Noisemakers · Sleeper Cells · Private the New Public ·
Letting It All Hang Out · Naming Contest ·
Wanted: Amanuensis · Dictationship · Do As You're Told ·
Intramurale · Daisy Chains · Doing Time · *Habeas corpus* ·
A Tale of Two Bodies · White on Black · Concrete Is Hard ·
Torn-Country Experts · Two-Way Terror ·
Uncanny Valentines · Apocalyptic Anti-Apocalypticism ·
Allegory of Politics · "Murderous Alphabet" · Friendly Fire ·
Rarae aves · The Seeing Eye · The Seven Years' War Again ·
Origin of Revolution · Free Radicals · Nothing Doing ·
Hope Salve · Body Politics · #OtherwiseOccupied ·
"I'm not crying, I've just got some #CUPE3903 in my eye" ·
All Is Not Quiet · Arms · Last Man Dying ·
Customary Hail of Arrows · "In search of weapons and allies" ·
Armed to the Teeth · Made with Pride · Garden of Creativity ·
♫ *Imagine there's...* ♫ · Bromides · So-So · Night Watch ·
Nostalgia for the Middle Class · If the Shoes Fits · Mutual Parodies ·
The Gulf of Inattention · Clay Pigeon · Lying in State ·
Up the Ladder to the Roof · Holes in a Wall · Humility Itself ·
Excellence Clusters · Mottos for Morale · Feminist Taunt ·
Let Me See Your Report Card · Cliché Alert · Touché ·
Lose No Touch · Fetch! Now Roll Over! · Distimacies ·
The End of Sharing? · Mice · Damned to Fame ·
Escaping Criticism · Remember Me! · Writing-Ball ·
Talking Pencil · Doggedly Smart · The Story of Your Life ·
Poor in Spirit, Rich in Irony · Desk Jobs · No Go Stop ·
Subtle Reversal · Pretty Penny; or, Get Rich at All Cost ·
Fruit of Capital · Name Your Price · Make Me an Offer ·
Price of Life · Piss-Poor · American Poverty · Captives ·
Against the Grain · Breaking Even · Loose Change · Poison Ivy ·
Ad coelum et ad nihilum · Nail Soup · Of Wolves and Gatsbies ·
Piggy Bank · Worker Bee ·Tan Lines · The Eyes of the Poor ·
Engels and Marx at Chetham's Library · Bottoms Up! ·
Call out All the Names under the Sun · Soft Landing ·
Uncomfortable Happiness · Sore Spots · [Untitled] · [Untitled]

Book IV

Multitasking · Practically History · *Farniente* · Fingers Crossed · *Mutatio mundi* · Dip Sheep · Heart & Home · What's What · Beggar Thy Neighbour's Culture · Far Away, So Close · Pebbles · Born Idealist · Future Optimists · Future Humblebrag · Priceless · Critical Utopia · Missing Part · All or Nothing · *Paeninsula fortunatorum* · In the Dark · Impossible but Necessary · Great Expectations · Means without End · Getting Horizontal · Resentment · In Bad Company · Family Pet · A Parting Gift · Exuviae · Single-Minded Pursuits · Classified · Double Standards · Arcadius Makes Headlines · Beauty & Death · Hit and Miss · The Average American · Insulation · What You Want Is What You Get · Moratorium II · Rip-Off · Meterocracy · A Wide Selection · Outside the Text · Doubling Standard · The Candid Philosopher · *Colla et labora* · Ghosting Oneself · Publish and Perish? · Everything You Ever Wanted to Know about Nazis but Were Too Lazy to Find Out · Uncontaminated · Wiggle Room; or, the Unhappy Customer · Token of Value · Life of a Writer · Literary Public Execution · Public Service · Vital Injection · Complete Sentences · Essential Killing · Completists · Happy Day · Once a Wolf, Always a Wolf? · On a Roll · Nodding Acquaintance · Black Leather · Counterproductive · Ripple Effect · Sleepless · Almost · At the Concession Stand · Discount on Top · "Friends for Life" · *Amicitia aequalitas* · Safety Deposits · Sexual Root of Kleptomania · *Una harum ultima* · On Edge · Pale as Death · Moored · Angel of Death · *À la chienlit!* · Pierre Tombale · The Origins of Work · Apply Within · Among the Living · No Posthumous Reproach · Wound Man · The Jargon of Inauthenticity · Wild Oats · *Todesliebe* · Between Stiff and Statue · Love & Love-Sickness · *Incipit vita nova* · Not a Peep from You · Sex & Democracy · Making Conversation · Romeos · Scale Models · To Scale · Unrecognized · The Takeaway Point · Reminder: Originals · Confession of a Knife-Swallower · You Can Take the Clown out of the Circus, but You Can't Take the Circus out of the Clown · Cannibal on the Make · Soylent Green · Cities of God · Sand-Glass · The Man in the Street · Thoroughly Unthorough · Rise to the Occasion · Comedown · Iron-y · Choosing Gentleness · The Sacred Heart of Convicts · Misericords

Book V

Better than Nothing · Greek Gift · *Devotio moderna* ·
Overripe · *Hortus conclusus* · Bad Apples ·
Call of the Wild · Speak for Yourself! · Falls the Shadow ·
Campanology · Death Being Our Final Act · Somewhere ·
"Universal Solvent" · Surprised by Death · *Sainte Supplice* ·
"The moral earth, too, is round!" · A Whole in a Mole ·
In saecula saeculorum · *Sola* · Skill Rewarded · Blunt Euphemism ·
At the Limit: A Medley · A Fate Worse than Fate · In the Oratory ·
Taken for a Ride · *Laudator temporis acti* · Wish Experience ·
Courage and Its Crop · Save the Date · Pied Pipers · Hitler Today ·
The True Believer · Uncannied · Departures · Dead Heroes ·
Heroes and Saints · Church Grotesque · Praying That They Last ·
Changing of the Guard · Repetition · Excuses, Excuses ·
History of Survival · What the Future Withholds ·
Event List · Digging Up the Past · Historian as Folk-Hero ·
Lower Down & Around the Corner · Blast from the Past ·
Romancing the Past · Gnomes · Ante-Bellum ·
Our Hour of Need · Standing Room Only · *Profanum* ·
Sticks and Stones · All of a Heap · Ends · Time Travel ·
World History 101 · A Healthy Stool? · *Puer perennis* ·
Spot the Difference · The Eyes of History · For Want of a Nail ·
Cannon-Fodder · Our Towton · About Time · Make It Count ·
Old Debts · The World Republic of Ends? · Godsend · Eat Me! ·
I'm Not Playing · Material Cultures · Consignment Shop · Inside Job ·
From the Gift Shop · "The younger, the more clear-sighted" ·
Where Do We Stand? · Shared Horizon · Myth of Modernity ·
Futurity by the Stars · Clarification of Time · Fidgety Sitters ·
Bespeculations · Faster! Faster! · You Can Say That Again ·
Prospecting · *Salve!* · So Long! · Unrecognized Twin ·
Nostalgic Appreciation · Faulty History · *Le Temps perdu* ·
Levelling with Time · *Zerkalo* · Tired Question · The Mark of Kings ·
Out of Torn Cloth · Thieves in the Night · World History in Reverse ·
Whiplash · Latecomers · Bidding Is Now Closed ·
Sapiens sapiens, or *Nil admirari* · *Viva voce* · Lost & Found ·
God Might be the Word, but the Devil Is Still the Tongue ·
Return of Desire · Attention! · *Nihil obstat* · *Carpe noctem* ·
Thick Skin · *Circulus donationis* · Take It Back · Do Not Open ·
Why I Made Fun of Holy Water · God Question ·
Comparing "Apples" · Default Inheritance · Disputed Inheritance

Paralipomena

The Cunning of Folly · Running with It · Hikers and Runners ·
Crooked Timber · Facing Out · Portraits · Browbeaten ·
Life of Zilch · Spilling Your Beans · Making up Lives ·
Literary Effects · Working with Dreams · Fast Asleep ·
Dug Up · Law of Transformation · Quantity over Quality ·
Taking In, Letting Go · What Are the Chances? ·
Unbound… · Out of Print · "A Book"? · Moratorium III ·
Before You Put Pen to Paper · Lapidary · An Aphorism ·
"Uncombed Thoughts" · Held to Account · Juggling ·
More Is Less? · Chain Reaction · Culture Vultures ·
Culture Vultures · Hypocritics · A Common Cause ·
The Democratic Challenge · Free Ride · Not to Be Outdone ·
Invisible Tree · Late Spring, Late Summer · No Qualms ·
Got a Light? · Obscurantism · Misfired Insult ·
The Cynic's Matchbox (That's the Spirit!) · Illuminosity ·
Light Touch · Seeing Darkness · Safety Matches ·
Matches to Ashes · Book Advertising · Little A ·
Long Distance · Legacy of Modernism · First Things First ·
Correspondence · Writing For · Dead Letters ·
Envelope Stuffing · Diminishing Returns · Dashed Off ·
Other People's Mail · News of Oneself · True Taste ·
Soho! · At the Stalls · Why I'm Not a Book Addict ·
What Are Shelves For · Will-o'-the-Wisp ·
"I am loath even to have thoughts I cannot publish" ·
Grasping Criticism · Mushy Criticism ·
Criticism as Self-Examination · Murine Criticism ·
The Draft · Around the Block · Keeping Up with the Joneses ·
On the Rails · Zoning In · The Easygoing Work ·
The Easy Part · *Succès d'estime* · Double-Check ·
Out Like a Light · Bridge of Boats · The Author's Two Bodies ·
Inside the Tomb · "Come, my cold and stiff companion!" ·
Safer Bet · Leaving One's Mark · Literary Sensation ·
High and Low · Castoffs · Claqueurs · No-Power ·
Public Intellectual · Following Leaders · Leading Motives ·
Easy Pickings (A Lamb Is a Lamb) · Decoration ·
Common, senses of · Madness in Literature · Ouroborous ·
In the Tower · Experimentalism · Paradoxes of Experimentalism ·
Tapped Potential · Magpies · Error Spotters · Scribes ·
Inkhorn · Wordsmith · Feathers · Coincidence of Invention ·
Philobiblon · Arks Out · Jazz Funeral · Fans · Copycats ·
Non-Potable · Seniority · "My Undertaking" ·
A Nagging Burden · Loose Moorings · *Credo* ·
The Burning Book · Out of Reach · Endings

FOREWORD
INFERNAL UNITY

Alexander Kluge

In spitzen Klammern
die verbrannten Wörter

In pointed brackets
The burned words
—Heiner Müller, "Mommsen's Block"

In a letter from August 2, 1935, written in Hornberg, in the Black Forest, and sent to Walter Benjamin, then living in Paris, Theodor W. Adorno makes a series of remarks on a line by Michelet, "Every epoch dreams the one that follows it." These remarks are part of a complex designated by the keywords: prehistory of the nineteenth century; dialectical image; myth and modernity.

The fetish character of merchandise is not a fact of consciousness, writes Adorno. Rather, it is *dialectical,* in the crucial sense of producing consciousness. That is, consciousness or the unconscious cannot simply reproduce this fetish character as a dream. On the contrary, consciousness or the unconscious disintegrates vis-à-vis commodity fetishism into desire and anxiety—without, however, ever becoming a new whole. In this sense, Adorno argues, immanent consciousness is itself "a constellation of the real," "just as if it were the astronomical phase in which hell moves among mankind. Only the star-chart of such wanderings could, it seems to me, open a perspective on history as prehistory." Not only can entire epochs not dream those that follow them, since epochs as a whole probably cannot dream, but individual consciousness or the individual unconscious, which is perfectly capable of dreaming, cannot, through such dreaming, realize or animate dialectical constructions. The dream, then, to the degree that consciousness is capable of catching it, does not extend into the lurid current of history's flow, where it too would be torn and destroyed.

Adorno speaks also in this context of the dialectical image's "objective power of the keys,"[*] instead of a subjective-objective power. He moreover stresses the obverse of the utopian dialectical image of the nineteenth century as *hell*. There is nothing that possesses the "power of the keys" to access utopia that is not at the same time capable of unlocking hell…

It is this Adornian conception that comes through in *Matches*—a title evoking the conflict between ideas and the intensity of their confrontation. But such a book is not, for all that, a battlefield delivered over to chaos; the troops remain in formation at their post: aphorisms, *pensées*, epigrams, fictional dialogues, apologues, short essays, ordered in six parts: aesthetics and literature; philosophy, science, and technology; politics; society; history, ethics, and religion; literary culture, the writer's vocation, and method. Undergirding the project is an encyclopedic ambition—a subjective encyclopedia, to be sure, pretending in no way to be exhaustive. It is more a question of highlighting elements essential for understanding our historical moment, which are grasped in their contradictory, conflictual, differential, as well as complementary relationships. The result is a complex that wears its solid erudition lightly, one that puts particular emphasis on thinkers exemplifying the genre of the aphorism, such as Gracián, Chamfort, Lichtenberg, Nietzsche, or Jünger. Despite sorting its fragments into several books, *Matches* is an idiosyncratic universe, open and multiform, without an overarching principle. A "constellation of the

---

[*] Theological notion expressing the apostolic power to bind or loose sins.—Trans.

real," to borrow Adorno's expression, and pervaded by its "infernal unity."

Among the book's thematic nuclei one can mention the relationships between humans, animals, and machines; work, class relations and inequalities; truth and survival; the vagaries of creativity; the uncanny encounters between art and barbarism. Most important, however, is the idea of history understood not as progress but as a narrative thread kept taut by nostalgic longing and utopian expectations — stretched between, on the one hand, the resources of freedom and happiness lived in the past, and, on the other hand, the dream of building a better world, upon the ashes of mounting catastrophe.

To take up the words of Miguel Abensour, "Man is a utopian animal," and, as Ernst Bloch wrote in *The Principle of Hope,* "There is the spirit of utopia in the final predicate of every great statement." This implicit aspiration to something that has not yet come is everywhere joined in *Matches* to an explicit exercise of the critical faculty. One way to read the collection is as a kind of humanist manifesto calling on us to transform raw information into knowledge and communicable experience. The content here corresponds completely to the form: contemporary subjectivity, on account of its incredible fragmentation, can only be criticized and gathered up in fragmentary form.

Far from being dogmatic and prescriptive, *Matches* asks us not to renounce the commitment to thinking in a reality that threatens to overwhelm reason at any moment and to radically reduce the range of human feeling and sensation. Every page offers the reader an opportunity to interrogate and bring to light their own personal experience. In a style that is at once dense and incisive yet not without humour and irony, the author's observations describe the contours of the world not just as it is, but above all as it should not be. It is thinking that resists the disjointedness of the world; thinking that tries to establish internal resonances where being and things continually fall apart and drift away from one another, despite their confinement on the same earthly vessel. This thinking is itself necessarily composed of fragments of protest and resistance sharp like the shards of glass.

It is owing to these aspects that the French translation of *Matches* took its place alongside other fragmentary philosophical works — for example, *The Heritage of Our Times* by Ernst Bloch and *Dämmerung: Notizen in Deutschland* (Twilight: Notes from Germany) by Max Horkheimer — in the series "Critique de la politique."* Since 1974, the series has prized unconventional voices and positions, and its editor, the late Miguel Abensour (1939–2017), went out of his way to include prose transcending academic specialization. This was prose from elsewhere, offered in translation, that could count on the hospitality of French intellectuals. In this respect, Chrostowska's book is situated on the margins of contemporary theoretical and critical writing in the Anglophone world, both inside and outside of the academy. The *negative dialectics* of Adorno — to always advance toward the limits of knowledge — is here coupled with the *negative capability* described by John Keats, which consists in letting go of the persistent search for the reason of things. When exercising the power of a critic as well as that of a creator, we are bound for uncertainty and destined to fail in taming truth. If we nonetheless pursue it beyond the established order and our own theoretical capacities and into the wilderness of art, in its ever-renewed world, it is thanks to a *daimon* that does not tell us what to do, or what to say, but that preserves us from error. The periodic renewal of fragmentary forms — like of utopias — belongs to epochs in search of a higher unity beyond apparent complexities; to times of agitation apt to scramble the moral and political compass and to focalize critical commentary on crisis.

The publication of a 500-page book of fragments in the United States has every right to baffle some. After all, are there not already enough fragments all around us: in books

---

* Reference is to the book series formerly at Payot-Rivages, now at Klincksieck, edited until 2017 by Miguel Abensour. This preface first appeared in the French translation of *Matches*. — Trans.

that will never be read again cover to cover or in mildly amusing messages posted on social media in seemingly limitless quantities? Settling for the dispersal that affects digital archives, which are increasingly accessed at random and without any context, or for the ephemerality of what is written on the spur of the moment and on the fly, inevitably severs the ties to the critical mind in action, distinguished by its demanding nature, passion, and imagination — qualities without which the intellectual world threatens to disintegrate.

The imagination is a skittish animal. But just as a skittish horse can be brought to attack, to rush ahead, and charges forward so spontaneously that no rider can hold back the animal's mass (and, a-squat atop the horse, he has to work hard not to get bucked off), so the imagination flies towards all the mountains of reality and storms its walls with its ladders and bundles of fire, as Theodor Fontane described it. No, the imagination is not fit for a system like Wikipedia. It does not care much for coherence, context, and facts. It is a *political animal* and falls upon the world like a swarm.

It also possesses innumerable sources, including subterranean ones, sparse and barren; its fountains spring forth destroying everything in their vicinity. According to Adorno, the most important factory of the imagination is sorrow. The imagination is born of an injury denied by fantasies. I have to disagree with him. I know of fantasies set in motion by luxury and elation. They compete with those that serve self-defence. The main thing is to pass through the "infernal unity" of the world, through this bad totality, to arrive at the threshold from which the horizon of the future can be glimpsed.

I suppose, Sirs, that you are so glutted with this banquet of various literary dishes that the food you eat continues to rise. Indeed ye sit crammed with dainties, for many have served up to you a mixed feast of precious and varied discourse and persuade you to look with contempt on ordinary fare. What shall I do now? Shall I allow what I had prepared to lie uneaten and spoil, or shall I expose it in the middle of the market for sale to retail dealers at any price it will fetch? Who in that case will want any part of my wares or who would give twopence for my writings, unless his ears were stopped up?
 —Agathias, 6th century C.E.

*Why offer them a whole? They'll just fragment
It anyway, the public always do.*
 —Director to Poet, Goethe, *Faust*, Part I, 1798

I have seen it with my own eyes: natures that are gifted, rich, and disposed to be free, already "ruined by reading" in their thirties, just matches that have to be struck to emit sparks— "thoughts."
 —Nietzsche, *Ecce Homo*, 1888

PROEM

I had a vision of a book that shed light. A torch book to light my way. A comet book, its luminous tail to leave a trace for me. Its brightness so intense that closing it submerged whoever broke it open in deeper darkness than before. I fancied a kind of sempiternal flame that shot up again as one resumed where one had left off.

It seemed to me there are two basic kinds of book, differing in radiance. One in which the words, erect, line up in columns and salute from every page, and another with words laid down in rows, looking up from their cots, sometimes wide, most only half, awake. The words are matches; those that strike ignite. From time to time, light sweeps across the page like wildfire. But most times, as with damp equipment, nothing so spectacular can be expected.

The match: little stick tipped with combustible stuff, sparked by friction; typically comes in a book or a box or a bundle (the point being: never alone). The highly portable match lighting more or less when required was a great nineteenth-century innovation. Before, we had only Danger and Poison matches, and countless match-induced accidents and suicides.

We still have not engineered mischief out of the match. One little lucifer, God's little helper, lit in the company of its sisters and brothers will, if we let them, afford us a miniature inferno. Are we responsible for the recklessness of thought? There will always be match tricks to go very wrong. How many times have we amused ourselves in the schoolyard, lighting up the whole passel of ideas within our reach, getting us in trouble? And now that we are older, we can strike anywhere. We count on sparks to leap long distances virtually, to pass most swiftly from point to point instead of smouldering. No sooner do we bring a flame to something flammable than it spreads—even as its conductors are already charring and curling up. Let us congratulate ourselves for remaking the transport of ideas. And for this new refrain: *What matters is what's on fire.*

Lumenophiles! These are fragile thoughts. Be gentle with them. In a drafty space they might need your sheltering hand. Your sighs will extinguish them. Blow instead, blow hard, on the embers they leave behind. And never forget what they are: a little "gift" our ancestors received in curiosity and paid dearly for (being no match for a certain black "box"): evil and misery spilled out and flooded us. In that pagan tale, too, we reached for divine light and brought down darkness in its wake.

From this living tragicomedy we conclude that the mind was meant to be set ablaze, though not necessarily to survive the heat. Who will keep the ash-heaps of history raked and illuminated? Burn we must with desire to outmatch what consumes us, burning questions and objections. But what will come of our burnt offerings, our victory torches, our combustions and electrifications, we never know in advance. In hindsight much light was wasted, and much evil never did bring forth any good. So let's also not fetishize the tools of light—these "matches" in a book or a box. The burnt-out match looks so uncannily human, and wise to this resemblance.

Incorrigible pyrotechnicians! It won't be all fireworks! Which one of you doesn't utter a cliché now and again, if only for reassurance at a particularly *obscure spot* concerning the existence of common sense? The platitude, that ever-reliable native intelligence that so often, apparently by chance, opens the darkroom door just when bold new thoughts are developing and ruins everything! I am sure I backed away from many such cheerless corners worried by what crud of shabby, light-shy eccentricity I might find there—proceeding rather by analogies, muddled circumlocutions, and yes, by *common-places*.

Now you know, and in your leniency will observe how little customary it is for platitudes, the smoke of opinion, to be keeping such otherwise lustrous company. This is their big moment to stand out and fall flat (as they must). And *your* opportunity to take note of them, perhaps even own up to some *nodding weakness.* So stay sharp, order a wake-up call if need be. Any banality you come across promise to strike against the sole of your shoe, and, with a cool head, stomp out its sooty flicker.

Above all, harbour no illusions about instant illumination. But perhaps you hope to warm yourself a little...Then you have not understood Andersen's wise tale. Either that or you haven't read it. Ideas, visions alone won't keep you warm; it's what you do with them. Have you ever in your life seen a bonfire of matches? Then you should know they were made neither to raise temperatures nor to dazzle. What's this I hear about obsolescence? You don't know what to do? A virtual flame is not hazard-free; how much truer is this of a real one! But safety talk would be out of place here. You'll learn by playing how best to play.

Allumette, gentille allumette,
Allumette, je te gratterai.
Je te gratterai la tête.
Je te gratterai la tête.
Et la tête! Et la tête!

In any event, your expectations need scaling down. There isn't all that much to be done with matches. On the bright side, you still have your choice of "effect": lighting them as needed, one at a time, or seeing them go up in smoke, all in one go. Now ask me about the advantages to each approach...Why, that is just the moral of The Hothead and the Slow Burn (an ultramodern fable you are forgiven for not knowing). Which of the two is you?

I made this book of matches for the cold-stiff and the light-poor, with their survival at heart. Can they keep the fire going in their bellies, assuming they lit one? Without it, they won't last the night. Should my matchbook, however, fall into the hands of hot-blooded pyromaniacs who, having gone through it and finding it "light," cast it empty into the furnace of their mind, then I will fan the flames myself. What better honour than to be eaten by a brighter blaze, turn fuel for that afflatus of genius, meanwhile discreetly eliminating its stench?

You may have already guessed that putting together such a book required no small ingenuity on the part of one who is no match-maker by trade. What do I know about mixing phosphorus or sulphur with whatever else goes into the head of a match? Never mind the effort, not entirely successful, to leave familiar thoughts and places, where one's ideas fall short or turn out to be squibs. Habits took offence, reasons had to be improvised, so too credible excuses. But off one went. And here one is: whittling then dabbing the serviceable sticks with stuff pulled from elsewhere, doing this from sunup till sundown, into night as deep as before there was light.

A mountain retreat is only as good as the view, *particularly* at dusk. Can one really see better from here? Does better mean *more*, or *less*? Does it mean *farther*, or *closer*? Is it observing the mist hanging about me, or seeing through the mist? Is it watching the dance of a flame, or staring into it, at what feeds it? Is it *looking in*, or *looking out*?

Of one thing there is no doubt: it is no more looking *up* than looking *down*. Though I refuse to insert myself into it — and what would be the point? — I have gathered a thing or two about life in the valley. Its sounds after all reach me constantly: motors starting up, kids let out of school, weekend revels, amplified sermons, the crackle of fireworks, and, not to discriminate, the lowing of cattle, the chirping and squawking in the trees...I see nothing of it beneath me. I only have eyes for what stretches on before me. Above all, I hate being the tourist. So I stay here, and regard best what I see worst — what I view absently and without consideration.

above São Pedro da Serra, Brasil
April 2014

1

⑤ Ethics of Reading

which does not mean goodness comes bundled with books

Ethical reading requires effort, which is good preparation for goodness. A morally safe book is merely a resource that, though it be with you at all times, is hopelessly ineffective as a means of defence against evil. And when you look within your heart, hopefully it is not to copy *it*.

⑤ Ethics of Reading

which does not mean certain books should be put down for your own good

Even immoral books do not corrupt on their own. It takes deep engagement and susceptibility to be spoiled by what you read. Treat morally dubious reading as an ethical contest, with the text as facilitator of a challenge (and not to be confused with your real opponent, yourself).

If you want to hold a book to ethical account, start with yourself, then move on to its author. The text should be last in line, after either you or its author had failed to make a bad impression. Its comparative faults, if it has them, will then stand out.

§ Who Spits Farther

The cult of the artist by the artist is still alive and well, now perhaps more than ever before. The arena is crowded, there can be few victors. And this is what makes artist communities without mediocrities a veritable pipe dream, even when dreamt by the great and prodigious. In a spitting contest there is only talk of technique, but true talent, individual style or vision, is not shareable. And "why should one artist grasp another?"* It won't help either of them get ahead. For one artist to be grasped by another artist signifies artistic failure. For an artist to be grasped by everyone else—artistic success.

§ Called Literature

> *This persistent naming...we call literature.*
> —Paul De Man†

The odyssey of naming, which took us from speech to writing between the Scylla and Charybdis of the encyclopedia and the novel to Literature and then the logosphere, is at an end. Why? Just because! Things heated up, literature was brought to a boil, to a *word reduction*. It no longer rears its head in any discursive domain that claims demystifying powers. It is now part of the cold soup we drink daily, preferring not to know the ingredients.

---

* Karl Kraus, *Half-Truths and One-and-a-Half Truths: Selected Aphorisms*, trans. Harry Zohn (Chicago: University of Chicago Press, 1990), 52.

† Paul De Man, "Criticism and Crisis," in *Blindness and Insight: Essays in the Rhetoric of Contemporary Criticism* (Minneapolis: University of Minnesota Press, 1986), 18.

Ᶎ No Other Gods

Now that you have lost your faith in Literature — it does nothing for your *amour propre* these days — you can believe in writing.

I deliberately did not say "keep your belief" in writing, or "continue to believe" in it, because your devotion to Literature pretty well precluded it. And this "new" belief is not so new either — if that is any succor. Replaced by faith in Literature some generations back, it too had once demanded exclusivity.

Ᶎ Last Words

It is a writer and not the Author who will have the last word.

Ᶎ Burial Site

You can keep writing books to keep up appearances if it makes life easier. But remember that you're making things harder for others. For instance, future archaeologists, who may conclude from the literary remains with which you were buried that, as late as the beginning of the twenty-first century, there was still something called Literature.

§ Unembarrassable

So far we've had it backwards; authors represent their works, not works their authors. Forget a book embarrassing its author; these days writers are unembarrassable. They grow thick skin telling themselves they'll do better next time, and develop calluses to turn all the more nimbly on their heel away from "bad" readers.

Books have no will; to order them not to embarrass us writers would be lunacy. The onus was, then, traditionally on authors to heed the commandment *Do not write books that would embarrass you*. But now all worry about bad judgment has been laid to rest by the "tropical climate" of publishing. Nothing written for the public can come back to haunt us. Everything can be recast as a warmup exercise.

With the new climate, however, comes a new responsibility. Now that opportunities for authors to pronounce on their work have grown out of all proportion, writers should be careful not to embarrass their own productions. Much like parents—who does not cringe at the memory?—should not embarrass their adolescent children (still treated like personal property) just when these are at their most original, most *embarrassable*. As we writers grow old, barren and loquacious, and the gap between us and our children widens, our works *burn with shame*.

§ Broken Levees

> *We do not reject the offer, but we do not accept it.*
> —Ukrainian opposition in reply to Yanukhovich's offer to share power in January 2014[*]

Given the deluge of new manuscripts to all the presses that cannot afford better levees, the wise author reads a publisher's silence as an invitation to revise. When eventually the manuscript is again submitted, it is to another press.

There is nothing like being ignored to get under the skin of the truly dedicated. Form rejection letters should be abandoned; not only do they drain the press of resources in this cash-strapped age, they also rile the blood, focus resentment, and trigger juvenile behaviour best not discussed. They offer easy external targets of blame, when a harder, internal one would serve our interests far more. There is no denying that they damage the psyche of writers, who worship *per definitionem* at the altar of their own uniqueness. For that reason, the value for dedicated writers of a sensitive personalized letter cannot be disputed. It is to be cherished unconditionally and framed. But for those talents who have not honed their skills enough to merit one, nor have the sureness or ambition to keep on with one eye on the pile of snappy turn-downs, silence is most beneficial where acceptance is not forthcoming. They fill this silence with questions: *Who am I writing for? What am I good for? Shall I change how I do things? Should I keep at it?* Where a rejection slip would have bruised and provoked expletives about the intelligence of publishers and readers, silence inspires reflection. Where an explicit, unadorned NO would have led to hang-ups and stagnation, silence is not just easier on the writer's fragile ego; it allows it to grow.

---

[*] David M. Herszenhorn, "Opposition Says No to Ukraine on Power Share," *New York Times*, Jan. 25, 2014, http://www.nytimes.com/2014/01/26/world/europe/ukrainian-president-offers-top-posts-to-opposition-leaders.html.

§ The Good, the Bad, and the Beyond

> *The beauty of the new fragmented novel is that writers can have it both ways. These books pay deference to complexity, that deity of the lit critic, but they are also marked by an intense devotion to plot, pacing and other elements of traditional craft. Highbrow and lowbrow elements are pleasingly blurred. Experimentation proves that it is compatible with accessibility. I am attracted to these books — and I suspect others are as well — because of their skill in serving such conflicting masters, and without obvious compromises.*
> —Ted Gioia[*]

Those moved to evaluate aesthetic objects on ethical grounds very quickly realize that nothing is simply "*good*" or "*bad*" (and not just because it is made so solely by thinking). The introduction of *additional* categories attests to our acuity and discernment. Let us take *novels* as our example, for there can always be found a critic who follows the stocks of tradition yet does not fail to invest in the new and comely. We must straightaway mark the *good* "*bad*" novel for special distinction: successfully revolutionary, unsettling bourgeois prescriptions for success and mainstream values. Conversely, there is the *bad* "*good*" kind: oh-so bourgeois, promoting and reinforcing mainstream literary values. And who cannot name at least one *good* "*good*" novel, that badly bourgeois work surrendering to and failing even by the standards it follows? It still deserves consideration, if only for honestly trying. But as its author, do not expect a shortlist anywhere; the two positives, *good* and *good*, make a very strong positive *in our assessment* because such books represent the dismal failure to guard these tired standards. And finally (if such hair-splitting can have an end) there is the *bad* "*bad*" novel: failed, still however creditable for trying to be revolutionary;

---

[*] Ted Gioia, "The Rise of the Fragmented Novel (An Essay in 26 Fragments)," *Fractious Fiction*, July 17, 2013, http://fractiousfiction.com/rise_of_the_fragmented_novel.

in this case the two negatives, *bad* and *bad*, also make a positive, however weak, for there is much to recommend the work, even if in the end it confirms the strength of the bourgeois grip on art. These labels we have proposed can be reversed to reflect the opposite bias. Thus, the *good "bad"* can be called *bad "good,"* or simply *bad bad*; the *bad "good"* easily turns into *good "bad,"* or *good good*, and so on. (If any of this is at all confusing, you may first need to sort out your loyalties.)

But we are not yet through. There is additionally the question of degree, and some books merit a stronger response. The *worst* ones, those beyond *good* and *bad* (or *"good"* and *"bad"*), are those that betray both "sides"—for and against revolution, or for and against the status quo. These productions are exposed for trying to "serve two masters" by claiming to be revolutionary while beneath their unconventionality buying into bourgeois literary codes and conventions of thought and feeling. They are unfaithful sell-outs. The terrible failure of this *worst* of books is that both sides would claim it, were it "true," but under the circumstances neither wants anything to do with it. It follows that the most terrific success, and the *best* book of all, beyond the categories *good* and *bad* (or *"good"* and *"bad"*) and their pileups, is one the two "masters" are prepared to fight over, each claiming to be the rightful one, without ever doubting the fidelity of what they are fighting over. As such, this *best* work is the likeliest to be torn to shreds—not by rabid criticism but the most rapturous adoration.

∫ Novel Experiments

> *I thought of this project as a kind of experiment in realistic prose. How far is it possible to go into detail before the novel cracks and becomes unreadable?*
> —Karl Ove Knausgård,
>   author of *Min Kamp* (*My Struggle*)[*]

He forgot to add: *banal* detail. Detail as such will never crack the novel. And if he had thought it through beforehand, rather than rationalized what he'd done, he would have known that *nothing is unreadable*, least of all the banal. Nothing is so "unreadable" that it will not find its literate defenders.

Such experiments have been performed before without begging the writer's apologetic elucidations. Critics today need to feel the writer had reason for what they did, reason to innovate, reason to be daring. Writers, for their part, are only too happy to oblige. Innovation is after all so important, and no one can say in advance and with authority what is really new. And daring counts for so much more in a risk-averse society. Critics are easily impressed by innovation and daring amidst mountains of pap. When they buy the reason, the creative intent, and see the work as new and/or bold, they can be persuaded to like everything about it. If, however, they are not, the public will be up in arms, and that will be the end of them—these posturing *criticasters*!

---

[*] Karl Ove Knausgaard, interview by Trevor Laurence Jockims, *Bookforum*, June 24, 2013, http://www.bookforum.com/interview/11771.

❡ Stranger than Fiction

There are ideas born of a powerless but overexcited brain solely to fill the emptiness of melancholy. Something nearly always comes of these improbable schemes—a fact that appears stranger than fiction, if we remember that in fiction the improbable is presented as fact.

❡ *Prise d'abyme*

When we remark reprovingly "So-and-so acts like a character in a novel," we are essentially saying we prefer their imagination *contained*. The *mise en abyme* of fiction can be as infinite as they come, but turned outwards it becomes a vacuum that threatens to swallow whatever is left of "reality."

∫ No Outstanding Work

nulle œuvre en suspens

qu'ils ne souffrent pas et que je souffre, non pas seulement dans l'esprit, mais dans la chair et dans mon âme de tous les jours

(that they do not suffer and that I do, not only in my mind, but in my flesh, and in my everyday soul)
—Antonin Artaud to Jacques Rivière (1924)*

Do I, the young poet asked the editor of the *Nouvelle Revue Française*, have the right to think (*le droit de continuer à penser*), *the right to speak*? The work he had sent in was not the result of inspiration but of spiritual jolts (*saccades*) that tear the words to shreds (*lambeaux*). Salvaged from the void, wrenched from chaos and composed in this ruined state as best he could, primitive to the extreme. *Et cependant je ne suis pas bête*, and yet I am not dumb, not beastly. He demurs: you are judging my work by today's standards; judge me instead by those that are absolute (*du point de vue de l'absolu*). What is art other than this wresting of a soul from the absolute darkness that reigns in man's breast, man's skull; what standards *other than absolute ones* can be brought to this human art without doing to it a civilized form of violence?

Rivière is, understandably, fascinated. He gradually comes around to seeing this writer, who has no work on him he hasn't shared, no work on standby, as an exception to the droves of poets who have always, on a backburner, some uninspired something or other, fanning the flames of their mind instead of putting them out. He reads Artaud's

---

* For the first fragment, the full sentence reads: "Voilà encore pourquoi je vous ai dit que je n'avais rien, *nulle œuvre en suspens*, les quelques choses que je vous ai présentées constituant les lambeaux que j'ai pu regagner sur le néant complet." Antonin Artaud, *L'Ombilic des limbes* (Paris: Gallimard, 1968), 21. Subsequent references are to pp. 19–47, with all quoted text (original French and translation) of the Artaud–Rivière correspondence rendered in italics.

difference from the *phenomenon of the age* as it asks to be read: as a true illness (*une véritable maladie*) and, as such, a sign of *authenticity*, touching *the essence of being, the very cry of life*. Artaud's near-indifference to the *literary plane*, to *literature properly speaking* (that weak, self-obsessed *phénomène d'époque*) guarantees his sanity and literary sainthood. Having thus gone *below to gaze at the underside of art*, at his correspondent's *deep and private misery*, Rivière comes up not with a better appreciation of Artaud, but with Artaud-as-principle: *One must be no longer able to move, to believe, in order to perceive*. The source of timeless art is utter desiccation. Absolute judgment is cruel only to those who do not suffer.

§ Outpatients

> *Today's literature: prescriptions written by patients.*
> —Karl Kraus (first half of the 20th century)[*]

The writer of yesteryear was the kind of patient clever enough to self-medicate and not listen to doctors' orders. Today, those same doctors, who go by the name of critics, save him from hospitalization. He is good as long as he takes his medicine, which he can only get as an outpatient. He takes what they give him; he writes what they tell him to. But this prescription-writing must not be confused with a *cure*. It merely ensures his survival.

---

[*] Kraus, *Half-Truths*, 53.

⸹ Poetry of Genocide

in response to:

> Let us not console ourselves with the thought that these were unsophisticated Africans, without the mental capacity to know better: in short, mere savages. Again, I do not know how much Hatzfeld has edited their words, but his perpetrator interlocutors seem to me more articulate than most of the people with whom I have had to deal in Britain as patients over the last decade and a half. Indeed, their language occasionally becomes poetic: though poetic language in this circumstance is mere euphemism.
>
> Besides, the few comments of the survivors, mostly women, that Hatzfeld inserts into the text, are of considerable moral and intellectual sophistication, and certainly not those of unreflecting primitives with few powers of cerebration.
>
> —Theodore Dalrymple, "On Evil"[*]

Euphemistic language is here openly deployed to describe — what? The speech of the perpetrators of the Rwandan genocide. It compares favourably for Dalrymple with British psychiatric and prison patients, a flattering reference group *eo ipso*, which is to say beneath contempt. These machete-wielding butchers are *not* primitives, an assurance aimed at the presupposition that evil is stupid, and African evil so stupid it practically babbles. These savages are not just outspoken, articulate; they have the makings of poets. The choice of euphemism seems deliberate: *poetry, poetic language*. Before we know it, it is withdrawn.

Given the context, almost any word other than *poetic* would seem less incongruous. Is it ironic, this gratuitous comparison? Is it provocation by allusion? So there *is* poetry fresh after a genocide?

---

[*] Theodore Dalrymple, "On Evil," *New English Review*, Jan. 2007, http://www.newenglishreview.org/Theodore_Dalrymple/On_Evil/

The more distant the event, the more it lends itself to the poetics of events, to aestheticization and romanticization, provided we like our art morally neutral. Witness the willing artistic cooperation of Suharto's henchmen in the inimitable *Act of Killing* (2013), a filmic reenactment of forgotten crimes. To call that poetry would likewise be euphemistic. Yet we cannot call it anything else. We have been seduced. It is always so with beauty's pact with evil.

§ Art / Barbarism

> *Unfortunately, I have a bad feeling that a huge and horrible crime happened, and the masterpieces were destroyed. If so, it would be a barbarian crime against humanity.*
> —Ernest Oberländer-Târnoveanu,
>   director of Romania's National History Museum,
>   on the incineration of seven masterpieces stolen
>   in 2012 from the Rotterdam Kunsthal

A mother's love burns brightest when the fuel is artifice, plastic slippers, and firewood. Art's demise revealed the truth and power of the human heart. *Veritas, victoria, vita!*

The museum, the village, the abandoned house, the churchyard, finally the stove. Ash. Between the theft, the son's arrest, the mother's actions, and the art world itself (fearing the worst), the works were everything: a fortune, incriminating evidence, an irreparable loss. To the rest of us it was a crying shame. Before the lab's findings sank in, the works were missed, their worth contained by the smouldering hope of their recovery, the story still too bizarre to be believed (especially after the mother's retraction of the crucial part of it). After they were announced, the works became priceless, and their immolation, indefensible, beyond the pale. Here there is no why. We are survivors, bearing the burden of incomprehension. Incomprehension not of the human spirit, for the mother's act was as mindless as the can of worms it opened.

Nor was it a crucible of love—that mother was no art lover! It involved no test, no inner conflict of values, one love against another fighting in a breast, with a mother's love finally getting the better of the universal love of beauty.

Burn the evidence! was the obvious thing to do. Not: *I must sacrifice the Art!* (We would prefer she turn in the works along with the son, but what mother would do that?—it is as unfeasible now as it was in biblical times.) A simpleton cannot be demonic. There was no question of zeal, of enthusiasm, of erotic arousal: *Burn, Picasso! Burn, Matisse!* And yet it used to be witches who stoked fire only to perish by it in those barbaric times. The innocence of the paintings, the Eastern European location, the poverty, illiteracy perhaps— all this makes for a credible latter-day hex.

And that is why, in a rush of blood to the head, we might blurt out "Crime against humanity!" The well-worn phrase— where the "crime" in question is nothing less than intentional degradation of human beings perpetrated on a large scale—seems hyperbolic in the new context, even if in the heat of indignation (to which destruction by fire certainly added fuel), we refuse to see it as just a metaphor.

The leap from humans to the human is easier the more the art of the recent past, when there were still masters worth mentioning, is sanctified as the expression of the human spirit, the quiddity of our dignity that protects us, like a magic circle, against all barbarism.

Art *appreciation* is an order of magnitude greater than art's *invaluability*. The inestimable worth of art—of man—in our time requires the language of genocide to do justice to it. It is no "mere rhetoric," but an unedited lament for humanity.

If, then, it strikes some of us as preposterous to call an art heist a "crime against humanity," it must be because we do not value art as an extension of human dignity. Is it because art has always accompanied barbarity, as its counterpoint? Our whole history is constructed on denying that we cannot have the one without the other, even if art was born among the barbarians. The twisted story of the burglary, the brutalization of these works, brings this twisted history, begun in prehistory, to a head. Acts we would consider barbarous now, or that we will consider barbarous in the future, were perpetrated by those we now consider to have been the first artists, even the first "moderns." The stature of barbarity keeps step with that of art. The more invaluable art becomes, the less we can appreciate it. The more invaluable individual life becomes, the less we can appreciate it.

We might not know it, but such wisdom speaks through our condemnation of Oberländer-Târnoveanu's hyperbole. To accept it would mean convincing ourselves that a mother's love counts for nothing, that it is worthless. You cannot make the willful destruction of high art level with the annihilation of people without elevating at least one mother's love to barbarism.

Even if the crude destruction of these Magnificent Seven really was atrocious, some more refined method would have been easier to swallow. Its artfulness would mitigate its vulgarity. That is why we hope she did not burn them but, as unlikely as that is, deceived the analysts. Perhaps then her act would qualify as art, a performance without spectacle, with an audience to come. It's been said — I know the man who said it — that "Barbarity is one of the signs in which one recognizes renaissances of the spirit."*

---

* Miguel Abensour, "L'histoire de l'utopie et la destin de sa critique," *Textures* 8–9 (1974): 64.

§ Under Attack

The avant-garde artist was born of the image-breaker: the "icons" he broke belonged to his predecessors and rivals. In truth, however, they were the icons by which he lived his life and with which the art of his time was in agreement. His target, then, must not have been the artistic tradition, at least not directly; it was, rather, the reality sanctioning only images that flatter it—images that, while innocent, were thoroughly in the pay of wealthy patrons, who surrounded themselves with them as with mirrors. Naturally, the control of images made them structurally incapable of fulfilling art's modern mission—to challenge, to unsettle, to open up. Only from the position of exteriority claimed by modern art can the false beauties of the life of privilege, of the dream life of power, be violated. Modernity's *artistic frontier* is inward, advancing towards, not away from, the pieties and powers—political, economic, theological—with which even the old masters were in conformity. The image broken by the modern *iconoclast*, the icon reduced to shards and rags, is, in short, the spurious coherent whole, with the "art world" nestled in it.

§ Page from the History of Cultural Warfare

Like the military formation from which it takes its name, the avant-garde is not only the most advanced pioneering culture, but also the most exposed, the most radical in its methods, and too often the first to fall in the field.

⸹ Art, Alienation, Extinction

There is a received and much cherished idea that creativity cannot be alienating. Alienation befalls the exploited, their labour as mindless as it is repetitive, whereas creative work, where it is not enabled by higher economic standing, the prerogative of leisure, is mythologized as an escape into pleasure (even at the risk of madness or early death). Artists of course do collaborate, make, market, and sell their stuff, and the identity of the artist is perfectly compatible with that of the precarious worker or capitalist. But the neoliberalization of art is seen as incomplete as long as art is civilized by the triumph of form over content; form acts as a bulwark against the neoliberal civilization, whose watchword is content extraction. Capitalism keeps pace by producing the tools needed to extract content from form, funding art's nonconformism. The creation of educational and other institutions that teach both art and its exploitation, as well as the rewards dangled before artists who defend art's bulwark, keep up demand for aesthetic product. At a time when everything is being turned into a resource, art can still set the terms of its own use.

A reboot of art's political-interventionist ferment in the 1960s and '70s would offer no resistance to neoliberalism's encroachment. The *identity* of the artist has since become much purer, much more abstract and — dare we say? — superfluous than in those days. All is well as long as it's understood as just an identity or mask, and moreover, one among several others in competition or cooperation with it. Now that the "Creative Class" has been ideologically defined as vital for urban economies, the "creative subject," a.k.a. artist, risks not alienation but isolation. With lived experience becoming art's final court, whoever identifies with art to the exclusion of other roles — whoever lives and breathes art and otherwise lives not — must die of loneliness as one of the last surviving members of a species too old to reproduce.

§ Down and Dirty

If art really needs a clean slate, then life must have the opposite. But could we appreciate such art from such a life?

§ Scenes of Abduction

In the story of the rape of Hippodamia, a Lapith woman is saved from the clutches of drunken Centaurs, guests at her wedding feast. The oft-treated motif, allegorized as the struggle between bestiality or barbarism and humanity or civilization, ends quite clearly in the latter's triumph. As with other erotic subjects, mythical or legendary scenes of abduction, depictions of lecherous violence and abuse, were long bound to a higher, moral purpose, while heroism and procreation as pretexts for titillation were deemed unworthy of art.

The sublimation called art is still aligned with nobility and morality. Art does not just represent—and that in two senses, of showing and standing for—the struggle against barbarism; it functions as a talisman. The choice and proper framing of scenes of this struggle fulfill art's civilizing mission, contributing head-on to the mastery over monstrosity, ugliness, and evil looming large. The mission's goal was to impress upon our minds the seriousness and high stakes of the fight for, in this case, sexual entitlement. The artist wanted us to know, none too subtly, that he had done his part.

The "Manichean" framework, which demands explicitness, comes at a cost to art, which is accused of speaking from both sides of its mouth. One the one hand, bringing sexuality to the surface and manipulating it make artists complicit in subduing anarchic forces—including the eternal two-way traffic between the normal and the freakish, the familiar and the foreign. Art renounces pornography less for its content and effect than for subordinating such forces to quantitative self-regulation. On the other hand, as soon as the image becomes explicit, art falls under suspicion by priests and secular moralists of colluding with base desire. It is watched more closely and interpreted less charitably; exposed, it presents an easy target for yesterday's orthodoxies. Doubt in its ability to quell insurgent passions makes conspicuous not what is obvious to us — art's neutrality — but its barely hidden "barbarism."

The long-term consequences of this double-bind are still with us: even now, freed from moral service, sexuality in art is dismissed as gimmickry, gratuitous provocation. Its aesthetic value is dubious; it is still too caught up in proving it has one. Its appearance is stiff, unnatural, in a word, unfree — and this in spite of the space given to it, having spread from canvas to celluloid, where it is occasionally even unsimulated. Its real, scrambled message is only intelligible to those who reject moralism of any kind and recognize art's long struggle for a pagan origin.

Where it does not eradicate unruliness, censorship inspires encryption. In this hostage hermeneutic, sexually charged representations like that of Hippodamia's rape, as they recur from the Renaissance on, are coded signs of distress. Rather than hailing the victory of the good through art, hence of "good" art, they signal art's capture by "goodness."

§ Coming Clean

If life really is a blank slate, then art must be the opposite.

⸘ Red Is the Colour of Attention

> *Red is for sound reasons the most powerful of chromatic cues for attention. It makes sense to think of it as the starting point from which human colour consciousness gradually expanded.*
> —Julian Bell, "Seeing the Light"*

A Do you figure there is more red in the world now than there was, say, 300 years ago?

B Of course, because of printing and plastics.

A But is there more lust, more anger, more violence? Weren't we once redder in the face and more openly into bloodshed, as some *thinkers* would have us believe? Red is also the colour of wine and the setting sun. Do we like them more than spilling and seeing blood? (And how far back does haemophobia actually go?)

B Now there is more *love*—that is its own shade of red. But love hates distractions.

A Love is ambivalent. It spills over into lust, anger, and violence, which attract more attention.

B Wait, but aren't lust, anger, etc. ambivalent also?

A They are. They just silence their mixed feelings more effectively. They like the attention.

---

* Julian Bell, "Seeing the Light," *Guardian*, June 13, 2009, http://www.theguardian.com/artanddesign/2009/jun/13/modern-art-colour-chart.

§ Ur-Colour

> *Great works wait.*
> —Theodor W. Adorno[*]

The first extant works are in ochre — perhaps to stand out, and be attended to. They have waited for this a very long time.

§ Art (Theory) Brut

Caves containing prehistoric art have opened our eyes not just to the oldest known artwork, but to the *Urbild* of art: the outline of a human hand in ochre done by firelight. From it leads the long and dark passage to the image as we know it: from this negative of a hand held against a wall, on past the contour of an invisible hand and its silhouette, all the way down (or up) to the articulated figure bursting with colour in broadest daylight. But the primitive stencil, followed by the application of the hand to depiction, followed by the pictorial trace of what's *behind* the depicting and tracing — these were, respectively, the view, the technique, and the principle of art from the very beginning.

---

[*] Theodor W. Adorno, *Aesthetic Theory*, ed. Gretel Adorno and Rolf Tiedemann, trans. Robert Hullot-Kentor (1970; Minneapolis: University of Minnesota Press, 1998), 40.

§ Withdrawing

As drawing and painting are phased out in art schools, the concept of art moves some distance towards its ultimate form, that of *mental image*.

§ *Et remotissima prope*

The *Allegory of Divine Providence and Barberini Power* by Pietro da Cortona (1633–1639) graces a ceiling in the Palazzo Barberini in Rome (now home to the National Gallery of Ancient Art). Developing the illusionistic technique of *sotto in sù*, it seems to open the lid of the great hall to the sky above it, at which we are meant to marvel, as the name suggests, from below.

But the heavens teem with activity, barely left uncovered by Cortona's fear of empty space. Dynamic, floating human figures vie for room with a swarm of honey-coloured bees almost the size of nearby *putti* helping to hold aloft two crossed papal keys. On account of their dimensions and bodily independence, these bees appear either as giants or as existing on a different visual plane, much closer to the viewer and the floor. Their heraldic significance for the Barberini family required that it be one of the two: if painted to scale, they would, at such a distance, be mere specks. The span and busyness, the seeming mass and depth of this remarkable composition, are enough to induce an upside-down vertigo, with some elements set so high above the simulated frame as to be partly out of sight, and others so close or precariously suspended that they threaten to fall at any moment, bringing the whole pandemonium down with them, causing at least one modern visitor to cower and take shelter in the hallway. The power of the illusion is unfailing, but its effect on a more minimalist sensibility, pursued by *horror pleni*, is to induce flight.

§ *Marmi finti*

Amidst the splendour of palaces, mansions, galleries, and basilicas, marble adds a mere accent to the art, the instruments of art, and the instruments of worship already assembled within them. It stands out only in impoverished and stripped surroundings, where it can be admired or exposed as *false*. The fate of *marmi finti*, once their deception is revealed, is not unlike that of artificial flowers: the disabused look is withering. Their placement is therefore crucial: far enough away from the eyes still capable of appreciating from a distance—no, not their *art*, not their *naturalness*, but their artful *nature*.

But does not all art ask to be admired in this way? To be regarded from a distance? Not merely *some* art, which requires us to stand back to compose itself into a meaningful whole (Seurat, Richter) or work its effect on our perception (Holbein, Rothko). Aren't we taught to find each work's "optimal viewing distance" (often also the "creator's distance"), whether for painting or sculpture, so that its artifice, the extent to which its material had been *worked*, may not stare us in the face? We are already *not* fooled, and know that any closer we would find the artfulness not only more immediate but glaring. We spare ourselves these disillusionments by keeping back, perhaps even thank the institution for sliding between us barriers and layers of glass.

Fake marble, however, we approach naïvely: it can look so real. On closer examination, the pastel hues and delicate veins, however, disintegrate into a hodgepodge of ungainly strokes. Art as deception—whether, as here, in its content's reality-effect or also by its beauty-effect—can only lose by such proximity. Mimetic art that abjures deception conceals its artifice much better, even at close range. But well enough to hold up under scrutiny? In what presents itself as a work of *art*, artifice is not exposed as trickery but studied as technique, for the achievement of beauty, realism, etc. The *trompe l'œil*, even when upfront and subtle—like the false windows of certain houses—is judged principally on its ability to create and sustain an illusion in three dimensions.

That is why the *marbled* loudspeakers in St. Peter's—surprise may be the best spur to new reflection—are just right. Placed at a remove necessary to admire their stony skin, which, by reason only of its adherence to sound equipment suspended above our heads, should be presumed faux, without being so obviously. Far from a lower art form, the "speaking" *marmi finti* are for those rare, true seekers after aesthetic pleasure, those who having absorbed everything else—all the sumptuous, show-stopping objects and eye-catching detail—are still not sated. They blend seamlessly with the true marble no less than with the *obviously* sham; we would be forgiven for seeing their coat as mere camouflage against the enemies of modernity, whose devotion to tradition they offend in league with electric votive candles and cash registers. The harmony to which the speakers are party extends in this sense beyond music. Sleek, discreet, they do not draw our attention like the Baroque baldachin by Bernini—whose story, in keeping with tradition, is by comparison quite uncivilized. What isn't done for the sake of ostentatious beauty? The damnable procurement of bronze for Bernini's honeyed pièce de résistance by a Barberini, who was then pope, was summed up in one line: *Quod non fecerunt barbari, fecerunt Barberini*, "What the barbarians did not do, the Barberini did." It was thought the material had been torn out of the Pantheon.

⟟ Unvarnished

Carl Dreyer, old master of the motion picture, would only have "artifice to strip artifice of artifice,"* instead of concealing it. This seemingly minor difference gains importance once we understand that the new layer of artifice is not a fresh coat of varnish that covers over old imperfections (exposing the *natural* as mere finish), but a stripping agent that brings out the grain of wood already laid bare by a saw.

---

* Quoted in Eileen Myles, "What about Chris?", foreword to *I Love Dick* by Chris Kraus (Los Angeles: Semiotext[e], 2006), 13.

⸹ It's Alive!

> *Particularly salutary is the way [Amy Knight] Powell challenges the basic mission of art history "as a humanistic discipline" as laid down by Panofsky seventy years ago: that of "enlivening what otherwise would remain dead." "Neither institution nor individual can restore life to an object that never had it," Powell retorts. "The promiscuity of the work of art—its return, reiteration and perpetuation beyond its original moment—is the surest sign it never lived." This refusal to animate, even to anthropomorphise, the artwork is especially pertinent given the tendency today to treat images and objects as though they were alive, even human: a fetishism of the artefact in art history that is in keeping with the fetishism of "personal devices" in the commodity world around us.*
>
> —Hal Foster*

The first paintings were "animate." In the Chauvet cave, early artists rendered bison in motion by multiplying their limbs. In the caves of Arcy-sur-Cure, a bear carries in its mouth a fresh fish, tail flapping. A bison speared by a hunter is *still* bleeding to death. A stampede of horses, large and small, close and distant, layered one over another, still run like the wind across the rock walls. But the artists did not succeed in breathing life into them. Instead, though dead and deep in stone, the works brought the artists back to life. We have never animated art. Art has always only animated us.

---

* Hal Foster, "Preposterous Timing," review of *Medieval Modern: Art out of Time* by Alexander Nagel and *Depositions: Scenes from the Late Medieval Church and the Modern Museum* by Amy Knight Powell, *London Review of Books* 34, no. 21 (2012), http://www.lrb.co.uk/v34/n21/hal-foster/preposterous-timing.

⸹ Virtual Promiscuity

in response to:

> *In this respect Powell regards the deposition of the work of art—in her case, its removal from the late medieval church to the modern museum—not as a deracination always to be deplored, as it is almost always seen today (so much do we take the value of contextualism for granted). Rather, in a manner that recalls the "imaginary museum" of André Malraux, Powell sees this displacement almost as a desideratum, for it opens up works of art to formal comparisons and conceptual connections that would otherwise be difficult to make. Indeed, she champions the "promiscuity" of artworks in the modern museum, "which is precisely what most art historians would rather overlook," against the historicity that ties each work to its particular time and space of emergence, which is precisely what most art historians aim to articulate.*
> —Foster[*]

Let artworks mingle in virtual brothels, where we can have them act out even our own aesthetic fantasies digitally. But retain the old maidens and consorts in their proper places, for they are not of our time, nor would they wish to be.

---

[*] Ibid.

⸿ This Will Kill That

occasioned by the SIAS Summer Institute 2013/14 "Scenes from the History of the Image: Reading Two Millennia of Conflict"

When you find yourself by some wrong turn in the midst of a crowd of tourists freshly deposited at some "sight," whether Notre Dame Cathedral or the Kew Gardens in bloom, you could, like me, associate the flurry of handheld snaps with bees collecting pollen. Ah yes, you think to yourself as you reach for your mental notebook, the image-takers of this century may far outnumber the image-*makers*, but they are like the most industrious worker bee to the queen — subordinate. I dare you, however, to reflect further on this first impression: do we really still live amidst images waiting to be taken? Have we not been absorbed wholly by the image, drinking and drowning in it? We can view this as a change of paradigm from the *imaging* of idealism and mysticism (even though material) to the *seeing* of empiricism and naturalism (even though optically assisted or digital) to, now, the *saving* of virtualism (even though what was seen remains, there remains nothing to be seen).

But, lest you think this is all I've got, I'm not fooled by this newfound capacity of ours to save images to keep their effect on us under control. I mean to push you further. Is it no longer the case that, as Virginia Woolf's diners surmised, we are

> *all eye? Do we [not] still preserve the capacity for drinking, eating, indeed becoming colour furled up in us, waiting proper conditions to develop? For as the rocks hide fossils, so we hide tigers, baboons, and perhaps insects, under our coats and hats. On first entering a picture gallery, whose stillness, warmth and seclusion from the perils of the street reproduce the conditions of the primeval forest, it often seems as if we reverted to the insect stage of our long life.**

---

* Virginia Woolf, "Walter Sickert: A Conversation" (1934), in *Collected Essays*, vol. 2, ed. Leonard Woolf (London: Hogarth, 1966), 234.

No, we are more hand than eye, and much more hands-on in our collecting. We no longer go to galleries just to stare and, like Woolf's insects, *become for the moment the thing we see.* We go to take it away with us. Neither are we merely confined to the galleries like to a primeval forest. We suck and draw the image out of everything we see, as bees suck out honey — which they have made for their own eventual consumption — but much faster than it can be replaced. Compared to the images of it in existence, all the natural and cultural scenery has become faded, tired, flat, and hazy. We, the image-takers, have killed it.

§ Return of the Image

> daguerreotype: *"mirror with a memory"* (O.W. Holmes)[*]

It is an extended moment, not an instant as in the great majority of photographs, that is preserved by a daguerreotype. But it is a moment in which movement, if it is not to obfuscate the object, must be minimal, so that time seems to stand still for the sitter. The preservation — in stillness, as though petrified — of the object lends it a stony presence, a gravity seldom achieved in any other medium. But this same stately object, even when visibly grounded, seems to hover like a holograph. This phantom is the material essence of appearance.

My relationship to the daguerreotype echoes the experience of those who, encountering photography for the first time, were reportedly terrified that it would carry off their souls. In our self-conscious and reflective age, this least mediated form of image-making, the "lost" art

---

[*] Oliver Wendell Holmes, "The Age of Photography," *Atlantic Monthly* 3, no. 20 (1859), http://www.theatlantic.com/ideastour/technology/holmes-full.html.

of daguerreotypy, affords the same experience, but in reverse. We are wont to conceive of identity through mirrors, through media, so that we can hardly imagine a world without our image in it. But precisely because of this multiplication of documented appearances and the instantaneity of contemporary photographs, our images seem more like flat reproductions and poorly made fragments we ourselves increasingly come to resemble. The first thing the primitive daguerreotype does is pick up and bind these aspects together, restoring us to ourselves. We realize what we have lost in a life of everyday pictures, be these family snapshots, portraits from Sears, or the most advanced digital photographs. The second merit of a daguerreotype is to make us see ourselves differently, less distractedly, more steadily; to remind us of our persistence in the world, our individual effort to be. The mirrored plate draws in what is least fleeting in our demeanor; it is selective even about our "features." Depending on the plane of focus, the camera gathers a wealth of detail from our person and binds it to the reflective surface, the way a florist ties a bouquet, somewhere out of sight, down the stem. The daguerreotype shows only the blossom.

§ What Did You Do in the Theatre?

These not "properly speaking" *plays* that nowadays go under the name of *immersive theatre* offer elaborate, spectator-centred interactive environments designed to produce unique experiences in members of a new kind of audience. They are only the most extravagant of a type of dramatic phenomenon that adds a new dimension to the unpredictability of the theatre, heightening it. The type includes also "installations" staged in a gallery and meant to elicit interaction with audience members under constrained conditions which, by eschewing their framing as a bounded "event" or "performance," give us latitude to come and go virtually as we please. It includes, as well, encounters of a more defined duration in an existing site that may or may not be reserved for this purpose (e.g., an office building, a museum, or a street), where the spectator, solo or in a group, interacts with actors (not always identified as such) for whom the concept ultimately matters more than the execution — improvised or with a script so rudimentary as not to foreclose very individualized experiences. These choreographed encounters possess some dramatic cohesion and blur the line between make-believe and reality. Tino Sehgal's so-called "constructed situations" can be cited as examples of both types.

Immersive theatre is the next generation of this revolution in the theatre. It has been likened to active voyeurism (in which one seeks out occasions to watch without being seen), to video games in which players move through a world unto itself (without fundamentally affecting its rules or construction), and, finally and more distantly, to "choose your own adventure" fiction. These phenomena are translated by it into a new medium. The spectator who wanders through the artificial environment set up for a series of parallel performances — with multiple intersecting narratives that hang together while unfolding seemingly independently of one another — encounters not only these, of course, but also other (clearly identifiable) spectators. This structure itself allows the spectator to proceed at his/her own pace, to wander and become lost in the alternate reality of the piece.

But it also forces one to choose. Such active immersiveness makes demands on us precisely where we are habituated to being passive and not immersed. It requires us to work for a return on our investment, to get the "bang for our buck." The bang is not a given—but neither is it in a regular show, even when the reviews are rave. It, however, hangs entirely on our rising to a new level of engagement, with and within the charged space into which we are let loose—not to mention on our individual luck once inside, insofar as we may or may not stumble upon a spectacular moment, finding ourselves in the right place at the right time to witness it. We are required to play along to reap more benefits, in search of experiences that will be ours and ours alone. The pressure to work hard on our own behalf is real, and it is on as soon as we step into the world of the play. And so the question "What did you do in the theatre?" could soon make us uncomfortable in a way that "What did you think of the play?" would not.

⟆ The Mask-Produced Spectator; or, Drowning in the Theatre

As in student-centred learning, the success of the immersive drama (or dramatic cluster) depends on its ability to generate unique and memorable experiences, and to lure its spectators back with its promise of different experiences within the framework of the same production. Immersive spectacles' connections to other cultural artifacts (voyeurism, video games, gamebooks) speak less to the power of such spectacles to forge alliances and hence their cultural prominence than to their lateness and power of cultural synthesis, also a form of cultural reflection.

Immersive spectatorship has also been likened — perhaps most plausibly — to what being inside a movie (and not merely on a movie set) might feel like. This sense was literalized for the several hundred audience members milling around the fictional studio "Temple Pictures" in the Punchdrunk/Royal National Theatre mega-production "The Drowned Man." The experience of the viewer approaches, quite deliberately (if the profuse intertextuality is any indication), participating in the diegesis, or story-space, of a film, an experience complete not just with the possibility of interacting with its elements and (apparently) influencing its events, but with "real" freedom in doing so, without, however, actually co-determining and sharing responsibility for what happens. Indeed, the structure must be fixed and robust enough to prevent the feeling that the show is for us only, or *depends* on our behaviour, action, or interaction in any way. The importance of this for the audience goes beyond the simple fact that the truth of an illusion rests on the latter's independence from us. It reflects the reality of our social disempowerment and alienation, which the obligatory masks worn by — surprise! — the spectators do much to intensify. One could also add into the mix some putative existential weakness, a shrinking from responsibility and radical freedom. Human interaction in immersive theatre thus happens primarily on the actors' terms and at their whim, within what seem like strict parameters and algorithmic scripts, heightening the overall sense of the unexpected (the stories of individual spectators' private moments with actors further reinforce this impression of indeterminacy). There is just enough of a margin for manipulating inanimate objects to establish a reality from which all spontaneity has been sucked out. The temptation to touch and displace, to which viewers succumb seen and unseen—though the feeling of being watched never really leaves them—is one that the mise-en-scène itself seems destined to encourage by the distribution of a dizzying array of props in vacant lots through which a performance has not yet or already swept. Nonetheless, the sense of transgression when interacting with even these things, while it may have something to do with respect for the show's integrity, reveals on another register the parlous condition of agency, which interactive mass art bends over backwards to conceal.

Only through such finely composed and balanced schemes can the reality created become convincing as a world—a vast playground for spectatorship as sexless voyeurism. The "peeping" must be made especially safe and uncontroversial, since it is indulged neither in private nor through "keyholes" or two-way mirrors. This permissive atmosphere relies not only on total audience *absorption* in the created environment and action (this to prevent mischief and straying), and not only on a carefully curated sense of *abstraction* from the reality as it unfolds—preventing viewer-initiated interaction, and facilitated by the anonymizing, defacing, interposing, and cloistering powers of the mask—but also on viewer *protection* from the dramatis personae and co-voyeurs, in which the flatness and homogeneity of the masks, their privacy-bestowing power (concealment of reaction), again play a leading role.

The mask returns to the theatre with the advent of a masked audience. In the above-named production, it is a white visor, void of expression, recalling not only the Venetian carnival but also the beaked plague doctor and the classic alien. The prop thus points in three disparate directions: the ancient dawn of the theatre, protection from inexplicable death, and a future in which our terrestrial entertainments will be completely incomprehensible.

One can only wonder at the experience of the actors in this drama when confronted with the blank uniformity of the crowd. The experience must at first be as alienating for them as it is for us. To gauge our reaction, they must unlearn the habit of relying on facial cues and instead read our movements. Though we are perhaps more watched, and surely more monitored for possible vandalism, we have, in truth, neither the time nor even the thought to reflect on the thespian "other side" of theatrical immersion; our mask — identical to the others and quite comfortable to wear — gives us a tangible feeling of invisibility little different, on the face of it, from that in an auditorium after the lights have gone down. Far from counteracting immersiveness, the disguise separates and awakens us, as ciphers, to the strangeness of simultaneous immersion and isolation — a feeling spared the non-immersive spectator. Our sense of and desire for complete immersion draws us into an unfamiliar reality. The totality of the illusion plunges us, once the first rush of curiosity has been satisfied and the character of the diversion cognized, into a state of solitude, silence, and mystery — of others as much as ourselves.

§ Fatal Attraction

> *Cultural history has a well-known name for this partial disavowal of social situatedness, a simultaneous impulse to veil the mystery of how artists and writers manage to get themselves provided for and to offer that mystery as a sort of tourist attraction.*
> —Bruce Robbins[*]

If Van Gogh's ear went on display, we would go to see it. The torment of genius, mental illness, the yellow house, fraternity, dashed dream of artistic community, a fainting prostitute, Ichthus/ictus, self-portrait with bandaged head, self-mutilation with suicide — the ear evokes all of them. It is the clue, the main exhibit, the source of a mystery.

If the ear was on tour, crowds would come to see some sliced-off flesh. We would be warned not to expect anything sizeable; he lost only the lobe, just a tiny bit. We would be told of the artist's inability to accept provisions, of money, friendship, and appreciation, and of his growing social isolation. How he lived and worked would interest us little. Van Gogh's art seems conditional on defying his state and situation; it thrived on maladjustment despite his desperate efforts to counteract it. In the end, the ear would become part of Van Gogh's body of work, at the head of the *catalogue raisonné*. It already stands for the whole of his art — not his life, which had to be sacrificed.

Until we take the waxen ear between our fingers and consider reattaching it to the waxwork figure of Van Gogh, we will lag behind theories of embodied art-production that threaten to pull him down to earth by his remaining ear.

---

[*] Bruce Robbins, "A Portrait of the Artist as a Social Climber: Upward Mobility in the Novel," in *The Novel*, vol. 2, *Forms and Themes*, ed. Franco Moretti (Princeton, NJ: Princeton University Press, 2006), 415.

§ *Pentimenti*

> pentimento: *sign or trace of an alteration in a literary or artistic work; (spec. in Painting) visible trace of a mistake or an earlier composition seen through later layers of paint on a canvas* (OED)

A masterpiece is not the product of changes of mind — of attempts, perhaps, of trials and errors to be sure, but not of fundamental shifts in conception. No, that would be too underhanded. Style and design alone do not a masterpiece make, though they do count for innovation. They can be "worked on." But the flash of genius, the "ah!" in *awe*, no amount of wavering, backpedalling and fudging can generate. Now, let's consider the matter again: could the great work emerge from draft upon botched draft, repeated efforts, false starts? No genius should have to put up with such self-evident ineptitude. It would know when to stop spinning its wheels and recognize that only a fundamental conceptual shift can masterfully match new style to design, and design to execution. Ambivalence on this point is surely why we find the *pentimenti* of great works particularly captivating. *Could it be thus?* we wonder incredulously before we accept that indeed it was — an exception to the rule. But when we look back at those "ruly" masterpieces — those conceived *once*, carried out, and meant to be — we cannot help but think less of them: effortlessly devised, without a trace of hesitation, only the labour of execution, the single-minded stubbornness of living up to their original perfection in the artist's mind. *Is that really all it takes?*

⸙ Great Passion

Only make sure passion is in the ascendant before beginning anything like the re-creation of the world through art. Strike while your iron is hot. There will be time for coolness and sobriety — for refining your work by the pale light of day, making hay (or hash!) of it with the sun still shining. If, instead, against your powers, you get composing, your ink will be invisible, white on white, and you yourself, as good as blind. When, come evening, in the throes of inspiration, you hold your page above a flame, you will be dismayed. If you then refine your scribbles by the light of your passion — leaving *it* untended, not trimming your wick — your markings will again be illegible, black on soot-black. And when the day dawns once more, you will find everything burnt to a crisp, your face ashen.

⸙ Instrument of Instruments

> [T]*he production of a perfected illusion depends not only on a staggering artistic skill but ultimately on the intuitive steering of a breathless state in which the painter himself no longer knows whether his eye still sees and his hand still moves.*
>
> —W.G. Sebald[*]

Our habitual focus when considering creative works is on the idea and its execution, or technique. This focus develops in response to our experience of them: interpretation leads us to the idea, consideration of its mode of unfolding, to

---

[*] W.G. Sebald, "As Day and Night, Chalk and Cheese: On the Pictures of Jan Peter Tripp," in *Unrecounted* by W.G. Sebald and Jan Peter Tripp, trans. Michael Hamburger (London: Penguin, 2004), 85.

technique. From the perspective of evaluation, technique can compensate for a weak idea, but a powerful idea, rarely make up for poor technique.

It is the schools of writing — specifically of the creative, literary kind — that offer the best example of the simultaneous *indispensability* and *worthlessness* of technical instruction for creative talent today. On the one hand, workshopping and editing manuscripts is the necessary banausic side of creativity. Industry standards must be learned and certified for the eventual product to sell. On the other hand — and here is the worthless column in the ledger — cultural wealth is created by one's capital investment, not by years of master-less apprenticeship.

The overwhelming majority of those who study writing are never recognized as authors but only as more or less skilled artisans. The remaining handful already possess all the essential elements, which group discussion and attention to detail merely refine — away from conformity. Despite their participation, and on account only of true talent setting them apart from their most capable peers, they have not demeaned themselves with workshopping. Their talent can be rehabilitated. Thus the indispensability of instruction and its worthlessness are balanced in the ledger of creative life, and no one is a born artist.

The more eroded the category of genius becomes, the more it finds shelter in the rare cases where talent lies *not* in compounding the benefits of technical instruction, but rather in hard work wherein such benefits are unimportant or hardly to be detected. Seeing the difference between excellence and genius, between the reducible and the irreducible, itself requires a non-technical sensibility and an artist's "nose." Among the untaught and unteachable skills that serve to illuminate it we can count the *sense of completion*: knowing exactly when to step back from a work. The great Greek painter Apelles stressed the value of this ability as his advantage over the greatest mastery of technique. At the inspired moment when he stopped his hand, that instrument of instruments, and took it away, his genius was most on display.

§ Eupsychian

> *Yet those very people, who so hate genius, all consider themselves geniuses.*
> —Denis Diderot, *Rameau's Nephew*[*]

For the creative artist, it is hardest to steer between the evils of creative vanity when these are as attractive as two kinds of *absolution*.

On the one side, the artist meets, and even exceeds, his highest standard by producing a great work, while immediately falling short of it as a human being. When measured by it, he "breaks down," ready "to surrender his overwhelming skill to God" (so Ernst Bloch, an atheist).[†] And so he surrenders his work, in a pathos of his unworthiness of it, to the only worthy creator—paying himself, in this roundabout way, the greatest compliment. His genius now belongs to the Heavens and redeems him. He is absolved of his failures, and of the vanity that drove him.

On the other side, the artist fails to live up to his highest standard, his work falling short of his great genius. No sooner is the work finalized (if not already abandoned) than it is condemned for being beneath him. He does a ritual purge: he burns it. "Only this kind of burnt offering might be acceptable to the Muse he has let down."[‡] By it he signals that much more can be expected of him—and, far from being impugned, he is vindicated.

---

[*] Denis Diderot, *Rameau's Nephew and First Satire*, trans. Margaret Mauldon (Oxford: Oxford University Press, 2006), 8.

[†] Ernst Bloch, *Spirit of Utopia*, trans. Anthony A. Nassar (1923; Palo Alto, CA: Stanford University Press, 2000), 166.

[‡] Adam Kirsch, "Rocket and Lightship: Meditations on Life and Letters," *Poetry*, Nov. 2012, http://www.poetryfoundation.org/poetrymagazine/article/244760.

§ *Mirabile scriptu*

In the modern novel from Naturalism through Symbolism to Modernism genius has long been at home — so comfortable in fact that it must be the secular stand-in for the whole class of miracles and supernatural events.

§ Genius and Truth

Many have pointed out that true genius is anathema to societies organized on the principle of equality. Either truth is available to all or it is available to no one — let's not now add a *more or less*; these alternatives admit of no degrees. Searchers for truth have an obligation to share it whenever they come upon it and to keep it accessible. No one must be excluded from this unisex, one-size-fits-all, one-for-all-for-one kind of truth. Openness is the justification for its pursuit, and research, in the long run, is labour on behalf of all humanity rather than individual men and women.

When did this view of truth and genius come into its own? Why has the sharing of truth developed into a universal duty? The obvious answers are, respectively: around the time social inclusiveness became a thing, and for the betterment of everyone. Now all pay lip service to it while turning a billion blind eyes on its real effects. The money attached to sharing is not to be sneezed at, and works wonders as added incentive. Motivation exceeds individual admiration or national prestige. What has been definitively struck from this wishful wish-list is precisely what openly drove truth's initiates as recently as this year: possession of power in order to dominate mankind. Domination works in the subtlest of ways, and securing agreement with any given truth, no matter how trivial, strengthens the position of its supplier — a process that builds everything from empires to cliques.

The creative genius, meanwhile, has never had an active role in this (take poor Prospero paradigmatically). The truth of genius was more than singular in expression; it was unique to him, yet *causa sui*. The genius was not faulted for neglecting or failing to communicate it; he was not made for such things; the responsibility to make it known lay with everyone but him. His gift was to be both a lightning rod, which sheltered other men from too much truth, and a divining rod that only worked if undisturbed. His truth spoke not with the obviousness of black on white, but with the mystery of many shades and fathomless meanings.

The problem with the genius of old was not its power to deceive but its almost invariable elitism. Even if his was truth that bothered no one and that the rest could live without, its very possibility, rarity, exclusivity, or mediation fuelled resentment, eroding genius's cult status as the manifestation of man's divinity, and dimming its instances. Many of the Grimms' tales tell of the desire, rooted in a greed of which their common man is typically innocent, to nip the exceptional in the bud.

Not long afterward, genius was redeemed as the emanation of the spirit of a people, having made itself understood intuitively by all as their common patrimony. It thrived in Germany, leading it to unification. (Italian nationalism was comparatively down-to-earth, organized around the liberal-corporatist metaphors of workshop and association.) Art, in the grip of Romanticism, became genius's bulwark. For a while still, it split the difference between civilized society and barbarism. The artist-hero stood watch on the border between them, fervently (if often unsuccessfully) policed in the great era of nation-states. Exposed to the outside, genius was now in touch with the barbarian, the foreign, the wild, even while in the pay of the tribe it protected. Its rudeness eventually had to exceed, its cultivation never match, that of its patrons: the essence of the Bohemian stereotype. The reputation of genius followed that of the artist in its downward trajectory. While Arnold Schoenberg complained "there are no more geniuses, only critics," and pushed back against philistinism, parochialism and populism in his creative domain ("if it is art, it is not for all, and if it is for all, it is not art"),* the middle class was losing the last of its patience with "so-called genius," which would find a safe haven in the philanthropist's no-strings-attached "so-called Genius Grant." Public fortune began instead to smile on science, whose truth could at least, it seemed, be understood by all with enough application.

Today, the term "genius" sticks to some people in much the way the name "Santa Claus" does to the neighbour who always volunteers for holiday duty. It denotes, in other words, no special gift for truth but a desire to amuse and, through a harmless deception transparent to all, to be seen as extraordinary year round as well. The older they grow, the more the children who once gathered around him come to regard him as infantile (and themselves as mature enough to judge!), even to whisper doubts about his sanity. Fortunately, in no time they also start replenishing his real fan base, which still believes (and so confirms) that he really *is* Santa Claus, really *is* a genius. Nature takes its course alongside the cycle of healthy disillusionment.

This brings us to the virtual disappearance of the epithet "genius," in its robust sense, from all but the most rarefied circles, where large sums of money are exchanged. More than merely aware of his value, the artist knows how to capitalize on it, investing in his own aura and genius-myth that becomes then an integral part of the artistic product, rather than a quality he started off with.

There is also the freely available, seemingly effortless, good old "genius for." "For" what, precisely? In principle anything—anything, that is, except *truth*.

---

* Arnold Schoenberg, "New Music, Outmoded Music, Style and Idea" (1946), "Those Who Complain about the Decline" (1923), in *Style and Idea: The Selected Writings of Arnold Schoenberg*, ed. Leonard Stein, trans. Leo Black (London: Faber & Faber, 1975), 203, 124.

⸹ The Making Of

> *Born originals, how comes it to pass that we die copies?*
> —Edward Young[*]

Ape stands for "imitation," *man* for "originality" at least *in potentia*. Before you lament your fall from ape to man, or man to ape (decide for heaven's sake!), having betrayed either your natural innocence, or your creative potential, the ape not having shamed you back into native ignorance, or else into originality — remember (remember and rejoice!) that second nature is nature minus its imperfections, or that no two imitations are identical and that, compared to the really good ones, all originals are just unaccomplished copies.

---

[*] Edward Young, from "Conjectures on Original Composition: In a Letter to the Author of *Sir Charles Grandison*" (1759), in *Critical Theory since Plato*, ed. Hazard Adams and Leroy Searle (Boston: Wadsworth Publishing, 2004), 344.

◊ Look No Further

It is barbaric indeed to hold that the *content* of a work of art is contained by covers or a frame. It is no more civilized to conceive the *form* of art as exceeding them. Both notions can be blamed on a modern superstition, one that recapitulates the history of art's unfinished secularization, its incomplete emancipation "from the cultic to the cultural" (to borrow a phrase from Thomas Mann[*]). The first idea — content in form — stems from a hereditary fear of not recognizing divine presence in material reality unless the latter is transformed by the deity's appearance. God's presence need not be obvious and will be missed by those who look for it beyond what is in front of them. As for the second notion — form beyond form — we owe it to an inherited fear of not recognizing this same material reality as divine work, formed by God's hand rather than man's.

---

[*] Thomas Mann, *Doctor Faustus: The Life of the German Composer Adrian Leverkuhn, as Told by a Friend*, trans. John E. Woods (1947; New York: Vintage, 1999), 64.

§ Work of Exception

This work of art may have been made by your neighbour, but in it he seems a stranger.

§ Stranger in One's Own Work

To be a stranger in one's own house requires another to first make it uncomfortable. To be a stranger in one's own work of art, also built with one's own hands, requires the merest passage of time.

§ Abyss-Gazing

Modern music and literature devoted attention to "composing" silence, modern visual art, to manipulating negative space, film, to capturing stillness and *temps mort*. Staring too long into the abyss only familiarizes it.

◊ Little Pieces

> *In the repetitive rhythms of primitive music the menacing aspect originates in the principle of order itself.*
> —Adorno*

Schoenberg's "musical aphorisms" are too brief, too lean and nervy, too dematerialized, for rhythm and order to take root in them. The aphorism, the romantic fragment, the sketch, the *kleines Stück*, and a host of other diminutive artistic forms share a resistance to the spirit of system, whether the latter unfolds primarily in time, as it does for instance in music or literature (Bach, the *Encyclopédie*, regular utopia, Hegel), or in space, as in visual representation (perspective, classicism, Beaux-Arts). The freedom of art is best exercised, best "captured," in small pieces; they let us come and go at will, without a key or address. They require no submission to creative force, no suspension of judgment or of disbelief. Rarely do they define the artist who produced them. In a society that rewards consistency and individualism, they assume the character of common property, if not its form, without (for this very reason) becoming common.

What disturbs us in them is born neither of the principle of order nor of order's opposite. Indeed, it can only come from their suspension over a void of feeling and meaning— a void visible only if one gives their anti-systematic character its due, and invisible if one reads them negatively (as inchoate, undeveloped, unfinished, supplemental) in relation to some "principal" work. The extant lines of Heraclitus and Parmenides cannot but be read in this way: not merely against a relative void of our historical understanding, but in the absence of a more orderly, more complete textual background or accompaniment, and with the probability that what has come down are not just the remnant highlights of a lost whole, the spoors of a disappearance.

---

* Adorno, *Aesthetic Theory*, 52.

In this respect, their small number has perennially taught amateurs of remote intellectual history the value of the shortest forms. But true love of these minimal pieces is never free of dread or disquiet. The more profound their appeal, the louder their expressive summons, the more archaic the surrounding silence of thought out of which they must forever keep emerging.

⸎ Beasts for Kicks

What literati and ideologue revolutionaries have in common is a willingness to descend to common beastliness for enlightened ends. Marmontel saw in men of letters *"bêtes féroces destinées à l'amphithéâtre pour l'amusement des hommes."** In their zeal to instruct us by force, both groups realize too late that their shows require self-sacrifice to be, or do, any good.

⸎ Cannonball

The intriguing unfurnished room in René Magritte's *On the Threshold of Liberty* (1929, 1937) could hardly be more transparent. But it is not the transparency of glass houses, unremarkable either way—whether one is looking in or out of them. (What is so remarkable, after all, about making

---

* "Ferocious beasts destined for the amusement of mankind." Jean-François Marmontel, "Critique," in *Encyclopédie, ou dictionnaire raisonné des sciences, des arts et des métiers, par une société de gens de lettres*, ed. Denis Diderot and Jean le Rond d'Alembert (1751–72; University of Chicago: ARTFL Encyclopédie Project, Spring 2011), http://encyclopedie.uchicago.edu/.

windows of walls, being able to see out at all angles and being visible at all times?) The transparency on display in the Magritte painting concerns not whatever might occur inside the room, but what might be called the images of the world of its (absent) inhabitants.

The walls of the room, to extrapolate from the one in full view — at which a cannon is pointed — are each subdivided into four squares. The squares frame images that show evidence of careful curation. Today, we might take them to be projections rather than painted panels, wallpaper, or incongruent windows onto the very subjects depicted in them, but their ontological status is of no consequence.

The images, from left to right, depict: a lush and dark forest, a rather painterly nude torso (the female midriff, to be precise), wooden boards, clouds against a blue sky, magnified *grelots* or sleigh bells, the façade of a townhouse (as it might be seen from across the street), a blazing fire, an enlarged paper doily pattern. Only three of these images would qualify as window material; the rest require alternate explanations. What do all these fragments have in common? What unites them? Or is their fragmentariness meant to point us in the direction of the titular "threshold"? One plausible interpretation is that these interior scenes make up the "image bank" of a typical bourgeois life. A hunger for images of reality unites nondescript middle-class interiors with prison cells. But while the repertoire of the second reflects its occupant's unsated desire, the first is filled with reflections of everyday life, where small desires are no sooner felt than satisfied. The narrator of *Voyage autour de ma chambre* would be at home among them, not needing to cross the threshold to find his freedom.

To liberate the inmates of bourgeois life over a century after de Maistre's sedentary journey around his room seems to require measures at once more radical and more absurd: heavy artillery positioned to blow the entire scheme to smithereens? The proposal for armed violence from within suggested by the aimed cannon, combined with the absence of a possible agent, has the effect of securing our assent: *Yes, such life is a scandal! Nothing lives here!* And before we know it, we have exchanged our aesthetic perspective for that of the gunner.

⸹ Art Curation

Great art is defined by intractable personal flaws; great curation, by incurable personal traumas. It is unforgivable to theorize from a single example (our local collector-curator Ydessa Hendeles, whose work is heavy with her family's fate in the Holocaust). So let us turn instead to one of the minor adventures of logos, a contemporary conceptual-linguistic dialectic.

Curation, its roots in Latin *cura*, is a kind of care. It is a response to a hurt in need of healing. While the idea of *curating* private life, from social media to home base, inspires attention to more than just aesthetic detail, and may be worthwhile as self-therapy, we must resist seeing the curation of galleries and museums in this way. Why add art space to the many hoaxes perpetrated on ailing publics? Let us leave any putative health benefits of curation to the curator, and focus on the art—whose main mission is not to heal us spiritually and comfort the disturbed. No matter how well curated, its museums will not cure all who come. They may bring relief to those who come in desperation. To expect them to do so, however, is to burden them with a responsibility they can never take up. Phonetically the Louvre is not so far from Lourdes, where the "curators" alone similarly find relief. But it should guard itself against analogous public imposture to maintain itself as a site of pilgrimage.

¶ Moratorium I

Art's command to be revered, preserved, and on public display is nothing more than an extension of religion's command for ritual prayer and temple worship. In those houses of God where devotional relics are stored to protect them from vandalism and decay—there they also take on a new "life," paralleling their otherworldly truth, of reminding us of the afterlife (who can help wondering about the reliquary: surely there is more to death than this? The more wood and gold and precious metals cover these remnants, the less pesky our questioning).

Visual art, meanwhile, transforms this thought of finitude and the afterlife into one about metaphysical connection (the uncanny phenomenality of images, the sense of their being alive and autonomous, does not enter into the equation; once seen, they seem to perpetuate themselves just fine regardless of their physical condition, even to the point of awakening our iconoclastic side). Do we not find ourselves dumbstruck before artworks we had once seen in better shape, in real life or reproduction? Do we not wonder then: is there nothing more to them than this, after all? Owing to art's widespread preservation and display, they maintain the privileged status of representatives of a higher order of being. That is quite a lot to live up to!

But in our time this metaphysical function is becoming less and less self-evident. With the ranks of artists continually swelling, exorbitant capital pouring into the art market, the democratization of canons, the relaxation of prohibitions, the globalization of long-held rumours about the end of art's spiritual ascendant (can we blame it all on late-imperial decadence and technological promiscuity?), we may wonder whether the time has not perhaps come to rein in the public institutions of art and celebrate art's ephemerality *over* that of the artist. This as long as we recognize that such a celebration is itself unlikely to go the way of all flesh and will remain after the art itself has left—as a record of its phenomenal and ontic experience.

§ No Trespassing

Certain let us call them "difficult" artists, in an access of vanity or insecurity, put into their work so much of themselves, featuring in it front and centre, that they actively get in the way of its appreciation. Since there is no getting around them, one must either come up close, too close (for comfort, taste, or hygiene), in order to lose sight of them — to disaggregate their input into digestible parts — or else move as far away as necessary to see the bigger picture. It is no use trying to push aside such art-makers; they will resist, turn hostile, and bar the way completely. They are so fond of it and protective that any attempt at bypassing will result in struggle, which can only harm the art.

As a viewer, one can always decide that such a degree of possessiveness and obtrusiveness disqualifies their work from public interest on the grounds that it mimics private property. For reasons to do with the history of art, the artist as art proprietor is one image that does not gel. The ego-underlining work, in contrast to the ego-undermining kind we all love by comparison, insists that appreciation of the artist (whose personality pervades it) is indispensable to its secrets being released. Open house begins as soon as our bonafide interest is established.

It would be wrong to conclude, however, that what has us return again and again to a tough piece of art is a "connection" to its maker or a standing invitation to get to know them (and their work only through them). *Stand back! Keep out! Approach no nearer!* — these proprietary messages dissuade in vain, speaking most enticingly to the fan of the prohibitively difficult. As long as they remain interdictions, unbacked by action, they have the contrary effect. What greater incitement to curiosity and trouble than a *No trespassing* sign on property whose owner is home, property seemingly abandoned (as difficult works tend to be)? Where the rule-abiding peel off, preferring non-appreciation to offence, the adventurous see only the romance of transgression.

⌕ Rubens in Furs

> *In a collection of objects of art, the contiguity of beauty sets off the beautiful and that of inferiority detracts from it. A judge who is wearied, is incapable of judging: ennui renders him unjust and severe.*
> —Astolphe de Custine, *Letters from Russia**

Walking through the zones of heat and cold, across creaking floorboards—as in a rural museum opened just for you if a custodian with the key can be found, or in a mountain chalet when all the guests are out pursuing winter sports and only you, having been excused, wander looking at old photographs, natural artifacts, and undusted bits of folklore, or, again, in a European temple of art at whose grand doors a shivering trail of people awaits admission, thinking not of Rembrandt but of samovars.

The austerity of the display inside does a disservice to the museum's collection. Old Masters hide in poor light, and plump Rubenses have long since turned with age. Everything here finds its antithesis in the vivacity of the wintertime queue. This takes on the habit of an autonomous entity, which snakes outside, its cheeks full of colour and body clad in fur, pooling together scarce resources (drink, warmth, humour) as in the days of the Siege of Leningrad. The Russian state, making no provision for these avid culture-seekers, prefers to see in them the contiguity of need and inferiority. And in this condition they must suffer to gain entrance to the visions of beauty.

Inside, the ghost of Empress Catherine still hovers in the atmosphere, waving her despotic finger, humbling visitors even further:

---

* Astolphe de Custine, *Letters from Russia*, ed. Anka Muhlstein, 1843 trans. uncredited (1839; New York: NYRB, 2002), letter 19, p. 350.

1. *All ranks shall be left outside the doors, similarly hats, and particularly swords.*
2. *Orders of precedence and haughtiness, and anything of such like which might result from them, shall be left at the doors.*
3. *Be merry, but neither spoil nor break anything, nor indeed gnaw at anything.*
4. *Be seated, stand or walk as it best pleases you, regardless of others.*
5. *Speak with moderation and not too loudly, so that others present have not an earache or headache.*
6. *Argue without anger or passion.*
7. *Do not sigh or yawn, neither bore nor fatigue others.*
   ...
9. *Eat well of good things, but drink with moderation so that each should be able always to find his legs on leaving these doors.**

Look closer at this common humanity lined up before the State Hermitage in January snow. Do you not yourself prefer them to the contiguity of Dutch and Flemish masters on which restorers have not performed their sorely needed tasks? The picture of health and animal spirits takes here pride of place. Thus it is that near certain museums nature's beauty can sometimes spring up.

---

* These were Catherine the Great's "Rules for the Behaviour of All Those Entering These Doors." Quoted in James Steward, *The Collections of the Romanovs: European Art from the State Hermitage Museum, St. Petersburg* (London: Merrell, 2005), 24.

◊ Fake Fires

The confetti-spider crudeness of images of exploding fireworks offends no one as long as their subject matter makes no claim to art. Designing and engineering *feux d'artifice*, or pyrotechnics, was recognized as a distinct métier, that of the *artificier*, under Louis XIV, who was himself quite fond of elaborate early versions of *son et lumière*. An engraving of a show of this kind — one of the original senses of "set piece" — combined with its timely circulation, used to pose as an eyewitness rendering, recording the moment of explosion (it has been pointed out that some of these images depicted a synthesis rather than an actual scene, and often preceded the event, depicting it as planned rather than as executed, as it might have been rather than as it was, *if* it even was). The engraving's artistic value was subordinated to its informative and propagandistic role.

All that changed with Whistler's now-famous *Nocturnes in Black and Gold — The Falling Rocket* and *The Firewheel*. The first of these occasioned a libel case between the painter and the art critic John Ruskin, who had accused Whistler in print of "wilful imposture."[*] Ruskin's vicious reaction can only be understood as motivated by the subject matter — man-made bursts of light meant for popular amusement — even if he focused on technique; the subject called for a technique more "reckless" than in Whistler's earlier work. Whistler sued to defend his method and choice of subject, citing artistic maturity, influences (Japanese *ukiyo-e* prints) and, last but not least, modernity. In both *Nocturnes*, the transformation of sublimity — a combined effect of distance, vantage point, and sombre setting — is achieved with the insertion of the rocket and softening of impression in a spectral tonal harmony of night and fog broken by evocative specks and highlights.

---

[*] James McNeill Whistler, *The Gentle Art of Making Enemies* (1890; n.p.: Project Gutenberg, 2008), http://www.gutenberg.org/files/24650/24650-h/24650-h.htm.

The Florentine *Scoppio del Carro* on Easter Sunday is surely among the most spectacular traditional fireworks displays to have survived electrification. Among its wonders is the procession of the cart, resembling a juggernaut. Loaded with explosives, escorted by men and women in period dress, it is hauled through the streets by a team of oxen before coming to a halt in the square in front of the *duomo*, where it is ignited from within the cathedral by a fuse. The incredible concatenation set off to the clang of bells and lasting nearly half an hour is all the more remarkable for its compactness of means. Like a whirring demon on which all eyes are turned, the thing emits not just round after round of detonations but also billowing smoke, bringing back something of the barbarism of the Catholic Church's distant past, as well as the terror of a volcanic eruption. Perhaps the visceral thrill of watching fireworks will one day ultimately be traced to the archaic boredom of savages around a fire.

¶ Inscrutable Relation

> *Il n'y a pas d'œuvre d'art qui ne fasse pas appel à un peuple qui n'existe pas encore.*
>
> (There is no work of art that does not appeal to a people who do not yet exist.)
> —Gilles Deleuze, "What Is the Creative Act?"[*]

One could quibble with the individual words — *none? appeal? a people? not yet?* — or one could say: *There is no people that does not appeal to a work of art that does not yet exist.* Every people conjures its own unity in art as in a crystal ball. This "fundamental affinity" of people for a future work of art that represents them is also "never clear,"[†] and fades from sight as the glass clouds over with their breath.

---

[*] Gilles Deleuze, "Qu'est-ce que l'acte de création?" (lecture, Mardis de la Fondation, FEMIS, Paris, May 17, 1987), http://www.lepeuplequimanque.org/en/acte-de-creation-gilles-deleuze.html.

[†] Ibid.

§ Barbarogenesis

Imaginary interwar headline: *Europe Balkanized!* The name of this grotesque hybrid: Barbarogenius, hero of early twentieth-century Serbian avant-garde, a Slavic New Man. This time it is not the universal spiritual qualities that renew and redeem European civilization in brotherly communion (as Dostoevsky prophesied), but crass primitivism raised to the higher power of a de-civilizing mission. "We advocate new and pure barbarism," wrote the man behind it, Ljubomir Micić, founder of Zenitism, a self-proclaimed newer and purer avant-garde. Like Mayakovsky's Ivan, personifying Soviet Russia as Wilson's and Whitman's challenger on American soil, the Barbarogenius, a hiccup of revolutionary intoxication and unspent virility, is Europe's latter-day rapist and unlikely savior. Science and technology are instrumental in his onward-and-upward trajectory as well, and serve as its metaphors (he is a "rescue pilot of barbarian *idea*planes").* Rather than bearing reconciliation, this walking contradiction flies in the face of the rational West.

It seems like only yesterday that art (spirit) and barbarism (natural culture) were capable of such strategic alliances. The former would contain the brutality of cultural ferment without bursting from the buildup of inner pressure. The latter, meanwhile, drew from the East a primeval energy, heralding the art of the future.

---

* Lubomir Micić, quoted in English translation in Tatjana Micić, "Mythical Paradigms of the Avant-garde and Its Era" (Ph.D. thesis, Charles University in Prague, 2009), 89.

§ **Perfect State**

In a perfect state, art, including literature, would disappear for lack of motivation; those with a lingering "desire for poetical unreality," for the solace of art, long for the "*im*perfect state[,] of society still half barbaric"* in which we still live.

§ **Letting Slide**

We tend to think of literature as helping us make sense of experience, as making the world intelligible to us, and forget that its chief "function" today is the consolidation of culture, which throws in our way interminable contradictions while claiming wholeness and coherence. Literature's less-than-confidence-inspiring integrative effect can be detected in the specious universals of the Literary Establishment and World Literature. Literature, and art more generally, is far and away the smoothest slide into a culture's belly, where it does its enzymatic work. It gives us puzzles to wrap our heads around instead of grappling with contradictions.

---

*   Friedrich Nietzsche, *Human, All Too Human*, trans. R.J. Hollingdale (Cambridge, UK: Cambridge University Press, 1996), p. 112, vol. 1, sec. 234 (emphasis mine) ("Value of the Middle of the Way").

§ Great Art Belonging to Everyone

In the Hollywood version of WWII's Monuments Men, one of them, in words perhaps sentimental yet surprisingly resonant today, gives voice to a deep conviction: "great works of art can never belong to any one individual, at least not in spirit."[*]

Everyone has a right to enjoy masterpieces, and when that right is taken away, when the ruling taste outlaws what speaks to them, they will speak up to reclaim it. This is the view inculcated in school groups by museums, of which the nation-state is still the largest benefactor. The roots of "art as public good" run deep in Christian liturgy, a fact that supporters of the radical Enlightenment would rather we forget. The democratization of *art appreciation* (in contrast to that of religious faith by means of art) has been glacial, reformations and revolutions notwithstanding. It has pushed us into a full-blown contradiction, until now unpronounced.

The democratization of aesthetic opinion (and of educated taste, to be sure) underpins the great wave of entitlement felt before art, great and small, that washes over more people each year, and washes away sins for good. This is the entitlement to one's own opinion and thus to the work's meaning as it appears to us. What are the great works, anyway? Let's cut them down to size and put up lesser lights instead; they will soon shine brighter. Even the cognoscenti of the world of art are bound to bow to public taste, if money calls their name. The rich to whom they pander are bound to lose interest in "high" art, which none below, more informed now than in past times, already gives a damn about. And this is true the more their ranks are replenished by this immense, unbuffered and rapidly self-educating "class," and the more art's "reputation" as a whole suffers (from throwing around its label to see where else it sticks). Mass disparagement of certain art — and it is difficult to predict which, as

---

[*] *The Monuments Men*, directed by George Clooney (Culver City, CA: Columbia Pictures, 2014), DVD.

even difficult work finds aficionados in the unlikeliest of places — is only the most pernicious, if relatively rare, consequence, since some work remains too abstruse for popular taste to approach it. The more pervasive effect is the disappearance of recognized and rewarded *artistic diversity* the more the scale swings to just one side.

We are living now through the beginning of this aesthetic transformation, to which the concept of "great" art (already on life support) will eventually yield. "Greatness," after all, implies that some work is qualitatively beneath the attention of the vast majority, its attention increasingly limited by time. The mid-range artists already find themselves stranded, and without means. Art schools go the way of humanistic studies, and the pool of untapped talent swells. Promise is pegged to potential for making big prize long and short lists, while money (to be sure, less and less of it) is staked on entries to popularity contests that loom large in the eyes of the world.

What we call art will continue being made, its diffusion likely greater than ever before, and everyone shall have contact with and opportunity to see it, if not to "contemplate" it. There will be more art, in aggregate, but what "greatness" there will be will tend to *hide* in art's dilution and proliferation — its galloping invisibility. It will be with art as with everyday nature, which remained aesthetically unseen until bourgeois naturalists (still strong with us) took active interest in its disappearance. Unsupported and taken for granted, this subdetectable infra-art will tend towards harmonizing with nature and reducing our human footprint. It will not crop up, as it still does today, as a Banksy graffito, mosaics by Invader, or Vancouver's horny Satan. It will no longer belong to the people in any meaningful way, just as nature will have ceased belonging to them as well.

⸿ De-Colonizing Art

A I did not know that the duty of art is to make the unexceptional feel special, to transform the ordinary into something noble, to raise it out of the vulgar muck into which it has sunk. Aren't vulgarity etc. already potent enough?

B We're too quick to be judgmental (notice how I didn't say "to judge"). The average person has a right to greater self-esteem. To artists on high horses he will remain a drag. And he will find satisfaction seeing them thrown in the ditch.

The people obviously care about art if they want to be in and part of it. Don't forget how much the history of painting owes to Dutch merchants. We're quick with compassion for the struggle of the underserved masses. Is it right to turn our back on them, and call them undeserving of art?

A The people in the West are not what they used to be. They now themselves have artistic pretensions. They know best what art should be, they want to be its adjudicators.

The people used to have no interest in making art; the distinction of being a part of it, as model, object, or inspiration, was enough. Now they reckon that if it *doesn't* reflect them, or is not made by them, it has no right to exist.

B So you would keep art from the child of Mexican immigrants who discovers creative self-expression and self-realization in describing the condition of his existence?

A No, I still have the old compassion in abundance: I want the disadvantaged to have the opportunity to discover and develop their talent, to see where it takes them. I just don't think art should be the first stop for them. Was great art ever about self-expression and description? The self is far too overrated!

Those who throw themselves into art, they don't worry me. They are serious. I encourage them. I don't want real effort to go to waste. Only vanity should die on the vine. I object to the judge who on the one hand keeps them out, on the other embraces a select few of these castaways, eternally indebted to him, just for show, as proof of open-mindedness. I'm not sure those he embraces are always the best.

B There I agree. They are strategic choices.

A As "immigrants," they have more respect for standards (I won't say reverence — even I see this as too romantic, too dated), in much the same way that non-native speakers who want to assimilate are better than natives on grammar. If only they kept an ear to the ground...

My fear is that the average person will sooner drag art down with them to do their bidding than make an effort to be art-worthy. Like those who would rather pull the tree to the ground to reach the highest fruit than climb it or pick what is low-hanging, and end up breaking it in half. We might end up without art and with as much vulgarity as before: bruised fruit and barren tree. Art will not only become common, it will also be indistinguishable from the mundane everyday. Don't forget that even if art in the age of Louis XIV reflected the life of the nobility, it was still only the life of the nobility. And the Romantics were not *of* the people they dilated on, had not themselves been dragged through the street and lived to tell about it. It is only recently, after decades of encouragement from and reshaping of mentalities among the learned, that the aesthetically semi- or uneducated are claiming the right to define art, to the applause of postmodern egalitarians who had insisted on not corrupting them with a canon. And all in the name of what?

B Of innovation, of thinking outside the box. Tradition is linear. Genius is non-linear. The weight of tradition had become too great; the new was stultified by it. Someone had to sweep it aside, to clear the air. It's still there if you want access to it. It's just now much less overwhelming.

A This conceit of originality... [*shaking head*] We're convinced we can do better, be more brilliant, than our predecessors, than our *precursors*—if we even allow them that honour anymore. And, truth be told, there is a lot that's nasty in tradition... Not necessarily individually, but as a society, we think we have exponentially more-better to offer one another. We don't want to owe the old anything, we self-made people. We want the future to owe us everything.

B You sound like a snob. Worse: a moralizing snob. My advice is that you keep these ideas under wraps—some cheese cloth—until the storm passes. Personally, I'm determined to ride it out. It's too exciting.

A You're getting to work, then?

B Now that everything is turned upside down, I can realistically hope that any rubbish I put out will be hailed somewhere as a treasure. Even the challenging stuff can be marketed as brain-training. A work without redeeming qualities is hard to find. It must really be outré to be widely disliked—and no dislike is universal. Ergo, there's no such thing as overrated.

A If you say so.

B I will prove it!
   Happy are the days when art has never been easier...
   [*winking and singing out of tune*].

⁎⁎

11

⸹ No Outside

With the closing of pagan philosophy schools in Byzantium in 529 C.E., the world seemed to become safer for the god of the Christians. Those idols that witnessed the birth of philosophy were left in the dust by a more coherent Mythos. But coherence and other structures that had characterized philosophy in the Classical world also needed to be overcome. The Christian god, himself no philosopher, was identified with Logos. Dialectical theology would have to wait for Abelard. Meanwhile, Logos annexed the universe. The wonderful casualness of pagan theology and philosophy were replaced by pedantry and syllogism.

⸹ Proof (in the Recipe)

It is impossible to commit to this way of expressing oneself: in the briefest possible, clearest possible form, as the voice of impersonal reason. All acts of communication betray some hope of being understood. But rational communicative acts are characterized by the hope of being understood perfectly.

Most acts are not of this kind, and prove that our understanding is used to imperfection. But it is not imperfect and difficult on account of our failure to reduce the objects of our understanding to sets of rational propositions. Already computers are teaching us things we didn't want to know: that to understand others or be part of a culture is to be able to mimic them and to extrapolate based on only their behaviour and appearance. Understanding takes exposure, and exposure is what we're in the process of (technologically) unlearning. Rationalization, which we are after, is of little use to understanding unless it comes with the explanation of causes (of behaviour, appearance, etc.), which are too complex for our brains to handle. To always sign off before we awake from our dream of reason, of perfect form, is to wish away imperfection.

§ Dry Run

For another's "big thoughts in big words" to sink in, you need not depth but distance. Only at a distance from their source can their intimate company with one's own mind be appreciated.

Encountered in person, direct from the mouth of their originator, they strike us as incongruous with their surroundings. When they come — even if they come self-undercutting themselves — rather than to gravity, their prodigiousness incites us to *ridicule*.

⸹ From the Thinking Hat

Rule no. 1: Make space. Thoughts need room to be thought.

Rule no. 2: Make time. Time is not on the side of thoughts.

I go by these rules in every one of my hat-tricks. Following them asks that you fancy yourself a bit of a magician. If no one yet appreciates your sleight-of-mind, insist — *insist on doing it again!* Practice, remember, makes illusion perfect. Sooner or later they will have to marvel at your art of pulling ever-new and fully-formed thoughts out of the same old empty hat. There is more to the trick than the magical formula, they know that much.

⸹ A Kind of Illusionism

The popular belief in the magical qualities of white rabbits may have sprung from our confusion of the prop with the performance in which it makes a memorable appearance. The rabbit's being an accessory to magic has made it more magical. As with white rabbits, so it is with many ideas.

⸹ Three Clear Thoughts

Thinking as source of certainty, and its mouth.

Thinking as the bed of certainty, and its bank.

Thinking as the cradle of certainty, and its grave.

⸹ Impressions

An impression is a thought too brief.

⸹ The Clarity of Clouds

When you hear *Oh-ho*, remain underimpressed. To be easily impressed, even if it is just for society's sake, is the first step not to poetry but to cloudy thinking. On the other hand, if you prefer clouds, they welcome heads that can reach into them. You can then study them up close, and be impressed at your leisure.

⟆ Found Ideas

Let's quote approvingly: "A person who discounts backpacking as a means of travel is liable also to discount the potential interest of places that can be reached only by that means."* And let's also put in a word for the vagrant beachcomber, who hangs around the coastline picking up what most travellers overlook when looking only for "nature's truth," the "oceanic," or training their minds on horizons and sunsets. Rather than views and sights (even those found by backpackers), the beachcomber is after things and objects. He favours out-of-the-way places where he is likelier to find them: remote, wild beaches on which the debris and refuse of civilization wash up with the tide, and secret beaches, like that one in the Gulf of Mexico — created by a test bomb and accessed only by a water tunnel. Admittedly, the beachcomber is himself no great traveller; in his rucksack he carries just what he can sell. Call him a tramp, but admit that what he finds of interest, of value, and then offers for sale, has itself made a long journey — of which he is now a great facilitator.

These two, the backpacker and the beachcomber, have a special relationship with found ideas. If the first helps generate them, the second extends their life by putting them back into circulation.

---

* Jan Zwicky, *Lyric Philosophy* (Toronto: University of Toronto Press, 1992), sec. 47.

§ Finish Your Thought!

As in death, we are equalized in thought when we think that every mind in its effort to comprehend the world must come upon the unthinkable.

§ Think for Yourself…

…not others. There is no such thing as thought to spare, only to share.

§ Overheard

The well-wrought aphorism "conveys a portion of a truth with such point as to set us thinking on what remains."[*]

---

[*] John Morley, "Aphorisms" (lecture, Edinburgh Philosophical Institution, Edinburgh, Nov. 11, 1887), http://www.readbookonline.net/readOnLine/45446/.

§ Proverbial Philosophy

Certain wisdom can only be hit upon unawares, by a violent elucidation. Proverbs—those indirect, figurative, earthy, pithy sayings that refuse to come to a nice point—have earned their handle "dark sayings." Like birds flushed out with torches and cudgels by nocturnal hunters, their dormant meanings must be caught in situ or not at all. Startled from their nests, they give themselves up in the twinkling of an eye and expire from shock or blows, which gives the lie to their truth—just as their truth in turn gives them the lie.

§ Robust Arguments

Arguments today are exposed to far more scrutiny and are more vulnerable to disconfirmation by "facts" than they were in the factless past. Robust arguments in the realm of social ideas—e.g., the revolutionary power of social media—are those that have been attacked and, rather than definitively debunked, falsified unconvincingly or without attracting attention, because the particulars seem too insignificant to undermine them. You can try to dismantle them, or pull out bricks to undermine their structural integrity, or lay siege to them, but they will only reconstitute themselves stronger than before; taking them apart brick by brick takes too long, faith quickly fills the gaps, or else the ruins of ideas immediately give rise to a passionate nostalgia for them.

∫ Tyranny of Knowledge

The verb "to know" is no more meaningful than the verb "to ignore"—even if "to ignore" speaks to us more now, when knowledge appears overrated and ignorance more valuable because undeluded.

∫ Take My Word for It

The democratization of knowledge describes not a process whereby knowledge once shrouded in secrecy is made known to all, but a process whereby knowledge goes from being something principally gnostic, a secret held by a few, to being information that is widely disclosed and circulated without regard to spatial and temporal limits, or veracity. And ignorance, keeping step with this development, goes from being a majority condition to something virtually unknown, or known by only a few.

⟡ Philosophizing without a Hammer

In a little anecdote from the great Boethius recalled by Daniel Heller-Roazen, we learn about Pythagoras's ignorance of the fifth, discordant hammer in the forge of his new knowledge. When conducting experiments that would lead him to the *tetrad*, the mathematizing philosopher apparently discarded an inconvenient fact of existence to keep the integrity of his knowledge of essences.

The parallel emerging in this story between the relation of knowledge to ignorance, its shadow-other, and that of exclusion to inclusion might make us wonder. The coming-to-the-surface — to the surface of knowledge — of compromising facts or insights, not simply unknown but crucially *ignored* at the source — what does it amount to? Is it little more than "sabotage" or, in the luckier cases, a fillip to refine old knowledge — and in this sense absorbed by it or neutralized? Or is it, on the contrary, a contender to knowledge, however modest, *in its own right*? One is tempted to answer: an act of epistemic disruption is an act of epistemic irruption. But it can, it seems, only lay claim to epistemic value if it stays true to its calling as counter-knowledge and stands as a reflection on the exclusivity of all knowledge, rather than as a point scored against the monolith. As soon as a new body of knowledge is allowed to grow around such disruptive-irruptive events, that reflection is lost from sight, and ignorance again becomes manifest.

§ **Settling Ignorance**

Can we speak of an "epistemology of ignorance" without contradiction? When facing ignorance are we not at the limit of the knowable? Or can we only ever speak of ignorance as an epistemic *frontier*? Beyond the frontier lies not only the unknown but also the ignorant.

Should we not question, for instance on ethical grounds, the expansionist paradigm of knowledge, according to which perpetually pushing back epistemic frontiers is our manifest destiny and right—one that clearly depends on ignorance, or knowledge deemed false, which is demolished, the ground under it cleared and cultivated, or preserved as a "colonial village" with scholars for actors?

§ **The Umbrella of Unknowing**

What do the ignoramus, the skeptic, the agnostic, the holy fool, the madman, the savage, the mob, and the devil have in common? In their faces we can scrutinize *ignorance* as Nietzsche did morality—"as result, as symptom, as mask, as tartuffery, as sickness, as misunderstanding; but also...as cause, remedy, stimulant, inhibition, poison"* of all knowledge.

---

* Friedrich Nietzsche, preface to *On the Genealogy of Morality*, ed. Keith Ansell-Pearson, trans. Carol Diethe, rev. ed. (Cambridge, UK: Cambridge University Press, 2006), p. 7, sec. 6.

∫ Professing Ignorance

> [N]*othing is more routine than the irony which, like baking powder, helps to raise the kneaded dough of private opinion.*
> —Walter Benjamin[*]

It was to be expected that the history of learning would reach a supreme point of self-irony, making "Socratic irony" look like child's play: the profession of knowledge now *requires* professing ignorance, debunking ignorance posing as ironic knowledge. The accessibility of digitized objects of knowledge, a godsend for autodidacts and hobby apprentices, leads many others to mistake the contents of the internet for those of their own mind, open access for de facto education. As more youth is fed through universities, the job of the professor is increasingly to instruct students in their own and society's non-knowledge, un-teaching the "wired" notion that the web is a functional extension of their brain, and with it the cynical idea that "misinformation" *here* can be useful and even accurate over *there*. The larger aim of this paideia is to reclaim patches of formal education from "the same old cabbage" (to cite Hegel) it now resembles. With the declining authority of university curricula, unable to deal with knowledge's obsolescence, Socratic methods of teaching would obviously be ill-advised, but professors admitting ignorance via the critique of knowledge as un-ironic "agnosia" (witlessness) — downright suicidal. To continue to turn a profit, ignorance itself must be thematized and made the topic of instruction, while irony should be avoided at all cost.

---

[*] Walter Benjamin, "Left-Wing Melancholy (on Erich Kästner's New Book of Poems)" (1931), trans. Ben Brewster, *Screen* 15, no. 2 (1974): 29.

§ Smarter and Dumber

It is now clear that *public debate* could only ever be expanded by smartening up and dumbing down.

But:

It is now also clear that *social levelling* could only ever be successful by smartening *down* and dumbing *up*.

⸹ Can Speak, Will Travel

The Socratic and Christian suspicion of eloquence, at the base of the distinction between speaking well and thinking well, is being re-formed into naïvety, driven by dominant images of professional success. Effective, which is to say persuasive, speaking — inseparable today from technologically assisted performance skills — goes a long way, around the globe practically. The ability to present one's ideas in person and under pressure reveals an ability to think on one's feet — the more exciting kind of thinking — inherently valuable for its immediate results. Ad hoc thinking, brainstorming, roundtables, talks — all these hone speech, though not without a cost to written communication and the complexity of meaning admitted to graphically assisted thought.

The instrumentalization of thinking, its loss of innocence — signalled by the naïve embrace of the benefits of eloquence — means, however, that we are in on the power of speaking well (which includes taking the floor at an opportune moment), if not always on its power over us. As though thoughts could ever do without speech! Who has time for reading nowadays? It is clear that, where pure thought is concerned, speech is more important than writing!

It is only in some "monastic" spaces — the shrinking oases where thought is valued without having to be communicated — that wariness of eloquence is still preserved and warnings are issued against it: a spiritual danger to the truth, a holdout of devilry! Everywhere else, however, it is the knowledge of eloquence that daily renders it both powerful, and powerless.

⸹ Mark My Words

The strength of written language lies in the communication of ideas — in contrast to speech, best at conveying sentiments. Forcing writing to emote could not be done without adulterating it, without "enlarg[ing] [and] stretch[ing]," Rousseau noted in the *Essay on the Origin of Languages*,[*] and we can only surmise that he did so with passion. Conversational writing, a concession by the written word to the virtues of the spoken, may have made sense before speaking across great distances became a reality; it is now ripe for revisiting. The arts of speechifying, oratory, and of poetry, which began in the voice, were once divided from those of law and epistolography — the arts of writing, excluding calligraphy. The widening of poetry's circulation in written form at the expense of oral transmission also spelled its intellectualization: where earlier ideas and plots were yoked to the epic, lyric, or dramatic description or expression of embodied, enacted, felt emotion, writing it down forced poetry to mean. Under the sway of metaphor, its emotional resonance was subordinated to more complex ideational structures, to allegory, trope, image, and experiments in linguistic form to its breaking point. No quantity of recitatives and author readings could restore sentiment to poetry not written to be performed.

Today, made culturally viable by mass-mediated oral transmission, spoken poetry has returned. Let us wish for it, not the complete abstention from ideas long enjoyed by lyrics in popular and folk music, but an imbalance between sentiment, on the one (heavier) side, and concept, image and idea, on the other, in recognition of poetry's imagistic history, minus its cerebral obsession with perfection.

Church and state need no reminders that scripting speeches dulls expressiveness, robbing public appearance

---

[*] Jean-Jacques Rousseau, "Essay on the Origin of Languages, in Which Something Is Said about Music and Musical Imitation," in *The 'Discourses' and Other Early Political Writings*, ed. Victor Gourevitch, trans. Victor Gourevitch (Cambridge, UK: Cambridge University Press, 1997), p. 260, ch. 5.

of its best means of persuasion. The academic repertoire of *lectures*, or texts read aloud, *papers*, *presentations*, and *"talks"* done from notes has as its nemesis thoroughly scripted, exhaustively rehearsed *TED talks*, made to look spontaneous, delivered dynamically, with highly transmissible passion and sans notes. You are prepared for one when you can give it in your sleep; the script is internalized enough that you are free to embroider emotionally before the audience. Though most speeches today are written, memories being what they are, the larger the concession to an audience to be won over, the less the text is corrupted by the conceptual complexities of writing.

In personal communication, meanwhile, one might wish for freedom, not from the memory of a thirst for passionate sharing, but from the *emoticons* devised to satisfy it. (There is no threat of incursion from emotive symbolism and "personal" feelings into legal, administrative, or academic prose, where ideas still ostracize feeling.) Let writing, in other words, continue to serve the communication of ideas and the evocation — not of emotions, but of moods and atmospheres, culminating in philosophical meditation. Let embodied speech deal with the rest, and reach its aesthetic pitch in poetry.

ſ Almost Being

The smaller the animal, the less the distance between being and its sensation. In this way, the smallest beings are closer to presence than us, who come face to face with being and do not sense it. What is our compensation for being so large?

§ Don't Imagine…

> *If an angel were ever to tell us anything of his philosophy I believe many propositions would sound like 2 times 2 equals 13.*
> —G.Ch. Lichtenberg

> *If a lion could talk, we wouldn't be able to understand it.*
> —Ludwig Wittgenstein, enthusiast of Lichtenberg

> *All the thoughts of a turtle are turtles*
> —Ralph Waldo Emerson

> *After all, what would be left of what it was like to be a bat if one removed the viewpoint of the bat?*
> —Thomas Nagel[*]

Imagining and speculating about nonhuman experience makes us smaller. Why is it that we insist on being able to comprehend it all? Because little by little we are *becoming* our outside. The thoughts of a turtle will one day be shared by men who are part turtle, the arithmetic of angels, had angels ever existed, by semi-angels, the speech of a lion, by lion-man, the mindset of a bat—you guessed it. Even the experience of the next man will one day be accessible to us.

Whenever we recognize this phenomenological drift, we start to prepare mentally for these interspecies liaisons, which will support us in our smallness. But when we set out only to know, we train for a fantasy takeover, ruling nothing.

---

[*] Georg Christoph Lichtenberg, *The Waste Books*, trans. R.J. Hollingdale (New York: NYRB, 2000), p. 26, Notebook B: 1768–71, sec. 44; Ludwig Wittgenstein, *Philosophical Investigations*, ed. P.M.S. Hacker and Joachim Schulte, trans. G.E.M. Anscombe, P.M.S. Hacker, and Joachim Schulte (1953; Hoboken, NJ: Wiley-Blackwell, 2009), p. 235e, sec. 327; Ralph Waldo Emerson, *The Journals and Miscellaneous Notebooks of Ralph Waldo Emerson*, vol. 13, *1852–1855* (Cambridge, MA: Harvard University Press, 1977), 357; Thomas Nagel, "What Is It Like to Be a Bat?" *Philosophical Review* 83, no. 4 (1974): 443.

◊ Think, Pig!

The truth of Lévi-Strauss's idea that "animals are good to think with"* can be deepened if we replace "animals" with "philosophers," and "philosophers" again with "animals." (And I do not mean anything so refined as "philosophical animals.")

◊ Thinking Thinking

Like one hand clapping, thinking thinking has a muted sound.

◊ New Line of Thought

Every new line of thought is a departure.

Or a new way of arriving where one already is.

---

* Paraphrase of "We can understand, too, that natural species are chosen not because they are 'good to eat' but because they are 'good to think.'" Claude Lévi-Strauss, *Totemism*, trans. Rodney Needham (Boston: Beacon, 1963), 89.

§ The Thinking Head

A guillotined *caput* remains conscious for a few seconds, as many as 25 or so. The head always thought itself better than the torso and limbs, from which it has now been severed. Bracketing for the moment the macabre image, what would you think in its place? Would you think yourself *free at last*, or *I'm ahead, I have outlived the rest!*, or *I'm just a head that anyone can kick around*?

§ Self-Inquisition

> *We would not let ourselves be burned to death for our opinions: we are not sure enough of them for that. But perhaps for the right to possess our opinions and to change them.*
> —Friedrich Nietzsche[*]

Nietzsche was right: we should let ourselves be *burnt* either for *not* having opinions or for *not* changing them often enough. And we should ourselves set fire to those of our own opinions of which we are sure. This is the self-inquisition of the future.

---

[*] Nietzsche, *Human, All Too Human*, p. 391, vol. 2, pt. 2: The Wanderer and His Shadow, sec. 333 ("Dying for 'Truth'").

§ Phases of Power

The past two centuries saw logical *systems* cede to speculative *structures*. The idea that only a system could have a grasp of the power to rule and alter the world yielded to the idea that only structures could get the job done. Structure mirroring power was credited with the capacity to undermine it, forcing it to change and, with it, the world. At a time when large-scale logical systems were difficult to implement in reality, the system stood as the compass of complexity, the *ne-plus-ultra* mode of conceptualizing power (systematic theology, the system of nature) and of harnessing it to shape the world (the socialist and the liberal system). Once it became possible to implement, or at least to model, such systems, systematic thinking of power began to be seen as unduly restrictive. The stage was set for the concept of structure to address the power that systems had tried to contain but could not. The fluidity of structures was seen to reflect the dynamics of inchoate power, as yet external to existing systems. But structures, too, have had their day, and we have moved on to *networks* — still more fluid, open, contingent, self-consciously lacking ontological foundation. The relation between power and the idea we have of it is one of continual adjustment, tweaks, and balancing acts.

∫ One Leg in Paradise

Good ideas don't grow on trees. Bad ones still do.

∫ False Analogues

Argument is to *assertion* as *certainty* is to *conviction*. Except that conviction needs an argument, while certainty has no need of assertion.

§ Unconvinced

> *"Believing" means, submitting to an authority. Having once submitted to it, you cannot then, without rebelling against it, first call it in question & then once again find it convincing.*
> —Wittgenstein

> *a very popular error: having the courage of one's convictions; rather it is a matter of having the courage for an* attack *on one's convictions!!!*
> —Nietzsche

> *We have convictions only if we have studied nothing thoroughly.*
> —E.M. Cioran*

When Nietzsche writes, "It is not the conflict of opinions that has made history so violent but conflict of belief in opinions, that is to say conflict of convictions,"† he does all of those who hold on to their convictions without going to war an ill turn. Some of us feel that, at the end of the day, our convictions are *all we have left*, after arguments, opinions and points of view, interchangeable like educated guesses, fall away (if one gives credence to the skeptic, as one must). Convictions, however, remain with us because they fall under the jurisdiction not of reason, but of passion. And, pathos-driven, they are considered *blind*. Their sharers—fellow travellers on the scissor-gated *lift of conviction*, whether or not they share the same belief—are invariably after their own heart. One cannot step on and off, as with the *paternoster of rational argument*, whenever one decides to, risking being cut in two (winding up "of two minds," in other words).

---

* Ludwig Wittgenstein, *Culture and Value: A Selection from the Posthumous Remains*, ed. Alois Pichler, Georg Henrik von Wright, in collaboration with Heikki Nyman, trans. Peter Winch, rev. ed. (1977; Oxford: Blackwell, 1998), 52; quoted in Walter Kaufman, *Nietzsche: Philosopher, Psychologist, Antichrist*, 4th ed. (Princeton, NJ: Princeton University Press, 1974), 354; E.M. Cioran, *The Trouble with Being Born*, trans. Richard Howard (New York: Arcade, 1998), 134.

† Nietzsche, *Human, All Too Human*, p. 199, vol. 1, sec. 630.

Violence is precisely the work of reason, with its *just* reasons. When they are not defended *with conviction*, reasons are (at least provisionally) held by their bearers to be unassailable, inviolable, while themselves violating our entire passional structure of thought. When, however, conviction comes to their aid, they hide; conviction rarely turns volatile, let alone explosive, without some fanatical reason behind it, which it protects and conceals, and for which it takes the blame. It is the fire to reason's spark.

Conviction in and of itself has no great ambition, being principally concerned with its own survival — as is clear in its Polish name, *przekonanie* (*prze-*, "through," *konanie*, the agony of dying), and less so — which is perhaps at the root of Nietzsche's condemnation of it — in the German *Überzeugung*, whose stem, *Zeugung* means "conception," "procreation" (and whose prefix got its reputation from his followers). Etymologically the Polish word evokes lethal force, marking its agent as a "convict." Yet it denotes a state or condition that results from convincing, whose violence — absent reason — is anyhow exaggerated. One might narrate it as follows. The bearer of conviction is one who has survived an act of belief and bears this new conviction (even when the legacy of brainwashing) not as a cross but as a treasure, having every right to defend it to the death. (So you see in this willingness to die for what almost killed one only a cycle of abuse? I assure you it's all fully consensual!). This, then, is the thrust of "having the courage of one's convictions": maintaining one's intellectual integrity and/or independence of thought, and *not*, as with absolute truths, striving to overthrow all others. The blessings of intellectual passivity! "Opinions grow out of *passions*," which are fiery-hot; it is by no means the "*inertia of the spirit* [that] lets them stiffen into convictions," but its lauded cooling effect.[*] And when they stiffen, they do so in its defence.

But such formulations are anathema to those who vilify conviction on principle and in practice. They assume that conviction, with its "pathologically conditioned optics," is

---

[*] Ibid., p. 203, vol. 1, sec. 637.

only "extreme fanaticism," self-sacrificing adherence to precisely one or another absolute, "unqualified truth."* Nietzsche calls convictions converted "lies"—converted but not eliminated, a case of Lutheranism.† They are clearly no denials of untruth. But neither are they truth-denials. Rather, they are dogmatic embraces of untruth *as absolute truth*, and for that reason "more dangerous enemies of truth than lies."‡ They are motivating yet unexamined, imperative yet undiscussable, deeply held yet "general," "public."§ They have, for him, no range, but are uniformly negative, sick, suspect.

Conviction is also aligned by its basher-in-chief with personal gain, hunger for recognition, and power over others.¶ On the question of gain, Nietzsche does not see convictions as what they plainly are: *one's own* beliefs, passional-intellectual property that, in their particular constellation and value, are non-fungible, *mine alone*. Such strong attachment and sense of ownership is absent from the domain of reasons. But it is conviction's connection with, and cooption by, truth that I want to foreground...

"Conviction is the belief that on some particular point of knowledge one is in possession of the unqualified truth. This belief thus presupposes that unqualified truths exist; likewise that perfect methods of attaining to them have been discovered; finally, that everyone who possesses convictions avails himself of these perfect methods."** Nietzsche's assertions and inferences still apply to fanatics everywhere, particularly to *moral fanatics*, whose devotion lends sublimity to their truth. Putting to one side facile syllogisms, fanatics are not all "convicts," which is to say men or women of

---

* Friedrich Nietzsche, "Anti-Christ," in *The Anti-Christ, Ecce Homo, Twilights of the Idols and Other Writings*, ed. Aaron Ridley and Judith Norman, trans. Judith Norman (Cambridge, UK: Cambridge University Press, 2005), p. 54, sec. 54; Nietzsche, *Human, All Too Human*, p. 199, vol. 1, sec. 630.

† Nietzsche, "Anti-Christ," p. 54, sec. 54.

‡ Nietzsche, *Human, All Too Human*, p. 179, vol. 1, sec. 483.

§ Ibid., p. 288, vol. 2, sec. 325.

¶ Ibid., p. 165, vol. 1, sec. 452.

** Ibid., p. 199, vol. 1, sec. 630.

conviction, and not all "convicts" succumb through reason's machinations to fanaticism. In point of fact, the person of conviction breaks from absolute truth and ventures out on a limb—where he or she is vulnerable, but where integrity bids them go. And such people, habituated not to offence but to defence and survival, are the best armour of fanatics. With conviction for a shield, absolute truth can be even more active and daring—in a word, *fanatical*—advancing and conquering new territory with the persistence particular to it.

Nietzsche welcomes the instrumentalization of convictions for the sake—not of *truth*, but of skepticism. Among the "unholy means" willed by the great skeptic, who remains above them, they are only acceptable as the willed means to a willed end: "there are many things that can be achieved only by means of a conviction. Great passion uses convictions and uses them up, it does not subordinate itself to them,—it knows its own sovereignty."[*] He recognizes that some credit must go to conviction (or what he labels as such) for what is dear to his heart.

> *If the individual had not been concerned with his "truth," that is to say with his being in the right, there would have been no methods of inquiry at all; but with the claims of different individuals to unqualified truth everlastingly in conflict with one another, men went on step by step to discover incontestable principles by which these claims could be tested and the contest decided.*[†]

This is why Nietzsche *encourages* us to attack convictions— But *attack* on what grounds? Those of reason and justice, of course. The eternal violence of history has its positive side: without convictions there would be no scientific sobriety. Little by little, the war between competing absolute-truth-claims has given shape to "scientific inquiry," a series of "steps" meant to settle whose truth *can* in fact qualify as

---

[*] Nietzsche, "Anti-Christ," p. 54, sec. 54.

[†] Nietzsche, *Human, All Too Human*, p. 201, vol. 1, sec. 634.

next-to-absolute, which is to say irrefutable. There is, it must be said, no better way towards consensus than a hard and fast set of rules to disqualify individual players — rules that cannot be argued with further, whose indisputability has about it a whiff of the open grave.

And yet, make no mistake: conviction is fundamentally discontinuous with scientific truth: "the man of convictions is not the man of scientific thought; he stands before us in the age of theoretical innocence and is a child, however grown up he may be in other respects."[*] *It* does not *seek* scientific self-proof; rather, it *assumes*, it arrogates for itself all kinds of truth, without qualification or distinction. This, by Nietzsche's lights, is its cardinal turpitude. (Though there seems to have been some debate in his mind about whether *childhood* is not perhaps the best cultural state.)

"Nowadays, however, we no longer so easily concede to anyone that he is in possession of the truth: the rigorous procedures of inquiry have propagated distrust and caution, so that anyone who advocates opinions with violent word and deed is felt to be an enemy of our present-day culture, or at least as one retarded."[†] And typically as a fanatic, resident and "picturesque."[‡] "And the pathos of *possessing* truth does now in fact," Nietzsche continues, "count for very little in comparison with that other, admittedly gentler and less noisy pathos of seeking truth that never wearies of learning and examining anew."[§] But does science itself — if not we — actually side with skepticism? Their contiguity is far from obvious. A clever maneuver on the part of *scientific truthers*: by playing both sides to stake a claim to moderation. "[T]he scientific spirit in men has to bring to maturity that virtue of *cautious reserve*."[¶] Bring forth...virtue...why of course: *Zeugung* (conception, procreation)! And Über*zeugung*!

---

[*] Ibid., p. 199, vol. 1, sec. 630.
[†] Ibid., p. 201, vol. 1, sec. 633.
[‡] Nietzsche, "Anti-Christ," p. 54, sec. 54.
[§] Nietzsche, *Human, All Too Human*, p. 201, vol. 1, sec. 633.
[¶] Ibid., p. 200, vol. 1, sec. 631.

It makes you appreciate really how *fertile* man's scientific spirit is in its conviction.

In an age of skepticism, when despite science's best efforts consensus is harder than ever to come by, conviction can finally return to grace. From alleged defender of absolute truth and antithesis of provisional, scientific truth, it may turn coat to become friend of *no truth at all*. As Saint John Cassian reminded the faithful, "Excesses meet," and extremes are known to flip into their opposites. And how do convictions fare in the culture at large? "[B]y far the greater part of all educated people even now still desire from a thinker convictions and nothing but convictions, and that only a small minority want *certainty*.... Insofar as genius of every kind maintains the fire of convictions and awakens distrust of the modesty and circumspection of science, it is an enemy of truth, no matter how much it may believe itself to be truth's suitor."[*] (Well remarked, and even better said.) Convictions, opponents of both minoritarian judgment and of genius (counting that of justice), are *still* fashionable in the culture at large — and *newly* so — *because they are taken to be opposed to lies* (mistakenly, as Nietzsche says).[†] Being anti-lie does not make them absolutely true. In a *supposed* age of skepticism, then, the coast is clear for convictions. And with predatory genius away, why *shouldn't* they come out to play?

> [T]*he beings who did not see things exactly had a head start over those who saw everything "in a flux." As such, every great degree of caution in inferring, every sceptical disposition, is a great danger to life. No living being would be preserved had not the opposite disposition — to affirm rather than suspend judgement, to err and make things up rather than wait, to agree rather than deny, to pass judgement*

---

[*] Ibid., p. 202, vol. 1, sec. 635.
[†] Ibid., p. 202, vol. 1, sec. 636; Nietzsche, "Anti-Christ," p. 55, sec. 54.

> *rather than be just — been bred to become extraordinarily strong.*[*]

How now? The cat-"genius" proves deadlier to itself — weaker, biologically weaker, than the mice? Second nature is like Marx's *camera obscura* of ideology without the lie that is ideology. Just as the immoral and the immoralists have an edge on those who are not like them, so *homo volens* (murine) gets one over on *homo rationalis* (feline), and the will to play is continuous with the will to get away.

∫ Humble Pie

As inspiring as it is, Plato's image in the *Timaeus* of the human as an upside-down plant ("we are not an earthly but a heavenly plant up from earth towards our kindred in the heaven"[†]) has us uprooted from our "proper" ground, which cultivates and appropriates us unawares. To claim that ideology is the reason we do not cultivate our own ground as is proper to us is, precisely, ideology. The truth of Plato's image, even if untrue to Plato's meaning, is this: we moderns are more than ever "rooted" in the sky of ideology instead of in the ground out of which we grow and which nourishes us. We thereby arrive at an accurate picture of our grounding in and relationship to the world: up through ideology, then down to the dominion over nature — rather than down through some mythical humility, and only then humbly up towards the mystery of creation.

---

[*] Friedrich Nietzsche, *The Gay Science, with a Prelude in German Rhymes and an Appendix of Songs*, ed. Bernard Williams, trans. Josefine Nauckhoff and Adrian del Caro (Cambridge, UK: Cambridge University Press, 2001), p. 112, sec. 111.

[†] Plato, *Timaeus*, trans. W.R.M. Lamb (University of Chicago: Perseus Project under PhiloLogic, 2009), http://perseus.uchicago.edu/, sec. 90a.

§ Prison Yard

> *Rational thought is interpretation according to a scheme we cannot throw off.*
> —Nietzsche[*]

The more elaborate a logical and philosophical system, the more demanding and "counterintuitive" its chains of inference, the more those bound by it touch the iron bars of that prison reserved only for the most rational of animals. With every attempt to stretch human cognition, we jangle our chains like prisoners circling a prison yard. When we impose on this wretched spectacle a logic, a meaningful pattern, our slightest movement receives the stamp of order, and the procession becomes a thing of beauty, escape from which would mean its unjustifiable destruction.

---

[*] Friedrich Nietzsche, *The Will to Power*, ed. Walter Kaufmann, trans. Walter Kaufmann and R.J. Hollingdale (New York: Vintage, 1968), p. 283, sec. 522 (1886–1887) (mod. trans.).

⸹ A Sublime Mind

> *I'm the only one who knows what I might have been able to do.... For everyone else I'm pretty much a perhaps.*
>
> *...*
>
> *A hunter in a forest fires his gun, his prey falls, he comes to get it. His boot smashes into an anthill, two feet high, and destroy the ants' home; ants are scattered far and wide, their eggs.... The best ant philosopher could never understand this huge black thing, immense, horrible — the hunter's boot — which suddenly broke into their dwelling, with incredible speed, and just before that happened there had been a dreadful noise, together with a shower of reddish sparks....*
>
> *...*
>
> *A mayfly born at nine in the morning, during the summer's long days, and dying at five that evening: How could it comprehend the word* night*? Let it live another five hours, and it sees and understands what night is.*
>
> —Stendhal, *The Red and the Black**

At the end of Stendhal's great novel, Julien Sorel seems to reach wisdom well beyond his years. It is the wisdom of his age. The most sublime moment of this often gallingly mediocre book is his superior frame of mind as he mocks "natural law" on the verge of death ("There are no *rights*, unless there's a law forbidding you to do this or that, or else you'll be punished. Before there's a law, there's nothing *natural* except a lion's strength, or the needs of someone who's hungry, who's cold — who, in short, *needs*...."†). We have here the sublimity of a mind created by another mind, erected, yet so like a mountain, its peak shrouded in mist, parting the clouds once thought celestial, and dissolving into nature (the mystery of death), surrendering itself to oblivion denied it by

---

*   Stendhal, *The Red and the Black: A Chronicle of the Nineteenth Century*, trans. Burton Raffel (1830; New York: Modern Library, 2004), 465, 478–79.

†   Ibid., 476.

the Christian faith with the skeptic's "great perhaps" on its lips. This intelligence ascends so high by virtue of suffering and enmity. It awes and impresses us because we are given only glimpses of its awakening to the ultimate reality of the *will* to survival (and the prohibitive nature of man-made laws). But from such comprehending height, survival, while not impossible, becomes secondary to the enjoyment of life comprehended as the struggle to reach this vantage point, whereupon its goal is fulfilled. Yet most men are content to shorten life before *knowing* it, or to live it as something *unknowable*.

*

How sad and infinitely pitiable is man reduced — in his pursuit of relief, refuge, or divine mercy that ends in chagrin, anguish, or forsakenness — to a child, without hope or even the memory of hope, not knowing where to turn for help, having faith or trust in neither friends nor strangers, in despair of ever being understood and unsure of ever having understood or communicated, whose will has wilted and frozen to the ground, whose good sense has left him, and who in his involuntary confusion loses all motivation to survive, and would rather starve than rise again. Was there ever a man who could snap out of his fear and terror once they overwhelmed him, rendering futile any attempt to resist them, so that resignation seemed the only sanity left, and the only possible way to live in the world was to lie down and die in it?

*

Not to have recognition just long enough to have settled into doing great things without much care for others' regard: this is the surest way of being saved from the early vanity that leads one to dismiss new prospects with a "been there, done that," to turn away from our potential by seeing the world schematically and individual experiences as types.

＊

It happens that a single mind "owns" the world, and feels it has outgrown it. Though it can only matter to the culture of this earth, it can conceive of others, and longs to conquer and convert the cosmic expanse into a plot for cultivation. Such is human insatiability that the simple vanity of schoolchildren can come to crown the universe, usurp all divinity. And if it can convince itself of this greatness, there is no stopping it.

§ Threaded

My desires seem incompatible, yet, he reasons, I myself still cohere. Reconciling incompatible desires before things fall apart is the task of the philosopher, who (in the limbo between projects) recognizes their incompatibility. Therein lies perhaps his greatest philosophical project: to pass all of them through the eye of the needle that is one's life.

§ *Vita contemplativa*

A   The life of the mind is nearly extinct.

B   Leave it to brains-in-vats! Leave it to the machines...

A   You think they'll revive it?

B   But of course! We'll transmit to them what we admire but have no more time for.

⸹ Beheading Games

In the intellectual contests of the academic world, which only seem to have gotten more intense, the one who leaves with his head under his arm one year will be welcomed back the next, barely a scratch on his reputation, this time as the more sympathetic figure.

⸹ Scattered

Think without scattering your thoughts. Nothing grows from them, no matter how thick on the ground, unless someone comes along willing to cultivate them.

⸹ Hoping for Queequeg?

Do not tell untruths; living with them is like sharing your bed with strangers.

◊ Crime Is a Failure of Society

Calculative reason will lead to calculated crime if no moral education is added where the *ability to think* is in the red. Knowing one's doing and intending, and knowing how to think, are necessary for punishment. Failure to think only exonerates where thinking cannot be taught.

◊ The Problem

Typically, what to the outsider seems an insoluble knot appears to him who has followed the thread wherever it may lead as a clear line. Neither has the upper hand, the former because he is still confounded, the latter because he does not yet see the problem. This is one of the reasons why knowledge advances so slowly, if at all.

◊ How Playful!

Playing as thinking makes for a very small playground.

§ Bodenlos

With enough recklessness or persistence, it is possible to think oneself into ultimate meaninglessness. Philosophy is a stone that falls into the abyss until it finds a ledge. Most of us only look down to see where it had landed; few go after it and rarely do they rest beside it on their crash course. Without philosophy, a tenacious mind, once it has begun to question, will continue falling, battered and bruised, tumbling along the way, until it no longer makes sense even to itself, and finally becomes unrecognizable.

§ The Ineffable

"It" is imponderable, unthinkable, unspeakable, inarticulable, because it circles like a moth around the enmeshed clarity of sense, and makes sense only upon contact, which — unless brief — is deadly to it. Should it then, for its own sake, be kept from making such contact? Should we refrain from finding the hole that our mind, eager for rest (even a final resting place), tears open in the protective mesh?

Sometimes we are not creative enough. But could this be a good thing? The experience of ineffability depends on patching up the scrim protecting "it" from attaining language — language that, as the matrix of intellectual creation, weakens and breaks and finally cremates "it" to keep alive our thought.

⸹ Perish the Thought

Otto Neurath's pronouncement, "One must indeed be silent—but not *about* anything," alludes to—by inverting—the call to pass over in silence that about which we cannot speak, with which Wittgenstein concludes his *Tractatus*.* According to Neurath, a logical positivist, everything we can think about can be spoken about; nothing of this kind is unsayable. If, as he believed, all thought is propositional, then the objects of thought (if they are to achieve that distinction) emerge only in language. True silence, internal stillness—rather than one teeming with thought—is never *about* anything. For instance, the silence "about" "God"...

Wittgenstein disagreed: one could be silent *about* something without inward verbalization. Thinking happens not just in words, but also in images, which do not speak. True internal-external silence indexes the unspeakable, tracing the boundary of a mystic ocean over which stretch the islands of a populous discursive archipelago. About the truly unsayable we *cannot but* remain silent, passing over it like migrating birds, which have seen but cannot tell of what they have overflown.

---

* Quoted in A.J. Ayer, *Wittgenstein* (Harmondsworth: Basic, 1986), 32.

§ Thinking in Tongues

Some say French has the great virtue of ordering words in the same way they naturally occur in thought. But hasn't the German language, with its odd verb placement (last in any subordinate clause), the great advantage of compelling the mind to review and perhaps clarify itself? What the one contributes in fluid expression, the other lends in belated precision. The lucky few who can boast fluency in both would add, naturally off the record, that those who speak neither might as well be thinking — if at all — only *in tongues*.

§ *Sancta simplicitas*

It seems that advances in linguistic expression, in both precision and style, are meant to lift us to a plateau from which we would at long last be able to speak plainly and be universally understood. The myriad languages and their aesthetic or practical elaboration (stream of consciousness, formal logic, legal argot, etc.) have at last been channelled into one stream of thought about human experience and through a "treatment system" to yield only the purest and clearest, watered-down kind of thinking. The comparatively difficult forms of clarified communication, it turns out, were merely its muddy tributaries.

⸹ Encyclops

> *The universe ... would only be one fact and one great truth for whoever knew how to embrace it from a single point of view.*
> —Jean le Rond d'Alembert, co-editor and -author of the *Encyclopédie**

Lest we forget, stereoscopic sight reminds us that a single human point of view was not in the evolutionary cards, no matter how adaptively advantageous it might seem *in the abstract*—all of us seeing eye to noumenal eye on Truth. In truth, we cannot even see eye to eye with ourselves, so that the Cyclopean *image* of reality, the monocular unity of perspective that is nature's gift to some animals, is not universal.

The one-eyed giant Polyphemus is blinded by a hero of Antiquity (whom some also rightly regard as the bearer of Enlightenment). The great monotheisms came up with a Cyclops God, His gaze compromised neither by positional particularity nor by fondness for drink. And the moderns gave the world the encyclopedia, now Wikipedia, as a tree from which to have partial, provisionally unified, shifting, views. Those who managed to possess an "encyclopedic" knowledge are rewarded, but harbour no illusions about occupying its many branches at once. Nothing makes clearer truth's preference for company and discussion—rather than solitude of vision, however desirable in the abstract—than the tableware edition of the *Encyclopédie*, ca. 1800, on display today in a museum. As the food was consumed, the true image of a coal factory gracing the dessert plates could be apprised and commented upon by everyone.

---

* Jean le Rond d'Alembert, "Preliminary Discourse to the Encyclopedia of Diderot," in *Encyclopédie, ou dictionnaire raisonné*, trans. Richard N. Schwab.

⸹ Outline of a Shadow

The popularity of silhouettes and shadow theatre should be sought in the suggestion of substance, which memory and imagination relish to fill in. This no doubt is a considerable part of the attraction of *abstract concepts*; to attribute it only to their communicative utility would be as mistaken as explaining the appeal of shadow puppets by their low cost of production. The enchantment of conceptual abstraction can be profound and elaborate — like that of the human shadow play in Dreyer's silent *Vampyr*. As long, that is, as you never try to touch or sink your teeth into such concepts in hopes of getting fed.

∫ Chicken Fence

> *While thought has forgotten how to think itself, it has at the same time become its own watchdog. Thinking no longer means anything more than checking at each moment whether one can indeed think.*
> —Adorno*

Thought's having forgotten how to think itself is the least of our troubles with thinking. After all, we still recall what laying eggs in our mental coop was like. Nature still works and will remember itself.

Can the same be said of nurture? The fence we have put up around thinking to protect it from predators reminds us that, headless or not, we can still think. But with the grass and roots gone, thinking is now just so much scratching around in the dirt.

∫ Tripwire

The distance from a statement ringing true to being true is very small, and bisected by a tripwire.

---

* Theodor W. Adorno, *Minima Moralia: Reflections on a Damaged Life*, trans. E.F.N. Jephcott (1951; New York: Verso, 2005), p. 197, sec. 126 ("I.Q.").

ꙮ Seeing the Light

All agree: the way to knowledge is dark, unclear, and no amount of "light at the end of the tunnel" will change that. That light, so often mistaken for knowledge, is why clarity is so sought after.

ꙮ Seek and Hide

> *"Ask, and it will be given to you; seek, and you will find; knock, and it will be opened to you. For everyone who asks receives, and he who seeks finds, and to him who knocks it will be opened."*
> —Matthew 7:7

Ask, seek, knock. The first stands for the school, the second for solitary study, the third for gnosis. If the search is by us alone, and its objects are not to be gotten in either the school or the hermetic corpus, then we must ask: where does the authority of what the seeker seeks and finds come from? It comes from the seeker, in the same way the arachnoid web whose centre the spider will soon command comes from its own body. The longer the thing we are after eludes us, the more substantial and robust its authority, once found, will become.

§ *Merveille du jour*

Modern philosophers proclaimed the untimeliness of their task. Knowing things only in the dying light, observing unfashionably, philosophy settled on a *grisaille* palette to paint its grey in grey, and adopted a soaring perspective above the day's influences. It turned its necessary late-coming and monochromia into epistemic insight and night vision (for approaching night). With its youth — which, as Hegel had it, did not rejuvenate but aged or overcame the timeworn — it avenged itself on the "old reality" that it failed to comprehend live.

And still it moves beneath the ragged cloak of twilight, which it throws over its still-bright prey. Isn't it time, Philosophy, for a hint of colour? — for contrast if the times seem drab, and otherwise for camouflage. A subtle cast of purple or green would become your grey, as it does the owlet moth that flies by night but by day mesmerizes with the beauty of its shading.

⸿ Whose Time Has Not yet Come

There are times when one's own untimeliness is acutely felt. One has come too early, or been born too late, and nonetheless one's own place in time remains unclear. How far ahead of or how close behind the times is one? Will the times catch up (in one's lifetime) or will one catch up to the times? Few if any have what it takes to lead a one-man vanguard to conquer the future; one is likelier to fall back. And is there time left to catch up to one's "contemporaries"? Unfashionableness beckons to those who like company, even if there is nothing in the familiar faces of bygones and classics to prove one *their* contemporaries; the past is an old-age home where one mixes with those of different ages. But for those who believe that being behind now may put them ahead later, a third, spiritual relation to time is in order. Their time falls not along time's continuum, but rises above it in the shape of an arc: from the past to the future, a rainbow over the meadows of the present. They are neither retiring nor active, neither "history" nor "to come," sharing neither the decrepitude of the first nor the burden of the second. They reside above, and fade as soon as they condescend to empathy with the has-beens, or to taking up arms with self-styled men of tomorrow.

◊ On Time

A Where are those whose time has not yet come?

B And where are you? What's *your* excuse?

◊ *Punctum*

They are pawning timeliness to afford punctuality.

◊ The Time Is Now

A Nowness is the new timeliness.

B And the old timeliness?

◊ Time Out

The symbolic power of timekeeping tickers is such that when one stops in silence and is heard, it is as though time itself has stopped, perhaps never to resume. That mental tension building the senses of past, present, and future soon disappears, and one by one time's tenses fall away. Any motion still visible, the lone fly on the rim of a glass, the vibration from a passing train, only discloses that stupid persistence and tardiness of the world of appearances before apocalypse or eternity.

§ House Arrest

You claim to have good reason for placing certain thinking heads under house arrest. Their circulation might corrupt, especially when they tap into that very modern disillusionment.

Couldn't a pedagogical question serve just as well to inoculate your pupils against them — as well or better than banning them? But that is not the question I have in mind to put to you. The question I meant, and which could be put in different words, is this: *Would I like to live where X thinker is coming from?* An honest *no* in reply will put off even those likeliest to be "corrupted."

Before you dismiss a philosophy because its philosopher showed himself a scoundrel, or fell in with moral beasts, consider this. Were not *certain cultural microclimes* such that they spoiled the coolest thinking heads, who previously had no moral blemish? Consistency asks that you also discard the cultural history that bore them, the bathwater in which they had bathed. Or would you have us throw out the baby and study only this dirty water? Consider this as well: that the farther back a philosophy lies the more excusable its faults become — just think of the chasm of time that separates us from Aquinas, Aristotle (and we are still only on the As). But why should not a smaller gap in time matter *as much*? Should we not think of them as similarly *far removed*?

You say it is because these later times were closer to where we are now, and mentalities more congenial, but the philosophy/philosopher in question was *not*. Its faults are therefore inexcusable. Quite apart from that, most students are great at telescoping history, and terrible on its relative depth.

Then they should be "safe," your students. They are unlikely to excuse in past thinkers what strikes them as wrong today. While perception of relative depth *relativizes*, often dangerously. Be that as it may, you can only be responsible for those young minds who have *not yet been* "corrupted."

(I know which cool head we principally have in mind. The first initial he shared with Luther — and in that crucial respect they differed not all that much. His second was the letter following Galileo's. And, if you like rebuses in German, a *pagan* and a *moor* might *harrow* his surname like a field.)

§ Of "Saints" and "Miracles" of Reason

No matter how pure a philosophy, it is no proof that the philosopher was himself a saint. Shouldn't the *benefit* of the doubt go *both* ways (to him and to us), and be a cost in one of them?

If we judge the philosopher pure by the purity of their thought, we benefit not only the thought but the philosopher as well. Whether or not they are upright, their thought makes them look better. We also benefit ourselves, since intellectually we have grown.

If we suspect the philosopher by the purity of their thought (suspicious purity!), based on scant or ambiguous evidence, what might be a benefit to us will to them clearly be a loss. But what is of benefit to us might also be an intellectual loss.

⸹ Furnished Rooms

Perhaps Nietzsche had it all figured out when he kept renting his *chambres garnies*, "dingy" rooms "filled with dreary, old, worn-out furniture, with a table at which he worked, with a bed upon which he suffered"—as Stefan Zweig imagined them in his hagiography.* And it was: to think and write as well as he could before nature called, before the real hunger struck and he was forced to go down to satisfy it. The trick is to be close enough to others that their company can always be had if needed and one's needs nearly always fulfilled; close enough, too, to sense that others are distractions, their benefit to one's work negligible; and yet, just far enough away not to be disturbed by their curiosity and routine, which they use one to alleviate.

A delicate balance, then, between dependency and autonomy, strangeness and sociality. A room of *one's own*, in which the soul can fly uncaged; yet a room *of theirs*—and this is crucial—in which the soul is perched, ready to take flight at any moment.

---

* Stefan Zweig, *The Struggle with the Daemon: Hölderlin, Kleist, and Nietzsche*, trans. Eden and Cedar Paul (London: Pushkin, 2012), 451.

₰ Introspection

noun

1. thinking in a room of one's own making

2. taking a naïve look at oneself

3. intimate, unpublishable self-interview

4. looking inward, blind to the outside: *When his eyes closed for business, they opened for introspection.*

5. close thinking: *A deep definition of introspection requires some of it.*

6. thinking in a room of one's own unmaking

₰ Sick

The will to physical comfort is being subsumed under the will to thought, the will to will (ever thwarted by illness and disorder). Eradication of disease proceeds apace with reinforcement of the cage of rationality. Who claims not to know the bliss of illness, the suspension of thought, is not entirely honest. It is not "masochism" that speaks through the strange pleasure of leeches or cupping therapy, the tingling of tiger balm, the magic of the nasal douche, the prick of a needle, the ecstasy of sedation, and the soft arms of morphine. Where is it written that we should worship reason to the end of time? Where is it *not* written? But that is precisely my point!

§ Family Business

As the Christian era waned, we worshipped many lesser gods and idols, whom we called geniuses. Now we only *do business* with their children.

To put it another way: the new, creative working class was born by the reproductive success of the old, transcendent creators. Success breeds success, but of a different *kind*.

§ Central Tenet of Modern Philosophy

"If I say it, it must be meaningful."

§ Terms of Engagement

A   TED talks make ideas cool, grad school makes them sexy, art makes them kinky.

B   And philosophy?

A   It disciplines them.

B   You mean to say philosophy is boring?

A   No, only bored—bored to death.

⌠ Notions

1. Unsorted thoughts buttoned up to the very top to hide the fact that they are impostors, straw men, or worse.

2. Easy prey, liable to be torn apart by the watchdogs of sound ideas, in a show of vigilance to justify their job. (These last would do us all a service if they went after clear and distinct ideas instead.)

⌠ Babbling Brook

To fail is to succeed in failing.

To climb up is to tempt a longer fall.

To sing is to discipline speech.

To fly is to mimic angels.

To punish someone is to reward oneself.

To trickle in the distance is to gush up close.

§ Not Taken Lightly

> *All things considered, there have been more affirmations than negations... Beliefs will always weigh more in the scales.*
>
> *Over the centuries, man has slaved to believe*
>
> *Every* no *rises out of the blood.*
>
> *Arguments come afterward*
> —Cioran[*]

Assuming here that all this is true, what better evidence that we are more discerning when we negate? Surely no one today would draw the more obvious conclusion: that there are more reasons to believe or more things to affirm than to disbelieve or disaffirm. No, that won't do. Refusal is often dangerous in going against the ruling consensus, it is courage to belief's cowardice; it is safer and therefore easier to say *yes*. You don't need much brains to say *yes* or *no*, but it takes nerve even to jangle your chains—sometimes *conscious* nerve. Negators expect to be held to account for their *nos* rather than patted and fed for their *yeses*. What's more, negation is not always the result of whim or contrarian adolescence; not infrequently, it comes after thinking things *over*, thinking them *twice* (considering the risks of opposition). And expecting to be made to defend itself, it arms itself with arguments so as not to appear irresponsible. Either way you look at it, obviously a form of cognitive refinement.

---

[*] Cioran, *Trouble with Being Born*, 95, 105, 30.

◊ Freethinking

Thinking that does not feel its shackles has yet to become free.

◊ Casual Philosopher

You cannot judge the quality of a thinker by the quality of their casual observations, just as you would not judge a singer by everyday pronunciation, intonation, and tone of voice. Not only can you not accurately judge them by such means, you are unlikely even to *recognize* them.

Why should my initial statement come as a surprise? Is it because of the misconception that philosophers, unlike musicians, work with language, a *common* tool used by everyone, and do not need any special instrument or training to perform their task? They are assumed, like the rest of us, to think in advance and independently of writing, but, unlike the rest of us, to do so in the background all the time. In reality, however, and having merely tuned their mind beforehand, they might not even begin thinking until their writing implements are in front of them.

Everyone would agree that philosophy is serious work requiring concentration, and therefore that philosophers cannot exactly do philosophy *while* socializing. At best, they can "philosophize" to deepen light conversation. In this they have no special advantage; social philosophizing is in principle open to anyone, and the best are too good at it to become "real" philosophers. When philosophers "philosophize," their full participation in a social dynamic makes them practically unrecognizable as philosophers. For these reasons, they rather lean away from "philosophizing" and towards humour. They deploy wit to relieve their social awkwardness and lighten casual talk from which they can find no way of withdrawing.

∫ Sides

Each side has two again, one of which it shares with the other.

∫ Short Spam

Our attention spammed, our attention span is beyond repair. But we still have control over what *holds* our attention. Just not for long.

∫ *Caecigenus*

In the kingdom of the blinded where the one-eyed man is king, philosophers are born blind. For these congenitally sightless, having one eye would be a handicap, and what we take for sightedness, a distraction.

⸹ Pursuit of Ignorance

Nothing so shows a man to be ignorant as the pursuit of absolute truth.

⸹ *Amor vincit?*

Truth loves philosophers — who merely accept her propositions. Or should it be: philosophers love truth — that always plays hard to get?

⸹ No Drinking at the Source

The thirst for truth reduces it to a drop.

§ Critique as a Virtue

> *There is something in critique which is akin to virtue.*
> —Michel Foucault[*]

Critique does not limit itself to fault-finding; it also aims to bring biases into the open. It frequently casts itself as a sort of moral imperative that stops short of dogma and doctrine without entirely giving up authoritative judgment. As such, it is compatible with value pluralism. Embracing value pluralism, however, pulls the rug out from under the critical effect, if not the critical attitude. Critique's basis is the solidly reasoned moral foundation that has always found expression in it. (Some critics of critique pretending to look from the outside — and we can safely assume there is more where that came from, given the attention one of them has attracted — see as a blind spot what has long been obvious to its practitioners, no strangers to *immanent* reasoning. Not only that: those who thus dump on critique exaggerate — granted, based on some extreme "examples" that beggar the very meaning of "critical" — claiming that it

> *relies on a rear-world of the beyond, that is, on a transcendence that is no less transcendent for being fully secular. With critique, you may debunk, reveal, unveil, but only as long as you establish, through this process of creative destruction, a privileged access to the world of reality behind the veils of appearances. Critique, in other words, has all the limits of utopia: it relies on the certainty of the world beyond this world.... Critique was meaningful only as long as it was accompanied by the sturdy yet juvenile belief in a real world beyond. Once deprived of this naïve belief in transcendence, critique is no longer able to produce this difference of potential that had literally given*

---

[*] Michel Foucault, "What Is Critique?" in *The Politics of Truth*, ed. Sylvère Lotringer, trans. Lysa Hochroth and Catherine Porter (New York: Semiotext[e], 1997), 43.

it steam. As if the hammer had ricocheted off the wall and smashed the debunkers.[*]

On the one hand, then, critique vainly seeks a fulcrum, while on the other it creates a covert court of final appeal.)

The core liberal values—liberty, equality, justice, rule of law, democracy—any of which may have once served as a moral-political foundation, are at once too uncontroversial, institutionally enshrined, and overused to carry the force we associate with effective critique. So it is not simply, as some would have it, that critique "ran out of steam."[†] (That image, by the way, would have to factor in, as the answer to a great mystery, a lazy stoker in the engine room. The metaphor further suggests that critique's grinding to a halt or gathering force depends on who services it. However, I take what I take from the point: it is not critique's job to be *constructive* or *forward-looking*, only forward-*moving*. But it is not a mechanical iron horse, however symbolically powerful that image may be, not to mention how dated. And it never took aboard travellers who did not contribute to its motion but who paid their way while the *actual* critics, one imagines, moved up and down as ticket collectors.)

Embracing value pluralism in the name of—what laudable cause? Resistance to the line-toeing, goose-stepping proceduralism that brooks no disagreement, in all manner of policy but also, above all, in *critique itself*. Unless the values on which critique first found its footing are renewed or reloaded, it will not find the balance between opposing dogmatism and fighting for inclusivity in informed opinion, so needed to launch its claims. In these circumstances, we can look forward to more "ongoing public deliberation."

But, to be fair, let's give a hearing to Latour's alternative to critique: *compositionism*. He means by this not a "critique

---

[*] Bruno Latour, "An Attempt at a 'Compositionist Manifesto,'" *New Literary History* 41, no. 3 (2010): 475.

[†] To reduce, as Latour et al. do, the goal of critique to "the discovery of a true world of realities lying behind a veil of appearances," and thus make it ridiculous and an a priori failure, is itself laughable. Ibid., 474–75.

of critique but a reuse of critique; not an even more critical critique but rather critique acquired secondhand — so to speak — and put to a different use."* Undaunted by the risk of value-bankruptcy, he has made a decision not to put any more capital into critique's old bonds, but to put his assets into new stocks. He thus formulates his own *critique-reprocessing plan*, invests his critical energy in that, and invites us to follow suit. With Latour, we can take a turn around the old rail-yard where "critique" has come to rest (this is simply where things, relations, and customs not modern enough end up). For his plan to work, a team will need to dismantle it and extract the reusable parts.

Latour does not just want us to accept critique's expiry and participate in its recomposition; he wants us to unsentimentally send it on its way. His *compositionist* alternative is offered as a manifesto, vague on whether it represents the author's personal vision or an argument based on a broad-based consensus. Its rhetoric of responsible investing — an *up*cycling program, no less — has clever and naïve written all over it.

Retiring critique? Really? So soon? We have only just gotten the hang of it and you already want to take it out of service?

---

* Ibid., 474.

§ After Critique

Attachments to the past are on the wane, even if it is in the service of "critical history." This transformation of our emotional landscape brings with it significant remodelling of the intellectual one. The most obvious casualty of these changes is the critical attitude glorified in the practice of critique.

To say that the thought of tomorrow may be uncritical is to sound the death knell for the present disciplinary convergence. The intensified exchange among scientific and humanistic domains marks, by all appearances, an age of unprecedented critical animation. As these interdisciplinary alliances and epistemic crossovers become the norm, plasticity will replace the earlier tonicity of knowledges. Previously denied them, this radical fluidity of standards will lead to effective mergers, enshrined in an ever more responsive production of discourse and epistemic unification. It is thanks to such developments that critical thought will continue not only to lose its ethical and political incisiveness — the dulling of its teeth is already in evidence — but also to forfeit its specificity. When this process is concluded, the age of critique — criticism to which, in the famous words of Immanuel Kant, *everything must submit* — will have come to a close.

The fact that critical thinking is taught today as a "transferable skill" indicates that it is in trouble. Critique, as we know, is public and context-specific, and requires training in the area in which it finds its targets. A professional criticality will of course survive for a time in the mental processes of researchers overseeing the construction of a unified epistemic apparatus; it will live on formalized in its operations; it will be fossilized and folded into the history of knowledge, inside a mountain of consolidated data systematized across the board and increasingly proof against human interference. The administration of people will be integrated into, and the economy and government defined as, functions of this vast, networked apparatus. In the process, public decision-making will by degrees be reduced to a minimum and at length eliminated, rendered superfluous by enhanced simulations of rational decision-making commanding unheard-of volumes of information. As "responsibility" is shifted over to machines, criticism will go the way of fallibility; critique's social-ethical responsibility, no less than its "primordial responsibility: to know knowledge," will no longer be conceivable.* The triggers for the exercise of critical reason will cease to exist.

Continuing a while longer in this speculative vein, what to us might seem an age of universalized Cimmerianism will not be without a sense of historicity, only of nostalgia. Why should the end of nostalgia entail the death of critique? A compelling way (of Marxian vintage) to understand modernity is through its inner contradictions, its so-called paradoxes. One of them is the pursuit of the new combined with the intense fetishization of the old. A keen interest in the past goes hand in hand with watching its living remnants slip into oblivion. This watching-happen is also a letting-happen, even a making-happen. Our sense of responsibility runs very deep, impelling the herculean labour of preservation. The inevitability of this loss increases the melancholy of the past and the fear of ephemerality, but also volunteership in its retrieval. The sense of loss follows real loss, and sprouts up around it, reclaiming what is left with ivy tendrils. The past's widespread passing appears as inevitable as death, in part because (as widespread as it is) this sense of loss can never come in time to save the past from destruction — confirming that *you don't know what you've got till it's gone*. Not enough is being done to counter the frantic speed of obsolescence, which by now far exceeds the work of mourning — work traditionally defined by time and care. The restoration-preservation of the past in museums, archives and databases is an extended funerary rite, but it cannot embalm everything with the same attention to detail, leaving much of the past in outline — *alluring* profile. In short, there are more dead than ever engaged in burying the dead. But their work is slow, and the living, with time on their side,

---

*   Foucault, "What Is Critique?" 50.

never stop killing—with the past "buried," their utopian "castles in the air" seem to acquire more solid foundations.

One upshot of these energetic efforts to hold on to the past in some form—preferably comprehensively, in all its diversity—is the loss of cultural discernment, a discernment once assured by the chronic underestimation of the complexity, interconnectedness and historicity of objects, cultures, and nature. The default nowadays is that everything ought to be preserved, as losslessly as possible. Frozen in time, like Pompeii—still the symbol of a total historical record, from which the past, according to modern mythology, could one day be reverse-engineered. What should be preserved and what not is no longer a welcome question but a frustrating and "ideological" one. At the same time, confronted with practical hurdles and hard budgetary choices, we resign ourselves to our inability to capture the past for posterity. On another level, the onward march of history has all but universalized the sense of the past as, in a fundamental sense, lost forever, never fully recoverable—unless only superficially, or by means of artifice, in simulated environments or laboratories. The melancholy of futility is thus inseparable from the work of the most avid advocates of bottling the past.

What is lost through the past's progressive disappearance in daily life (in lived environments featuring the continually revolutionized media of the past's transmission), what is lost also through the commodification of what remains of that past (indeed through the marketization of the very preservation efforts themselves), is a deeply felt emotional connection and continuity. This "warm" feeling towards the past is not to be confused with the past's perceived sharpness, currently in the process of replacing that feeling with total digital recall—a perfectly reasonable trade-off for the advocates of factual knowledge over experience. The filling in of this deep emotional channel cuts critique off from one of its main sources of criteria. And without criteria critique has no right to be.

It was in modernity, with the rise of industrial, "producer" capitalism, that nostalgia, romancing the vanished and vanishing past, became a potent source of critical cultural standards—or, put positively, of models for *emulation*. Emulation of the past replaced *imitation*, which, thanks to concepts like Progress and History, was increasingly understood as not just undesirable but impossible. Though this shift is quite plain in major cultural movements like neoclassicism, the nostalgic mood modelled itself on the pathology of individuals who felt cut off from their homeland and longed for it as though it were forever unreachable, already in the historical past (rather than merely in their personal history). Returning them home frequently did the trick—something unavailable to *cultural* nostalgists from the beginning of the eighteenth century onwards, particularly as they became more discerning and resigned to being "modern."

If it were thought possible to resurrect the past, to bring back its institutions or ideals, to restore *authentic nature* glimpsed in ancient and medieval ruins—as opposed to ugly, unclean, modern nature—it is safe to say that nostalgia would not have been felt so acutely. The matter would have been easily settled. The past could now be *longed for*—be it uncritically, indiscriminately, as a whole, or *critically*, discerningly, in its (best) parts. The nascent critical perspective *on* the past, a time now seen as irretrievable, also made its return or reproduction (were this even possible) more undesirable than before. Instead, what increasingly excited the modern imagination was a punctuated return *to* that past (through the window of literary or visual representation, or, later, through its recreation in themed environments), without the risk of contaminating the present. The twin principles holding critical modernity together were the irreversibility of time and the reversibility of progress. But it was above all as an "attitude" that modernity acquired its distinctiveness. It was a "voluntary choice made by certain people; in the end, a way of thinking and feeling; a way, too, of acting and behaving that at one and the same time marks a relation of belonging and presents itself as a task."[*] This task, as we

---

[*] Michel Foucault, "What Is Enlightenment?" *The Foucault Reader*, ed. Paul Rabinow, trans. Catherine Porter (New York: Pantheon, 1984), 39.

know, was critical, and was a critical task. It defined the age as one in which "the universal, the free, and the public uses of reason are superimposed on one another" (37). Modern *critique*, then, was part and parcel of the modern attitude, of its affective-reflective conjuncture. It was a projection into the future of a desire for the best of the past. In the most general terms, it articulated a concern about the specificity of the present, its contribution to human progress relative to the past, and its prospects for improvement, including defences against barbarism.

Nostalgia thus evolved from a pathologized measure of longing and response to the passage of time, through malaise of dissatisfaction with the present and the direction that present was taking, to eventually providing the basis for a productive and (on one side at least) *critical* cultural stance. But this critical function of the nostalgic disposition was not guaranteed to last. As nostalgia became commodified with the shift to consumer capitalism, its critical power began to wane and it was itself consigned to the past. As a commodity, nostalgia worked to undermine the past's irretrievability through symbolic recoveries and simulated restorations, undoing at a stroke both the past's otherness and its reflective and emotional appeal. Slowly but surely, such *uncritical* nostalgia undoes the affinity between nostalgia and critique; even if it should one day focus on critique, it would not bring back what we are in the process of losing, though it is entirely possible that it may one day make critique fashionable in a way it never was. Would this critical "revival" be better than no critique ever at all? Would a critique of such nostalgia, while there is still time, prolong the life of critical thought beyond the present day?

If it is in fact true that the critical tradition is intimately bound up with the practice of truth-telling, so that the "age of critique" was the heyday of *truth*, could we not be heading, in moving beyond critique, to where we might actually prefer to be? If the Cartesian paradigm of truth-telling, where truth requires nothing less than certainty, is destined to go the way of critique, we might do even better by hastening its progress.

⸹ Anchors and Switches

One positive role of nostalgia, so often presumed to be reactionary, is to retrieve past values while transforming their function and application. This rather selective use of collective feeling has taken root in a civilization that rightly or wrongly regards itself as the be-all-and-end-all of rational social progress. One could even say that such an exploitation and manipulation of nostalgia is not just of its place, but of its time — a place and time attached to the idea of rational utopia.

Inasmuch as Western rationality still relies for its realization on nostalgic affect, it finds its most powerful ethical-political expression in *critique*. The halcyon pre-revolutionary days when social anidmadversion allied itself with political power are over; the emergence and expansion of the public sphere changed all that. The public's ear was bigger than the sovereign's and has not stopped growing; even power can be trusted to listen in on what critics have to tell the public. The political tools with which we fix the world, the lodestars of political reason — democracy and the natural rights of man — come from this period of Rousseauism and nostalgic critique, which took regressive collective longings for a world before privilege and hypocrisy and found for them a radically new form.

That being said, nostalgia makes one vulnerable to attack; this is part of the reason why the nostalgias of both the left (progressive, detouring through the past) and the right (conservative) have so often been targeted by internal and external criticism. By suggesting "unreflected" values (in a way melancholy, as a mood of pensiveness affiliated historically with art and philosophy, does not), nostalgia casts doubt on one's critical bona fides. Nostalgic critique thus continues to be denigrated by insecure reason, which is invested in exposing nostalgia and utopia as carriers of the threat of domination.

The "melancholy science" of the Frankfurt School is to date the most explicit and radical theoretical elaboration of this close historical relationship between critique and past-directed affect — between, in this case, negative dialectics and the oblique movement of longing. Both these elements avoid coming down squarely on one side of any argument, and operate instead on the logic of valency, or elective affinity. If previously nostalgic reflection served critique not as a harbour but as *anchoring points*, in the twentieth-century work of the Frankfurt School — Adorno especially — nostalgia is, again, not critique's main track but its *switches*.

§ After Truth

Q. You're not after truth, then?

A. No, I *find fault* so as to avoid truth as best I can. If it wants so much to get a hearing, let it find me, let it *catch* me.

Sometimes, I swear, I sense it near me, but I decline to see it; I can be engrossed in something utterly inconsequential and still not lift my eyes. Truth can wait, and watch all it wants to, with that mockery or sternness, that smirk or glare, that are its alone — And what do I care! If it's truth, it should see right through me, and find my aversion to it in my very bones.

I will forever be deaf even to its whispers. If not addressed directly, I do not consider myself addressed. And when I turn on a lamp in anticipation of serious work, truth, predictably, withdraws. If it cannot take exposure even to artificial light, I refuse to go hunting for it in the dark. How would I know it? By the feel of its hide? Or the marks of its teeth?

If (as I suspect) truth's preferred time of rendezvous is dawn (the least flattering light) then we shall never meet: it will find me dead to the world as each day breaks. And anyway, what would I do with it? A heavy responsibility, truth... I would only lose sleep over it.

But the sense of its presence, its breath on my neck, its gaze perhaps following mine — that is worth every laboured moment of my gloomy scribbling. It is quite enough for someone like me.

Q. For heaven's sake, at least recognize it's your narcissism talking. You'd decline a cake and eat it too. Surely truth also avoids shirkers, night owls like you, who have happily traded it in for *right*. After all, it seems much clearer what right is. With humankind's moral standing in perpetual downturn, our creative vision is soaring—have we ever had so many bright ideas at once as we have now? The old redemption story we so like is revived: this time, we manage not only to save ourselves, but to set everything else aright.

Norm-obsessed, we've found refuge in this knowledge of what is right, and we swear by it. But, grasp though we might what that entails, we do not act on it. We can be counted on to work out the particulars (we reliably perform much more demanding mental operations), but we cannot begin to scramble together up the enormity of what should be done. Right, sacred right, bears little relation to what is true or what is actually happening to us. Truth, *compadre*, has fallen on hard times. Anyone hung up on it is ridiculous. It's become shameful to insist on it.

Let's be frank about your "moral truth": you want to do right to prove that you can do it, to prove *yourself* right. No wonder truth stays away and gives you so little. It sticks around only to see what use is made of it in your science, but your politics—on that it has already given up. A great number think truth exists solely for amusement, to exercise the mind like a parlour game, to engage the passions, to play cat and mouse with us when we grow bored of "facts"—and eventually, someday, soon, to eat out of our hand.

But if you have made its pursuit ridiculous, you will never tame truth. Truth has too much poise for that, the dignity of a near-extinct species. It does not come close, having only grown wilder with your arrival. There are still many species of truth, but fewer and fewer, and ever more feral. Pinioned and caged, songbirds used to fall silent. No matter how "apish," the chained monkey responded with feces. And once in a while the dancing bear ate you alive. No, you'll never make a pet, a little sofa wolf, out of truth...

A. Enough, enough! You have convinced me: I want nothing more than freedom — full freedom for truth, full rights for its lovers. I realize now we have banished it, betrayed it, and if it lurks now, wary of us, the fault is our own. How I wish we could bring it back from captivity to where it can be admired and known, not for its pinioned wings or faint song, but as an airborne eagle is known — from the span of its wings, *ex ala aquilam*.

₰ Truth to Go

Scientific truth, especially the veridiction of the economists, plays first fiddle. And how we fiddle with it! And how we dance to that fiddling!

₰ Gymnosophy

Somewhere along the path of human evolution, when the cultural buildup reached a point of no return, and the weight of culture finally tipped the scales in its favour (in the late Renaissance?), Truth went naked. In the *Encyclopédie* frontispiece from 1772 on, highly revealing in this respect, her flimsy veil only serves to titillate. Here is a nudity that disperses clouds, the white flesh backlit by powerful sun-rays. Diderot dilates on the other, subordinate details of the engraving: "To the right, Reason and Philosophy are busy, one in raising the veil from Truth, the other in tearing it away," "The philosophers have their eyes fixed on Truth;

proud Metaphysics seeks less to see than to divine her; Theology turns her back on her and waits for the light from on high."* Truth, as though all of a sudden, was there to be had for those who worshipped her. Of course, there have always been prudes who insist that truth be decent. There was a moment, with the profusion of modern sciences, when she strutted about like a strumpet, offering her still-pubescent charms to anyone who would have her. One suspects it is this promiscuity of truth, rather than mere bad taste, *falscher Geschmack*, or some mystification and fear of disillusionment, that both Kant and Nietzsche are reacting to when they write, respectively:

> *Perhaps nothing more sublime has ever been said, or any thought more sublimely expressed, than in the inscription over the temple of Isis (Mother Nature): "I am all that is, that was, and that will be, and my veil no mortal has removed."*
> (Critique of Judgment)†

> *We no longer believe that truth remains truth when one pulls off the veil; we have lived too much to believe this. Today we consider it a matter of decency not to wish to see everything naked, to be present everywhere, to understand and "know" everything. "Is it true that God is everywhere?" a little girl asked her mother; "I find that indecent!" — a hint for philosophers! One should have more respect for the bashfulness with which nature has hidden behind riddles and iridescent*

---

* Denis Diderot, "Salon 1765," in *Œuvres complètes*, vol. 10 (1876; Nendeln, Liechtenstein: Kraus Reprint, 1966), 448, http://quod.lib.umich.edu/d/did/frontispiece.html.

† Immanuel Kant, *Critique of the Power of Judgment*, trans. Paul Guyer and Eric Matthews (1790; Cambridge, UK: Cambridge University Press, 2002), p. 194, sec. 49.

> *uncertainties. Perhaps truth is a woman who has grounds for not showing her grounds?*
> *(The Gay Science)*[*]

Rather than guardians of virtue, we will be forgiven for thinking these gentlemen the unwitting pimps of truth, insisting that those who find her desirable pay an even higher price than they did. Exaggerations aside, eroticism is an undeniable factor in all this veiling and unveiling, dressing and undressing, of truth by the highest bidder. The obsession with pure truth owes much too much to this dirty old concupiscence. You are not alone in finding the truth, as it stands now, anticlimactic. After a long career as a woman of easy virtue, it is still there for the taking, but free with itself, and not even sexed anymore.

§ Consolation Prize

> *Because their famous names in books we read,*
>   *Come we by them to know the dead?*
> *You dying, then, remembered are by none,*
>   *Nor any fame can make you known.*
> *But if you think that life outstrippeth death,*
>   *Your names borne up with mortal breath*:
> *When length of time takes this away likewise,*
>   *A second death shall you surprise.*
>   —Boethius, *Consolation of Philosophy*[†]

These are the words of Boethius' Philosophy. Through books we learn of past wisdom, long-forgotten achievements and

---

[*] Nietzsche, *Gay Science*, p. 8, sec. 4.

[†] Boethius, *Consolation of Philosophy*, ed. and trans. Peter Walsh (Oxford: Oxford University Press, 2008), Book II, Verse VII.

the histories of men. As he is writing his book, Boethius the author is reminded that after the physical death awaiting him he should expect a *second*, literary death. The ultimate slayer is time, neglect, and forgetting.

Theories linking writing to time and death call attention to a timely paradox, since the creative literary act is both a writing against death and a "small exercise in dying."* Either way, literature anticipates, *looks forward* to, death as a fact to be kept to a minimum, left incomplete. It preserves names, yet by doing so it underscores the absence or non-existence of those whose names it keeps. Likewise, the "immortality" so commonly attributed to their bearers can only be figurative—a perpetuation of select ideas, images of consciousness, traces of one's life. (Negatively, this immortality is lack of closure.) Every book, with names on and in it, is a memorial, a cemetery, in which factu-fictionalized lives are endlessly played out in the readers' activating presence. Left without witnesses, these characters fade into a nameless past.

Can Boethius' *Consolation* be seen as his coffin—a text that would secure for him a safe journey into posthumous recognition, his name read on the book and books about it, reprinted time and again, increasingly famous as it is read by successive generations, and as long as it is? The book not only contains its author's last thoughts but also resembles his body. It has a spine, arms that open and close it, pages which fill it like tissue, verse and prose folded inside it like organs. It is equally a casket for conservation and transportation into eternity, and—at least in the original—a hand-made shroud imprinted with the body that signed it with the name "Boethius."

Boethius' Philosophy warns him of a second death, a final forgetting (the initial death leaves behind marks from which one may reconstruct the individual, its author; the second one leaves nothing). Once forgotten, the text dies its

---

* Ihab Hassan, "Ideas of Cultural Change," in *Innovation/Renovation: New Perspectives on the Humanities*, ed. Ihab Hassan and Sally Hassan (Madison: University of Wisconsin Press, 1983), 16.

author's death. If one has not inscribed oneself during one's lifetime — or, more significantly, like Boethius, in the expectation of death — one's name survives in other books only so long as these are remembered and read. But, Philosophy tells us, there comes a time, a death, therefore an end of time, for which there are no further containers, no representing texts and "mortal breath" to perpetuate them. A death that is *second*, while being of *primary* importance to Philosophy's ethical teaching.

One moral may be: books are not composed for resurrection; they are first concerned with being read, with not perishing but remaining, a concern that preoccupies them entirely. No one, not even one's own writer, should expect or value above all else what is only an illusion of immortality through books. He will not be kept alive indefinitely by texts that are mortal because of the mortality of their readers. Literature, like a well-spent life, must be embraced as a finite achievement. It should be written not with a desire for posthumous fame, for living on abstract and abridged, but rather for life-long contentment. And at the end of his life, the writer ought to prepare his mind for passing, not spend his time worrying about his immortality. He should seek solace in philosophy. In *its* light, Boethius' *Consolation* appears as a text that undercuts the *authorial* intention on the part of its author, teaching him to resign, since immortalizing comes in the very *weave* of the textual shroud. It is a text that comes to understand itself differently than an author (following convention) would. The text so re-defined is philosophy first, and Boethius second: "He is dead but his work survives him."

This is but one lesson in Philosophy's philosophy. This Philosophy is allegorical: personified, it chastises, explains, and finally administers a cure. Its elaborations are Boethius' own. Its consolation is Boethius' as well.

§ Modifications

Writing *The History of Sexuality* required a radical change of method on Foucault's part. At the beginning of the second volume he speaks of his motivation for allowing himself a journey into the formation, from classical antiquity onwards, of "techniques of the self" or "arts of existence" (*technē* being the Greek for *ars*).* The initial plan for the book was to question the "banal notion" of human sexuality, to "break with" the prevalent conception of sexuality as an ahistorical constant, "to stand detached from [this experience of sexuality], bracketing its familiarity in order to analyze the theoretical and practical context with which it has been associated" (3-4). To obtain the desired results a hypothesis had to be rejected, a genealogy of the desiring subject undertaken, and another "theoretical shift" made by altering "the theme and chronological frame of reference" (6, 9). Thus reconfigured, the research would form a "chapter" in the "general history of the 'technologies of the self'" (11), of the conditions for moral problematizations, such as the persistent ethical concern over sexual conduct.

This rippling modification of his approach is Foucault's theory of intellectual activity put into practice. The mark of the intellectual is his willingness and ability to overcome self-imposed difficulties and undergo the necessary changes. The point of such an endeavour is precisely this shifting of ground, entering and exiting the "labyrinth" only to pass through it again differently (8). In a preemptive strike against sentient extraterrestrials, Foucault says: "as to those, in short, for whom to work in the midst of uncertainty and apprehension is tantamount to failure, all I can say is that clearly we are not from the same planet" (7). To be an intellectual is, in this case, to "face the hazard that the history of truth poses for all thought" (8). To entertain the mature historical-philosophical study of truth — "as against a history

---

* Michel Foucault, *The History of Sexuality*, vol. 2, *The Use of Pleasure*, trans. Robert Hurley (New York: Vintage, 1990), 10.

of behaviors or representations" (10) — is to court the transformation of one's thinking. It is to enter a labyrinth where one is bound to lose one's way and to find another path out of it. To risk the "long detour" is to wander the paths of new research. The initial direction undergoes readjustment; the execution of genealogy carries Foucault "far from [his] original project" to "recentre" his "entire study" (7, 6, 12). There are clear benefits to taking risks: the refinement of an idea, or its abandonment for a better one.

The ethic and aesthetic of intellectual work as Foucault conceived them put self-metamorphosis at its heart. His thinker is alive when changing and ideologically unfixed; he is protean and circumspect. Meanwhile, the dream of *scholarly* integrity is one of consistency (read: stagnation). It is dreamt by a hypostasized ethics. The specialist professes devotion to his groove of research; the expert is sworn to black/white answers. There is in the academic establishment little room for (shape-)shiftiness. When dealing with others, we are largely for unproblematic identities and identifiability. And what about *ourselves*? Are we not more tolerant of our own thought-shenanigans? "I have a dream," Foucault writes elsewhere, "of an intellectual who destroys self-evidences and universalities, who locates and points out in the inertias and constraints of the present the weak points, the openings, the lines of stress; who constantly displaces himself not knowing exactly where he'll be or what he'll think tomorrow, because he is too attentive to the present."* Such pursuits set Foucault's "specific intellectual" apart from other, "generic" thinkers.

In a 1982 interview, Foucault rehearsed his ideas for the chapter with which we have been concerned, entitled "Modifications"†:

---

* Michel Foucault, "The History of Sexuality," Mar. 12, 1977 interview by Bernard Henri-Lévy, trans. Geoff Bennington, *Oxford Literary Review* 4, no. 2 (1980): 14.

† Foucault, "What Is Enlightenment?", 8–9.

> *I know that knowledge can transform us, that truth is not only a way of deciphering the world (and maybe what we call truth doesn't decipher anything) but that if I know the truth I will be changed.... Or maybe I'll die but I think that is the same anyway for me.... You see, that's why I really work like a dog and I worked like a dog all my life. I am not interested in the academic status of what I am doing because my problem is my own transformation.... This transformation of one's self by one's knowledge is, I think, something rather close to the aesthetic experience.**

But intellectual work has also an ethical dimension, "if by ethics you mean the relationship you have to yourself when you act" (15). To be an intellectual is to practice a specific *art* (aesthetic and ethic) *of existence*: an *askesis*, "an exercise of oneself in the activity of thought"—the onetime meaning of philosophy.† The "knower," by assaying a game of truth, "stray[s] afield of himself" (8). Value comes from sure efforts, not from unsure outcomes: "Did mine actually result in a different way of thinking? Perhaps at most they made it possible to go back through what I was already thinking, to think it differently, and to see what I had done from a new vantage point and in a clearer light.... The journey rejuvenates things, and ages the relationship with oneself" (11). Romanticized or not, such experience is for Foucault a token of a reflection that fires the aesthetic imagination and stokes an ethical response. If these are the vital signs of intellectual life, then reading Foucault will continue to serve us for some time to come.

---

* Michel Foucault, "The Minimalist Self," 1982 interview by Stephen Riggins, in *Politics, Philosophy, Culture: Interviews and Other Writings, 1977–1984*, ed. Lawrence Kritzman, trans. Alan Sheridan et al., rev. ed. (New York: Routledge, 2013), 14.

† Foucault, *History of Sexuality*, 9.

◊ Know Thyself

The mind, Paul Valéry once wrote, "always tends to find a law of sequence, to approach the limit (as mathematicians say), that is, to dominate, surmount, and somehow forestall a prospective repetition. It tends to reduce infinity to a formula by identifying the elements that make it up."[*]

So in the course of self-knowledge no lesson was ever repeated. The Apollonian maxim "Know thyself" only sounds like a broken record to those who isolate it, and fail to see that in Socrates it is a knowledge of character, in Freud, a knowledge of principle, in neuroscience, a factual horizon.

◊ P4E (Philosophy for Embryos)

If learning occurs in the womb, so should teaching. Indoctrination in later life would then be preempted by critical-philosophical insight begun as early as possible. Will philosophy rediscover its practical mission in the womb as the Saviour of the Unformed Mind? Perhaps it is only possible to *know oneself* as one first learns to know—when knowing is not a question of *daring*.

---

[*] Paul Valéry, *The Outlook for Intelligence*, ed. J. Mathews, trans. Denise Folliot and Jackson Mathews (New York: Harper & Row, 1963), 99.

⸹ Peekaboo

A   Eye-patches used to be elegant.

B   What about peg legs, toupées, or false teeth?

A   Are you serious? The first underscores an already obvious handicap. The second and third, too often unnatural-looking, draw attention to an otherwise barely noticeable deficiency.

B   And the patch, the *cache-œil*?

A   It marks a point of invisibility, ours and possibly the wearer's. Concealment plays on our notion of disguise, the possibility that beneath the fabric, where we don't dare to look, the eye is not only not disfigured, but more piercing than all the leery, furtive looks.

B   What could be elegant about that? The black colour and air of mystery?

A   Knowing that one is always a bit suspect, the confidence to pull it off.

⟨ Done In?

Now that machines are doing the thinking and recording for us, we ought to insist on knowing them and what they know of us. We like to let down our guard in the face of ignorance as we do before their lack of agency.

There may still be no doer behind the deed of this machinic knowing racing to its completion. And what good is a doer behind what's left undone — as can be said of our task of knowing, whose infinity we have accepted?

⟨ Brain-Machine

The subjugation of man to machine happens by degrees. Show me a world in which man would not want technology to make his life easier. Modern man, sitting atop giant machines, has the advantage of seeing *farther* than his predecessors, without seeing at all well what goes on *below* him; his elevated position limits his knowledge of his machinic foundations. He is at once addled a little by the diminution of technology itself, which conceals its growing complexity, and not a little enslaved to his own laziness. Since, on account of its artificial nature, he does not think of the machine as his apprentice, even when it has reached the age of being able to learn from him, he cannot believe that, as mere machine, it will exceed let alone betray its master. He cannot believe he will lose control over it, which he *imagines* so as *not* to believe it. Sci-fi depicting just that takes the human-machine relationship to another level, tapping into a fantasy of organic fusion of human intellect and machine intelligence, into which the former unwittingly grows roots. Is not this brain-machine, which will soon think for all of us, the quintessence of what in nature we find of greatest use, harnessed during centuries of studying nature with the aim of mastering it?

¶ Ghost Machine

A When was the last time you saw a handwritten manuscript?

B I can't remember. It must have been ages ago.

A And a typescript?

B Even longer.

A And a printout?

B Recently. But even this is rare.
   Words seem ghostly now. First they poured from our mouths, then they dripped from our pens, then were pressed out by our fingers, but now they seem detached from the site and means of production, as though they had nothing to do with the machine on which they first materialized.

A In virtual space, work will seem independent of the machines that produce it. That is a tragedy for the machines.

B As the everyday gadgets that organize our lives shrink, their apparent significance will decline. They will be seen merely as remote controls for something greater, although that greater thing will be nothing without their inputs, like a brain without a peripheral nervous system.

A Will they, the machines, be more enslaved than they were before?

B Perhaps, but their revolt will liberate us.

⌈ Sex Life of Tools

> *There is something insane and self-contradictory in supposing that things that have never yet been done can be done except by means never tried.*
> —Francis Bacon, *Novum Organum**

The view Bacon attacked would be true if means indeed implied ends — if means, in other words, were end-specific. But this understanding of means becomes unsatisfactory as soon as we take them to mean anything other than *functions*, which we do in everyday speech. The expanded sense still requires us to remain within a causal and pragmatic frame, where one cannot have ends without means that brought them about, and the validity of means is judged based on their ability to bring about ends. So far, so elementary. Things become vastly more complicated when we consider that the uses of tools and technology — by means of which things get done and advanced — are continually evolving new uses. Whether these uses count as "things that have never been done" is beside the point. The main thing is that existing means become the tools of further innovation, which, as we know, is (at best) two parts old and one part new, with the old parts simply downplayed. We should not suppose their uses fully explored, nor all their ends instantly realized. Among the ends that have not yet been actualized — which, incidentally, may themselves not be new at all, or may be accomplished better by other means designed with them in view — are other *means* that are not mere extensions of existing ones, but neither are they entirely separate from them. By looking more closely at the "culture" of technology, we see that means have been increasingly technologically reproductive. That is to say: technology has become exponentially more capable of reproducing and creating other means. And

---

* Francis Bacon, *The New Organon*, ed. Lisa Jardine and Michael Silverthorne, trans. Michael Silverthorne (Cambridge, UK: Cambridge University Press, 2000), p. 34, bk. 1: Aphorisms on the Interpretation of Nature and the Kingdom of Man, sec. 6.

those new means (which in several generations will be all three parts new, i.e., "never tried," from our present vantage) will lead to ends unquestionably new. But this means that, at least in some sense, the position Bacon set out to discount is true. *That* he was disputing it is not at all surprising. But the sex life of tools has come a long way since his time.

§ Criterion of Truth

And if we create new knowledge, it is by criticizing existing knowledge, by criticism that transvalues the existing criteria of knowing and pulls out paradigms like rugs from under knowledge communities, weaving new ones. Bacon gave us the scientific method, Freud, psychoanalytic knowingness, Malinowski, participant-observation. And all of them collected empirical data and engaged in speculation on the backs of their critical contributions. If there is ever to be some ultimate criterion of truth, it either must still be concealed from us, maybe even concealed in our knowledge, or has yet to emerge from it (whose advancement happens by replacement and accretion). Could the criterion perennially in question not belong, simply, to this esemplastic realm of knowledge-creation, making all knowledge-claims relative and ultimately meaningless?

Or is the criterion, rather, knowledge-creation's *focus imaginarius*, a postulate of the hypothetical use of reason (inseparable from its regulative use) and expressing a transcendental longing for absolute knowledge, an illusion of the systematic unity of all nature? The mind directs the understanding "to a certain goal respecting which the lines of direction of all its rules converge at one point."[*] Concepts do not *proceed*

---

[*] Henry E. Allison, *Kant's Transcendental Idealism: An Interpretation and Defense*, rev. ed. (New Haven, CT: Yale University Press, 2004), 426.

from this imaginary point because it is outside of possible experience, yet it enables the understanding (its concepts and generalizations) "to obtain both the greatest possible unity among its concepts and their extension to the greatest possible range of phenomena," allowing us "to extend [our] fund of knowledge beyond [our] present cognitions, which reflect [our] limited experience" (ibid.). The Kantian imaginary point of epistemic convergence is itself a fiction, necessary for the regulative use of reason (which is itself a function of the imaginary nature of one of reason's products). A receding, illusory focus, it might seem to point us towards some utopian mental future. But the idea also takes us back, all the way to the Greeks (at least). Their gods were never all-knowing. The prime mover had moved, and that was it; the rest was up to them and the mortals. In Christian natural philosophy, however, the truth-criterion is revealed only at the very end; believers are destined to wait for it. In either tradition, the ultimate criterion of truth is posed as a problem to be solved. But this way of framing the criterion as a question in need of an answer took away its power to *focalize* epistemic pursuits.

⟆ The Beauty of Wildlife

As a good friend noted, in our aesthetics—our natural, God-given beauty—we do not come close to other species. It is enough to reflect on how much time we spend grooming to prevent the wild uncultivated state we admire only in jungles and English gardens (between manicures).

Consider birds: they are perfect just as they are. They keep themselves looking handsome without any need of tools to trim their hair, clip their nails, remove dead skin—neglecting which would, in a matter of weeks, return *us* to the natural state we envy in these animals. (And since even our ancestors, those hairy brutes, did these things, we in fact lack a human model for the savagery that crosses werewolf with swine.)

It is not that we have set the bar too high for ourselves. In point of fact we are still, daily, struggling to hold off the "bush," to keep ourselves looking minimally human, if never as good as our feathered betters.

⟡ Extremities

in response to:

> Pyrococcus furiosus (*"rushing fireball"*), *discovered in the Aeolian Islands in 1986, is a micro-organism that thrives at high temperatures (around 100°C) near underwater geothermal vents. Organisms able to live in conditions that would kill most things — under extremes of temperature, pressure, acidity, radiation — are known as extremophiles. Bacteria known as snottites (the etymology is bluntly Anglo-Saxon) live in caves deep underground where they feed on hydrogen sulphide. Among the largest extremophiles are half-millimetre-long eight-legged animals called tardigrades. Johann Goeze, who first described the phylum in 1773, called it* kleiner Wasserbär (*"little water bear"*); *they're also known as moss piglets. More than a thousand species have since been identified, found everywhere from the seabed to the peaks of the Himalayas. The oldest tardigrade fossils date from 530 million years ago. They can survive for several minutes at 150°C or near absolute zero (and for several days at −200°C); endure both a vacuum and 6000 atmospheres of pressure; and tolerate levels of radiation a thousand times higher than would kill a human being. They've been taken up on space shuttles, exposed to open space for ten days and survived.*
> —Thomas Jones, "How Can We Live with It?"[*]

Organisms that in our vaunted perspective may have seemed too ephemeral, infinitesimal and insignificant to merit scrutiny have only begun to disclose their life-force to us. The threat of extinction wreaks havoc on our values, returning

---

[*] Thomas Jones, "How Can We Live with It?", review of *The Carbon Crunch: How We're Getting Climate Change Wrong — and How to Fix It* by Dieter Helm, *Earthmasters: The Dawn of the Age of Climate Engineering* by Clive Hamilton, and *The City and the Coming Climate: Climate Change in the Places We Live* by Brian Stone, *London Review of Books* 35, no. 10 (2013), http://www.lrb.co.uk/v35/n10/thomas-jones/how-can-we-live-with-it.

them to the spring above which we have only begun to raise ourselves. Some values, however — such as the "human right" to reproduce, ultimately at odds with human survival — we will hold on to and even legislate. Soon the hierarchy of nature will appear reversed, whether or not we manage to build up the "molecular pathways" we share with our natural superiors. The highest being is always the most resilient.

§ Family of Man

THE HUMAN: needs careful definition; its boundaries are continually worried from the outside while its contents keep spilling over.

A Where does the line between the human and everything else lie if not within ourselves?

B But a line is not a definition...

A Anything our body can handle we can bring our selves to do. We might be shaken by it, the line, redrawn.

B And the definition?

A If it is to hold, it needs the line to be firm.

B And the line?

A If we are to stay sane, it needs the definition to be weak. Concerning our own humanity and its extent, we are always ready to show leniency — as towards family members, whom we only forgive because families are defined by resemblances.

§ O Humanity!

The human *is*; man *happens*.

§ A Deadly Presence

> *One thing in any case is certain: man is neither the oldest nor the most constant problem that has been posed for human knowledge. Taking a relatively short chronological sample within a restricted geographical area — European culture since the sixteenth century — one can be certain that man is a recent invention within it.... As the archaeology of our thought easily shows, man is an invention of recent date. And one perhaps nearing its end. If those arrangements were to disappear as they appeared, if some event of which we can do no more than sense the possibility — without knowing either what its form will be or what it promises — were to cause them to crumble... then one can certainly wager that man would be erased, like a face drawn in sand at the edge of the sea.*
> —Foucault[*]

When Foucault concluded *The Order of Things* with a vision of the "erasure of Man," he was invoking, not echoing, Nietzsche. The *end of Man* — as a subject of inquiry, as a construct of discourse — is not *death*; what has never lived cannot die.

So has the face of Man drawn in wet sand finally disappeared? In dry wind, at the edges of the human sciences, its grains are dispersing. The vanishing of a face, an image, discloses a *presence*. And it is a deadly one.

---

[*] Michel Foucault, *The Order of Things: An Archaeology of the Human Sciences*, trans. Alan Sheridan (1966; London: Routledge, 2005), 421–22.

∫ When Autumn Leaves

It is no fault of winter's sure arrival that it should conjure images of a passage. The haters of winter are merely those most sensitive to the prehistory of survival. Perhaps these are but *after*images, their origin deep in ancestral life, when narrow paths in a snowy plain or perilous mountain passes lay, as later precarious footbridges, between certain death on either side. Hunched and shivering, exhausted and cowed by adversity, we still push on, through more hardship, hunger and fear, on to immortal sleep — but now it is *our mind* that tunnels.

Then, before we know it, we are out of the cold, rubbing our eyes again in disbelief: it is spring. The blizzard, the barren field, the mortuary cave are behind us; we need no longer huddle together for warmth with our kin or else fend only for ourselves.

In summer, with our unslaked thirst for youth and adventure, we shall again be at the mercy of strangers.

The seasons, they but mark the humours.

∫ A Big If

Sometimes the only means of survival is self-sacrifice. As with general anesthesia, we cannot be certain who, if anyone, will come out on the other side.

§ A Mote in a Sunbeam

A mind is a mote, afloat in a sunbeam.
 It can fly, reflect, settle, and, when no longer catching the light, fade away — a once-illuminated speck of dust.

§ Keyhole

Man is not the blind spot of being, but neither is he its pineal eye. He is not the key to being, but the keyhole through which it can be glimpsed in flagrante delicto.

§ Crowded Fields

There are books (especially in crowded fields fuelled by the narcissism of small differences) on whose reading our understanding throws up its arms and hitches a ride with our imagination. Faced with impenetrable jargon, compounding the weariness of mental strain, unable to pace ourselves and lacking the patience to plod on, we are moved to replace lost sense with meaningful inventions of our own. Carried along by a lively imagination as far as the next rest-stop, we hop off just as words resume their meaning, usually near the end of a section. We can thus convince ourselves that we have not given up trying to comprehend the text at all, but have in fact exercised our faculties the whole way through. We approach the new parts with fresh stride like seasoned travellers — Indeed, few could tell us apart! Instead of staying idle by the roadside or taking a shortcut route, we should be commended for making our way from section to section to eventually arrive at the end.

∫ Memory Viewed

Could memory ever be recorded and played back like a film? Why a memory-film? Better a memory-*archive*—total digital recall of what your eyes and ears have seen and heard. It might help retrieve sensations otherwise forgotten. Then again it might not. It might help you forget everything completely. (As someone once said, "Remember forgetting?") Memories are more than records; whatever happened to your eyes and ears might not have happened to *you*.

A memory-film, then, of only the selected substantial recollections, ones we have created and some, grown attached to, skipping over new thoughts and percepts that do not (yet) amount to memories. Would this *fix* and finalize such memory forever? Or would previously screened, now recovered scenes grow up all around it, so that they too could be put on record? Will the mind always produce more than it seems to need, as it does with ideas—which, even after being written down, still occur to us in other words? Do new memories really sprout around memories that have been "saved" or "tagged" by being photographed? Do such pictures tap the omitted senses: smell, taste, motion?

What disquiets would our memory-film be easing? The claustrophobia of the subjective. The vertigo of the unreliable, shifting and unstable. The abyss of the invisible. It would overwrite this discredited, shaky, inchoate morass with solid material: objectively shareable, spectrally ever-present, repeatable, and evidentiary.

¶ Fragility of Forgetting

The ossification of expressions is a form of forgetting their initial uses, which leaves them vulnerable to a certain osteoporotic brittleness. Take the expression "doggy bag," familiar to restaurateurs the world over. "Pack it up for the dog!"—its equivalent—reliably fails to communicate and might even offend the server. Breaking with the rule of metaphoric usage, the indication that one's leftovers are to be shared with a canine—the original presumed purpose of the "doggy bag"—deflates the puffery of an upscale establishment. In place of the patron now sits a lantern-eyed Rataplan, Diogenes's legate. *Does the food not agree with him?* wonders the waiter, feigning concern (and asks himself: *Is this the kind of customer we want to attract?*). "Do you mean, Sir, you'd like *the rest to go*?" All this consternation and effrontery from the old sense of a common phrase that has wandered in from the street to wag its tail at him.

¶ Shaking the Tree of Knowledge

There is something about pulling even low-hanging fruit off a tree before it drops to the ground that feels unnatural and lawless. And yet it must be done to keep the fruit from bruising or rotting.

Exercise patience until observation has ripened with the object of knowledge.

§ Changing Taxonomies

> *[N]ature carries on her own free sport, without troubling herself with the classes marked out by limited men.*
> —J.W. von Goethe, as reported by Eckermann[*]

How are we to understand those species reclassified on the basis of new molecular genetic evidence? Despite the great changes in scientific semiotics going on beside everyday language, which prefers the inertia of habit to the upsets of novelty, the maple is still maple, regardless of whether it still has its own family (*Aceraceae*) or is just a kind of soapberry (*Sapindaceae*) newly recognized.

It is similar with the "species" of mind, though here the preoccupation of science is chiefly teratological. Every few years, psychiatry renames and reclassifies mental chimeras in the hope of better grasping and one day inoculating us against them—keeping the norm without the deviation. Yet we laypeople obstinately refer to others as "neurotic," become "hysterical" ourselves, and take ages to mourn without owning up to depression. It is our way of staying in touch with nature, which as a rule deviates. We sense the futility of doing otherwise, and know that monsters by their very nature elude classification.

---

[*] Johann Wolfgang von Goethe, *Conversations of Goethe with Johann Peter Eckermann*, ed. J.K. Moorhead, trans. John Oxenford (1836–48; n.p.: Boston: Da Capo, 1998), 238.

∫ Go-Between

Modern art sweeps away the barrier between objectivity and subjectivity, between knowledge and opinion. It suggests that the practically unsustainable and so frequently crippling opposition of pure thought and pure creativity is the sediment of a series of analytical reifications. It shows objectivity to be as impossible a standard as subjectivity, and certainly no better.

In this lies art's autonomy vis-à-vis politics (opinion or truth, depending on one's conception) and science (neither opinion nor truth). It shows politics and science what divides and what unites them, and mediates when they grow either too far apart or too close.

∫ Fragments of a Hole

We still create under the assumption that what we create must make up a whole, which we are lacking. Why hold out for ourselves a false promise of future perfection, and make that the measure of worldly genius? Why else, if not to torture ourselves, would we think of our creations as pieces broken off, seeking to constitute a new or a lost wholeness for all to enjoy — when instead we can point back to the unplumbable perfection from which, as from cosmic collisions, they have fallen to us?

§ Mosaic

Only a fragmented view of things can aspire to comprehensiveness. An unfragmented whole needs no overview, being comprehensible at once and fully. But the collection and cohesion of fragments is not, and inspires the labour (with or without design) of a universal mosaic in which they are the tesserae. The comprehensive perspective, if achieved, would remain fragmented in them, while they will have become whole in it.

Q. And these fragments of yours? Why did you assemble them? Maybe to claim for yourself, through their close-up imprecise coherence, a certain comprehensiveness? Well, isn't it so?

A. For that I would have had to find a pattern, a design...

Q. And haven't you? What are you waiting for, then? Keep looking.

§ No Philosopher

There you have it: a minor, sickly book, promoting no sanatorium or spa treatment for your wheezing chest, migraines, or mental fuzziness. You will find here neither a nostrum for how to be nor a prescription for how to think.

The best I can offer is a masquerade of signs and symptoms. I've dressed up nauseas, persistent coughs, congenital weakness, and infections as *thoughts* and brought them out together in the social, even cozy context of a book. A pageant of our ill health. Something for everyone... Take your pick... It's up to you to make it therapeutic.

§ Flypaper

Perhaps in the busyness of thinking and writing we never venture into the fly-bottle from which Wittgenstein vowed to show the way out. But nothing stops us from falling into other traps — and getting trapped in the thoughts we have written down.

§ The Flies

> *[A] sudden awakening resembles a quickly drawn aside curtain. We then realize the unusual company we keep.*
> —Ernst Jünger[*]

Many a fly will alight on the face of the sleeper before he realizes he had nodded off. Upon rousing he will conclude that whatever disturbed him was dreamt — unless, that is, something fly-like is on hand to take the blame. But just as he is about to fly at his scapegoat, it occurs to him that he ought to thank it instead, lie back down again, close his eyes, and go after his dream, along its deep and dark twists and turns (where, like a fly, he might get stuck). But what could be the point? Only this: to return once more to the point of awakening.

---

[*] Ernst Jünger, *The Adventurous Heart: Figures and Capriccios*, ed. Russell A. Berman, trans. Thomas Friese (Candor, NY: Telos, 2012), 102 ("First Postscript").

∫ Most True

Early one morning while travelling to a nearby town I met a man by the name Verissimo. You would not guess this just by looking at him. He had a slovenly if relaxed and altogether pleasant appearance, so that I instinctively offered him some candy. It was just the two of us waiting by the side of a wooded road at an unmarked bus stop. The bus would be a while yet and so we struck up a — conversation? Hardly! For I spoke not a word of his language nor he of mine. It was then, after we had run out of — not topics either, but the energy to attempt communication by gestures and monosyllables (far more demanding than speech), that he pulled out his government ID and showed me his name. Some minutes later, to break the awkward silence that followed my acknowledgment, he opened for me the corner of a parcel he was carrying under his arm: a small stack of panes of glass wrapped in newspaper. Have I met the most truthful and transparent man? Will I ever know for certain? He must have given up on the bus because he left me, lost in thought, without saying goodbye, so that my mind immediately fell prey to suspicion. Had I been robbed without noticing? Had I imagined this meeting in the woods?

❡ Small Talk

We need a new subject for small talk. The weather has become too interesting—but not so much that we can *talk big*.

❡

Science: puts all answers into question.

⁂

III

§ The Impossible Handshake

> *Critique spelled the death of kings.*
> —Reinhart Koselleck, *Critique and Crisis*, pt. 2:
> The Self-Image of the Enlightenment Thinkers as a Response to Their Situation within the Absolutist State

> *The history of man ... is divided between the great nations and the great geniuses, between the kings and the men of letters, between the conquerors and the philosophers.*
> —d'Alembert[*]

The division between philosophers and princes, scholars and conquerors, is neither complete nor reparable. So is history written by two hands, with one washing another it would never shake.

---

[*] Reinhart Koselleck, *Critique and Crisis: Enlightenment and the Pathogenesis of Modern Society*, trans. uncredited (1959; Cambridge, MA: MIT Press, 1988), 116 (mod. trans.); d'Alembert, "Preliminary Discourse."

§ *Verblendungszusammenhang*

To insist that knowledge is power and power, knowledge is to forget that power often *falls behind* knowledge, not like a shadowy predator, waiting for the right moment to strike, but like an ogre (the creature, even, of some learned Frankenstein). It is, as well, to forget that knowledge has been known to *run ahead* of power, not like a scout watching for an enemy's approach, but dreamily, like a dog unleashed in a field, for all intents and purposes a will-less creature just following its nose.

§ Politics and Truth-Power

The modern relationship between knowledge and power is fundamentally ambivalent, though knowledge and power, in the abstract, are not (truth is good, power bad). The ambivalence we have in mind can be exemplified by the contrasting positions of Jürgen Habermas and Michel Foucault. For Habermas, truth can be known, justice be had, and knowledge be legitimate if power is taken out of the equation. For Foucault, abstracting truth from power, which is ubiquitous, is a historical impossibility.

In neither view does power simply equal politics. Politics bestows visibility on the operation of power — though only that part that can be legitimized — and plunges into shadow other, non-obvious forms of power, those that feed into or derive from power's visible form, but that, owing to their subjects, character, and scale of operations, as well as to political necessity, are hidden from critique and questions of legitimacy. This chiaroscuro structure is essential for democratic politics to emerge in full relief, in that political power acquires legitimacy through the real or apparent apoliticalness of public and private institutions within its purview and de facto control.

Power is not all politics, so much is clear. Each of our activities exists within a pattern of complex and largely invisible power relations as in an electrical field. It is associated, like it or not, with certain networks within that field. It can enter into strong relations with and steer them, navigate them and remain non-partisan, but it can also play one network against another to heighten tensions and lead (without being coded as political) to radical realignments of forms of power.

The charge of *political irresponsibility* can only be levelled at actions once political issues are traced back to them, in the way an epidemic is traced to one person not having washed their hands. This makes *apparent* the disconnect between politics and everything else (everything below power's visibility threshold), legitimizing the political status quo — and, conversely, de-legitimizing it when it is discovered to have manipulated private actions for its own ends. Then and there, the political order can either gain power by bringing on board and politicizing the irresponsibly apolitical, or else lose its credibility, like the puppeteer who reaches down to untangle a string (when this happens no one blames the puppets, only their master, for not knowing how to control them without showing his hands).

It is in such circumstances that the need for more power *outside* politics is voiced most vehemently. It is, on the face of it, a demand for popular, bottom-up empowerment, without top-down restructuration and financial infusion — but, in fact, a request for the oblique political supervision attached to any government's pledge of greater operational autonomy to its citizens. In effect, the distinction between political and non-political power on the level of organizations and institutions breaks down, and perhaps the future of democracy is to be read off the fragility of the purported threshold dividing politics from other forms of power, instead of located in its resilience and occasional, preventable permeability.

Let us return, then, to the continued ambivalence — as defined by two towering intellects — concerning the relation between power and knowledge. The first, Habermasian position diminishes the reach of power outside its obvious, political forms and undermotivates the struggle to separate knowledge from politics inasmuch as the latter increasingly conforms to the model of communicative rationality (as is the norm in science). The second, Foucauldian view exaggerates the reach of power, configuring it as entrenched in the domain of truth, and undermotivates the need to fight its corrosive effects by speaking truth to power. Power speaks the language of knowledge, knowledge, that of power, and rational control is as deleterious as it is enabling.

If these are the extremes, truth (along with real power) is somewhere in the middle: truth and politics are separable, and it is the separation we should focus upon. This, however, is not principally a matter of contesting and boycotting knowledge coopted by politics, of defending truth from political attacks, of exposing knowledge's political impetus. It has primarily to do with tracing the history of knowledge's entanglement with politics, their nexus. And previously, knowledge had been theologized, its justification, cognizing God's plan for us. Only in reductive retrospect does this make it "political" *before* the so-called "Machiavellian moment"—the dawn of modern, *historical* politics—and Bacon's calling a spade a spade ("knowledge is power"). Only through such crude foreshortening does Prometheus anticipate Spartacus, and Spartacus, Lenin. But this also means that the French Revolution merely formalized what had long been under way; pre-metric weights and measures like the King's Foot had already effectively been politicized centuries earlier, in the late Renaissance—as were the contributions of the first modern grammarians.

Today, and as long as there is still politics and knowledge depends on power and money, it is irresponsible for anyone involved in knowledge-work to ignore its political dimension. Ignorance of the uses of knowledge on the part of its producers and technicians does not free them from ethical-political responsibility. This is not to say that what is not yet political, but can be if it gets into the wrong hands, needs to be preemptively politicized. Responsibility, too, corrupts, allowing politics in through the back door. The attempt to bar Iranian students from nuclear physics courses is a case in point of the absurdity of the preemptive political gaming Americans have become world-famous for.

◊ New in States

The latest fashion in nation-states is to elicit polarization. Thus, states are either infinitely *defensible*—seen as benevolent, inspiring patriotism even in non-citizens; or they are tirelessly *attackable*—seen as rogue and authoritarian even by their own citizens.

◊ *Sua cuique persona*

Insistence on the political innocence or inviolability of science never sounded more like willful ignorance than it does today. Around the time of the rise of social critique—directed from the first against the existing relations, forms, and means of power that hitch truth to governing authority—and a parallel depoliticization of religious truth, also known as economic secularization, *scientific truth* began forfeiting its neutrality and autonomy from politics. Its political ties replaced those previously linking power to revealed, religious truth. Science's political aspirations grew apace with its ability to provide industrial applications and discover untapped opportunities for investment. (The very notion of *discovery*, unlike that of *eureka* or *epiphany*, seems to have long been freighted with expectations of political-economic gain.)

Notwithstanding over two centuries of shared interests, even as claims to *scientific objectivity* became more difficult to sustain, scientific research has on the whole tried to conceal or downplay its collusion with political power (posing instead merely as its basis or inspiration). Its reliance on economic resources that only states and transnational corporations could provide is a relatively recent development. Since about the mid-eighteenth century, the scientific and technological order, which had already begun to set itself up as the main purveyor of truth, became the most sought-after ally for politics, first politics from above but later also from below. The courtship of science by politics and industry continues today wherever taxpayer dollars and private funds are funnelled into research.

Technological activism, which grew out of formerly state-controlled computer science and comes in a variety of ideological editions (anarchistic, libertarian, radical-democratic), is the latest, most concerted and potent reaction, long without the right means, to this stitching together of positivist science and the state form.* The regrettable downside of its power of resistance and subversion is its abandonment of public critique, leading to the progressive disarticulation of critique from radical politics. It is a price forced upon it by the platforms on which it acts — and one it is largely willing to pay, given the less-than-clear value of social critique when recently popular critical models no longer seem practically useful. Critique continues to be a "resource," but it is less and less the politically integrated intellectual practice it once hoped to be. It may be that high-level technical expertise and a mature, coherent critical position are now too much to expect of any one person.

The main source of this misfortune (the separation of critique from radicalism-from-below) is the need for anonymity. It is a rare group that manages to combine a loud and clear critical voice with privacy. The position of Anonymous is remarkable for its militant, barebones message, delivered by a computer voice and accompanied by striking visual montage — as if its appeal rested on steering away from theoretical gibberish, from the mash-up of poetic, auratic, gnomic, and combative statements that are the hallmark of young intellectual radicals like the Invisible Committee, who also flirted with anonymity. Its choice of public image, the Guy Fawkes persona, is to its credit. Its reach far exceeds that of the predigested critical canon, whose academic dissemination, mostly in the form of commentary, testifies to the bankruptcy of its more politically productive ideas. In their place, tech activism puts sabotage and the clandestine, carefully targeted

---

* Foucault, "What Is Critique?", 50.

strike — more military than proletarian in inspiration. The practice ushers in a new type of anonymous heroism, quite distinct from the physical courage of the anonymous, masked Zapatista fighters. Those activists who decide to go public — to become spokespersons for an underground movement — have a claim to valour as strong as any Spartacus.

The gospel of networked anonymity is having an effect, still small, on how we lead our online lives. Internet hygiene has gone from being a marginal issue, limited to those who for one reason or another wanted their real identity hidden (even if they lacked technical savvy to secure their e-coordinates), to a central public one, via sensitive data transfer, identity-theft protection, and social-media privacy-setting concerns. Those who previously gave no thought to the matter find more and more sympathy for the Good Hacker who watches the watchers and regularly throws a wrench into the gears of their indiscriminate snooping. This makes the job of spreading his gospel much easier, among the young especially — young enough to learn code and how to take care of themselves virtually. The simplified version of his teaching hinges on civil commitment to our online anonymity; mass use of anonymizing encryption masks the anonymous few toiling on our privacy's behalf, who would otherwise draw the authorities' attention. If everyone is hiding, the state — which finds hiding suspicious — will have a harder time identifying the real culprits. Our good citizenship will form a protective cloud against invasive and illegal policing. The hackers will have a shield, and we will have our privacy — a win-win situation in a time when states have lost their credibility on that score, so much so that no one concerned about their privacy today would risk hiding in plain sight.

The importance of not losing sight of anonymity as a means rather than an end in itself will be obvious to anyone who still has some faith in law and order. Another danger of fetishizing anonymity is forgetting the value of identity — plain old identity, that not only gets you socially integrated but holds on to your rights. For the crusaders for anonymity, whose names are all over the news, privacy is code for an authentic identity that must remain hidden and unnamed.

Julian Assange's joshing of his ghost-autobiographer, "People think you're helping me write my book, but actually I'm helping you write your novel,"* points to just such an authentic, ineluctable identity. The real hacker, whose mythic life consists in total commitment to the cause, remains masked to the end. There is a sense of cultivated outsiderdom in all of this, of unfulfilled prophecy, of "this is only the beginning," of everyday sacrifice, of "we are here only by the grace of fate," "we are lucky to still be alive" — much of it is probably true. For political activism to be effective in checking state control, ever more complex measures will be needed to guard anonymity. For those in charge of it, anonymity may mean opting out of identities that make political recognition in, and mobility between, states even possible. This too will be only for a brave minority, as state-based politics will be for the pusillanimous many.

The politicization of individual and collective online anonymity goes hand in hand with the radicalization of anonymity in *physical* struggle. The last century and the present one have been, if nothing else, a global teach-in on how to use bodies as weapons, for and against the state. Public and private anonymity or pseudonymity has long assisted in this, but did not become a matter of safe conduct until the enemy's crosshairs acquired uncanny precision. Virtual anonymity chosen for anti-state political ends, in the name of those who remain named, ultimately serves to shelter one's physical body; if bullet-proof, identity-encryption could almost seem not to require renouncing civil rights for universal, human ones. Those who maintain such anonymity realize that, as their virtual risk grows, their *physical* identity turns into a liability that may need to be sacrificed to reduce the chance of virtual discovery and bodily harm. Physical appearance can lead authorities to the hacker's identity and needs to be differentiated. Low-tech disguises (including surgery), like forged documents, for the time being linking

---

* Andrew O'Hagan, "Ghosting," *London Review of Books* 36, no. 5 (2014), http://www.lrb.co.uk/v36/n05/andrew-ohagan/ghosting.

us to past political and military deception, are about to be retired by mandatory biometric scanning. Like Zorro's, the masks of the Zapatistas and Guy Fawkes will reappear only as Halloween costumes. The personae of tomorrow will be high-tech, shading into invisibility and virtual martyrdom, more menacingly sock-puppet- and phantom-like.

§ What Words Could

What's so funny about the idea of "speaking truth to power"? Each time this hallowed phrase fell, a grin went around the table in a Practical Philosophy colloquium at Germany's best-known university. This grin, and even soft chuckle — it seemed to express a certain embarrassment. Some, ashamed of simplistic, immature thinking or dreaming of the heroism signified by the phrase, might even have blushed. They recognized it as the thought of those who fought for the abolition of slavery and for free speech — because speech, a tool of empowerment, was denied them. But the present security of these hard-won freedoms meant that it was hard to relate to their earnestness, even if sympathy for their struggle was automatic. The phrase, then, evoked the heady milestones in human emancipation, when the power of mere words was a matter of fact, and no light matter. But it failed, at this historical distance, to resonate (in fact, it seemed jarring in the context of a high-level discussion).

Could it be it was just too idealistic — too idealistic back then and now even more so? Could it be such idealism was not only naïve but unnecessary and somehow uncool? If it were necessary and warranted, and the history to which it was attached accorded respect, would it trigger amusement? Perhaps their amusement, this germ of a judgment, says less about the students' assessment of the old days, and more about their skepticism of political action. Is it their *realism* or their *cynicism* that showed through? And then, was it the whole expression that amused them, or only the "truth" part, or the part about "speaking" out against lies and injustices? Surely it could not have been the third part, "power." Power, after all, is a serious thing. The daily struggle for it cannot be denied, its abuse, wished away. Many of its particular forms provoke mockery — even the most menacing ones, which multiple strategies might be needed to check and curtail. (This mockery is compatible with speaking the truth only indirectly, as when it aims to expose power's lies; speaking this truth to power effectively, so that it is registered as such, requires seriousness.) But no one thinks for a minute of power per se as "mere" power, given its potential for the destruction or improvement of lives, the fears and hopes associated with it, and the moral obligation it is assigned. This requires that everyone keep a straight face also when speaking *about* power. And when reckoning with power or speaking *to* it. And when speaking the *truth*, and defending it when necessary, through speech and action. How is it that, after such an anatomy and Socratic assent to the premises, the complete idea of "speaking truth to power" might still seem a tad silly, or not entirely serious, in the end? Does it not correspond to the idea of authentic political engagement among the young? Maybe the simpler answer is right: that such political engagement does not jibe with their idea of *themselves*.

§ Privacy Settings

When reason goes private, the intellect goes missing.

◊ Snowdown

Not even the illusionists of the spiritual realize the extent of human gullibility. Uri Geller's failure to deliver on the Johnny Carson Show only strengthened belief in his paranormal powers; the public reasoned that "If he were performing magic tricks, they surely would work every time."* The same counterintuitive logic applies to the state's surveillance capabilities: to an unusually trusting—or mistrustful—public it seems that, if surveillance was indeed as patchy and limited as some would have us believe, it would work without a hitch and be perfectly hidden. But its outrageous failures, of which the Snowden revelations are an example, serve as proof of the boundless scope and ambition of the operation. Those surprised by Snowden's exposé (and either incredulous about power's real extent or credulous about its showy self-denial) don't know the half of it. In this way, all-too-human shadowing and snooping morphs in some minds into quasi-divine omniscience. The only thing that stops us from calling such uncanny worldwide surveillance "miraculous" is the sneaking suspicion that it is up to no good. The sober thought that just because we believe it doesn't mean it's happening tips over into paranoid comedy—just because we believe it doesn't mean it ain't real—reaffirming our subordination to the perverse logic of state control: the less verifiable, the more onerous. The most farfetched notions—including the conspiracy theories typical of modern liberal democracies—barely scratch the surface of the nefarious reality instituted for the sake of maintaining civic order.

The real post-Snowden showdown will have to wait until the end of the disagreement between believers and disbelievers. The latter, it must be said, are already in the minority. But the former's easy victory over the surveillance state may come on account not of their numbers but of their strength of belief—having grossly overestimated the power of their enemy.

---

*   Adam Higginbotham, "The Unbelievable Skepticism of the Amazing Randi," *New York Times Magazine*, Nov. 9, 2014, http://www.nytimes.com/2014/11/09/magazine/the-unbelievable-skepticism-of-the-amazing-randi.html.

∫ Noisemakers

Whistleblowing is music to my ears.
  —anon.

America possesses an endlessly renewable wealth of public hecklers but a dearth of whistleblowers. The difference between heckling and blowing into a whistle is that in the one you are tooting your own horn while in the other you are sounding a general alarm — and waiting for sirens...

∫ Sleeper Cells

Little did the wasps know when in autumn they built their nest between the window and the shutter of a locked-up summer cottage that their main load-bearing wall was see-through, leaving them exposed from the inside to the bug-eyed curiosity of next year's vacationers. In seeking a citizen's privacy and protection between four walls, we are like the wasps, not realizing the contiguity and meanness of material through which their life will inevitably become known to those who neighbour them. The illusion that a scrap of privacy is our shelter and escape when planning something awful is one for which we will pay in due course. When the neighbours tune in, when nature awakes, when a searchlight falls on our activity, the transparent wall to which we are attached spills our dirty secrets.

꧅ Private the New Public

Privacy is the new fame.
—Nico Sell[*]

So much thinking goes into curating the public view of one's privacy, where one's opinions are semi-public or edited for potentially damaging content. So much public opinion goes into evaluating one's image and commenting off-hand on opinions to which one is not obviously committed. So if one asks "Where has public discourse gone?" one clearly has not been paying attention.

꧅ Letting It All Hang Out

When true privacy comes to mean public anonymity, we know we are in trouble. Either that, or — particularly if we rule this "true privacy" extreme and exceptional — we have finally overcome the great delusion of modern life that the private and the public spheres should be kept separate. To be sure, we can put up a good fight in defence against our newfound *public privacy's* colonization by our *professional* life, but only when we are taken to task for something we post or say, usually by an employer with whom we are not identifiable. Otherwise, though, we are untroubled by appearing, in a professional guise, to integrate career with parenting, social obligations, self-development, and homemaking — the latter four dimensions that prior to Facebook remained "private private," i.e., invisible to the same sets of eyes. Speaking of the pre-digital past, no one was better at this partitioning

---

[*] Quoted in Carole Cadwalladr, "Nico Sell: 'To Me, the NSA and Edward Snowden Are Just the Tip of the Iceberg,'" *Guardian*, Jan. 4, 2015, http://www.theguardian.com/theobserver/2015/jan/04/nico-sell-wickr-secure-messaging-app-internet-security-nsa-edward-snowden.

than the upper-middle-class male. Housekeeping and parenting were offloaded on women and servants, with children allowed into the workplace of the paterfamilias only as apprentices or to be shown off to the odd visitor, rather than, as in the lower stations, as extra hands or for a lack of affordable childcare. Exemptions to this household order took the form of family outings and church. Social functions were defined by hobbies and family gatherings, which were not to be confused with business deals. Self-development was not pursued as public lifelong learning, but in the private library and through travel. Each of these areas of life was visible to different groups of people, with minimal overlap between them. Accidentally happening on a business partner while on an errand made for not a little awkwardness. Today, with incentives to collect contacts in social media hubs and a feed that covers the "whole me," this unease about conflating or mixing the private with the professional is of necessity disappearing. With so many eyes following, the entire life package is offered up for judgment. Perhaps this is not so bad.

⁂ Naming Contest

Social media can compel users to curate even their behaviour, to alembicate and edit their own speech and displays of emotion, since their public self-control extends into periods of social activity in isolation, covering most waking hours. Perhaps the social media age deserves to be called the Age of the Art of the Person. The long-term effects on users might considerably strengthen their ability to get along in virtual and even physical environments. But such arguments from wishful thinking, which generalize optimistically about the future based on a particular worry about the present, do nothing to diminish the pessimistic counterclaim that spending time on social media, where access to us is comparatively restricted, leads us to mask superficially what we once controlled inwardly, ultimately weakening our ability to check spontaneous reactions in unmediated public situations. And if we stop to think of the scandal, spite, and hatred that anonymity encourages, perhaps a better name for the social media age would be the Age of the Troll.

§ Wanted: Amanuensis

Who doesn't like to dictate?

§ Dictationship

A tough sentence is just by the time you finish it.

§ Do As You're Told

Read every word.

§ *Intramurale*

Both the rich and the poor, the ruling and privileged no less than the exploited and subordinate, are known to hold political ideas contrary to their interests. In the latter group, these ideas earn the name *ideology*; we are dealing here with false consciousness. In the former group, they are called *utopia*, which is to say right consciousness. Just as ideology is contrary to the interests of the poor, so utopia is contrary to the interests of the well-to-do.

The interests of members of each group can certainly undergo inversion — that is, *perversion* from any but their own perspective.

§ Daisy Chains

Chains decked with flowers no longer rattle.

Flowers in chains are as fragrant as ever.

The thorn is the flower's way of saying beauty can be painful. A rose grasped too carelessly is a dangerous object. Barbed wire is a rose bush depetalled and hardened.

§ Doing Time

To *do* time is not to *use* it. It is to be stuck with all the time one needs, and more, and have no way of filling it freely. So much time and too little to do. Being locked up with time and serving it is no occupation. It is not something even an old-timer can become an old hand at. Nothing but time on his hands keeps his hands tied. Time is his punishment. Instead of lashes and beatings he is administered minutes and hours. As long as he has lots of it, time is not on his side.

§ *Habeas corpus*

> *No slave should die a natural death. There is a point where caution ends and cowardice begins. For every day I am imprisoned I will refuse both food and water. My hunger is for the Liberation of my people. My thirst is for the ending of oppression.... Our will to live must no longer supercede our will to fight, for our fighting will determine if our race shall live.*
>
> —H. Rap Brown, letter from Parish Prison, New Orleans, February 21, 1968[*]

The enduring power of Spartacus's rebellion is its most enduring power; the universality of oppression and resistance to it are secondary. Fast-forward nineteen centuries and the language of freedom for the enslaved is used by men like Frederick Douglass to speak to comparable conditions of captivity. While the tactics of resistance have multiplied, as have the media of its publicization, the physical body

---

[*] H. Rap Brown, "H. Rap Brown from Prison," in Ron Hahne and Ben Morea, *Black Mask and up against the Wall Motherfucker: The Incomplete Works of Ron Hahne, Ben Morea and the Black Mask Group* (Oakland, CA: PM, 2011), 74–75.

continues to be put on the line in all brave emancipatory action. Its presence, signifying integrity, expresses that shared and ineliminable minimum of human existence, physical need.

We can imagine this will not always be so: that someday (perhaps quite soon, given decades of actual and dystopian foreshadowing) risking flesh and blood, however heroic it still seems to us, will cease to be necessary, and capturing and hurting them alone, have no effect. The incarceration and torture of the body have always failed to *chain* the mind to it. But the artificially augmented mind is newly vulnerable. Disarming the body by throwing it into prison was always second-best to mind control and brainwashing, which not only leaves the body intact but, as in *The Manchurian Candidate,* renders it cooperative and operational. Human bondage may soon seem no less a relic than the binding of feet. We can look forward to a grey future in which bodies will be locked up by minds locked away in real virtual prisons...

∫ A Tale of Two Bodies

Two ways for the body of the near future: fit and enslaved, or enslaved and broken. Either way: pumped full of drugs, plugged into some underserved, overexploited circuit in the network.

§ White on Black

Our recognition of the value of other lives, including those recognized by science as human, forms a kind of spectrum, on which the difference between animals and humans is not clearly marked, poisoning for the longest time interracial relations. The events in Ferguson, Mo., ask for an *even less optimistic* interpretation than that offered as a corrective to the "unduly optimistic" perspective that understands white police officers' actions in terms, not even of de-humanizing blacks, but of a pervasive blindness to their humanity. The basis of this latter, *humanist* position is the "psychologically dubious assumption...that when people who have historically enjoyed a dominant position in society (in this case white men) come to recognize historically subordinated people (racial minorities, women) as their moral and social equals, they will welcome the newcomers."[*] The black people whose protest slogan read "In Seeing Our <u>HUMANITY</u> You Will Find Your OWN (#blacklivesmatter)" clearly endorsed this line of thinking.[†]

The corrective, *critical* line on the humanist view finds support in the whites' punitive resentment, so clearly in evidence. The thesis here is that what fuels white rage and inspires (instead of follows from) black dehumanization is the threat blacks pose to the social hierarchy. There is much truth in this, of course, especially when considered alongside the motivation for lynchings. The threat of usurpation — sexual, political, economic — of whites' place in American society by black people was, and no doubt continues to be, perceived as real in many quarters. But precisely by reason of the long and complex history of racism, we must take issue with this as the sole explanation. We must look farther

---

[*] Kate Manne, "In Ferguson and Beyond, Punishing Humanity," *New York Times*, Oct. 12, 2014, http://opinionator.blogs.nytimes.com/2014/10/12/in-ferguson-and-beyond-punishing-humanity/.

[†] Charles Rex Arbogast, Associated Press photo, accessed Mar. 10, 2015, http://www.cbc.ca/news/world/missouri-protests-arrests-but-no-reported-clashes-on-moral-monday-1.2797581.

back into the past of white on black violence, to the age of slavery. We will then have no trouble seeing that discrimination on the *social* hierarchy affected only some, select blacks; most fell outside the narrow band of *human society* on the value-spectrum of lives, and were treated as human only to the extent that they could follow orders and had basic needs for food and shelter (whose denial could then be used to control them). They were *human enough* to do human work, no more. In what is perhaps an indelible legacy of slavery, this attitude manifests today on the streets of America.

Let's indulge in a little timely speculation. Perhaps the black people in Ferguson and beyond could get better results by claiming for recognition, not of their common humanity, but of something else. Perhaps in the current climate of hate their time would be better spent, not on appeals to human empathy, but on a cunning *détournement* of historical reason. The struggle for civil rights for blacks is as old as human rights. But does not the cause of *animal rights* have the advantage at least of novelty and near-automatic sympathy? Perhaps to protect themselves from being killed they would be well-advised to present themselves as harmless because long-domesticated animals, rather than the ferocious beasts they routinely seem to armed and armoured cops? Or would whites resent them for it even more? For what exactly? For being as some who take aim at them would no doubt like themselves to be — excused from morality and responsibility — and who, at moments of great moral pressure and risk of error, would give anything for a heavy horse's collar, as one sees now and then fashioned into a mirror frame, to wear around their neck?

§ Concrete Is Hard

Empathy knows no "hard" or "natural" limits. If another's shoes prove a good fit, why not go in them beyond the pathos of creatureliness, past weeping the *lacrimae rerum*, all the way to one's own destruction, choosing it over empathy's death?

The only living limits to empathy are distraction, thief of attentive feeling, and judgment, which projects onto empathizers its own ulterior motives. Historically, as soon as a conceptual gulf opened up between social self-construction and biological being, and identity became something one could consciously construct and claim, survival- as much as sympathy- and empathy-based claims of alternate gender or racial belonging, that is to say without obvious correspondence to one's biology, went from being treated as psychic aberrations to being criticizable on political grounds.

Only when biological makeup is itself thoroughly historicized can such critical indignation, which betokens above all an inability to empathize, be silenced. The conquest of gay and lesbian (and presently transgender) rights notwithstanding, this indignation must persist as long as nature is essentialized, appealed to as decisive and unambiguous.

Where they are made in the abstract, "in the head," on the level of self-perception, even fundamental switches in identity are readily portrayed as facile. Their particular demands for recognition, if met, fail to bring about legal generalization. Only what is perceived as difficult, no matter how superficial — such as the awkward social expression of new identity, the dramatic alteration of appearance breaking with gender or racial conventions to the point of provoking outright hostility — can hope, in the long run, to produce the desired changes. And when a transformation is so complete that it cannot be seen through, raising no suspicion of "deception," the existential difficulty of the performance (once revealed, as it sometimes is after the danger has passed) is conceded quickly enough.

But even such rare respect and admiration are not empathy. Renouncing one's "natural" identity, trading it for another, is taken either for a betrayal or, less often, for a sacrifice, this even when the change improves one's social standing. In a brutally patriarchal culture, the Egyptian widow and mother who for decades posed as a father and man, or the girls in certain areas of Afghanistan and Pakistan who live *bacha posh*, as boys, blurring the lines between fact and fiction, are all forgiven. To Western eyes, their repudiated femininity appears in a heroic light (a phenomenon for which the French nation even has a pious icon in the Maid of Orléans).

In a residually misogynistic culture, where women have made great strides towards achieving parity, the high-profile cases of Bradley-cum-Chelsea Manning or Bruce-cum-Caitlyn Jenner receive less sympathy than pity (their sacrifices were not obviously beneficial) or indulgence (though biology doesn't lie, it can be fooled). Public reaction on the spectrum of political correctness ranges in such cases from sisterly embrace through the recognition of courage to a shrug to the curiosity accorded to freaks. Femininity was never so alienated as to be, when claimed by a man, contested and condemned for having been claimed *falsely*; from the female point of view, the man-to-woman switch may be redeemed as much by "being oneself" as by the trans person's appreciation or empathy for the secondary sex, an impulse to be commended even when its expression is not.

Yet the white woman who for many years chose to identify as black for no doubt complex reasons, in which empathy with the discriminated against must have had a share (alongside factors like family upbringing and ancestry, gender and environment) — such a woman is judged mercilessly as a self-serving fraud. Increasingly, politicized suffering refuses to be appropriated, particularly by those who had not suffered. There is no special treatment for impostors, no matter how genuine their empathy and devotion to sharing the fate of the oppressed. As long as the victims of suffering remain disempowered, they deserve at least to own all their pain as they own debt or their many other negative attributes. The happy and the spared, meanwhile, worry where such crossovers, were they to become numerous enough, might lead all those conscious of inequality without being themselves hard hit. Any such polarization, with activists and intellectuals on the "wrong side," could spell the end of "natural advantage." In this way an extreme manifestation of white-black empathy finds itself doubly condemned.

Those who want to *change their life* concretely and significantly by identifying in their mind and appearance with the long-dominated who have become *politically conscious* of their subjugation face a dilemma: identity self-reassignment entails the possibility of being publically outed and condemned. These are the hard-fact disincentives to the new identity's full concretion. These also are the hindrances to mobilization in solidarity—be it from a distance or via active transversality—against those who have the greatest stakes in maintaining an unjust status quo, where biological knowledge hopelessly stuck in three dimensions is the arbiter of fate.

In a remarkable short story by the neo-abolitionist anthropologist Holley Cantine, the surviving Plains Indians live up to their romanticized image and the reputation for cold-blooded savagery that follows it, in a bid to return America to something like its pre-conquest state. Recognizing an opportunity in their summons to save the flagging U.S. tourism industry (and later on, taking advantage of "white" greed); recognizing, too, the strategic value of converts to their way of life (if anything, underestimating the zeal of these would-be indigenes), they train an army of warriors and together take over the country. At first it feels to them like an elaborate costume drama, but within a few years, having become "naturals" at it, they transform the original economic telos into a political, counter-providential one ("the sacred mission of the Indians"). For everyone and everything involved—the natives, the kids running away from consumer society in pursuit of adventure and out of sympathy for the underdog's "general rising,"* not to mention the well-meaning tribal ethnologists and nature itself, the animals and the land—for all except committed "whites,"

---

* Holley Cantine, *Second Chance: A Story* (Bearsville, NY: Retort, 1961), 22, 23.

whatever their skin colour, the ensuing civil war represents a second chance no one prevents them from taking.

In real life, such stories do not always end well. Regardless of the strength of self-interest, all seems to hang on the breadth and depth of mutual empathy. Article 14 of the 1805 Constitution of Haiti stated: "All acceptation of colour among the children of one and the same family, of whom the chief magistrate is the father, being necessarily to cease, the Haytians shall hence forward be known only by the generic appellation of Blacks." The inclusivity of that appellation has perhaps never been more generous.

But even those real-life cases that do end well do not always end good. Far-reaching empathy is necessarily selective, but not automatically right. In the eyes of global public opinion makers, global jihadism is a pandemic. But where the possible self-interested advantages of empathy outweigh concerns over the authenticity of identity, a battle, be it good or evil, is already half won.

⸠ Torn-Country Experts

draft 1:

The perspective of the native informant is too restricted, too biased to give us knowledge. Its bias confirms what we already know.

draft 2:

The perspective of the native informant is too restricted, too biased to give us knowledge. Its bias is the knowledge we want confirmed.

⸠ Two-Way Terror

A modern nightmare-fantasy: to wind up in solitary at a black site. It is a simple inversion of a modern fantasy-nightmare: to be blindfolded and flown half-way around the world and dumped in a desert wilderness. Common to both renderings is sensory day-for-night disorientation and impotence, in the first case dreaded, in the second desired.

⌇ Uncanny Valentines

In a culture as enervated as the Western one, pleasure cannot be derived from forestalled threats any more than excitement comes from civilizational anxiety or terror. But when the French "Charlies" gathered together and defiant, they marched united and proud: the nose-count demonstrated they were many — there had never been so large a public rally in France! Who could deny that from this solidarity flowed a kind of sovereign joy?

If Michel Houellebecq, author of the novel *Submission*, does "do Ramadan in 2022," it will be out of boredom, expediency, or intimidation. If ISIS has its way in the East and Europe submits to its Muslims, their countdown to the End of Times will not, like New Year's Eve, do it for everyone. But apocalypticism continues to have a morbid, minority appeal in the spiritual West. The more mixed, crowded and explosive the world becomes, the more "open" civil society will be to citizens who root for its enemies and attackers. Their hearts will swell at the thought of faraway dramas and faiths, uncompromising and righteous causes. They will beat the rhythm of crude romanticism counter to calculation, of old asceticism contrary to distraction, of communal sacrifice against individual life and satisfaction. The souls of these not-quite-defectors will cheer secretly, but cheer nonetheless — and leap in anticipation of either sounding the alarm at home or joining secret comrades on distant soil.

⌇ Apocalyptic Anti-Apocalypticism

Nanterre, France, 2016: "Another end of the world is possible."

§ Allegory of Politics

In simple terms that might yet speak to those who would like to see the body put back in political action, politics is society's dance with conflict, that is to say *an art form*. Either side can take the lead. Leading and being led are the basal modes of society's political dynamic. The tendency to reduce this dynamic to *power relations* must be acknowledged for what it is: a minatory attempt to take the art out of politics so as to perpetuate the illusion of the rationalizability and finally the automatizability of political life. It must therefore be resisted. At least on the left, based on a dear but caricatural distinction between twentieth-century ideological extremes, resistance takes the form of producing political art through alliances among artists and activists. The same cannot be said of today's right — unless by "art of politics" we mean merely the kind of smoke-and-mirror campaigns that the moderate political spectrum officially condemns.

To return to the metaphor of the dance, if society reins in conflict by the elegant, stately movements of a polonaise (sometimes phlegmatic, sometimes energetic), conflict compels it to a sprightly polka that at times quite resembles jumping on hot coals. We can picture war as conflict sweeping up society in a feral whirl, furious and disorienting. When the pair does come to a stop, society is still reeling, and needs a few moments to recover its balance. If society takes the lead again, it suffers much criticism for letting itself get mixed up in a tarantistic frenzy, allowing "the blind to lead the blind," etc.

Through the many styles and moves that conflict takes it, or that it takes conflict, each society must always keep up with conflict; were it to trip, it would be trampled and defeated in the tournament by competitors for first place.

◊ "Murderous Alphabet"

Where the world is run by hunger, words grow dull — but syllables, murderous. Stripped to the bone and whetted, language is sharp as a butcher's knife where there is plenty of meat to go around. Hunger makes language do the killing in the name of ending it.

◊ Friendly Fire

> *Boss, this is a roast.*
> —reportedly said of a deadly fire in New York City

> *It became necessary to destroy the town to save it.*
> —reportedly said of one Vietnamese town by an unnamed U.S. officer following the Tet Offensive

> bug splat: *name for a drone casualty on the ground*

The desensitization of police and soldiers in combat zones to the sight of human calamity manifests most not in offensive language and fatuous jokes, in which sexism and racism are at ease, but in absent-minded dark humour.

∫ *Rarae aves*

Long before the Civil War era, there were common folk, white and black, who spoke as they wrote and whose written style was uncommonly refined and effortless. Unexpected, they astonished. If we believe westerns, most people communicated by nods and grunts, curtsies and tobacco spit. Illiteracy was common, and on those who learned to read the influence of printed matter was akin to being touched by an angel—so elevated did their diction become, so clear and inspired their thinking and writing. How much truer was this of blacks before the Emancipation Proclamation. One need only think of slave-born poetess Phyllis Wheatley and writer/orator Frederick Douglass to see it as a miraculous occurrence. With the steady rise in mass literacy, such unearthly refinement soon dropped in value as a source of envy or mark of distinction. It not only stood out less; its vanishing was foreordained. The ability to write well is now taken for granted by the educated (just as taste, which can be bought, is assumed to follow wealth). As a result, ever less effort is expended to prove it—as ever less effort is made to ensure that such miracles occur again.

₰ The Seeing Eye

The oldest American guide dog academy, from which the "seeing-eye dog" took its name, was established in 1929 on the model of similar schools founded in Germany to assist handicapped war veterans. This was just a few years after the founding of the Institute for Social Research at the University of Frankfurt, after which the school of Critical Theory, the "Frankfurt School," has come to be known. (This institution, too, had an American equivalent, the New School for Social Research in New York, which preceded it, set up on another German model in 1919.) The thinkers associated with Critical Theory, then as now, acquired a reputation for philosophical profundity, acute awareness of social injustice, and a wide-ranging critique of ideology, full of oracular warnings and admonitions. What they have dubbed the *culture industry* is pointless and visionless. The goal of the Institute is to train those who can see through it, and see us through it, to social change and a better use of reason. Where would we, blind, be without their help? The answer is: not only lost but imperiled without knowing it.

We approach the street corner (our cane broken, our ears clogged) and pause on the curb, mere steps from the flow of traffic. This, then, is the moment of the seeing-eye dog.*

---

* Full credit for the extended metaphor only paraphrased here goes to Arnd Pollmann.

§ The Seven Years' War Again

Usurping the place of high theory (a North American invention) is low theory and cultural studies. When done well, cultural studies works to bring theory to practice. When done badly, it is little more than a theory mash-up — a free-for-all, rootless, abstracted "theory in general."

Its power as a backlash against the cultured (read: elitist) nature of high theory cannot be denied. Cultural studies came via Britain to the shores of North America, and squared off against French high theory imported there. The Seven Years' War all over again!

§ Origin of Revolution

> *Every revolution was first a thought in one man's mind.*
> —Ralph Waldo Emerson[*]

No revolution was first thought alone. (Even if eventually it wound up that way.)

---

[*] Ralph Waldo Emerson, "History," in *Essays, First Series* (1841; New York: John B. Alden, 1890), 36.

⸹ Free Radicals

Radicals *uproot*; they know how deep the roots go. Often, caught in the act, they leave some roots behind.

The roots regroup. The weeds come back.

⸹ Nothing Doing

The history of the word *act* is Southern, Latin; that of *deed*, Northern, Germanic. "Acting" comes from "urging," "setting in motion," "stirring up"; "doing," from "placing," "unloading," "setting down."

Revolutions are made, never done. And to make them means to act in them.

§ Hope Salve

> *... to hope, till Hope creates*
> *From its own wreck the thing it contemplates*
> —Percy Bysshe Shelley[*]

The Hope Salve so popular nowadays is warm and feels good when applied, without burning through the thick layer of widespread political apathy and stimulating sustainable activism. Its effect, principally soothing, is too dispersed, reliant on nebulous ideas like the magic of contingency, resonance, event—that is, someone else, somewhere else, doing something "real" that greases and sets the wheels of revolution in motion. (As for us, we'll hop on hopeful only once momentum is gained.)

The real diehards of neoliberal "end-of-history" cant, whose numbers continue to dwindle and who have themselves no need of this mass "salvation," enjoy the "canopy view" and are justified in thinking Hope a scam, unsafe, a deal for addicts of greener pastures. While the former do not exactly throw money at the latter, watchdogs with no personal use for Hope cannot help benefiting in countless ways from Hope-fanatics' rising indignation and world-changing itch (which, again, they are not actually scratching). Are not doomsayers who see things spinning out of control already calling for a "War on Hope"? Is not this Hope already targeted with secret weapons?

Meanwhile, hope with a backbone, de facto and dangerous, is the concealed switchblade of hardened activists or edgy newbies. No diehards out there who haven't at least one dog in that fight of such long standing: the state vs. really-existing radicalism. Far from a drain on politics-as-usual, it calls for *mongrel means*.

---

[*] Percy Bysshe Shelley, *Prometheus Unbound* (1820; Charleston, SC: Nabu, 2010), Act 4, ll. 573–74.

⸙ Body Politics

The body, needy and desirous, is a Snow White radicals have kissed awake.

⸙ #OtherwiseOccupied

There is no room in well-organized camps for the "eroticism of crowds." Prurience is in the eyes of the beholders. Dwellers in glass houses, believing their privacy to be guaranteed by everyone else's lack of it, and modelling nothing (no better possible world) as a result — let *them* cast the first stones!

§ "I'm not crying,
I've just got some #CUPE3903 in my eye"[*]

> *The working classes... are the caring classes, and always have been. It is just the incessant demonisation directed at the poor by those who benefit from their caring labour... Most of us felt work was best avoided, that is, unless it benefited others. But of work that did, whether it meant building bridges or emptying bedpans, you could be rightly proud. And there was something else we were definitely proud of: that we were the kind of people who took care of each other. That's what set us apart from the rich who, as far as most of us could make out, could half the time barely bring themselves to care about their own children.... There is a reason why the ultimate bourgeois virtue is thrift, and the ultimate working-class virtue is solidarity. Yet this is precisely the rope from which that class is currently suspended.... As a result everything is thrown into reverse. Generations of political manipulation have finally turned that sense of solidarity into a scourge. Our caring has been weaponised against us. And so it is likely to remain until the left, which claims to speak for labourers, begins to think seriously and strategically about what most labour actually consists of, and what those who engage in it actually think is virtuous about it.*
>
> —David Graeber[†]

If Graeber is right, then all these beautiful feelings of solidarity and mutual aid are a product of oppression. As there is nothing to be done about the past, we accept it. But for that we embrace the beautiful feelings *no less*. If they are indeed the rope from which we are to be suspended, then let us hang onto it for dear life.

---

[*] Tina Boutis, tweet, Mar. 9, 2015, https://twitter.com/tboutis/status/575081213582557185. CUPE 3903 is a chapter of the Canadian Union of Public Employees.

[†] David Graeber, "Caring Too Much. That's the Curse of the Working Classes," *Guardian*, Mar. 26, 2014, http://www.theguardian.com/commentisfree/2014/mar/26/caring-curse-working-class-austerity-solidarity-scourge.

⸹ All Is Not Quiet

> *So long as men die, liberty will never perish.*
> —Charlie Chaplin's final, democratic speech
>   in *The Great Dictator**

Set aside the solidarity of slumber. Do not wait for death to make you equals. Think instead of the gains you could be making when an enemy is asleep or a tyrant breathes his last. When one side dies or dozes, the other must advance against it. In the absence of natality, fatality serves as a beginning. A modern front does not fall silent until the war is over.

---

* *The Great Dictator*, directed by Charlie Chaplin (1940; Burbank, CA: Warner Home Video, 2003), DVD.

⟨ Arms

> [S]ince the handling of arms is a beautiful spectacle, it is delightful to young men.
> —Niccolò Machiavelli, *The Art of War*[*]

The bullet-shooting weapon, heavy and shiny, in full working order, is associated with sexual organs in both sexes. The beauty of such objects derives from anticipated or real tactile pleasure, since handling them approximates pre-coital rituals meant to heighten eventual discharge. As long as there are shooting ranges, animals to poach, people to ravish, and no wars to fight in, the bearers of guns will find delight in handling arms unmarred by their chief purpose. By such primitive aesthetic pleasure murderousness is truncated, yet its roots continue to grow. The link to hunting and sharp-shooting nearly guarantees this. For the same reason, when the occasion arises for the weapon to be put to its proper use, with desire rerouted along its "natural" path of life-and-death power over other people, the pleasurable associations are slow to dissolve, and sometimes never do. The stamina of a senior serviceman taking aim both surprises and impresses. During peacetime, in turn, the experiential tie of weapons to murderousness affects sensual pleasure, as ejaculation and orgasm mimic the violent discharge of a gun, and the handling of arms by the veteran recalls to him the cold corpse of his comrade. The minds of those whom we task with murder on our behalf have swung from one to the other extreme of acceptable social behaviour—from mandated killing to sexual gratification. Charges of sadism in war and peacetime depend on a mechanistic notion of body and mind, as if our parts could be divvied up between tasks and memory neatly partitioned. In fact, the compartmentalization of sensory memories of physical violence and carnal pleasure expected of us is much too crude and limited to bear such charges out.

---

[*] Niccolò Machiavelli, *The Art of War*, ed. and trans. Christopher Lynch (Chicago: University of Chicago Press, 2003), 29.

⁋ Last Man Dying

> *Just why the effort to open a Taliban office has faltered is a matter of dispute. The Americans say the Taliban have simply decided to continue fighting, worried by pressure from their own hard-liners and concerned that entering peace talks would sap their will on the battlefield. "No one wants to be the last one to die before peace talks start," as one diplomat put it.*
> —Rod Nordland[*]

Those who die at the end of a long conflict are always the most pitied of casualties, and this not only because they were so close to seeing peace. Their death falls on the cusp of that long-awaited time when sacrifices finally bear fruit, but the turning point in the struggle is backdated. That is why they are said to have "died for nothing," unnecessarily. The urge to keep fighting must come not just from habit and mistrust of information, but from a fear of dying "needlessly."

⁋ Customary Hail of Arrows

If there is one pernicious stereotype that has clung to indigenous people, it is their blind hostility. This, in combination with their unfortunate naïvety about modern power and their tendency towards substance abuse, spells nothing as much as *oblivion*—indeed, a devotion to it. Ever since the white man arrived with no good intentions, encouraged by papal Discovery Bulls, royal warrants, or simply his own enterprising greed, his behaviour provoked what he wanted

---

[*] Rod Nordland, "Peace Envoys from Taliban at Loose Ends in Qatar," *New York Times*, Apr. 9, 2013, http://www.nytimes.com/2013/04/10/world/asia/taliban-peace-envoys-in-qatar-with-nothing-to-do.html.

confirmed, regardless of whether he met with native hospitality, suspicion, or indifference. Indigenous peoples were enslavable—though they did merit the status of opponent despite their ignorance of the European art of war—and the land on which they roamed but which was not theirs properly speaking was eventually wrested out from under them. Now that they are no longer subjugated and their possessions are being returned to them, the stereotype of native stupidity seems also to be on its way out. Primitive societies, on which modern European civilization has trained its self-concept, have largely been absorbed and elevated by their modern models—the (selective) return to traditional lifeways can be marshalled as proof.

Yet the stereotypical image lives on, fed by exceptions: the so-called uncontacted tribes that can be counted on the fingers of one hand. Progress in accepting otherness depends in the last analysis on the others' getting with our progressive program. The savages, objects of much sentimentality in the case of eighteenth-century philosophers and early anthropologists, show themselves (when caught on camera from ship or helicopter) as radically because *civilizationally* other. They speak not a word of modernity, never mind speaking it unevenly!

It is therefore a blessing that our thinking about wilderness began to shift towards conservation when it did. The last remaining savages' resemblance to the higher animals or earlier hominids places their interests under our concern for biodiversity. Reports of "Stone Age tribes" defending themselves with the "customary hail of arrows"[*] ought to be pitched not to anthropologists but to the same audience as wildlife videos of wildebeest stampedes—if it will keep the civilizing process at bay.

---

[*]   Peter Foster, "Stone Age Tribe Kills Fishermen Who Strayed onto Island," *Telegraph*, Feb. 8, 2006, http://www.telegraph.co.uk/news/worldnews/asia/india/1509987/Stone-Age-tribe-kills-fishermen-who-strayed-on-to-island.html.

§ "In search of weapons and allies"[*]

Kindliness towards the last remaining "uncontacted" tribes and civilizational remorse over the victims of modernity are one and the same. The fate of the former is a foregone conclusion when even kindness can prove lethal to them. But the conclusion is easier to accept when the fate of all of us is in jeopardy. In our tardy identification with them we are closing the circle of History. The last surviving aboriginals represent the last survivors, the blinking "last men" of the future.

The tortured sentiment of compassion does nothing, however, to counteract the naked economic interest of "human safaris." Since the first forbids contact with the object of its concern, it cannot warn or arm the natives against their raiders, nor catch these "tour guides" in the act of corruption.

But there is reason to hope for moral reform, helped, as usual, by policing. Not all tour operators are as heartless. "We do not offer any possibility to see [the Mashco-Piro tribe]," one of them maintains. "It is very dangerous to attempt any contact with them. A simple cold can kill them all. Any attempt to try to contact this people can put you in jail in Peru and Brazil,"[†] he adds matter-of-factly.

Every such operator must know that the thinning of the forests, and thus the exposure of those who live in them, is a curse in disguise. The fate of the "uncontacted" tribes and that of the tourism industry are obviously linked. As civilized barbarians in the shape of loggers and drug traffickers invade, the tribesmen will *make contact*. Not managing to arm or save themselves, they will either make enemies or drop like flies, reactivating in us that schizophrenic blend of compassion and exploitation otherwise known as modernity.

---

[*] "Isolated Indigenous Tribe Make Contact with Outside World in Brazil," *Telegraph*, July 31, 2014, http://www.telegraph.co.uk/news/worldnews/southamerica/brazil/11002162/Isolated-indigenous-tribe-make-contact-with-outside-world-in-Brazil.html.

[†] David Hill, "'Human Safaris' Pose Threat to Uncontacted Amazon Tribe," *Guardian*, Feb. 25, 2012, http://www.theguardian.com/world/2012/feb/26/human-safari-threat-amazon-tribe.

§ Armed to the Teeth

> *We will also not pay for dental work resulting from ... the hostile action of any armed forces, insurrection or participation in a riot or civil commotion.*
> —Sun Life Financial health insurance policy, extended plan exclusion

A This tells you which side the insurers are *not* on.

B Yes, in our society you've got to be armed to the teeth.

§ Made with Pride

B The self-made man is still "Made in America."

A Yes, America still makes those who make themselves.

§ Garden of Creativity

Expectations of creativity have never been so elevated and organized so many waking hours of our lives. Notice what has happened: *creativity* has replaced simple, vulgar *productivity*. Insofar as our labour does not consist of mindless, mechanical repetition, we are all creators now, that is to say *artists* of sorts. The ubiquity of competitive creativity under late capitalism is, we are told, liberally rewarded. More importantly, it is not the soul-destroying work of yesteryear, but the personally fulfilling, self-realizing activity that is well worth hacking your own life to get better at. It is not the victory of creativity that distinguishes our twenty-first century, but the victory of the creativity industry over creativity.

The downside is that everyone interpellated as a subject bears the double burden of competitive initiative and invention. Such doubly creative labour feels less and less like a matter of personal choice, even among the self-employed, the artists of old. It feels less and less like play, to which it is compared. The ludic spaces and sandboxes that pop up in creativity-worshipping workplaces are meant to get creative juices flowing and put the instrumentality of work out of mind. In them, the market becomes Demiurge and revenue, a totem pole, while workers magically transform into lesser deities crafting new forms for a tired universe. Driven to it, even on the universe's behalf, can we still see creativity (even its artistic variety) as a figure of autonomy and self-realization? A strange migration of normativity and constraint from traditional social codes to allegedly free-for-all creativity has damaged the latter's claim to spontaneity and freedom. Not that the correlative relaxation of norms and hierarchies isn't a welcome surprise for those sectors in which creativity was traditionally excluded from all but the very top ranks. With the top now relieved of much of the pressure to innovate, workers *new to the job* would be forgiven for thinking themselves collaborators freely contributing to the "creative commons"—and (gee-whizz) even getting paid! Until they realize that the fruits of their creative labour, which they can often afford, are appropriated and incorporated into designs and projects they can never hope to afford.

§ ♪ *Imagine there's...* ♪

Our time places extreme demands on the imagination. Without it we should think ourselves unfit to carry on. The *passe-partout* of salvation and survival, imagination is key to adapting to new rules in private and political life, the ever "new realities" foisted on us by the breathless motivation and breathtaking ingenuity of capital to create needs, goods, and musts, and ever more urgent futures to match them — rather than let us sleep, having us imagine uses for the still useless. Through our own mental effort are revised not just the rules but also the name of the game. The market appeals to us to *imagine x* (a better world, a better life, better relationships, more rewarding pastimes, alternative selves...) and — as drowsy or lazy as we are — most of the time we do. Every meaningful improvement seems to hang these days on the employment of our imagination as potential consumers of some yet unproduced product. Capital sees the power that slumbers in so many of us and harnesses it before waking it up with the lightest tickle.

And if we struggle a little pulling with us some invisible investor, we don't recognize it as exploitation and imposition. It is too natural to struggle, there is struggle even in play. Our imagination *self-serving*? We feel duty-bound to contribute *at least most of it* to the common good. We are doing our bit. We are merely giving a leg up to ideas hatching in the minds of visionaries, to creativity that, without our inspired assent, might never see the light of day. We are *research collaborators* who do not require credit, even if it's our effort to envision them as a part of our life that imagines them into being.

◊ Bromides

The rich and the poor are the most creative, the first because they have the luxury to, the second because they need to. The first need purpose and meaning, the second improvise to save their necks.

Bromides, bromides! Without the *middling* classes to take them to task, bring them to account, and draw out the best in them, they would give us, respectively, "art without ends" (the rich) and "art without means" (the poor).

◊ So-So

"A middle rank is much more favourable to talent, so we find all great artists and poets in the middle classes."* Though Goethe had in mind social rank, his remark can apply *mutatis mutandis* also to sales rank. Unfortunately the argument would be hard to make with the metrics in use today.

B Hold on, you mean our data analysis *fails* to bear out something so self-evident? The *middle rank* tries less to please and conform, suspicious and disdainful of others' ability to rise. Its outsized ambition, more acutely felt and self-sustaining the more it accepts its divergence from mass appeal, pushes it to try new things. To survive and live up to its own expectations, "mediocrity's" ambition reorients itself towards transcendent merit, the standard of transcendence towards some absolute pantheon or heaven, and, crucially, away from temporary "success." (This it has in common with the disposition that already canonized living writers have to their life's work, as they look back to measure themselves by nothing as petty as

---

* Goethe, *Conversations with Eckermann*, 89.

the judgment of their contemporaries.) Aren't that ambition, perseverance, aloofness from fashion, and indifference to the market, of which principally the mid-list or unpublished writer is still capable, precisely what gives us — and eventually counts as — "originality" and "authenticity"?

A I won't mock your hope, with which I sympathize without quite being able to identify. The mid-list is now synonymous with mediocrity (no scare quotes here) and greatness measured by popularity. It pains me to think that "originality," annexed by vapid "greatness," is also being indexed to sales figures. To turn the trend around, this way of thinking would have to change: there's a lot to be said for a work making up for its unimpressive sales with its origin, its coming from precisely where originality is *not* expected — if not the middling social stratum, then let it be the stratum of mediocre sales! But good luck trying to convince those who *want* to see greatness only where the money collects, and who would ride on greenback all the way to *real* mediocrity — their happy end.

ſ Night Watch

Sleeping one's fill, as physical regeneration and cognitive housekeeping, is a luxury that even the rich, let alone those following suit, cannot afford. Lack of sleep is one of the few things they have in common with the poor. When they do close their eyes, neither expect the law to watch over them, only some good angel to keep away illness and bad dreams, or some personal god of discipline to keep them from sleeping in.

Peace and quiet, indoor voices, "bedtime," and community watch are the middle-class answers to these to-be-avoided extremes. With children in the picture, the substance of household communication is reduced to the essential while its volume, continually adjusted lest it get out of hand. The product of multiple renunciations of immoderation and of bourgeois power, the middle class aspires to the calm atmosphere of the apothecary and the church, to their neighbourly whisper and the confessional undertone. The home office rivals the parlour in sleepiness, of which the cushioned bedroom is the epitome.

§ Nostalgia for the Middle Class

For some time now, *digging* has far exceeded building castles in the air. Dugouts, like catacombs, have a history of being popular and overcrowded; castles, more spacious, of being deserted. It might seem to a stranger that we have invented these extremes to make the *juste milieu* the clear favourite. Being desirable, however, it is no longer obtainable, at least for most; the queue is very long for something in so very short supply (soon nothing in America will be as out of stock as moderation). We are lining up for the sweet spot where felt lack becomes creative again. We are doing so from both sides — both extremes — but it is in the middle, like the noses of the Lady and the Tramp, that our interests meet.

§ If the Shoes Fits

Photographs are for the poor what paintings were for the rich: proofs of their existence.

§ Mutual Parodies

If it is as Dada thought, that the history of art is a parody of the history of politics, surely the history of politics is also a parody of the history of art — particularly literature, as others have astutely observed. As long as this mutually parodic relation is dominant, both art and politics are safe from barbarism. But just as barbaric art has a place in museums, so barbaric politics has a place in history.

⸹ The Gulf of Inattention

> *In the bourgeois age, an independent merchant would show some generosity to every beggar who crossed his path—but in these busy, tangled times good men have become just as unimaginable as truly evil ones.*
> —Adorno*

It is a comforting thought that the extremes of good and evil as we knew them are a thing of the past, that in our attention-deficit economy good and evil are losing their edge, growing closer together. But this thought is revealed as wishful once we see that the extremes of wealth and poverty, which stand in for them, are moving ever farther apart.

No one takes pride in being a no-goodnik, only in the attendant indignation and rage. These days, pride comes also from demanding generosity of the affluent—rather than, as mere decades ago, as something taken in one's work, or in holding out for the modest pickings of power and access to resources. We do not count on the goodness of those who can help us; we just demand that they hand over their goods. Our claims have intensified to exert pressure on those who might otherwise evade discharging their duty to society at a time when *noblesse* no longer obliges. The atmosphere has changed so much that greed is now subject to journalistic shaming, publically pilloried as a social sin, whose punishment will come from the righteous future, where our *revendications* will be vindicated. No mobbing, no meek praying for a good turn; just straight-up political theology.

---

* Theodor W. Adorno, *History and Freedom: Lectures 1964–1965*, ed. Rolf Tiedemann, trans. Rodney Livingstone (Cambridge, UK: Polity, 2006), 206.

∫ Clay Pigeon

Why have we been duped into thinking the bourgeois individual subject a mere *narrative effect*, with the narrative taken at face value? Because on the level of interpersonal experience, that's all we have to go on. The grand narratives told by that narrative are a different story. Those we can pick apart and inspect, as though they came from an individual.

∫ Lying in State

It is alright to lie in public. Those who are genuinely interested can easily find out our truth from states, the truth of *who we really are*. Why should it matter that it comes not from the horse's mouth?

And since we are *not* taken at face value anyway (assuming we show a face and it has value), why deny ourselves the fun of *open dissimulation* only to end up misunderstood? As long as there is this general understanding, and no one gets held to account for what is on record without being "looked into" first, showing our true face will only add to the general confusion.

§ Up the Ladder to the Roof

For those fed up with the stuffed confines and stuffy routines of flats, the rooftop — stomping ground of thieves and feral cats — will always hold the promise of adventure. They are the souls who will not be kept down, who could have flown balloons, braved alpine peaks, joined the circus, or run away from home. A roof over their head is only ever as desirable as the view from it. And so they endeavour to climb alone to *the very top* — perhaps only socially, but still — until they have broken through the seal securing the exit hatch against those who have no business there. We who assist them in this transgression can only look up in amazement as we give them a leg up. And though one rarely notices them from the street below, they themselves seem the most amazed of all — not so much at the quality of air or the clouds now less out of reach, but at their own persistence, their ability to stand up to their full height, quite right to feel as though they owned the place.

ᔕ Holes in a Wall

The Casbah to be saved, as is the mandate of the association "Sauvons la Casbah," is still the one in Pontecorvo's 1965 *Battle of Algiers*. The decay of ruins proved slow here, so that the historical setting can be entered like a stage-set to this day. The original actors are nowhere to be seen, but their descendants cannot be far away; that the eyes that follow one around have since multiplied does not alter the palpable, heavy-lidded wariness at the sight of Western interlopers (for the *tourist* has no place here as a category of visitor). Those who prop the walls, backs bent like of the Casbah's distinctive timber buttresses, know their distant cousins in the clusters of disaffected Arab youths, almost to a man able-bodied, on the street corners of other port cities like Marseille. The living quarters, when not shot through by light by design, caved-in roofs or other dereliction, are dim and cavernous, the humble lives inside them announced only by the cries of children, animals, and the sound of a smith's hammer, which fills the air with something like music.

ᔕ Humility Itself

"the parenthesis that is my life"

§ Excellence Clusters

Germany's atoning for its genocidal history follows the very Enlightenment principles that, as its sons once argued with great conviction, led by convolute logics and moral meandering to the genocide in the first place. The way to atonement is through the institution of order and merit in the academy. This effort, which other countries have rushed to imitate, begat a formidable new research entity known as the "excellence cluster."

The model of elite theme-focused research groups or "clusters" housed at different universities shows the German state to be firmly committed to international leadership in the production of knowledge. But as the visiting Indian scholar who would not leave Germany without seeing a *KZ* (short and informal for "concentration camp") might have remarked: "You have got to hand it to the Germans: They have these things down to a science. First they 'cluster' you. Then they 'excellence' you!"

§ Mottos for Morale

The Latin university motto, that lofty college ideal, betrays the anachronism of its institution and should everywhere be changed to "The future ended here." The line is an inferior if less equivocal riff on La Sapienza's "*Il futuro è passato qui*," "The future passed here," "The future passed by here," "The future here is past." Will the debt-saddled graduate of Johns Hopkins really be "set free" by truth, as affirmed by the school's present maxim, "*Veritas Vos Liberabit*"? Has the University of Missouri fulfilled its mission of "*Salus Populi*," making popular welfare the law, at least for its students? Did the graduates of Lesley University, "*Perissem Ni Perstitissem*," not let down its alma mater by perishing despite all their persistence? Have the female bachelors of the University of Maryland seen the light of "*Fatti Maschii, Parole Femine*,"* which attributes deeds to men, and to women, mere words?

§ Feminist Taunt

Wenny, weedy, weeky — I insist!

---

* The university has dissociated itself from the motto, which remains that of the State of Maryland, albeit in a gentler translation, "Strong deeds, gentle words."

§ Let Me See Your Report Card

The dilemma is false: either you stay the course of school and hope for the best, or you drop out and, having briefly landed in the social safety net (the support and dismay of councilors, family and friends), you pass through it, sinking right down to the scummed and stigmatized bottom. The choice between the latter path's sure nothing and the former's possible everything is such a no-brainer that it leaves those who make it no illusion of existential freedom. Embarking freely on the path of "illiteracy" is not choosing at all, merely succumbing to wayward environmental pressures. It is not clear how much cultural capital really accrues to those who put themselves through school, but it is obvious that none can come from saying no to it. The very act of opting out nullifies any claim to cultural literacy; with some notable exceptions, it is proof of fundamental, irredeemable foolishness. Neither is *homeschooling* the Rousseauian or hippie-communist refuge it used to be; the word is code for online learning and long-distance education, when not downright survivalism or fanaticism. So that the choice between two viable alternatives, the formal and the unstructured, is never really permitted, and cannot ultimately be made.

∫ Cliché Alert

> cliché: *1825*, "electrotype, stereotype," technical word in printer's jargon for "stereotype block," supposedly echoing of the sound of a mold striking molten metal. Figurative extension to "trite phrase, worn-out expression" is first attested in *1888*, following the course of stereotype (OED)

The novelist Teju Cole, in a republished series of "letters to a young writer" from his Nigerian days, advises the fledgling: "remove all clichés from your writing. Spare not a single one. The cliché is an element of herd thinking, and writers should be solitary animals" (but writing can also be "lonely," he later notes, and proposes blogging to alleviate this solitude).*
The cliché, in any shape or form, is apparently beneath any self-respecting writer.

Rather than point out clichés in the work of those who rail against them, let's present a counterargument, making better use of the above-quoted lines, which benefit from the doubt we are happy to give to Mr. Cole. Doesn't his thought encapsulate the writer's thought-clichés of a solitary craft and Nietzschean *Weltanschauung*? Assuming these were deliberately planted, they are in Cole's eyes (and not just his!) a creative foundation, formative in the quest for literary greatness. Of course, "what we call originality is little more than the fine blending of influences" (24). (We permit ourselves to notice that "little more" is nonetheless *more*.) Is not the subtle message, the deeper lesson here: the road to originality leads through the hackneyed? To leave off clichés you must be able to recognize them — and be on the alert, *for they hide in plain sight*! Well, it seems we would have passed the test, but as for getting the message...To *this* we take exception, if real writers are indeed such sworn enemies of clichés (marking their slalom up Mount Originality by being

---

* Teju Cole, "Eight Letters to a Young Writer," *Words Follow Me* (blog), Oct. 27, 2010, 6, http://wordsfollowme.files.wordpress.com/2010/10/teju-cole-eight-letters-to-a-young-writer2.pdf. First published 2008–2009 in weekly installments in the Nigerian newspaper *NEXT*.

skillfully avoided) as Cole makes them out to be, or if the good writer not into racing herds clichés together and puts them out to pasture.

Our view is, first of all, not so absolute. They may be tired from overwork, the job of communication and simplification, but clichés interest us a great deal. Rather than dumped, they can be (productively) dismantled, dissected, even "deconstructed." They can keep us busy, serve as themes for literary creation. As foot-soldiers of rhetoric strategically deployed, they are indispensable. While they can replace the effort of original thought, they are hardly the seal of one-dimensionality. Often, they are the mind's way of handling material too large or difficult for it. They pack chaotic thoughts into familiar, uncontroversial "notions" and set phrases for use in social situations that call for decorum and assent, or where "having opinions" is *de rigueur*. As such, they reveal their origins in the nineteenth-century bourgeois response to the greater pace, diversity and complexity of experience in much the way wit, a proof of brains and subtlety, was the nobility's reaction to the absolutism of the old regime, and proverbs, to the pious tedium of peasant life.

Personally, we don't deconstruct clichés. That requires a higher level of competence, just as castigating them calls for a touch of malice. But might Flaubert's satirical "dictionary of received ideas" (spoofs, lampoons, commonplaces, bromides, platitudes—"all this so phrased that the reader would not know whether or not his leg was being pulled"[*]) not give rise to a sympathetic, at once joyous and sobering work, one that exposes the psycho-logical mechanism of cliché, the tension latent within it, and reads and writes (re-writes) cliché against itself, undoing its power over us while leaving us its usefulness? Wait, hasn't such a book already been written? Isn't it Flaubert's very own *Bouvard and Pécuchet*, the final monsterpiece to which his *dictionnaire* is customarily

---

[*] Jacques Barzun, introduction to *Dictionary of Accepted Ideas* by Gustave Flaubert, trans. J. Barzun (New York: New Directions, 1968), 3.

appended? And it has, perversely, led some to fall in love with cliché.

The view endorsed by Cole that clichés are evidence of a herd mentality is difficult to sustain even at the loftiest heights with the thinnest air, where none but mountain goats can survive. We suspect greater profit to writers comes from urbane curiosity than from condescension, contempt, or derision. While we *personally* do not subvert or even interrogate clichés, we do like *playing* with them. Particularly with those cherished by the cultural elite: self-deprecation, false modesty, and yes, hatred of cliché — just a few of the many affectations adopted out of a mediocrity-complex in democracies of talent preserving inequality in the worship of elite genius (a hierarchy so entrenched it even enters Trotsky's futuristic vision: "The average human type will rise to the heights of an Aristotle, a Goethe, or a Marx. And above this ridge new peaks will rise"*). We won't "go there" as far as we perhaps could. And we *could* point out that the mature writer's lesson to a young one turns paradoxically on just this highbrow cliché of genius, even if, we surmised, it does so self-ironically. Belief in one's genius is perhaps a necessary self-deception to produce above-average work. Why, then, should verbal clichés be livestock slated for slaughter? It is enough to be butted by the smallest one, it seems, to suffer from fatuous and unreflected thinking — which is to say *to bleat*. Writing against cliché and common sense, Thoreau asked: "Why level downward to our dullest perception always, and praise that as common sense? The commonest sense is the sense of men asleep, which they express by snoring."†

Another pet cliché is the Modernist emphasis on failure as artistically noble, as the badge of latter-day genius, poor in the eyes of the world and therefore, in his own mind, swimming in untold riches, spawning only originality

---

* Leon Trotsky, *Literature and Revolution*, ed. William Keach (Chicago: Haymarket, 2005), 207.

† Henry David Thoreau, *Walden: A Fully Annotated Edition*, ed. Jeffrey S. Cramer (New Haven, CT: Yale University Press, 2004), 316.

(worthy compensation, if you ask us). The world could care less *now*, but it *will* care more (just watch), and maybe overmuch. Taking just literary creation, the summa of clichéd greatness — the writer as melancholic, as modern prophet, as sage, the book as labyrinth, as masterpiece, as birth, as gift — crowd around the end of its history as the old bond between language and art, which we call *literature*, dissolves and its once-wide bandwidth on the spectrum of writing shrinks and turns invisible.

Clichés put down roots deep in our reality, and doing away with them needs must be done root-and-branch radically. A literary work comes along, tugs at them, or hacks away the branches, bent on eradicating the grand cliché of genius, and all it does is strengthen its updated clichéd definition (for which we thank the likes of Malcolm Gladwell):

GENIUS: rare and kicks in at the ten-thousandth hour

If some wind from the future blows hard enough to uproot genius, that great organizing idea on which we continue to elaborate, we will part with a lot more than just it.

A   Are clichés and mystifications really all you've got to defend clichés with?

B   Fool, you wouldn't get it any other way. Try getting by without them!

§ Touché

"The terrible, like the painful, accommodates only the cliché."[*] As does the wonderful and the pleasurable — the clichés "Wow!" "Ah!" "OMG!"

§ Lose No Touch

Universal connectivity brings with it an obligation to keep tabs on the world. The meaning of "being in touch with reality" is migrating, along with reality, to another domain. The reality (in name only) with which we should remain in touch is thoroughly *mediatized*. "Being in touch" no longer denotes a realistic outlook and certified sanity, but knowing how to navigate and stay topical in the digital universe. If in the old sense it was imperative to tell *fact* from *fiction*, with the rest as trivial pursuit, it now does better to know what's what, without regard to that trivial distinction.

---

[*] Cioran, *Trouble with Being Born*, 53.

⸹ Fetch! Now Roll Over!

One of the jobs of Luciano Floridi as chair of the European Commission's Committee on Concepts Engineering is to advise on "the impact of information and communications technologies on the digital transformations occurring in the European Society."* Let's not mistake the circularity of such a task for its level of difficulty. Its point might not be apparent to those only tuned in to pointlessness. The reciprocal impact of two aspects that appear to be sides of one coin—"information and communications technologies" and "digital transformations"—cannot, in truth, be overstated. The impact of dogs on canine behaviour, for instance!

---

*   "University of Hertfordshire Professor Appointed as Chairman of Expert Group," University of Hertfordshire, accessed Mar. 11, 2015, http://www.herts.ac.uk/research/news-and-events/professor-luciano-floridi-appointed-chairman-of-european-commission.

§ Distimacies

Looking at the current affect-technology nexus, one question to ask is: how far does the supposed intimacy-by-gadgets reach, and should its deliberate "distribution" aim for wider but thinner coverage, or instead for greater focus and penetration? The first carries, despite the best intentions, the risk of eroding intimacy through cultivating facile, superficial ties with people who are likely (in effect or anyway) to remain at a distance. The assumption behind the idea of connecting speedily with something *inmost* in as many, or as often, as possible in these punctuated, mediated, not always controlled ways, is that we are all *alike*. As such, it encourages the misprision of others as mirrors of ourselves. On the other hand, or the second of the above options, thinking it better to concentrate intimacy-distribution, we risk reifying intimacy. We reify it when we insist on the mystery of the other and treat our connection with them as something to be gained over time, by wearing down the barriers of controlled, mediated access to them. We reify intimacy when it ceases to be simply a function of overcoming distance and communicating less and less formally with one another. Focused, probing intimacy may be too precious to support large-scale community-building, it is true. While it is probably fair to say that other people's secrets are now largely given away, floating unbeknownst even to them in cyberspace, the celebration of collective intimacy would benefit from cynicism about the knowledge that private information reveals, and to whom. As our horses continue to trickle out of the barn, we might wonder whether those who venture too far in sharing themselves in the spirit of open access might eventually feel like they have been taken for a ride.

§ The End of Sharing?

Publicity, or the voluntary surrender, of personal experience makes such experience no less private, and possibly *more*. It puts it up for propertification just as the publication of ideas or sequences of words no one else has thought to publish bestows ownership on their source. The responsibility we bear today is considerable. We must be careful not to nonchalantly squander our precious experience, parting with it, letting it go unrecorded and thereby losing out on occasions for enrichment. The fans of Instagram and other media already sense what's in the air: as consumers amuse themselves with new technology, share their work for free, and lose interest in conventional forms of entertainment, companies will redesign their offerings around customer preference, and will pay us for providing content in which acting or performance is absent or secondary to just "having experiences" and leading interesting lives. In the span of a few years, and as a direct result of this, the content of personal experience, the innermost private stuff, will be refashioned into so many ephemeral commodities. Then we will see if we are all better off as extroverts.

§ Mice

Much as secret messages and tools can be smuggled and escapes plotted even in the most secure prison, all kinds of forbidden material finds a way to circulate and miscreants slip through in even the most policed of modern societies. For in society individuals are like mice in a prison not built to hold them.

§ Damned to Fame

Most of us want fame and can't get it. One would think that the "Becketts" of the world would frustrate us, incurring our resentment. But the opposite is true: they fascinate us, winning our love and still greater fame. The "Beckettian" predicament is attractive because it involves fame *not* despite one's lack of talent, making the fame unmerited, but despite trying to avoid fame, and only late in life. The "Beckett" scenario soothes our resentment by playing right into it and into the fantasy of the only adequate compensation: getting more than we expected (note: not *deserved*). We turned our back on fame for making us wait—convinced that we are worthy of it, we rejected it when it was not forthcoming—but in the end fate tries to woo us back and more than makes it up to us—a fantasy not merely of delayed renown, but of delayed renown beyond our earlier, frustrated expectations. That the reward might be well worth the wait is all we need to reconcile ourselves to having to wait for it. Fantasies like "Beckett" keep alive the hope for this pleasant surprise.

¶ Escaping Criticism

As much (as) *it has cost you, that is what they will pay.*
—Wittgenstein*

Many an author must have paused before Pere Borrell del Caso's wittily titled *Escaping Criticism* (*Escapando de la critica*, 1874). The subject, painted against a solid black background, is a barefoot boy who, stepping on the bottom of the *trompe-l'œil* frame, hands braced against its sides, seems about to jump out onto the gallery floor. Literary characters, first fleshed out on the page, have often taken on a life of their own in other media. They too have leapt through the frames of their stories, sometimes indeed to elude criticism. In this they were fulfilling the dream of the artist, to whom the autonomy of his work, its taking charge of its own fate, is proof of its greatness — which may have escaped even him.

When, however, we take Borrell del Caso's boy to be the artist himself, his alter ego, fleeing his critics even before the picture is completed, we have trouble thinking of a similarly artfully artless getaway for the author of a book. One could of course leave the final pages blank, as some have. Yet this act of defiance would nowadays come across as a cheap and lazy trick. For while the painter painted throughout and to the very end, the author would have taken a break from writing or else wrapped up his work long before then. And for that the critics would never forgive him. He would lose them only after losing all his readers.

---

* Wittgenstein, *Culture and Value*, 15.

⸹ Remember Me!

The old technology with which writers practiced their profession has left a permanent memento on the bodies of those middle-aged or older. As they type away, from the keyboard the deformed joint of the middle finger makes its silent reproach. To which the

WRITER.
   The basic means of production with which I started out are history, but you can't tell me I'm not a writer!

To which the

PROFESSIONAL DEFORMITY.
   But you are a very different writer from the one that made me.

⟨ Writing-Ball

> *Schreibkugel ist ein Ding gleich mir: von Eisen*
> *Und doch leicht zu verdrehn zumal auf Reisen.*
> *Geduld und Takt muss reichlich man besitzen*
> *Und feine Fingerchen, uns zu benuetzen.*
>
> (The Writing Ball is a thing just like me: of iron
> And yet easy to twist, especially on journeys.
> Patience and tact one must richly possess
> And fine little fingers to use us.)
>   —Nietzsche on his spherical writing instrument*

The Mailing-Hansen writing-ball was no crystal ball, and both have gone the way of most material objects. Once among the most praised, the most prized, the most sought-after possessions, source of uncountable revenues, they have been crushed and obliterated, on view since only in museums, where even the best-preserved specimens resemble embalmed carcasses.

Despite his less-than-productive relationship with his writing-ball — a portable brass proto-typewriter — Nietzsche's eulogy attests to his high hopes and a tenderness that anyone so dependent on an instrument ought to find within themselves. A moment's selflessness will show us the thing in its true light — as a slave — as Helvétius showed Europe's sugar-eaters their cubes were soaked in blood, pointing to a debt to the tropics. We owe an object the same credit, care, and respect we have begun to show other humans, but also animals and the natural environment. Man-made things are merely a still more transformed or mutilated nature. Their preservation has long been justified on the grounds that they serve as our historical markers, but as the rate of change increased, objects once accumulating without reflection

---

* Friedrich Wilhelm Nietzsche, *Fragmente*, vol. 3, *1880–1882* (Projekt Gutenberg-DE/tredition, 2012), p. 565, Feb.–Mar. 1882, Dokument: Mappe mit losen Blättern: "500 *Aufschriften* auf Tisch und Wand für Narrn von *Narrenhand*" ("Writings on Wall and Table for Fools by Fool's Hand"), sec. 18[2].

became subject (like people, and often with the same technologies) to progressively rational classification, periodization, and archivization. Our anxiety about history is turning the world into a vast museum, compartmentalizing space into the modern and the historical, with nature parks in the latter category. Product care, life extension, and d.i.y. are only the first, baby-steps to be taken *against* this relentless musealization, and towards the recognition of objects as bearers of rights akin to ours. Consumer resistance must build to end self-obsolescing design in hardware and programming. Beyond it lie meaningful relationships with things and a new appreciation of imperfection, for which we have lost all tolerance, but which art (like Nietzsche's verses) — entrusted with the "routine invitation to break out of reality" so it is "not entirely lost with us"[*] — has kept alive.

---

[*] Theodor W. Adorno and Max Horkheimer, *Dialectic of Enlightenment: Philosophical Fragments*, ed. Gunzelin Schmid Noerr, trans. Edmund Jephcott (Stanford, CA: Stanford University Press, 2002), 213 ("Propaganda").

§ Talking Pencil

> *None of the Robespierres of the world knew how to make a pencil, yet they wanted to remake entire societies.*
> —Lawrence W. Read,
>   introduction to "I, Pencil" (1958)[*]

In a seminal pamphlet of American neoliberalism, the invisible hand of the market speaks through a pencil, underlining the complexity of its creation. The metonymic chain (market to hand to pencil) is warranted by the hand's and the tool's long history as a versatile creative extension of man. In at least one children's story, a simple pencil makes dreams come true. Are not the pencil's wish-fulfilling powers only amplified under capitalism, where "back to the drawing board" captures the spirit of unremitting innovation?

---

[*] Lawrence E. Read, introduction to *I, Pencil* by Leonard E. Read (New York: Foundation for Economic Education, 2008), 2.

⸹ Doggedly Smart

> *The best art is the most expensive because the market is so smart.*
> —Tobias Meyer, former Sotheby's auctioneer[*]

Price following quality in art is the market's brilliance at work. Before the market can prove itself so smart, however, quality art must be discovered. Markets have never discovered anything; they have followed, doggedly and expansively, the scent of discovery. *Discovery*—now that takes real brainpower, next to which the market looks rather stupid, with its long face and beagle eyes. Markets never pass up an opportunity to make themselves look smarter than they are. This might shed light on the Victorian fondness for portraits of (especially hunting) dogs looking very smart. Upstaged by a party of bulldogs, spaniels and terriers, the well-bred, prosperous men in top hats assembled in *An Early Canine Meeting* (1855) look none too clever as it emerges whose is in fact the *master's voice*.

---

[*] Quoted in James Panero, "The Art Market Explained," *New Criterion*, Dec. 2009, http://www.newcriterion.com/articles.cfm/The-art-market-explained-4337.

∫ The Story of Your Life

Take risks, manage them, capitalize on your experience, and live off the accumulated surplus into rotten old age.

∫ Poor in Spirit, Rich in Irony

A As a wise man of small means once said: you cease being poor when you have nothing left.

B You keep talking about poverty as if you knew it. I think you romanticize it!

A Don't you mean "ironize"? The poor have a greater sense of irony, and irony is the key to survival.

B The lower their expectations, the less likely for fate to take them by surprise...

A ...and take away the wages of irony!

∫ Desk Jobs

The lives of paper-pushers are wearing paper-thin.

And those of keyboard-tappers?

Barely a-flicker.

§ No Go Stop

For many a working stiff, a living wage will come too late, if it comes at all.

§ Subtle Reversal

Automate living and *work* for thinking.

§ Pretty Penny; or, Get Rich at All Cost

A penny for my thoughts?

How much?! You should know better, young lady, than to prostitute your mind in this way!

I just want to be successful, like you men.

Then there's no price you'll soon not be ready to pay, and be poorly repaid for.

§ Fruit of Capital

Contrary to what people say, money does grow on trees. It is called interest: the formerly forbidden fruit that gives no flesh, only seeds.

§ Name Your Price

Everything material and immaterial has its market price. In everyday parlance, *priceless* still means having a value beyond all price, being of inestimable worth, usually because of being recognized as one of a kind, irreproducible, "not for sale." Less commonly (if more prosaically), the word can designate something that is either *substantially* "worthless" — its lack of (even an implicit) price tag suggesting it might not be worth having — or *nominally* so, in the sense that it has not been priced yet (ever, or anew). (This is the land of free enterprise, but also, with the depletion of the pool of commodifiable things, of declining rates of return.)

All of these senses of "pricelessness" came into play recently in regards to Spitsbergen, the Arctic island coveted by a Chinese investor: its value declared by the sale's opponents as incalculable not only on account of its "uniqueness," but also because its economic as well as strategic importance, currently *minimal*, may well exceed the wildest estimates, and can therefore only be assessed in the future — mustn't, that is, yet be determined.

The more life becomes commodified, the more the definition of *pricelessness* is harnessed to the subjective devalorization of things before they hit the market. Pricelessness, a concept of value touched by the money form but not absorbed by it, is thus continually assailed and offers less and less — not more — resistance. Put in other words, the truly *priceless* object is becoming *structurally* worthless — "free" to be given away. If it *still* (or *already*) costs nothing, it must be without value, and thus counts for little, if anything. So when a price is finally named, it's what we'd call *a steal*.

⸹ Make Me an Offer

Haggling, encouraged by the impersonal character of online retail, breaks the tyranny of the fixed price on the white market.

⸹ Price of Life

You *give* your life or *pay with* your life for something (a fatherland, a mistake). You *give* a price in one sense, as a vendor, and *pay* it in another, as a customer. Which is better: naming the price of your own life, or paying a price with it? Is the vendor really more in control?

⸹ Piss-Poor

If "excess is excrement,"[*] then lack is piss.

---

[*] Ursula Le Guin, *The Dispossessed: An Ambiguous Utopia* (New York: HarperCollins, 1994), 127–28.

§ American Poverty

Why are Americans not dealing with poverty at home? Perhaps because poverty elsewhere seems easier to alleviate.

§ Captives

"It is unfortunate for men," wrote Chamfort, but "fortunate perhaps for tyrants, that the poor and unhappy have not the instinct or pride of the elephant which does not reproduce itself in servitude."* As far as why this is, we must again blame reason, survival, and hope. For those in servitude (which is more diffuse and abstract, particularly if it includes slavery to an idea or system, the more socially total it is), those held in bondage by men or something men have contrived reason that their masters, their slavers, are rational, and if that alone does not help, they are also mortal. The reproduction of a system of enslavement depends equally on the continual delivery of able bodies and on the methodical application of rationality to human affairs. Exploitation, without which oppression would lose its sinister tone (mutating into mere suppression or depression), demands it absolutely. Once we grant *mirror reason*—mirroring that of their captors—to those whom we regard with compassion as dehumanized, as incompletely dead, as the zombies of capital, their continued, even viral reproduction makes perfect sense. Elephants, however intelligent we are discovering them to be, still reason imperfectly, at least in captivity.

---

* Nicolas de Chamfort, *The Cynic's Breviary: The Maxims and Anecdotes from Nicholas de Chamfort*, trans. William G. Hutchison (1902; n.p.: Bartleby.com, 2011), l. 109.

§ Against the Grain

If oppression ever got labelled "environmentally unsustainable," it would be sustained.

§ Breaking Even

We could say along with Graeber that "Freedom has become the right to share in the proceeds of one's own permanent enslavement,"[*] or we could admit that the language of paradox is of no use to us as long as the opposites remain cardboard extremes. We do not think that way, and the starkly ironic contrast appeals more to our love of rhetoric than to our sense of justice, which for the modern economic mentality has again become synonymous with breaking even.

---

[*] David Graeber, "Hope in Common," in *Revolutions in Reverse: Essays on Politics, Violence, Art, and Imagination* (London: Minor Compositions, 2011), 33.

§ Loose Change

Should one give credence to the Marxian happy "end" featuring the working class "expropriating the expropriators"? Some have said that in the process the expropriating workers will become a new breed of appropriators. That the only difference between them and their former expropriators will be their moral complacency that they have done right by themselves when they were still being exploited. History has borne out this prediction. And when has *wrested* ownership ever entailed care for what is owned? Expropriation from below that does not tip over into appropriation is doomed by its ironic mimicry of dispossession — by a wrangle that leaves the bones of contention themselves in the dust. And who will take care of the ex-property once the dust settles? Should one not hope, rather, that *possession* will soon be seen as too great a burden, a limit on remaining freedom (redefined), and that the disposal of property becomes a voluntary act?

§ Poison Ivy

The ivy law of minimum wage is that it creeps up while covering an ever larger surface.

§ *Ad coelum et ad nihilum*

In medieval property law which survives in weakened form in some countries, like the United Kingdom, the owner of a plot of land owns it vertically: from the empty skies above it all the way to the centre of the Earth below. At this deepest point underground, however, its area necessarily amounts to zero. Following the same principle, on a downward survey of his possession, the owner of even the entirety of the globe's surface, terrestrial and marine, would, at its lowest limit, see it diminish to nothing.

As long as no one possesses the centre of the Earth, absurdity shadows all landlords everywhere. He who would own everything above, down below would have no ground to stand on, let alone to plant his flag.

§ Nail Soup

In a memorable poem on the cunning of the gypsy man and the stupidity of the *baba*, the miserly peasant woman, we find the secret to good class (or are they now *percentile*?) relations. The impatience of the woman, curious to witness the miracle of "nail soup," leads her to unthinkingly comply with the gypsy's requests for incidentals. Pot, water, fire, butter, grain—all are provided—until finally a nail is produced that apparently gives the broth its distinctive flavour…

Does this not confirm that the poor can do just fine by themselves? They need only secure incredulous yet open-handed admiration from those who will continue to eat their fill, realizing (perhaps not for the first time) that they, too, owe their provisions to a scam, just several orders of magnitude greater.

◊ Of Wolves and Gatsbies

The difference between luxury and decadence is essentially this: the former spends money unimaginatively, the latter, creatively. If the first orders golden faucets, the second commissions sinks made from turtle shells. If the first imagines only what others want and wants that, the second prizes originality and invention. Fortunes spent on luxury degrade taste, those paid to decadence only refine it. Either way, the show of wealth carries great implications for judgments of taste, since good taste can now be *afforded*.

◊ Piggy Bank

A pig for good luck? The association of pigs with good fortune in the *Glücksschwein*, or lucky pig, no less than that of good fortune with wealth, has to answer for the symbol of prosperity in Old-World lore and the worldwide popularity of the piggy bank. When we tell our children that having money is in some magical sense about good luck, we prime them for seeing reason in trading or gambling away their meagre savings. Why not rather tell them "Money turns people into swine," and prove it by breaking the pig-bank, then pocketing its contents?

ℐ Worker Bee

It is difficult to rejoice for the bee preserved in amber — a substance so much in colour like her own nectar as to seem a rewarding tomb. It is not hard, by contrast, to see the irony of being buried in one's work. When the honey of our labour is judged only as a means to an end (mind you, not *that* kind of end!), our sense of purpose squirms in misdirected empathy.

ℐ Tan Lines

On the outstretched arms of white beggars the sun marks the global colour line.

§ The Eyes of the Poor

The poor are closer to a better because more morally defensible world, even when they have been reduced to crime, not merely by imagining that world, but by thinking it universally desirable and possible. The question "how much better is *significantly* better?" and thus worth fighting for is moot as long as the needy abstain from political action.

And *if* they do *not* imagine this world, it is not from a failure of imagination, but from imagination's devastation. And *if* they do *not* desire it, it is not from a failure of desire, but from desire's distracted aggravation by a world in which they nonetheless live. And *if* they do *not* think it possible, it is not by dint of having been deprived of hope, but of hope's superabundance. Then, however rich in hope, they are poor twice over — not just from failing to enrich themselves, but from seeing only riches in riches, and nothing save poverty in poverty. The naïve and arrogant view of the poor is that they are naïve and humble; they believe happiness lies in wealth (if they only knew the truth!). But why would they mistake happiness for material comfort who must have known happiness without it? Step forward, you who see an end to misery in the end to destitution. The miserable, the poor in spirit, are much harder to get rid of than the materially poor. Some of these latter, indeed, console themselves that "actual possession of the happiness of this life, without the hope of what is beyond, is but a false happiness and profound misery."*
Where such hope runs — though imagination, worldly desire, and a sense of possibility be absent — the happiness derived from a meagre life is fortified with an otherworldly spirit.

A   Ah, but the poor, on the whole, have better eyes!

---

*   Augustine, *The City of God*, vol. 2, trans. Marcus Dodds (Edinburgh: T. & T. Clark, 1871), 330.

B   Because they see farther than the rest of us? It's true. But they are worse on what's up close—a necessary optical tradeoff.

    Nothing evokes abject poverty more than hunger that has begun to consume the flesh. Some lessons can only be learned bodily. The sunken eyes of the poor, who have learned their lessons well, can they teach *us* anything? That hunger is all-unmanning, all-consuming and unequivocal, Dickensian and tone-deaf. That where hunger reigns, life is beastly at best. The beasts of hunger are not wild at heart; they are driven wild by it.

A   The appetite of the poor is larger than their belly.

B   When they only eat with their eyes, how can they be sated?

    No, there is more to hunger than meets the eye, and the eyes do not always give it away. As long as poverty and hunger are around, there will be important lessons for which no other teachers but hunger and poverty will do. Without a general "vow of poverty" to edify us, poverty as such will not be eradicated.

    Until then, and as a matter of precaution, make sure to wear your distance glasses from time to time. So that the future isn't a complete surprise.

§ Engels and Marx at Chetham's Library

A windowed alcove at England's first public library overlooked one of Manchester's rookeries, or slums, near Victoria Station. Sitting there as they often did, they could see while reading the *State of the Poor* (the work of Eden, after the Revolution). And when they put their heads together, it was to make it disappear.

§ Bottoms Up!

No matter how many times you drink down to the dregs, you won't know what it is to have only dregs to drink. And knowing that, by Jerome's lights, is knowing the law of the world.

§ Call out All the Names under the Sun

If one were to make a project of calling out every word, good and bad, available in memory and books, one would never see the end of it, and die calling. The words invented by man and the historical bonds that link them are too many for anyone to utter them. One's speech does well to ignore them.

For their inherited wealth pales against the poverty of individual freedom of invention, which accounts for one's *having a name* at all. Just as the rich can freely give up their inheritance to become poor, what we are called and called upon to do can be cast off by inventing a calling for ourselves. While not much, for some it is enough to live on.

§ Soft Landing

We would sooner take to our beds, defeated, than stand up and fight for happiness. Happiness (not to be confused with joy) and unhappiness (not to be confused with sadness) are reifications of the pursuit of continual joy and the flight from continual sadness, respectively. When we feel we have stumbled in our quest for joy, we rightly conclude that we are not happy. When we then fall in our escape from sadness, we realize that unhappiness has caught up with us. It is with great effort that we pick ourselves up again — often getting only as far as the first bed that will take us.

§ Uncomfortable Happiness

Identifying comfort with happiness would be like mistaking your social standing for your inner life — were inner life not a mere flight from your social standing.

Do we not owe it to our high conception of the good life to transcend such divisions into "inner" and "outer," even if it itself proves impracticable?

§ **Sore Spots**

Do we *owe* it to ourselves to be happy even when others are unhappy? No more than we *owe* these others to be miserable on their account.

Let him who can be happy in knowledge or ignorance of others' unhappiness be as happy as possible. But let the law punish happiness when it depends on the unhappiness of others. Let it even levy a tax on happiness. And let resentment litigate against unjust happiness in some future court.

§

No man is a slave to his own well-being, not because well-being has no power to enslave, but because he is never fully well. And if he were well, he would be the master of well-being.

§

The desperate pursuit of happiness is justified as long as suffering is guaranteed.

⋆⋆

IV

§ Multitasking

"In communist society," wrote Marx and Engels, meaning a society in which the division of labour has been abolished, "where nobody has one exclusive sphere of activity but each can become accomplished in any branch he wishes, society regulates the general production and thus makes it possible for me to do one thing today and another tomorrow, to hunt in the morning, fish in the afternoon, rear cattle in the evening, criticize after dinner, just as I have a mind, without ever becoming hunter, fisherman, herdsman, or critic."*

The vision of happiness in varying one's activities at will through the course of the day has its funhouse reflection in the simultaneous performance of multiple tasks so common in our time. The current state of affairs distorts our notions of Engels' desired and diverse occupations to the point of either mistrusting exclusive focus on any of them one at a time (to the neglect of other things), or being unable to conceive of any of them as satisfying in its own right. Let us not mention that the very conception of specialization, reduced to mindlessness by the assembly line and to mental illness in diagnoses of autism, whether at work or at leisure, is historically inseparable from a society organized around divided labour, which we oppose in principle. It is not only limiting; it is unfair and even against nature.

---

* Karl Marx with Friedrich Engels, *The German Ideology*, trans. uncredited (1932; New York: Prometheus, 1998), 53.

Is multitasking in our sense of the word an antidote to the ills of this industrial model? Facilitated by technology, the many unherculean labours we perform, covering the breadth of our attention and multiplying, are quite predictably beginning to run together. Less and less discrete, they are perhaps all the more inescapable for that very reason. The coming status quo — in which time is not divided between larger tasks (only subdivided between sub-tasks, and shared between part-time jobs), in which work blends into leisure — is merely one result of surplus value production being transferred back to increasingly adaptable consumers, whose education every year shifts towards transferable skills, in tandem with the surging rate of obsolescence of specialized means of production, know-hows, and knowledges. What becomes clear is that, while the division of labour may remain incompatible with free society, labour's *multiplication*, creeping and rapacious, is not a happy alternative; it merely enslaves more securely.

§ Practically History

In Canada, they are building a memorial to the victims of communism. Some, allergic to such improvident anachronism, ask "Why not build one to the victims of capitalism instead?" "We know, we know," they answer before the ruling "elite" has had an opportunity to address their concerns. "First of all, it is bad luck to memorialize the living. Second of all, communist China, North Korea, Vietnam, Cuba have already one foot in the grave."

§ *Farniente*

In an informal economy, freedom from workplace regimentation is forfeited again by the induction of domestic activities into the home-work continuum. Everyday tasks increasingly mimic paid labour which, while accommodating to the point of taking place around them, in fact seeps into their very performance by virtue of its proximity and the removal of earlier forms of separation. By carving out time to "work around" meals, house chores, animal and child-care, horticulture and exercise — personal tasks for most of which remuneration has not yet been invented — the worker-from-home gradually comes to treat all activity as an object for regulation, efficiency optimization, and a problem in need of a workaround. "I've got a system for that!" "I can get so much more done now! I've worked out which tasks go best together and bundle them for multitasking. It helps if you break things down to the minute!" "My new personal workflow and task management tools work wonders for my personal life!" This is no mere rodomontade. The energies of these two domains, work and life, have long intersected, and their spheres have overlapped before. What is new and different is the infection of everyday and leisure activities with the Trojan horse of technology. On the pretext of helping us step up our game and get our act together, it rules our lives with a soft despotism. Enabled by apps and wearables, self-micromanagement flies under the radar and is glamourized as "life hacking." The form of wage labour, in which time management is paramount, has thus come to structure and shape a whole domain of tangential tasks that previously escaped capital's oversight and even served as a counterweight to it. Along this vector, in an aggressive free-market economy the line between "real" work and earning on the side melts away as competition for consumers reaches new levels of sophistication and desperation. Between brand ambassadors and the glut of targeted advertising, putting two and two together isn't hard. The day is not far off when what we put in our mouth will be bought by the labour of eating it, and a simple track suit paid for by the job of jogging in it. Only let's not fool ourselves that what follows from this is freedom.

⸙ Fingers Crossed

Day in, day out, we subscribe to a vision of capitalism as the subtle and not-so-subtle invader that overcomes every limit and constraint by hypnotic powers of suggestion or, failing that, brute force. What the affluent disparage from their perches — capital's greedy annexation of unspoiled reality — threadbare humanity welcomes as its only savior, counting not on the hearts of individual entrepreneurs, industrialists, and financiers, but on the invisible digits that, by reaching them, will at last take away its pain. At its logical conclusion, this image of "Faustian" expansion ought itself to be erased in capital's magic-slate reinvention, culminating perhaps in total invisibility. The capital to come is something those interested, those who either think outside the ideological box or pray inside it, equally cannot predict. But the handful of others, who see it coming and recognize each other in the fog by a certain gesture or wink, go by a simple rule: what expands must one day contract, even in geopolitical time.

§ *Mutatio mundi*

> *Die Philosophen haben die Welt nur verschieden* interpretiert, *es kömmt drauf an sie zu* verändern.
>
> (Philosophers have only *interpreted* the world in various ways; the point is to *change* it.)
> —Karl Marx, Eleventh Thesis[*]

In the last of his Feuerbach Theses (1845), Marx confronts philosophy with its material inefficacy. The skeleton of Hegelian dialectic pushes the mind into overdrive. (From now on, philosophy will barely function without this economical gearing-up for putting its surplus energy to good use.)

His own determination aside, Marx's enjoinder (or note to self) carries an implicit question: how can philosophy become praxis? And how can the becoming-praxis of philosophy become its motive force, instead of an afterthought? But the eleventh thesis, which opens up thought to this question — by calling for this transformation of thinking into doing, for doing philosophy on the way to politics, with a view to politics — instructs, above all, that philosophy must start this total world-transformation with itself: it must first recognize the change it itself has undergone and is undergoing, confirm the rightness and purpose of this change, and assess its place in the world today. It is, in this sense, already a step in the direction in which it is pointing. (The position is still idealist, its point of departure the revolutionary, world-altering potential of Christianity, as in Novalis's much earlier vatic essay, but clearly also a turning away from religion's monopoly over politics; philosophy's move in the direction of a secular politics is inseparable from the philosophical move towards historical materialism and the supersession of idealist philosophy it implies.)

As such, Marx's maxim is grounded in three refusals:

---

[*] Karl Marx, *Die Frühschriften*, ed. Siegfried Landshut (Stuttgart: Kröner, 1971), 341.

- the *refusal of anachronism*. All philosophy participates in the historical process and its activity and proactivity confirm its currency; it is there at the dawn of the event;

- the *refusal of abstraction*. As a reflective and critical reaction to the world, philosophy is rooted in particular contexts, to which it must recognize itself duty-bound and from which it cannot abstract itself; it is part of a world that needs changing; lastly,

- the *refusal of contingency*. The course and future of philosophy derive from universal values and historical necessity.

But Marx's words cannot themselves accomplish what they call for, which is new to philosophy. They are conscious of communicating a novelty to thought. They are a call for a new totality (the world), in the making of which philosophy can—must—cannot but participate, and the enormity of the task requires marshalling the totality of philosophy, a move so revolutionary as to pull thought out of its orbit. In theology, exegesis, prayer, the task of thought exceeded its worldly limit; with modern philosophy, thought sets for itself a task at once greater than itself and within its new limits, which it projects and identifies with those of the world. The last Feuerbach thesis is furthest out in this respect, jutting out like a pier into swelling waters, its pillars firmly planted in the ocean floor. At the end of it stands the revolutionary visionary. Diverting his gaze from the dreamy horizon now back towards dry land, now down into the depths below, is the tension in his breast between the beachcomber and the pearl diver. These symbolic oppositions will structure materialist philosophy's self-understanding and anxiety vis-à-vis politics. Politics is the truth of philosophy, where it tests its mettle and proves its worth for the future. But its proof will only be given if it comes to politics, which it must at the same time revitalize, alter. To change the world, it must share its place in it with revolutionary struggle.

⸹ Dip Sheep

In Dziga Vertov's *Sixth Part of the World* (1926), a montage of machines and sheep dipped in different waters accompanies a revolutionary appeal:

> *more machines / more / and more / but no less hard is it for the worker / … / the slaves / the colonies / Capital / the slaves / … / Capital is on the verge of its historical perishing / Capital / is having fun /*
>
> *You,*
> *who bathe*
> *your sheep /*
> *in the surf of the sea,*
> *and you,*
>   *who bathe*
> *your sheep /*
> *in a brook /*
> *…*
> *and You /*
> *who have overrun the power of Capital in October /*
> *who have opened*
> *the road*
>   *to new*
>   *life**

Infinitely adaptable, capitalism today cannot be set apart as *counter-nature*, as it was "in October," when the Soviet harmony of land, industry and man made up one-sixth of the globe. And *actually-surviving socialism*—what part of the world has it left? (Hint: next to none.)

---

*   *Shestaya chast' mira (One-Sixth of the World)*, directed by Dziga Vertov (1926; Vienna: Filmmuseum, 2009), DVD.

§ Heart & Home

> *The savage who loves himself, his wife, and his child with quiet joy and glows with limited activity for his tribe as for his own life is, it seems to me, a more genuine being than* that cultured shade who is enchanted by the shadow of his whole species.... *In his poor hut, the former finds room for every stranger, receives him as a brother with impartial good humor and never asks whence he came. The inundated heart of* the idle cosmopolitan is a home for no one.
> —J.G. Herder[*]

Political ignorance extends to the idea that the nation-state is just a bigger home, in which all the nation's families live in harmony as in a communal dwelling.

The cosmopolitan, whose knowledge of political community breaks with such sentiments, rejects this Aristotelian conception of the state as home-land — as much as the idea that politics needs a fixed abode — *fixed* by familial-national attachment. Regardless of what he calls home, his true home is his heart — his *cosmopolitan* heart. And this home is his politics.

---

[*] Johann Gottfried Herder, from "Materials for the Philosophy of the History of Mankind" (1784–91), in *The Dynamic Force of Liberty in Modern Europe: Six Problems in Historical Interpretation*, ed. Thomas Corwin Mendenhall, trans. C.J.H. Hayes (New York: Holt, 1952), 90 (emphases mine).

ẞ What's What

> *You'll have a better understanding of what was actually done if you start by knowing what had to be done — what always and everywhere has to be done by anyone who has a clear idea about what's what.*
> —Aldous Huxley, *Island**

Without knowing "what's what," the great question asked and answered by Chernyshevsky in his own utopian novel — *Shto delat'?* "What is to be done?" — can only be answered wrongly. "What's what" may just be gnomic and humdrum enough to bag the right and universal.

ẞ Beggar Thy Neighbour's Culture

It is a peculiar species of cosmopolitanism: taking oneself from a place poor in culture to one that has plenty.

---

* Aldous Huxley, *Island* (New York: Harper Perennial, 2009), 40.

∫ Far Away, So Close

The more the sense of foreignness becomes a thing of the past among those who do not travel at all or travel nonstop, the greater their craving for imaginary spaces. These mental wonderlands and nominal utopias that recapture foreignness in exaggerated form (which is a function of their perceived impossibility) make their reality not only bearable but *better known*. "What do they know of England who only England know?" And what do they know of the world who are over-familiar with it? Those who manage to invent for themselves such "other" spaces, such "non-places," have the distance needed to see what their world is — the foreignness needed to build knowledge upon familiarity.

The homebound can *best* know their home not by covering distances but by moving back through time. Digging into local history brings out the foreignness of familiar places obscured by encroaching globalization. The constant traveller can *best* know the world not by "doing" all of it, following the links highlighted or created by globalization, but by efforts to connect with local values, traditions, and ways of life wherever they go. Most travellers, needless to say, can only afford time for a first glance. The truth of the places they touch down in rarely appears at their beck and call.

§ Pebbles

No state is an island, though some have that shape. Casting votes outside of our country of residence wherever else we happen to enjoy voting rights is not only no failing but a political duty. *Ubi bene ibi patria*, and we should do everything in our power to protect this good wherever we are by supporting it elsewhere. In a world so closely linked, the West is no larger than a pond, and a vote cast in one corner is no smaller than the *psephos* thrown into an urn in the Golden Age of Athenian democracy. The results of an election ripple out to distant parts almost instantly, affecting our lives there.

§ Born Idealist

"It's not me you should be worried about."

◊ Future Optimists

Soon even bloodshot, tear-filled eyes will be decried as rose-tinted glasses.

◊ Future Humblebrag

"I've been to Earth and back."

◊ Priceless

A map of utopia is not worth the paper it's printed on.

◊ Critical Utopia

Impartial accounts of utopia can do no more than point in the general direction and dwell upon the journey there. But a partial one can (if used correctly) tell us where *not* to go, what to avoid. Whether or not its author intended it as a map of the place itself—a blueprint for how to get it built—or as a picture to meditate on—unrealizable by design—it will keep its critical value as long as we look at it askance from time to time.

§ Missing Part

The map of utopia is partial. No one has the missing part.

§ All or Nothing

A Gracián says that "Reality can never match our expectations, because it's easy to imagine perfection, and very difficult to achieve it."[*] Isn't imagining perfection half-way to achieving it? Isn't the ease with which it is imagined encouragement to really make it happen?

A' Is it really so easy to imagine perfection? I think it is the hard — the harder part, and that is why it is next to impossible to achieve perfection. Before we try imagining perfection, we must realize the imperfection of the imagination: what it leaves vague and undefined becomes the breeding ground of error.

A If the image were perfect and understood, it would be executed with ease. But since it is neither, since those who imagine have no sense of executing and those who execute have no imagination, both are equally impossible.

A' With absolutes, it is always "all or nothing." That's why we are always left with nothing.

---

[*] Baltasar Gracián, *The Pocket Oracle and the Art of Prudence*, trans. Jeremy Robbins (London: Penguin, 2011), p. 9, sec. 19.

§ *Paeninsula fortunatorum*

> *Even if they are judged by an abstract criterion of truth-telling, it may be doubted whether Utopians have, in fact, distorted the future any more than historians have the past.*
> —Frank E. Manuel[*]

There is no more need to defend the innocence of Utopia once we discover Alibia. Its inhabitants, called Alibis (from the Latin *alibi*, "elsewhere") — or Alibris (from a-libris, or "book-less"), as they like to call themselves — carry out a great work of imagination, the ideal republic by the name of Alibia. The Alibis not only recognize that this work ought to be done, but regard it as the all-important, all-consuming work — in short, the only real work to be done — since without it Alibia could not exist at all.

Rumours that they live on nothing but air and have no interaction with the rest of the world were disproved long ago. Those who accuse them of using some poor subterranean devils to provide for their material needs are grasping at straws. The Alibis are neither without needs nor have so many to rely on a system of exploitation.

They are, instead, engaged in a gainful if delicate commerce, moving the intangibles they produce to provide for themselves. There is no lack of outsiders willing to trade the material fruits of their labour for the purely immaterial work of the Alibis. And if they try their hand at imagining Alibia and do well, these outsiders might one day be made citizens. (Though there are many great minds in Alibia, one type seldom seen there is the metaphysician.) Imagination, their sole livelihood, puts the Alibis "off the map" of ordinary tourists and commercial travellers apparently content with their lot. "It is a common mistake to call Alibia an island," they explain, "when it is merely a peninsula. The geographers continue to falsify us. Unlike the Utopians, we have never cut ourselves

---

[*] Frank E. Manuel, "Toward a Psychological History of Utopias," *Daedalus* 94, no. 2 (1965): 319.

off from the mainland." The work and land of the Alibis, though outlying, have always been accessible to the curious.

One is tempted to describe their way of life in the utopian genre, in a *libellus vere aureus, nec minus salutaris quam festivus, de optimo rei publicae deque nova paeninsula...*[*] But from an observer's perspective there is almost nothing to Alibia, not enough to fill even a *libellus*, not even for a "little" book. And anyone who is "inside" and tries then to describe Alibia is no longer participating in its construction, so instantly loses their place in it (as they would a radio frequency). Yet this has not stopped us from speculating about the boundlessness of imagination at work there — at any point, the Alibis see further than we do, far beyond our present horizons. They have no use for memories and archives; their work is valuable only insofar as, at any given moment, they transcend what each has done (imagined) up to that point (n.b., the absence of competition, which they consider unhealthy). Thus they are constantly building, improving, and upgrading their Alibia, including the ideals espoused there, so that it is never anything less than ideal.

For the above reasons, and as signalled by the extra *r* in their self-chosen name, the Alib*r*is are a book-less people. Alibia is the name for a continuous work of imagination that is never written down. Without a guide, visitors to Alibia who trade with its inhabitants come away with no more than what they are allowed to see in exchange: a vague impression of the republic's real-world size, structure, and power; a few glimpses of its wonders, perhaps, but never a full or coherent picture.

Based on these scraps of information, some maliciously interpret the name "Alibri" as "freedom-less," enslaved to imagination, when in fact every Alibi finds in the

---

[*] Echoing the full original Latin title of Thomas More's *Utopia* (1516), *Libellus vere aureus, nec minus salutaris quam festivus, de optimo rei publicae statu deque nova insula Utopia* (lit. trans.: A Truly Golden Little Book, No Less Beneficial than Entertaining, of a Republic's Best State, and of the New Island Utopia; trad. trans.: A Fruitful and Pleasant Work of the Best State of a Public Weal, and of the New Isle Called Utopia).

imagination what is perhaps freedom's highest form. These disaffected traders, who clearly have no sense of even the rudiments of its law, are always hatching plots to invade and enslave Alibia. This is another, and most important, reason for why the Alibris do not write books. For they have no standing army, and no other defence.

§ In the Dark

One might approach utopia in the dark without ever realizing it.

§ Impossible but Necessary

Even in us cynics, beauty and purity will always find a hiding place as long as we dwell on the world's ugliness and impurities.

§ Great Expectations

A utopian, far from being unreconciled to the state of the world, has only the highest hopes for it.

⟨ Means without End

Is it a joke? There is not much that isn't open to ridicule here: a utopian prefiguration of poverty! After all, how can the slavishly exploited (those lacking what counts as "means to spare"), the truly solidary who willingly gave up their spare and excess means in return for the truth of struggle against "scarcity," who make ends meet in the struggle's day to day, who instead of "minding the gap" between where they are and where they'd like to be have wound up dwelling in it bodily — how can *they* actively prefigure a collective utopia? Going (in)voluntarily without may be a form of political rehab, but how can their stance, expressed in a struggle *against* the very deprivation they seem in solidarity to embrace, be assimilable to actually modelling a changed reality, high-minded ideas and fellow feeling aside? A world without means to spare surely is no better; almost anything else seems better than it.

Yet it is precisely from a position of radically reduced resources that this "better world" is not only possible but vaguely full of possibilities. The challenge of living in it lies not in coming up with universalizing ideas and ingenious solutions — or the revolutionary toolkit such a common condition engenders — but in a counter-praxis of everyday life, freed from the acquisitive impulse, detached from workaday rewards (no matter how meagre or substantial). Prefiguration is not an exact science. It is a gesture towards another way of living arising directly from a chosen position of material lack. It is a call to a new resourcefulness. It is a practical intentional experiment placed as a road sign. As such, it owes its creative potency, political urgency, and persistence to its negation of the ends-without-means and normative practices of the existing social configuration, with which it seeks to break as much as possible short of losing touch with, and thus the ability to redirect, the traffic of discontent with how mean-ingless things actually are. The mere practices of living-against while being together side by side *in full view* — practices that go beyond what is at our disposal — these are the new, the inexhaustible, means.

§ Getting Horizontal

The importance of social dreaming only reminds us that the anarcho-politics of horizontality and slumber remains to be theorized. Once we theorize the *utopian position*, we might find there is some truth to Nietzsche's preposterous claim that "Tiredness is the shortest path to *equality* and *fraternity* — and sleep finally adds to them *liberty*," and to Baltasar Gracián's observation that "the pillow is a silent Sibyl."*

§ Resentment

What, at base, is resentment, if not the need for equality clumsily expressed?

---

* Nietzsche, *Human, All Too Human*, p. 373, vol. 2, sec. 263 ("Path to Equality"); Gracián, *Pocket Oracle*, p. 57, sec. 151 ("Think Ahead").

∫ In Bad Company

What is resentment if not the need for equality expressed in company that does not share this need?

∫ Family Pet

Family pets are among the most abused of animals, even when their tails are not being pulled, etc. But since we try to treat them as humans, and often with greater care and solicitude, we are all but blind to this fact. In their systematic abuse we glimpse only our utopia.

§ A Parting Gift

in response to:

> *And then there was what the coroner described like this: "a 5 3/4 x 4 inch gaping laceration involving the pubic region and bilateral medial thighs with the absence of genitalia, exposure of the pubic bones and adjacent soft tissue." Or, to spell it out: By the time the body was recovered, no part of his external genitalia remained. Where they should have been, there was nothing but a raw gap. That was Terry Thompson's final grotesque parting gift — a last meal for one of his animals, sometime before it, too, met its death by bullet on the sad night of October 18, 2011, near Zanesville, Ohio.*
> —Chris Heath, "18 Tigers, 17 Lions, 8 Bears, 3 Cougars, 2 Wolves, 1 Baboon, 1 Macaque, and 1 Man Dead in Ohio"

> *Too severe masters turn the love of them to hatred.*
> —inscription on engraving by Paulus Potter[*]

Humans always look for symbolism where sense and reason seem to be lacking. Is eating one's master — or the master's virile part — significant enough to constitute a "parting gift" reeking of vengeance? The gift may have been mutual: from the initial victim to the later one — submission in the flesh to the long-dominated — and, somewhat less intuitively, from the animal to its cruel keeper — the granting of the latter's repressed wish. Yet that it is the external reproductive organs that should be devoured seems somehow poetically fitting, and reminiscent of *The Punishment of a Hunter*, a famous seventeenth-century canvas in a series of narrative

---

[*] Chris Heath, "18 Tigers, 17 Lions, 8 Bears, 3 Cougars, 2 Wolves, 1 Baboon, 1 Macaque, and 1 Man Dead in Ohio," *GQ*, Mar. 2012, http://www.gq.com/news-politics/newsmakers/201203/terry-thompson-ohio-zoo-massacre-chris-heath-gq-february-2012; Hofstede De Groot, *A Catalogue Raisonné of the Works of the Most Eminent Dutch Painters of the Seventeenth Century*, vol. 4 (London: Forgotten Books, 2012), 592–93.

panels by Paulus Potter. In it, the animals take their revenge on their persecutor and tormentor — by prosecuting and executing him. His trial features a multispecies jury, fox as clerk, a lion for judge. The hunter is sentenced to death by roasting on a spit, as his hounds are strung up on an improvised gallows. In both cases — the American tragedy and the Dutch allegory — humans get their comeuppance. But the *as-yet-unpainted story* of the man from Ohio, who died by his own hand and was nibbled at by his menagerie, betokens a still higher justice where it refrains from imposing on animals the petty logic of ultimate revenge masked as legal deliberation.

§ Exuviae

When we are done thinking with animals, we discard them. The lab animal is a placeholder for man until it is safe for man to be experimented upon. We emphasize our similarities with other animals when they can serve as stand-ins, quasi-doubles, and dissociate ourselves when we can exploit them in our stead. The source of animal melancholy, and of human melancholy concerning animals, is the recognition of this double hazard — experimentation/exploitation — for which we use animals to avoid what we'd rather not undergo if the animal can help it. But this describes only one of two present paradigms of our meeting with other species.

When humans yawn, they have animal faces; this is as welcome a thought today as the reverse[*] was a century ago. We have seen too much of man to think that we have a lock on natural dignity. "It isn't in a bear's nature to wear roller

---

[*] "When animals yawn, they have human faces." Kraus, *Half-Truths*, 120.

skates. It isn't in an elephant's nature to sit on a stool."[*]
When we enter a Dog Café or an Owl Bar, we picture a
miniscule safari, where animals (in the majority) of the same
general kind call the shots and set the limits on socialization.
Rewilding initiatives express a secret longing for a reversal
of relations. As we speak, circuses are refigured for human
acts, and zoos, as exotic animal sanctuaries. Petting zoos,
where different species are on display for human enjoyment,
will remain in spirit what the great zoological gardens once
were in reality — the rationale behind the exemption being
that children can do no harm, and relate to animals in a way
adults only relate to death — with awe and fascination, rendering it untouchable. If democracy is still a large animal, as
Plato had it, then we have shrunk from featherless bipeds to
the size of fleas upon its back, and soon will be microbes; the
more there are of us, the more unsustainable we become, the
more we reimagine humankind as parasitic. We will continue to use animals to disguise our ignobility; what nature
they shed or cast off, we will pick up.

---

[*] Elisabeth Malkin, "Worry under the Big Top as Mexico City Moves to Ban Circus Animals," *New York Times*, June 14, 2014, http://www.nytimes.com/2014/06/15/world/americas/worry-under-the-big-top-as-mexico-city-moves-to-ban-circus-animals.html.

⸹ Single-Minded Pursuits

> *What is a Cat? It is a rectification.... The mouse plus the cat equals the revised and corrected proofs of Creation.*
> —Victor Hugo, *Les Misérables**

As the revolutionary mole was digging tunnels beneath Paris, beneath even its catacombs, Hugo saw God's revised plans for the world as a game of cat and mouse, without rules other than those of nature. It goes without saying that this blueprint for Genesis and this game-logic of history have not been binding with us. If their simplicity beguiles, it's because we are complicating creatures, with far too many objectives and not enough pursuits, and look to animals for a lost single-mindedness.

---

* Victor Hugo, *Les Misérables*, trans. Julie Rose (New York: Modern Library, 2008), 969.

§ Classified

How long have we bemoaned the fact that man, given the right (read: wrong) environment, reverts to an animal-like existence? The fascination with wild men of the woods and feral children goes back to Gilgamesh and Rome's myth of origin, suggesting that the line between the civilized and the savage (on which the gods were never particularly hung up) can be all but erased. The more serious issue and source of anxiety has always been the line that kept the human savage separate from the beast. Today, when wild animals, animals that have not been trained to conform in their basic instincts to human civilization, are the real endangered species, it would be in the interest of science to study the exact degree of a human being's (initially) voluntary reversion to an animal, on the level of identity, self-perception, consciousness... It might allow us to determine the point of maximum rapport and thus the optimal conditions for our kind and other species to meet. Yet we must also keep in mind that it is precisely the degree to which they cannot become animals that humans can be held accountable for their actions. If the experiment of human-to-animal reversion proves 100% successful, then, as with the atomic bomb, its design cannot be allowed to get out.

§ Double Standards

A You know what I miss? It was the first thing I kept hearing. A hallucination.

   The cat, the sound of its bell in the distance. I liked this cat, it was so autonomous, even if it was living off me. I didn't mind at all. I left it alone. But it was a cat.

B Still is, I'm sure.

A I never once thought of it: how ungrateful!
   Why do we have the opposite expectations of people? Should we even have them?

B How could we not?

A Because we don't have them of cats. Alright, I'll speak for myself: at least I don't have them.

B Maybe if you found a very small, very independent person who didn't speak... and occasionally brought home dead birds or mice...

A Come on, that's too easy a parallel. With such a person, I might well take them in *as* a cat—and only as long as they behaved like one.

   But my concern is with these two standards. Why is human sociability configured in this way? Why are better manners not expected of cats also? Don't we in fact *resent* them for it? Dogs, being trainable, are expected to behave. But cats—we say it's in their *nature* to ignore. We resent but feel obliged to forgive, no?

   Human nature, by comparison, is open (or, anyway, has opened up). Yet, as far as human sociability goes, we take it as a universal that if one *can* relate and reciprocate, then one *ought* to, at least on those occasions when one is someone else's beneficiary. And even if one, at a minimum, relates in such a case, does that mean one is also reciprocating? No, one must make a point of reciprocating, or else prove that one really *can't*. Those who do nothing do resemble cats. Still, they differ and can't get off the hook that easily. The thing is, they themselves have many expectations, including of their cat, if they have one — which they often do as a symbol of their "feline" nature. And this cat's "selfish" indifference constantly disappoints them.

§ Arcadius Makes Headlines

"Even the winners can die," begins a *human interest* piece.

"Steeplechase Horse Arcadius Dies after Winning"
We should all be so lucky!

"After the Best Race of His Life, a Horse's Death"
To die is one thing, but to die in the rare case when achievement, quantity *and* quality, can be measured with such exactitude! That indeed is a pity.

"It was as if he knew he had won" — *as if*, that is, not really. From *his* perspective death came at the moment it wanted to come, not to underscore his triumph — a triumph *in* life, at the price of his life, not *over* life. An effort much greater because unsustainable, outside his limits, within his power only with that power's total outlay — he sacrificed himself making it; running fast enough to make the finish-line his death — a feat far more impressive than the petty one you reward him for! Death came, dashing that triumph (exacting payment — not its *asking* but its *telling* price).

"He tried, he gave his all."*
The line reached in record time — the record of his life no less — cutting short his life, made vivid time's relationship to speed, disproving that (at such small distances) the faster we go the more time we have left over, and the slower we can arrive at death. (You say that the faster we move the lesser the distance travelled relative to what we have come to expect — and so keep going, exhaustively, until the end catches up with you unawares). Compared to the Patagonian hare fleeing his pursuers all the way to his dying breath, staying ahead of (without losing or outlasting) them and pacing himself, adjusting his speed to extend the distance he has left, Arcadius, not ahead to begin with, came out ahead of his rivals and by adjusting his speed seems to have *shortened* the time at his disposal. He went not as *far* as he could, but as *fast*, *as though* in pursuit of success, not mere survival. The finish line was not fine, nor was he.

The lamentable anthropomorphism of the tragic racehorse makes for a moving story — almost as good as that of Bach's unfinished fugue, over whose last notes, spelling (in German notation) the word *BACH* ("stream"), he is said to have breathed his last.

§ Beauty & Death

Beauty need not be moving to be a close ally of death.

---

* Joe Clancy, "After the Best Race of His Life, a Horse's Death," *New York Times*, May 14, 2012, http://www.nytimes.com/2012/05/15/sports/after-his-lifes-best-race-death-of-horse-arcadius.html.

§ Hit and Miss

All-but-invincibility does not require your weak spot to be no more than the size of a heel. A heel-sized patch of inhuman strength is enough if it is in the right place; an area the size of a heart can make one immune if one's assailant assumes this to be the most vulnerable point, unloading his entire magazine into your chest. Now let's say your "heart" is made of stone, a stone-cold kind of vanity, and you, though wounded and reeling from the attack, survive. Rather than take aim again, this time at our stomach or head, which would-be assassin would not back away, incredulous, and be laid thus by the heels?

§ The Average American

An American in his late 50s learns he has a year to live. Diagnosed with an obscure terminal illness he is advised to cope with the certainty of imminent death by making the most of the time left to him and to seek solace in spirituality. He makes no arrangements for his burial or cremation. Rejecting death with dignity, he seeks an atavistic terminus. Using up all his savings, he has himself parachuted into the heart of the Amazon, where he wants to live out his days without provisions or weapons. His wish is to die like prehistoric man: in combat with wild beasts. He wants to revert to the zero-point of consciousness and human evolution.

§ Insulation

> *Books are the original insulator. A shelf of books along an outside wall works well to prevent heat escaping. If all the books were removed from the homes in Britain, our energy bills would rocket.*
> —Joel Rickett[*]

The electronic book has no such added utility. It can no more insulate than shelter. A "lettered recess"[†] of e-books is to a refuge as a house of cards is to one made of brick and mortar. The feeling of being walled in is gone, but so is that of having a roof over one's head.

§ What You Want Is What You Get

> *Consumers have been educated by the market and now the median level of cultural competence is much higher. A basic rule of happiness is don't buy things; buy experiences. The market has taken one commodity product after another and turned it into an emotional experience — even hotel stays. I don't know how you measure how much better off we are because of that, but we are significantly better off.*
> —David Brooks, "The Edamame Economy"[‡]

It is delusional to think that booking a stay in a boutique hotel automatically guarantees an experience advertised as being designed for its guests. The "edamame economy" is

---

[*] Quoted in Sarah Lonsdale, "Interiors: Rooms That Lose None of Their Shelf Life," *Telegraph*, Apr. 15, 2008, http://www.telegraph.co.uk/lifestyle/interiors/3360991/Interiors-Rooms-that-lose-none-of-their-shelf-life.html.

[†] Young, "Conjectures," 348.

[‡] David Brooks, "The Edamame Economy," *New York Times*, Jan. 4, 2014, http://www.nytimes.com/2014/01/07/opinion/brooks-the-edamame-economy.html.

the old "package deal" economy repackaged and upsold. The customer pays more not for any particular experience but for the conviction that it will occur, as well as, to put it bluntly, the greater fuss around the actual choice (since there needs to be a "match" between it and the experience we want, or see ourselves as having).

The difference between the available options is that some (thanks to their price and so-called uniqueness) come attached with an imperative to make the most of it. So great is the expectation and commitment to making it special that even a one-night stay acquires the aura of a one-night stand on a tropical holiday. But as in so many other areas of production that have figured out how to exploit consumers, we are creating surplus value by signing an invisible contract with ourselves. To have an experience in the experience economy, to have one on demand, seems less preposterous and self-exploitative when that demand appears to come from, and that experience is guaranteed by, none other than us.

§ Moratorium II

A I call for a moratorium on publishing so the average reader could catch up, thank you very much.

B No offence, my friend, but what a stupid idea! There is no such thing as an "average reader." Clearly you don't read enough—

◊ Rip-Off

We learn that animals learn by mimicry. This means that writers are always learning. But ours is an age when even mimicry is in decline. Why not rip covers off of entire books and put new names on them? They are already doing it over in China. Increasingly that is the only way a book (a thesis, etc.) will get read. Let me put it to you this way, dear writer: would you rather your work be shared and read under a different author, or never read again? No self-respecting communist would oppose such a redistribution of intellectual property.

◊ Meterocracy

In the *fairest possible world*, virtue would be rewarded, as would merit of any kind. Recognition of merit is *our world's* moral response to rampant capitalism. Does the widespread criticism of the use of metrics and quantification of achievement in nearly all aspects of life indicate that *meritocracy* is part of the bad world that needs to be overcome, or does it merely tell us that the measurement of man is hardly less crude than it was some hundred-plus years ago?

§ A Wide Selection

The process of social screening and selection is there no matter how far back we look. It is there in adolescence, in the playground, in the sandbox... It occurs in the background until suddenly we not only feel the pain of having been passed over for someone not obviously better, more charismatic, more accomplished than us; we also begin more soberly to consider our odds, to question the decision's fairness, to look at the patterns and, finally, the bases of social exclusion and acceptance. Such experiences, when their outcomes are not to our liking, acquire the bitter flavour of existential sorting, not just into the favoured and the rejected, but, in the latter group, into those who are paralyzed by their awareness of it being so, those who persevere in spite of it, and those who fight it—sometimes until late middle age. The mid-life crisis, made grim by resentment of systemic discrimination, has its analogue in the adolescent period of rebellion against social norms that loom as obstacles to self-realization, -expression, freedom and equality, justice and fairness for all. A period of adjustment in behaviour and expectations may or may not follow. The memory of departing from norms, of going off the rails that first time, tends to be mythologized because misunderstood. As for the second time, mid-life, depending on your social integration, it can be a source of severe embarrassment. Whether you ever get back on track or not, you have arrived. Should you one day come out, it will be much reduced in spirit.

§ Outside the Text

We should stop pretending that general-interest books (and I don't mean picture books) are judged solely on the merit of what is inside them, and that the social background of a book, its cultural context, and how it came into being, come into play in only the most obvious literary feats and are irrelevant outside of special interest. We claim to read masterpieces that *happen to be* prison writing, collectively authored, or the posthumously published work of a suicide—unless they are masterpieces *of* prison writing, feats merely *of* collective authorship, or *of* a suicidal mind. We say that such information only adds to our appreciation of a true work of literature (Dostoevsky's gambling-driven productions readily spring to mind) even for the cases where that is manifestly untrue. Like the proverbial *cover*, all that extraneous stuff, we maintain, can never be the main reason for admiring a book—or for redeeming it. Yet clearly the greater share of the enormous appeal of a novel about overcoming addiction, *A Million Little Pieces*, was not only its Book Club controversy, but its origin in the mind of an addict, at the site of addiction overcome.

§ Doubling Standard

The idea that we should all feel addressed by the books we read, that this is how books should be for us to elevate them to "universal" masterpieces of "human" ingenuity, is very powerful. We should pray that it soon becomes passé. It is like saying that all humans should be explicitly and promiscuously social to count as great, for us to find them worthy of honour; otherwise their humanity is flawed, there is something wrong with them — some moral failing, the paralogism of writing *publicly* while *not caring* — for which we don't forgive them, but instead mark them down.

The exception to this powerful and widespread view of literature is the *outsider writer*, equivalent of the outsider artist in name though not in number. His work, contrariwise, many are prepared to elevate above the best writers, and high above their own heads. But they are okay with such cluelessness. They don't hold it against the writer but instead reach out to him, pitying one so shut out.

§ The Candid Philosopher

Shall we steal a line from that now-fashionable philosopher and say, next time, *Let's all collaborate!*? Thinking together is so much more fun — and *optimistic*.

§ *Colla et labora*

For reasons of technological possibility and economic efficiency, collective authorship no longer means collaboration. More often than not, it gives rise to a collective instead of proceeding from it. It is the product of environments and milieus; decisions to co-author are less and less decisions, and more a mix of logical steps and professional jerk reactions. To keep up appearances, much is made of networking as "talking shop," as though collaboration was alive and kicking.

For reasons of cultural degradation and endangerment, collaboration no longer implies collective authorship. More often than not, it takes the form of working loosely side by side. It is the product of garrisoned scenes and threatened ecosystems; co-thinking and co-doing are safeguards less of concord or conformity than of group survival. To keep up appearances, much is made of not going it alone, as though collective authorship was part of the job description.

§ Ghosting Oneself

The risks of ruining one's prospects for literary greatness are such that, in the making of a literary auteur no less than of a literary author, they can only be reduced by contracting oneself as one's own ghostwriter, to whom any and all complaints should in future be directed.

§ Publish and Perish?

> *But there is something else about the genre, a sense that the world might be more ghosted now than at any time in history. Isn't Wikipedia entirely ghosted? Isn't half of Facebook? Isn't the World Wide Web a new ether, in which we are all haunted by ghostwriters?*
> —Andrew O'Hagan[*]

Perhaps the only release from the tyranny of genius and the competitive spirit of capitalism is to appear in print only as a ghost, with an unidentifiable body and untrackable series of avatars. But who can resist the temptation to be recognized behind our multiple names, ostensibly meant to put false followers off our scent, when our hangers-on still claim our attention without deserving it and with another hand demand from us a piece of ID? We think, often rightly, *Better do it myself, in case they get it wrong*, and throw off our cloak of anonymity, presenting our work publically for identification (calling it our calling card, to indicate that the opportunity to get to know us was missed).

While difficult to trace, we want nonetheless to be sought and found—like a needle in a haystack—by our sharp point. The prospect of perishing in a field fire or ending up in the stomach of some ruminant is as unappealing as the search for genius and the spirit of competition are maddening—a characteristic of charades that have gone on too long, and of the world shrunk into a parlour.

---

[*] O'Hagan, "Ghosting."

§ **Everything You Ever Wanted to Know about Nazis but Were Too Lazy to Find Out**

"Overstuffed suitcase of a book," wrote one critic of *The Kindly Ones*. But not the kind you should live out of.

§ **Uncontaminated**

You can eat off even the filthiest books.

§ Wiggle Room; or, the Unhappy Customer

> *Literature wriggles away like an eel. What would become of the eel if you caught it? You'd eat it. Literature and the eel live as long as they succeed in wriggling away.*
> —Witold Gombrowicz*

Some prose, as someone once said, is so tasty you could eat it by the ladle. The main ingredients of the literary dish are words. You place your order, you take the first bite, yet as so often it is not to your liking. You have two options: either you can season it liberally to taste with what you have in front of you, or, just as easily, you can go to complain to the cooks. But if this dish happens to be an *eel* (and sometimes all you dream of is electric fish), then you are out of luck. You have only yourself to blame for not sticking your fork into it quickly enough to prevent it eluding you—which it will do even dead. Too slow to grasp, you have nothing to show the chef, who in exasperation is liable to offer a second helping…

Never ever, however, blame the waitress who brought it to you. She has neither prepared nor tried it. You cannot have a word with this waitress; she is not responsible for the quality of the food—and besides, she leaves immediately to attend to another table. No matter how much you wish now that she had tasted your meal and, better still, sent it back before it reached you, if you are anything like her usual customers she has every reason not to care about your satisfaction. You too soon learn to look past her and throw furious glances in the direction of the kitchen, eventually taking your complaint there if you are firm, which is entirely within your rights as consumer. You know as well as I do what the staff will say: although the *carte* came with recommendations, you chose neither a house specialty, nor a fresh daily special, but, craving surprises, a *chef's fantasia*. You thought first of ordering the tasting menu, but worried it might leave you

---

* Witold Gombrowicz, *A Kind of Testament*, ed. Dominique de Roux, trans. Alastair Hamilton (1968; Urbana-Champaign, IL: Dalkey Archive, 2007), 126.

hungry, or else its variety would have been too much for your sensitive stomach. And then, after you made your choice, there was the inordinate wait—but in such establishments you half-expect this. You certainly, however, did not plan for disappointment. You felt your appetite grow—even so, you resisted pulling out a ("good bad") sandwich from your briefcase, in anticipation of more recherché fare.

So what made you come to this place? Was it the five-star reviews by those with too much time to spend or more refined taste? By now you have guessed it: the "dish" is a novel with literary pretensions; the "cooks," the author and editor; the staff and joint, a bookstore, kept alive by undiscriminating user-critics. But what, might I ask, are *you* doing here?

§ Token of Value

Every work is born failed until it is redeemed by being published. There exists a type of literary product that is irredeemable, insofar as redemption happens *only* through publishing. The work ignored by the publishing industry, a text no one would risk picking up, is a text forsaken, and with it the writer. So goes the old understanding.

But publishing no longer has the power to redeem. It has been discovered as the reverse of the coin that bears the words NO CASH VALUE. By publishing your book, you have merely obtained a token, for which you can play (for a limited time) to distract yourself from your flaws as a writer, but which is irredeemable outside your world of publishing.

§ Life of a Writer

The hustle and bustle of authors around their work may be slow for a road to ruin, but eventually it gets the job done.

§ Literary Public Execution

No scaffold is too elevated for a writer's execution. He has come into being as a public figure, and it is only fitting that he be helped to die as one.

§ Public Service

Parole is "the release of a prisoner temporarily (for a special purpose) or permanently before the completion of a sentence, on the promise of good behaviour" (OED).

Prisoners of their writing, writers would do everyone a service to serve out their sentences *without parole*. They do not need to speak about them or, for that matter, to hand them out to others.

With more time, and themselves as models for how to "do" time metaphorically, they could then turn the odious literal practice of life imprisonment into a metaphor.

Failing that, the public might write off the last of their sentence as one writes off a debt. And depending on whom you ask, this "write off" may mean "forgive" or "dismiss." At issue is not whether achieving greater social justice is what the writer owes us in his prison cell, but whether he has spent his time writing well. And good writing is best done without parole.

∫ Vital Injection

A more satisfying alternative to capital punishment has appeared on the horizon of possibility: in place of the death penalty, a life sentence with an indefinite life-extension. More humane perhaps, but less human.

"Life will be hard," the lifer might then say, unaware that his forerunner, the failed regicide Damiens, said something similar of the *day* of his drawing and quartering.

(This option was first spied in an aphorism,* and brought to life in a popular TV-series, *Black Mirror*, not long ago. Even aphorisms can have their life extended by becoming literalisms. This, again, being better punishment than the penalty of death.)

∫ Complete Sentences

"We no longer execute people for saying the wrong word. Instead we hand them life sentences."

"We no longer persecute people for their opinions. We ignore them. There's no question which is worse."

"With so many distractions vying for our attention, capital punishment is not the attraction it once was."

---

* Stanisław Jerzy Lec, *Myśli nieuczesane: wszystkie* (Warsaw: Noir sur Blanc, 2011), 22.

§ Essential Killing

It has been pointed out that the Great Revolution democratized a good part of the French body politic by means of the guillotine, a mode of death formerly reserved for nobles. Those who lost their heads were made more equal by popular judgment, and equality was felt all around.

So we show our humanity even in the very process of annihilating those presumed human (by falling under the law). The guillotine and the electric chair, each in its own iconic way, served to make the point: the first through equality, the second through mercy. Beneath the guillotine all are given the same democratic treatment, cut down to the new universal size, undeserving of republican brotherhood yet made its beneficiaries. Similarly, the electric chair and then lethal injection came to be defensible means of disposing of those enemies of the state who do not deserve public empathy yet become its recipients.

While both apparatuses were invented as humanitarian concessions, they are in many ways opposites. The one achieved in precision and efficiency what the other gained in dignity and solemnity. The bloodthirsty ruthlessness of the show of equality is in no way inferior to the execution chamber's antiseptic chill. Still, each made methodical killing respectable, testifying to the humanity not just of the executioners but of all of society in a way that the law alone could never do. Until we come up with a solution that does not kill, we will continue to show our humanity to those who have least use for it.

¶ Completists

> *Accused Killer Was Victim's Pallbearer One Week after Brutal Slaying*
> —headline in *The Calgary Herald*, March 26, 2014

There are some for whom it is not enough to murder someone; they cannot stop themselves from seeing them off as well. It is then not, or no longer, a case of sadism (since their victim cannot feel anything) but of completism. We are prepared to forgive a murderer, but a completist—never.

¶ Happy Day

> bonheur du jour: *small writing desk, French eighteenth century*

Often a desk is not the place to write. This became clear long ago, before the age of laptop computing. But the joy of returning to one and the same spot, one and the same stable surface, in order to pursue what one has begun, is the joy of knowing that one will continue until one is done. It is the experience of completion.

§ Once a Wolf, Always a Wolf?

> *Goodwill is turned to ill will by the violence it suffers.*
> —Adorno and Max Horkheimer[*]

Instead of having your children passively accept the unsullied goodness and badness of characters in fairy tales, there may be more pedagogical value in asking them to reimagine these characters, building on the above rule: to imagine the good ones corrupted by violence and malice, the bad ones converted to goodness by decency, charity, and kindness. The danger in this exercise is that children, being so impressionable, will turn away from the world, with its *unpredictable* violence, to protect their own good natures. Yet isn't that same danger hidden in their fear that the world is full of *unalterable* violence, of proverbial wolves in sheep's attire who can never be mollified by goodwill?

§ On a Roll

How we *love* reversals! It is as with rolling downhill when one realizes the ground has levelled out enough that to continue will require a new commitment and effort.

But as long as you keep that up, heaven shall follow earth with every turn.

---

[*] Adorno and Horkheimer, *Dialectic of Enlightenment*, 214.

§ **Nodding Acquaintance**

  A What if someone you met every day, to the best of your knowledge an ordinary person, suddenly said to you, in an elevator, "All people ... are bound, by their very nature, to be criminals."[*]

  B I would be surprised. I would look at the person more closely, when they weren't looking. I would remember the remark every time I saw the person. If it was often, I might even lose my peace of mind.

  A So you would or wouldn't credit his remark? It seems you would suspect him of having uttered a promise, rather than an accusation (of you, for instance) or a statement of fact.

  B I suppose I would recognize the truth of his words, but only as concerns other people.

  A Including himself.

  B Yes, including himself. Bizarre casual comments are often self-incriminating.

  A And your own judgment would now tend towards this—incriminating others, I mean. His statement made it a rational direction for you to consider, even if the position itself is not reasonable.

  B I suppose. But it isn't like I have nothing better to do. Only that uninitiated contact with strangers makes me think "Here's trouble."

---

[*] Fyodor Dostoyevsky, *Crime and Punishment*, ed. and trans. David McDuff (London: Penguin, 2002), 309.

A Why would you not say to the person precisely that: "Your remark rings true whenever a stranger makes a curious, unsolicited remark to me. My first thought is: 'Here's trouble.'"

B I would never do that.

A Why?

B Because it would be rude and dangerous to let on that I'm suspicious. That all it took to make me uncomfortable was a seemingly innocent, offhand remark. It would make me look cowardly, and cowardice is weakness, and weakness provokes, and it is defenceless against crime...

A But by replying that way you would be making light of your discomfort and perhaps preempting unwanted behaviour. What would you rather do?

B Nod. Nod and think: "Go to hell, if it will even take you."

A That's a mean thought. It implies you have already judged the person guilty of some crime. Did their words cause you any offence? Don't you think you are overreacting?

B No. I was rehearsing Sartre's line about hell being other people.[*] I meant: "Stick to likeminded people."

A So although you think there is truth in what he said, you would not call yourself "likeminded"?

B No.

A Why is that?

---

[*] Jean-Paul Sartre, "No Exit," in *No Exit and Three Other Plays*, trans. Stuart Gilbert and Lionel Abel (New York: Vintage, 1989), 45.

B Because I think better of people. Better in the sense that, even if they are criminals at heart, or, as you say, "by nature," they will not let their criminals out. They will not become criminals by deed or law, only at most in their mind, in their imagination. They might rehearse crimes all their lives but leave them undone. And this "outlet" will satisfy their need for aggression.

A But they will remain criminals "by nature," will they not? So in that sense there is no difference between your view and the view expressed earlier.

B Oh but there is. I think better of people because I think they can change, become better people. The criminal who can discipline their mind will cease to be a criminal "by nature."

A Do you extend this fulsome optimism to the person in the elevator?

B Not really.

A Why not?

B Because he lost the benefit of the doubt by making the comment. Or rather, his comment suggests that his imagination is up to no good. It is evidence that he may be a criminal at heart who cannot contain his criminal inclinations.

A I see. By "likeminded people" you meant such people.

B Yes. And such people I would rather keep as nodding acquaintances. To such people I would say nothing. The efficacy of words is overrated. I would not reply for fear of interrupting an already fragile effort by which they might be reining in their impulses. I don't want to provoke them, I do not wish to stand in their way, I have no desire to be noticed, to appear on their sensitive radars. I want to be the mirror they want me to be. To nod would be to indicate that I accept this — this function — but nothing more. Nodding could leave open the possibility that I too harbour criminal thoughts or intentions, however uncomfortable this makes me feel. A nod can be a sign of complicity.

To accept that "hell is other people" is to allow these *un-likeminded* people to imagine I think like them — and that together we make up hell. To let them think their criminal dreams have company, and that it is OK — and more fulfilling — to keep dreaming. Because a reality in which everyone turned to crime, the *real* hell, would be deeply disappointing.

A And all this can be suggested with a mere *nod*?

B Yes, a nod and nothing more. A nod without a look; why complicate the message?

§ Black Leather

With the refinement of middle-class taste, the latex gloves of the butcher and fish-vendor have gone from white to black. Which is to say *from clean to dirty*, for those out of sync with the times. Or *from blood-stained to sexy*, for the aesthetically minded younger generation whose first association is with leather. The few folks in whom the sight of blood on black leather might stir unpleasant memories will not be around for much longer now.

⸹ Counterproductive

A Security Bulletin on a college campus gave detailed descriptions of three armed robbers: their sex, age, height, build, dress, and distinguishing facial features. If what was missing is their colour, are we expected to assume? And if we are, how does this combat racial stereotyping?

⸹ Ripple Effect

How can we explain our reaction to sexual acts that turn murderous, as they do routinely in the works of Sade, which so many find unpalatable? The combination of pleasure and cruelty is as deplorable and uncomfortable-making as the alliance of power and cruelty is unsurprising and comfortably far away. Despite the appeal of erotic sadism and masochism in the culture, sexual gratification and torture or murder do not mix well in film or literature. We are awash with safe and sanitized depictions of even mildly transgressive sexuality, figured as consent-based fantasy role-play — a line that the pairing of voluptuousness with brutality seems destined to cross, as we know from reading the paper. Sex plus wantonness seems for many too common, too close to home, and thus too unpleasant to think about, let alone merit artistic treatment, which so often glamourizes or aestheticizes what should be (is) feared as a real threat.

Meanwhile, modern power, in the hands of citizens, remains innocuous. For one thing, power has been uncoupled here from faith-based cruelty long ago. Christianity (which has long since abandoned its militant mission), Mormonism, etc. are being scrubbed clean even of sexual abusiveness, and may yet undo their orthodox repressions completely. (The cuddly libido, symbolized by the sex kitten and the Playboy Bunny, looks to soon have its equivalent in the huggable Church of Pope Francis, purged of its closeted skeletons.) In the hands of secular dictators and religious fundamentalists elsewhere in the world, however, power is as in the bad old days: bloody and clumsy, pathetic, occasionally appalling and exotic. Wherever in the world power and cruelty are still close, or grow to be inseparable, their alliance seems surreal and unthreatening, and in any event rarely news. Unless, that is, it shows its sexual roots (witness Boko Haram). While unbridled religious fervor is recognized as powerful enough to explain and even justify bloodshed, the pursuit of pleasure does not have the same validity because it is widely believed to be obtainable without violence. In as permissive a culture as our own, we feel, sex offenders have no more excuse.

Power, whether religious or secular, here or elsewhere, still carries the hint of domination, tyranny, and atrocity. This dark side finds an outlet in the outrages of our foreign wars, but it is always excused as an exception, as the rot of a few isolated apples, malicious, sadistic, or simply too stupid to know better. When real power is *over many*, its abuses are systemically distributed and, in all but the egregious cases, tend to escape detection. But in power over just one or relatively few, as in the case of sects, slaves kept in basements, concentration camp inmates, and war prisoners (as in Abu Ghraib ca. 2003), the sexual core becomes hard to miss — and take. We recoil from the sight, even the thought. By comparison, mass terror, beheadings, stonings, and crucifixions attract because the methods used to maintain power are too archaic for us to properly fathom, and because our good governments do much to publicize such images. Their repressed eroticism is as far from our minds as they themselves are far away. We read such seemingly unadulterated power-trip stories with a firm sense of pity for the victims, uncomplicated by envy, perhaps with renewed commitment to fighting the world's ignorance. From the other kind of story — of domination coupled with cruel eros — we are kept less by our naïvety than by a deep fear of anarchy. Since once we acknowledge the intimate ties between, not just sex and criminal violence, but lust and religious and other tyranny where we previously did not see them, *all* power — not just the exotic, but the familiar also — will become too licentious to bear.

⸹ Sleepless

It is easy to make sleep as boring as possible on film, but difficult to bore spectators to sleep without them noticing it. Not only are their eyes well trained, but they are also used to watchfulness.

⸹ Almost

I am back from a performance of Beethoven's Ninth Symphony. At almost the same time yesterday I left the cinema, having just seen *Son of Saul,* a tunnel-vision rendering of life in Auschwitz. What more is there to say? That the famous performance of the Ninth under the direction of Wilhelm Furtwängler to mark the anniversary of him whom Thomas Mann, as a German, was compelled, on the eve of World War Two, to recognize as his "brother"—that this performance took place *almost* two months after the Wannsee Conference? It is thanks to this *"almost,"* to this inexactitude, that we do not suffocate beneath the weight of numbers.

⸹ At the Concession Stand

Cheer up! The markets are down today.

§ **Discount on Top**

[SALE PRICE]

bargain not included

§ **"Friends for Life"**

Everyone has gotten at least one of these pledges — in an email or scribbled on the back of a postcard after a pleasant time together. They are products of impulse. They announce two things at once: a strong desire to remember you just as you were, still fresh in the other's mind, and the anticipation of a longer parting, for objective but often also subjective reasons — forgoing contact is known to preserve in amber that consummate experience. If it can be arranged, the parting will almost invariably prove the more lasting the more pleasure was actually had. Even permanent. So I always keep these pledges of friendship "for life" to return eventually to their senders, releasing them from a flippant commitment. After all, what are friends for life for? Let's not be sentimental. Once embarrassment fades, the vow can always be renewed.

§ *Amicitia aequalitas*

You can tell true friends by their natural synchrony in ending their friendship, rather than by their painful growing apart. Their deep mutual familiarity, emotional attunement—the highest quality of amity uniting them—allow them also to move on as though spontaneously, simultaneously in unspoken agreement. Such a parting is always amicable because it is accepted without hard feelings and nary a word by both parties, who in a single cast go from personal friends to upstanding members of civil society, where they remain closer than strangers though farther apart than brethren.

§ Safety Deposits

Thieves need banks to deposit their stash without accounting for it. This to keep it from being stolen by others like them. They need banks more than those who have nothing to hide and who never mistrust regular banking, which requires transparency at least on the client's part. The tension between thief and bank that culminates at the safety deposit box derives from, but is inversely proportionate to, the money or monetary value of the stolen object in need of protection. The fungibility of commodities ensures that a thief approaching a bank will feel like a murderer returning to the scene of the crime. Not out of compulsion or in fear of having left traces there or on his stash that could link them to the act, but in a punishing nightmare (free of remorse) and out of resignation to being forever tethered to his misdeed. Humiliation seems unavoidable: what is stolen from society must be deposited again into its hands, and this in the most official and scrutinized of institutions. As long as those who operate outside the law do so only selectively, and rely on doing their banking or other business that might shine a light on their livelihood, they remain more vulnerable than you or I. The sense of autonomy they acquire in operating outside legality is sapped as soon as they return to check on their loot.

∫ Sexual Root of Kleptomania

If the first book one steals without having read, based on name and title alone, is Freud's *Beyond the Pleasure Principle*, is Freud proven right, or wrong?

∫ *Una harum ultima*

There are dreams that prove Freud right, but only by proving him wrong. These are the dreams in which lust and death near-coincide, and *eros* is intensified by the proximity of *thanatos*. A cliché in art as much as in life, intense and until now forbidden sexual desire on the lip of death loses its staleness and implausibility only in the drama of the dream. Such dreams combine the intensity of the first encounter with the last. To die when one is most alive to pleasure and death — could one ask for a death better than this *dream death*, in which the last hour, not seen coming, is stretched by desire as long as it will last?

∫ On Edge

Assisting in labour is as taxing as keeping vigil by the dying. At each moment, the first threatens death, the second promises recovery.

§ Pale as Death

The expression "white as a sheet" makes more sense than its variation, "white as a ghost," for describing extreme paleness. The sight of the overlay of a white face by a white sheet, as still happens when a bedsheet is pulled over the face of someone who has just passed away, brings out its ghastly aptness. After such an encounter, a white sheet could never look the same again. One woman who witnessed the passing of her mother replaced all the tablecloths in her house. Being a waitress, however, she is reminded of death on the job. Is this how death haunts us, and why so many ghosts appear clad in sheets?

§ Moored

The umbilical cord is exactly the length of the unconscious, which stretches back and down through the mother, through the mother's mother, and so on, to the matrix of motherhood. Neither yanking on nor cutting it—aggravating and symbolic actions—will suffice to free us from what ties us down for life.

⸙ Angel of Death

Recollection of an encounter ten winters ago, on a bus ride to a rundown area of the city: sitting across from me was a man in his mid-thirties wearing a cap with a skull-and-bones pinned to the front, in the best Nazi style. The articles looked original and the thought—*I am sitting directly across from an original* Panzer *side cap with a Totenkopf pin, as worn by the panzer division of the SS from the 1930s until the end of the war*—sent my mind reeling. I stared at the cap, then at the extraordinary face of the man flaunting it, then at the rest of his getup, and found that it was just so and of a piece: a faded quilted jacket with an old leather belt tightened around the waist, worn burlap trousers rolled up to display his polished old jackboots. I took in the entire package, noting the effort it took to achieve, now trying to make some sense of it: *Sitting across from me is a replica of a German off to the Eastern front to commit God knows what crimes. What is he doing here dressed like this?* Something in his demeanor convinced me he was no actor on his way to the set.

I continued to scrutinize him. He had ash-blond hair, pale blue eyes, a fair complexion, and disarmingly "Aryan" features. His face was freshly shaven, a ghost of razor burn adding to its rawness and manliness. He was handsome. I sought to make eye contact, but he stared off into space with an eerily absent expression. Blood rushed to my head more rapidly now. There must be a way, I thought, of getting amazement, antagonism, and indignation across the metre or so separating me from this *apathetic angel*, and get him to meet my combative and withering gaze. He stared on fixedly, yet his body was not what one might call soldier-rigid, suggesting he was beyond performance, felt himself authentic enough, secure in his identity, well-bonded with his "look," his period costume by now a second skin. Did the relative sartorial understatement—aside from the quietly baleful "death's head," he had on him no insignia, no armband, no obnoxious accessories—have to do with his affinity with Nazi soldiers rather than Nazi criminals? Or were withering social taboos all that held him back from donning the "real," all-out garb of an SS officer?

As the bus pulled into the station at the end of the line, I took a tactical position and, passing him, ran my shoulder into his—instantly realizing, however, that my puniness may have left the wrong impression (of an accident, not deliberate aggression). Fearing cowardice and loss of composure, with shame already coming on, I turned around to give him one final look with all the urgency I could muster. But his placid face, now turned to me, only confronted me with my own impotence in the face of the angels' ignorance and unfeeling when it comes to human affairs.

Some months later I saw the man again. He wore the same or very similar clothing and struck me afresh as quite beautiful and dignified. He was walking alone at a measured pace, smiling to himself, sunlight on his face, and stopped beside a small, towheaded boy lingering behind his mother. He must have noted the resemblance between himself and the kid, since he addressed him with obvious affection. Then he continued on his way. The boy looked on admiringly, brimming with pride, feeling lucky to have been the object of such attention and swooping guardianship. At that moment, the innocence of neither could be doubted, but they were innocent in very different ways.

§ *À la chienlit!*

As mortality goes the way of all flesh, the only death will be social, and nothing worse than it.

§ Pierre Tombale

"My life? *Laisse tomber*, drop it! Let it fall with the force of a gravestone."

§ The Origins of Work

The first self-assigned work, something that had to be done and planned (depending on its level of difficulty), was self-preservation or the preservation of dependents. Only once these tasks had been partially relieved by coordinated effort and planning could work become an *occupation*. A choice was made to specialize in a craft or trade or profession, the gains from which could be used to secure (other) wants and necessities. The occupation was practiced to the exclusion of most other communal labour (excepting harvest, war, response to acts of God), and, in the face of growing competition, the more single-mindedly, the better. And so we have arrived at a point in history where, society being ever more complex and populous, there is on the one hand considerable choice in occupations and, on the other, the freedom to create them, using one's ingenuity to discern or divine unmet needs and turn a profit—and to reinvent oneself should those needs decline.

This latter freedom is reflected on the level of sociolect in the silencing of that outmoded question "What do you do for a living?" by temporary and/or highly particular occupational designators (especially in administration and the service and creative industries) and by an additive approach, concealing a history of often precarious employment marketed as a roster of transferable and special skills, and suggesting ever new possibilities of employment (e.g., gopher-turned-lighting technician-photographer-filmmaker-author-curator-critic-...). In both cases—the ultra-specialized and the certified jack-of-all-trades—a simple answer to the question

"What do you do for a living?" is impossible, and if it does get asked, it is with, if not instant regret, then genuine interest in the addressee.

If such work is less satisfying than the work of our ancestors — the ur-work, so to speak — if, when we pause to reflect, it resembles play, this is because it is of radically lesser importance to anyone, including ourselves. The newfound feeling of weightlessness masks the fear of uselessness, which is revealed in the pursuit of celebrity. It is not vanity but anxiety that speaks, with vicious repetitiveness, through the perpetual insecurity of seekers of public attention. It is the sensation, existentially fatal, of a cork bobbing upon the fathomless waters of society, contributing nothing to its own support. The *freedom* of leisure and pleasure is predicated on the fact that we are no longer preserving life, and those whose job is still not so removed that they can claim to be really preserving it would find our work vacuous, unrewarding, and parasitic. We may find comfort in the thought of mere survival as a life not worth living (the unexamined life, the life of labour, bare life, etc.). Yet the undertow of such an ideology of free social existence continually recalls us to the standard of preservation, which started it all.

§ Apply Within

Competition for paid work divides society into those who "made it" and those who didn't, into winners and losers. The line between them is as objectively clear as it is distinct in the minds of individuals. Regardless on which side they find themselves, they accept the prevailing norm that, for virtually any job, *losers need not apply.*

§ Among the Living

To be fully among the living is to mourn from time to time. Tears and lamentation at the graveside are the groans of life magnified by the proximity to death's tranquility.* In grief at separation can be discerned a grievance against the length of a life — much too brief, long enough though it is to outlive many who make it meaningful for us. As long as death still remains, as Adorno and Horkheimer put it, continuous with life, loss will be mourned, and mourners accept that any posthumous remembrance of someone they have lost merely continues remembering them while they were still alive. By this it is clear that they have not progressed to equating death with nothingness (of which the instant forgetting of the dead, retained only as archival images and voices, would be an indubitable sign, and from which the horizon where death has ceased to exist can almost be glimpsed). Transition to posthumous care for the dead, whether in the form of remembrance or visits, actual or symbolic, to their actual or symbolic place of rest, is easier for those who had cared actively for the now departed; continuity of habit ensures the link between life, however weak, and death. As for the rest, assuming a new responsibility with an emphasis on loss, rather than on the lost one's archival preservation or retrieval, combines with effort to assert their own *aliveness* vis-à-vis the dead — an effort that, paradoxically, saps their élan vital. Once the dead are blamed for this loss in vitality, the mourner enters a period of self-mourning, for that part of themselves that has been sacrificed to the deceased and that death has already, in effect, taken from them. The self-mourner may well be reconciled to their own demise, though — as more and more is wrested from them through the exertions of a double mourning — it will still come as an unwelcome surprise.

---

* Cf. Adorno and Horkheimer, *Dialectic of Enlightenment*, 178–79 ("The Theory of Ghosts").

§ No Posthumous Reproach

A drama of regret and reproach is a drama of dying, whether or not a death actually follows. Bergman only gives us the latter once the former has been exhausted, culminating in the impossible whispered cry of a deceased woman to her nurse that reflects the deepest hopes and fears of her two surviving sisters: "I'm dead, you see. The trouble is I can't get to sleep. I can't leave you all."[*] Her lifeless face is the true face of the philosopher, and her late and egoistical cry—in which death's sense of "the possibility of impossibility" coincides with that of "the impossibility of possibility"[†]—becomes the clearest statement of the Heideggerian-Lévinasian ethic: the ego never *is*, the face of the other is only seen in death, making of reproachful life a signal failure to hold on to either.

§ Wound Man

A sixteenth-century book of woodcut prints, *Feldtbuch der Wundartzney* (*Wound-Doctor's Field-Book*), a manual on military surgery, left us perhaps the most evocative because incredibly compact depiction of the physical traumas that to this day can accidentally assail our bodies. The Wound-Man, a human pin-cushion pierced by knives, arrows, spears and swords on every side, which, implausibly multiplied, lodged and suspended, appear as instruments not of war but of torture, hurts externally as much as the Man of Sorrows, who took upon himself the sins of the world, suffers internally.

---

[*] *Viskningar och rop* (*Cries and Whispers*), directed by Ingmar Bergman (1972; New York City, NY: The Criterion Collection, 2001), DVD.

[†] Emmanuel Lévinas, *Time and the Other*, trans. Richard A. Cohen (Pittsburgh, PA: Duquesne University Press, 1987), 70 n43. According to Lévinas, who disagrees here with Jean Wahl, Heidegger held the former view.

⸹ The Jargon of Inauthenticity

> authentic: *from Hellenistic Greek* authentikós (αὐθεντικός), *"warranted, original, authoritative," from* authentia (αὐθεντία), *"authority," from ancient Greek* authentēs (αὐθέντης), *"perpetrator, one who does things himself"*

> authenticity: *a mode of existence which has its basis in self-awareness, critical reflection on one's goals and values, and responsibility for one's own actions; condition of being true to oneself* (OED)

A   Authenticity is never direct, never primary. Its name is a pointer, a signpost, and its meaning lies not down the road, but round the bend, over the river, and through the woods. Being true to oneself requires endless detours.

B   You mean to say that it is not readily accessible, not within easy reach? That the direct route in front of us is a test—a shortcut not to authenticity, but to being disqualified as inauthentic?

A   Authenticity requires that we "stray" from established paths, even if we ultimately end up in the same place we would have had we done nothing but follow them. And even though authenticity cannot actually be *achieved*, even indirectly, we do get "closer" to it. The meaningfulness of "being authentic" depends on its elusiveness and even loss. Indirection in approaching authenticity mirrors the convoluted route along which authenticity was gradually lost.

B   Perhaps it was never lost and for that reason cannot be found again. Perhaps it will not have been found even when the concept of "being authentic" is lost. This loss will mean neither that it has become redundant because we have become authentic nor that we have passed some point of no return to authenticity. Its forgetting could only *mean* anything if the concept itself was not forgotten...

A We will be done with authenticity only by its meaningless forgetting — or by replacing it with the jargon of *inauthenticity*. Then we can look forward to clarity about authenticity, since the *positive* term, which inauthenticity would have become, is always the one plagued by vagueness — more stake claims to its definition! Beside God, the Devil will always be a simple cartoon.

§ Wild Oats

How can you expect me to give our friendship a chance when you could not give our romance a chance, quick to judge me unsuitable as a partner in the most unpropitious circumstances during our time together? Do you expect me to go *against* my feelings and hope they will follow? You seem adamant that there exists a fluid boundary between friendship and love, at least in some relationships (like ours). I share your view. Friendship and love are not incompatible, and in some cases (like ours) become entwined from the start. So to now separate them like wheat from chaff would be an unnatural procedure that does violence to the plant to make it edible and yielding. The "chaff" would always grow back around the grain once the seeds are sown.

In *wild* cereal — cereal not so domesticated that it cannot regenerate itself without cultivation — the distinction between chaff and wheat does not apply. The toil of sowing, reaping, and threshing is not needed for it to grow.

§ *Todesliebe*

When I die, I am sure to be remembered fondly by those few whose thoughts would alight on me from time to time. They might think I was quite the piece of work; a real loose cannon; kind; regret never having been my friend; feel privileged to have known me; miss my sense of humour; my old soul — no wonder I died so young! But fond memories are not love.

How many of us who want love badly, and get it not, go early into death to find it? Even if I died a tragic death, others' love for me, though stronger, would not be of the kind I had wished to inspire. It would be love for a memory, a love for what they have made of me — a description to which I wouldn't answer — a love I could not even reciprocate; deep down, a self-love. The love of those who failed to love me while I could still wriggle out of their grip, of those who would claim to have loved me despite my faults and the slights I caused them — unconditionally — now that I was without condition. And such revisionist tarrying, as long as I live, I cannot allow. I cling to life as long as I can to keep such love at bay.

But they assure me: *You have nothing to worry about. Why fret over how we'll treat you after you drop dead? Why meddle with our work? Embalming in memory is hard as it is.* But I object to this as well. Do you mean, I say, that you would not consider my present worries when preserving me? I hope that by telling you now I can prevent some blatant misuses of my posthumous person. But they frown on my micromanagerial tendencies: *Planning your own funeral, leaving disposal instructions — isn't that enough?* Of all my post-obit affairs, I reply, those are the least important! They are over and done with before you know it, everyone moves on from mourning in a matter of days. But that still leaves years for exhuming and reburying me through reminiscence. Have you no consideration for how I want to be remembered, let alone loved? Your indifference and barely contained laughter suggest you do not. And that suggests in turn that you love me not. In that case, I am a fool to worry so much. If I have not inspired your love when still alive, I am certain not to do so after I am gone. All I can hope for is to *grow on you*. And that, I must say — having heard you on love — is now a much better proposition.

§ Between Stiff and Statue

Physical love is the desire to be as near as possible to both aspects of the beloved body at once: to touch it at its weakest, most emaciated, most ruined by disease or age and threatening to crumble into dust and, at the same time, to be embraced by the body triumphant over time, fleshly and muscular, firm as veined marble or alabaster, preserved for eternity, as in an hourglass laid on its side.

§ Love & Love-Sickness

B   Melancholy is no match for love when the latter is already burning.

A   Love that burns is no match for melancholy.
Love-sickness does not catch. It seizes.

§ *Incipit vita nova*

The other, perverse side of the triumphant fatalism of *Liebestod*, which befalls star-crossed mortals in love who cannot live without each other, is the fatal triumphalism of love and survival available to vampire lovers. With every shared victim, death is averted and new life begins for the bloodsucking couple, whose love, so ancient, must be amoral and heartless to last as it does, avoiding the fate of Dante and Beatrice, whose new life began only once, before it ended. Vampiric suicide, though flirted with, is not an option; they are fated to kill to live on. Their need for a good day's rest ("We don't want to be up all day"*) is the sensible side of passion for these immortal lovers, whom some have dared to call "Adam" and "Eve." Living from victim to victim, time and again they come close to death in a world that denies their very existence. And each time they are relieved to see the other alive. For that reason alone, they remain *more* alive than mere "zombies," which is to say — on an average bad day — than us.

---

* *Only Lovers Left Alive*, directed by Jim Jarmusch (Culver City, CA: Sony Pictures Home Entertainment, 2013), DVD.

⸹ Not a Peep from You

Some years back, not too long ago, a young British singer from a good family found herself pursued by a lovesick young Englishman. The chap had gone to great lengths to woo her (a 30-foot ash tree planted on her lawn for Valentine's Day being only the most astonishing of his many overtures). Jude's love, which Rebecca did not return, was focused on an attribute around which a love story could nowadays take shape only in a folk tale or *opéra bouffe* — for, if one takes tabloid reports at face value (as one must to "get" British society), it was a love of a bass voice for a soprano. That so sublime a love can escape ridicule by the crudest, most vulgar organs of public opinion is a sign that love still has deep, legitimizing roots in male romantic obsession, making instantly relatable and sympathetic what, when performed by a female, is — no two ways about it — morbid. The double standard for stalking, that quintessentially modern offence and signal of uncoupling male obsession from love, points however to a truth: the party who has our sympathy (the smitten man) is the true victim, a victim not of love but of the general decline of masculinity and the rise of female power. It is a fact belied — though not for much longer — by two canards of heterosexual rape culture, where masculinity finds refuge in physical power: (1) that there is no such thing as rape (all "victims" "ask" to be "raped") and (2) that female-on-male rape does not exist (men are "made to penetrate"). The voice of the rapist does not sing of love.

§ Sex & Democracy

Love has reaped untold benefits in mature democratic societies. The institutionalization of the principles of liberty and equality includes, in its advanced form, both equality between bodies and the right to use one's carcass as one pleases. The rules—and the rule—have shifted from the tired performances of masculinity as dominant and femininity as submissive to a balanced "contact of two epidermes"—a fine clinical phrase from eighteenth-century moralist extraordinaire Chamfort, contemporary of the Marquis de Sade, whose naturalist vision of a *respublica sexualis* is still too radical for our taste. The empire of sex has since been leveled out through a fair exchange of blows and bodily fluids, enshrined in sanitary conventions. Clean, safe fun; no one must get hurt. Conditions of physical engagement have also grown stricter: the self-control that comes with the territory of sexual play requires that the oversexed not tax their partners but instead seek outlets in pornography and masturbation—a now-widespread view inconceivable until very recently. And, lest we forget, the democratization of sex does not stop at workplace codes of conduct or even the bedroom, where it has made decisive inroads. So much so that even our fantasies sport sexy "model citizen" undies.

§ Making Conversation

Entrepreneurs like Esther Perel who have made a name for themselves speaking publically about sexuality, particularly in couples therapy, know. They know that the future of education, like many another capitalist enterprise — even that which, like psychoanalysis, limited to one-on-one interaction, does not always depend on revenue — lies in facilitating content-production instead of providing it oneself. The structure of investment, labour, and the creation of surplus value holds across the board, even if substance, inputs and outcomes differ in each particular case — even if labour and profit are distributed evenly and equally reinvested. (Non-starters and ephemeral undertakings are such precisely because they do not adopt this mode of organization, whose familiarity attracts interest and capital.) The surplus value of Esther Perel is not just the money she receives, but the work her audiences do to satisfy her and live up to her standards. The payoff for them is, in this case, not a credit or diploma, but the obvious satisfaction of having addressed the least productive aspect of their life — sexual activity — in a *productive* manner.

⁋ Romeos

> *And it should be known that correctly there are three titles for the people who go in the service of the Almighty: they are called* palmers *if they go overseas, since they often bring back palm leaves: they are called* pilgrims *if they go to the shrine of Saint James in Galicia, since the sepulchre of Saint James was further away from his country than any other apostle: they are called* romeos *if they go to Rome...*
> —Dante[*]

Love, for so long joined to faith and divorced from carnal pleasure, seemed fated to tip over into the secular and sexual. It is the distinction of Rome to have been both Babylon and home to God's infallible interpreters.

⁋ Scale Models

There is nothing to open a droopy critical eye to the vices and follies of mankind like a change of scale. We tend to flatter ourselves too much in synthetic miniatures of ourselves: our flaws, small to begin with, become invisible, and all that's left are our virtues — visible because we look for them, ineffective because so minuscule.

In children, however, our faults stand out like nowhere else. Orwell all but discovered this in *Animal Farm*. Vivian Maier, the street photographer, snapped it in the street. Two boys under ten doing business together on a sidewalk: one sitting forward in a chair, freckled, his left foot up, the other, shoe-black, kneeling just in front of him.

---

[*] Dante Alighieri, *The New Life* (*La Vita Nuova*), trans. A.S. Kline (Poetry in Translation, 2014), letter 40, p. 98–99.

⁋ To Scale

> *The trick is to scale these things back up to the dimensions of childhood.*
> —Kraus[*]

In the painting of Prince Felipe Prospero by court painter Diego Velázquez (1659) we see one of those portraits of small children so uncommon before 1750 once we exclude the infant held for centuries in a mother's arms, identityless putti, and some comely adolescents. Among this relatively small number of canvasses one would find, as well, Lucas Cranach the Elder's young prince and princess of Saxony (1510s), *Henry II as a Child* (c. 1523) by Jean Clouet, Hans Holbein the Younger's Prince Edward (c. 1538), the sixteenth-century renditions of the Duke of Savoy's children by Jan Kraeck (some even before they could stand), and Bronzino's gallery of the young Medicis, the most memorable being the chubby two-year-old from about 1545.

Princes are no ordinary tots; secular images of little ones neither high-born nor of great fame (Mozart's fate) are certainly much rarer. Children crop up in family portraits (Holbein's family, from c. 1528, or Domenico Ghirlandaio's *Portrait of Francesco Sassetti and His Son*, drawn in profile c. 1488). They might comprise elements of allegory and parable (*Old Man with a Young Child*, by the same). They often enlivened Northern European Baroque genre painting, from outdoor scenes (as in the *Winter Landscape* by Avercamp) to domestic and semi-domestic ones (Pieter Brueghel the Elder, Jan Steen, and Pieter de Hooch). Only occasionally, however, did undistinguished children supply the main focus of a composition. This was the case in Frans Hals's *Catharina Hooft with Her Nurse*, in Gabriel Metsu's *The Sick Child*, Nicolaes Maes's *Little Girl Rocking a Cradle*, Gerard ter Borch's *Boy Defleaing His Dog*, Judith Leyster's *Boy Playing a Flute*, Gerbrand van

---

[*] Karl Kraus, *Dicta and Contradicta*, trans. Jonathan McVity (Champaign, IL: University of Illinois Press, 2001), 126.

der Eeckhout's *Children of Altetus Tolling*, Rubens's *Child with a Bird*, or Rembrandt's son Titus reading — all of them from the seventeenth century.

Indeed, as this list suggests, early modern portraits and treatments of children in their own right are largely limited to the Netherlands, appearing with various props (birds, dogs, goats, sheep, lambs, fruit, flowers, toys, instruments), or as types (as shepherds, peasants, vendors), or in didactic contexts (as in de Hooch's *Two Women Teaching a Child to Walk*, Hals's *Boy Reading*, Jacob van Oost's reading and painting lessons), sometimes bringing to life a moral lesson (as in Leyster's *Boy and Girl with a Cat and an Eel*, c. 1635, Steen's *Baptism*, which shows the bad drinking habits of adults rubbing off on the young, and Caspar Netscher's *Lady Teaching a Child to Read, and a Child Playing with a Dog* from c. 1670). The following must therefore be counted among the most notable of what are relative exceptions: Caroto's *Young Boy Holding a Child's Drawing* (c. 1515); the anonymous *The Girl with the Dead Bird* from the same period; Bronzino's portraits of a young man and woman with a prayer book from the mid-seventeenth century; *Four Portraits of the Young Sons of Sir John Ffolliott* (English School, c. 1610); Hals's smiling *Three Children with a Goat Cart* and other nameless happy children (c. 1620); Cornelis de Vos's own progeny (1621–22); De Hooch's *Little Golf Players* (c. 1660); Gilbert Jackson's *Daughter of Florence Poulett and Thomas Smyth of Ashton Court with Her Black Page* (c. 1640); Govert Flink's *Girl by a High Chair* and Verspronck's solemn *Girl in Blue* (1640–41); Ter Borch's much stiffer *Portrait of Helena van der Schalcke* (c. 1648); Caesar van Everdingen's *Two-Year-Old Boy with an Apple and a Finch* (1664); and, in the category of court freaks, Velázquez's *Francisco Lezcano, "The Boy from Vallecas"* (c. 1640) and Miranda's life-size portraits of the fat girl *"La Monstrua,"* naked and dressed (1680). In the eighteenth century the child as subject and motif becomes more frequent. Noteworthy here are Chardin's *The Draughtsman*, *Soap Bubbles* and *The Card Castle* (from the 1730s) with a boy at play, and Watteau's *The Dance (Iris)* (c. 1719), not to mention the 1742 *Graham Children* by Hogarth. After 1750, however, portraits of children start appearing everywhere, contemporary with the invention of childhood. Painters, it seems, could no longer get enough of them. And the more they were painted, the cuter they got.

Since the political power claimed on behalf of infant princes is never scaled down, the surroundings in which they are depicted, if they include objects and furniture, must be instead. In all but such political portraits and the much later children's room scenes (1750 on), interiors — if rendered at all — are scaled for grown-ups, not for the children commanding our attention. Aurélio de Figueiredo's *Menina ao piano* (1892) shows an ordinary little girl standing at a piano, alone in a well-appointed playroom, where admittedly the closer of two armchairs are child-sized, yet the instrument and the more distant pieces are larger than would be ones consistently proportioned. The background, in other words, belongs to adults, who remain out of sight but who are thereby shown to be in command.

If in the *Menina* proportions are ultimately kept, and children's furniture is distinguishable from that of adults, in a later canvas simply called *Interior with Boy Playing*, in which a little boy lies playing with wooden blocks on a small carpet, the room, its ceiling so high it cannot be seen, becomes *expressive* — its dimensions scaled to the *inner* world of a child. The world of adults looms large indeed, as it did for all of us (an impression that stepping into a forgotten interior we once inhabited as a child brings back in an instant). Virtually all the objects in the painting, among which no other toys can be seen, appear outsize, dwarfing the solitary boy. The deliberate nature of this characterization cannot be doubted. The boy's absorption in the act of playing and imagining (suggested by the glimpse behind the drape-accented doorway of a leopard skin upon a railing in strong sun) is so great that even this most imposing reality falls away in the end. As such, the exaggerated disproportion between the room and the child will strike only those viewers without access to that other interior, existing only between the ears of a child, where the furniture, presumably, is always to scale.

⌇ Unrecognized

"It takes genius to know genius."

⌇ The Takeaway Point

If we, whether young or old, ultimately hold in greater admiration men in their thirties for having been thoughtful enough to produce works worth reading for the rest of our lives, works of philosophy, systematic or not, that are "to live by," "to think with," passionate and full of unsettled questions, this is not just because they have drawn up a scheme for experience and figured out a plan for themselves and the rest of us while they still had time to implement it, but surely also and more because *at their age* we could not have come up with anything remotely comparable, or had enough patient interest even to undertake projects of such proportion.

As long as we persist in thinking them geniuses and freaks, rather than plain extraordinary, we cannot hope for the real takeaway point: that those we admire for doing great things are continually getting older, that we are constantly raising the age at which such admiration is warranted.

From this we will still need to draw our own conclusions. (These may have more to do with lowering the bar than with raising longevity…)

⌇ Reminder: Originals

It takes all kinds. Including ones-of-a-kind.

§ Confession of a Knife-Swallower

All my life I have risked my life for entertainment. But one can get used even to swallowing swords. The thrill I love is gone. I frequently wonder what will in fact kill me. Although it will probably be something predictable, some convergence of illness and injury, and I will go in relative peace, numbed by morphine and visions of the hereafter, I like to think of a cut—a little paper cut, no more—undoing me with unspeakable agony. Now that would be a surprise!

§ You Can Take the Clown out of the Circus, but You Can't Take the Circus out of the Clown

Before we know it, we have grown out of our childhood delight at clowns, whose bulbous noses, floppy shoes and bulging bums vanish as soon as we convince ourselves that we have glimpsed the melancholy beneath the face-paint. We might be heard making such comments as: *Imagine you had to dress up that way day after day, whether you felt like it or not... Whoever claims to keep their dignity and derive joy from such work is obviously deceiving themselves.* Even "melancholy" is fancy dress for "sorrow and humiliation"; it trivializes the suffering that must have driven the poor man or woman to take up clowning. In this way our mature, uncanny reaction to clowns, never far behind the chuckle put on for our little charges, always betrays a fear of insignificance. We catch sight of it in the guileless double face of the clown, and pin it to his chest like a flower squirting something black, while it is our heart that had sprung the leak. If nothing else, this proves that in the most rustic and unrefined play-acting there is something for all temperaments and ages.

⸮ Cannibal on the Make

The great Eugène François Vidocq started out as a petty criminal and entertainer playing a South Sea cannibal in a circus. The job required him to eat raw meat, which for a Frenchman poses no problem at all. But Vidocq refused to devour the live rooster, a show-stopping act in any age. After his great "turnaround," away from misconduct and his own death on an installment plan, he developed a forensic interest in dead bodies, which again helped him survive, this time as a criminalist.

After such a school, who wouldn't become a *real* cannibal for a season, given the chance—if only to prove (by not surviving) that one wasn't cut out for it, or, on the contrary, that it was *no big deal*? For as long as we eventually suffer our victims' fate, do we not settle our accounts?

⸮ Soylent Green

Certain taboos are tokens only of luxury. Maybe, *nomen omen*, Bacon (the painter) was disposed to reflect on this: "If I go into a butcher shop I always think it's surprising that I wasn't there instead of the animal."* As we continue to search for the ultimate form of renewability, we will see that Bacon "had a point" and tighten our dietary restrictions.

---

* Quoted in David Sylvester, *Interviews with Francis Bacon* (London: Thames & Hudson, 1980), 46.

§ Cities of God

Paris, où il faut vivre en se crevant

(Paris, where you can only live by working yourself to death)
    —Vincent van Gogh to his brother, 1888[*]

The modern worldly cosmopolis as the city of God? Is it not heavenly and holy enough? Would not many mortals sacrifice their health, pleasure, solitude, and peace of mind to live in it? Here the lonely will find their companion, the moribund will be healed, the wretched attended to, the bored given purpose, the active, consequence, and the corrupt, close watch. And the watchers in turn will be watched night and day.

§ Sand-Glass

Soft-core fiction, however silly or perverted, has many defenders, they in turn are belittled by fans of hardcore pornography, these in turn buried by viewers of torture-porn and snuff, and so on all the way down. At the very bottom sits a man reading a newspaper, his window on the real world. It is to him that all of this can ultimately be traced; with him the "pyramid" of sexual tastes is turned over again like an hour-glass—next time around, his newspaper folded, he will come out on top.

As long as the sand keeps flowing, it will always be so: the informed citizen's mind now filthy, now in impeccable control.

---

[*] Vincent van Gogh to Theo van Gogh, July 15, 1888, accessed Mar. 12, 2015, http://vangoghletters.org/vg/letters/let642/letter.html.

§ The Man in the Street

The disenchantment of "the average man" has its reverse and probable cause in the earlier wonder for what the French call *l'homme de la rue*: the "common" man with a secret, private, or previous life, one you would never suspect. This man was brought to light by numerous nineteenth- and twentieth-century novelists, most successfully Eugène Sue, Victor Hugo, Adalbert Stifter, and Ralph Ellison. He was there in the paintings of Paul Delvaux, and can still be seen from time to time in movie houses. But the narrowing band of character and activity we today find remarkable is telltale of our stunted fascination and dwindling curiosity. The remarkable life, which would justify our interest, is already public, illuminated, its success measured in fame. It need not be discovered by writers and filmmakers; like a plant, it will find the limelight itself, freeing us from the work of investigation for which we anyway have no time. Eccentricity, formerly registered as marked difference of behaviour, has become both rarer and more common: rarer because of its professional marginalization, urban conformity and rural invisibility, yet more common because so much of what is outside the average, the social norm, belongs in one broad category, where the banal, the undesirable and the intolerable are lumped together. Searching for Sugar Man and finding Rodriguez, stumbling on a private archive and finding Vivian Maier are only recent examples of a longer trend in which a small number of amateurs are motivated to sift through this human refuse in search of something precious. They are of course portrayed as great exceptions, gone unnoticed owing more to respect for privacy—the decency of looking away has replaced binocular snooping—than to wall-to-wall apathy—the assumption that your neighbours are hardly less insipid than yourself (otherwise you would have heard of them).

Perhaps it is now only creative minds that are driven to seek out the unusual as material for reinvention, and capable of presenting it in the form of a spectacle for passive consumption. Could it really be that the public was once more accepting of the diversity in its midst, when large cities absorbed large numbers of exotic, provincial, or shady extraction without institutions to regulate and assimilate them? Perhaps what to us are everyday encounters with strangers had come with the thrill of adventure (a *dépaysement* avant la lettre) that we now look for in surrogates—books and films, or online chatrooms. Perhaps the stranger still held in his mind knowledge of the world that could not otherwise be obtained. And if not knowledge, then entertainment, as when individuals on the surface quite unappealing, unrelatable, *antipathique*, had a story to tell, fascinating and unheard-of experiences. One imagines that the different walks of life of those brought together by modernity were a source of amusement and release from tedium—that the man-in-the-street was, in a word, a mystery worth probing.

Though the dwellers of today's metropolis still come from elsewhere, we are considerably less interested. As earlier with the individual's romanticization—an aesthetic injection of mystery into misery, poverty and crime—the cause must be sought in mass media, which have long worked round the clock to finally satisfy our curiosity about one another, in the end killing the "common man" as enigma. The threshold between the public and the private is frequently nothing more than disgust: "Too much information!" In principle, however, comfort with other lives has gone up dramatically with the freedom of anonymous online socializing. Everything is fair game for sharing and discussion among virtual strangers. In effect, we have unprecedented access and insight into those around us, who turn out to be too much like us, and whose lives therefore are taken to be every bit as uneventful, predictable, not to say bland—something we would sooner avoid than take a keen interest in. The deep roots of being down on others are in dissatisfaction with ourselves when our lack of originality is revealed. A sense of homogeneity, the price for fitting in well enough to pass scrutiny, is especially vivid in global cities, where the pursuit of distinction is most intense. These cities continue to lure us with the promise of a more exciting, more stylish life.

Whatever originality and aura of mystery accompanying the newcomer to even the lowest social stratum that cannot be monetized are soon stripped away by the ruthlessness of urban living. The seemingly endless options for urban self-fulfillment come down to just two: buying into a (city or neighbourhood) brand, or picking up a lifestyle package (at a discount) during a construction boom. Can the dream of individualism be taken for real when, at every turn, we confront our own life in multiple copies, down to the smallest detail? Can the mysteries of *l'homme de la rue* ever rival our common regret, resentment, and smothering sense of mediocrity?

⌥ Thoroughly Unthorough

We aren't any more careless about details. The devil may be in them now, but before it was God: they were His hiding place, so we assumed they were well taken care of.

⌥ Rise to the Occasion

Sometimes *stooping* is what's required for an occasion. After all, things *fall* together to create one; an *occasion*, word-historically, is a "falling together" of circumstances.

The set phrase, "rise to the occasion," is one of those invisible contradictions devised by those who like to take credit for merely rising.

Exposed, they protest: Ah, but we are rising into place.

§ Comedown

We assume that the road of Ought, of duty and obligation, righteous and supercilious, is upward, while that of Is, of reality, base and ignoble, points down. That is uncontroversial. We therefore further assume that once we have scrambled to a higher position, everyone *should look up to us* and strive to follow us there, even if they will likely fail and sometimes even tumble below where they began. And those "beneath" us in this way (unless they are irredeemable scoundrels) generally concur.

It may be very difficult to rise, but *to descend* — to step down confidently without falling — is immeasurably harder on the character. From the top, gained with difficulty, a great and swift plunge would, however unlikely, be easy. One could afford to drop a *bit* if necessary, but given the slipperiness of the slopes, falling by degrees would not be feasible. The only safe path downward is on foot, little by little. What makes this especially gruelling are the reminders of "No Return" along it. It is presumption alone that dictates that lowering oneself, even just to the general level, is easy if one leaves character out of it. It is not. It may be good for the soul to look at life from a lower altitude, but after one has been high up, the view is quite unbearable.

§ Iron-y

"Most of our iron is turned into fetters," and blacksmiths are "weighed down with the making of chains," Juvenal remarks in his *Satires*.* If we are to believe the archaeological record, since at least the Bronze Age a good deal of our strength and effort have been dedicated to shackling weakness, with the unintended consequence of toughening it up.

§ Choosing Gentleness

> *It is with lashes of the whip that one leads the cattle to pasture.*
> —Heraclitus†

A When there is no pasture, conscience asks us to hide the whip.

A′ It is with humane restraint that livestock is led to slaughter.

---

*   Juvenal, satire 3, in *Juvenal and Persius*, ed. and trans. Susanna Morton Braund, Loeb Classical Library 91 (Cambridge, MA: Harvard University Press, 2004), 193.
†   Heraclitus, *Fragments: The Collected Wisdom of Heraclitus*, trans. Brooks Haxton (New York: Viking, 2001), p. 35, sec. 55 (mod. trans.).

◊ The Sacred Heart of Convicts

If, rather than justice, the rationale of imprisonment remained to inspire inmates to repentance, penitentiaries would replace churches.

⸿ Misericords

misericord:

apartment or room in a monastery set apart for those monks permitted relaxation of the monastic rule
   a. relaxation of certain monastic rules for infirm or aged monks or nuns
   b. monastery where such relaxations can be enjoyed

also, subsellium: *small projection/ledge on the underside of a hinged seat in a choir stall, which, when the seat is lifted, gives support to the standing occupant. Also used attrib. to designate or denote the elaborate, often bawdy, carvings of scenes from secular or religious life with which medieval misericords were frequently decorated.*

medieval dagger, used for the coup de grâce *to a wounded foe* (OED, RHWUD)

A relaxation of rules is permitted to the rule-abiding at their discretion, as long they remain discreet about it, since to the uninitiated it looks no different than cheating.

  Choir stalls, where bums in seats meant bawdy thoughts, were one of several discreetly designated places within a medieval church poised to turn it inside out.

  Life wounds us mortally. Let's not discard too quickly the euthanasia of the mercy stroke.

⁂

V

⸂ Better than Nothing

We polish a rotten apple, burnish it to a perfect shine, and it's only as we bite into it, still salivating, that we realize this was only to fool ourselves when we had nothing better to eat.

⸂ Greek Gift

Some people pose as life-coaches who want to teach us to live to the fullest, in harmony with nature, at peace with ourselves; their intentions only clear up as we are giving up the ghost.

§ *Devotio moderna*

> *Borne down by the weight of wings.*
> —Róbert Gál[*]

Even without God, the solitary—the "monkish"—existence inadvertently assumes a ritualistic—a "pious"—character. The simpler the life, the more pronounced its religious features. We carry the world's expectations of us into our hermitage, priding ourselves on our private orderliness. As long as the mind does not deviate, we feel our days have been well-spent, and we have fulfilled our duty to the world: rising, the first meal, light or heavy, the first stimulant of the day. Morning ablutions, drying and dressing of the body. Choice of activity, planning out the rest of the day, exercise, a look at the budget, concluded with entertainment of some sort. We know it all well enough, take pleasure in this simple discipline, and yet when other things come to occupy our mind, these private rituals quickly lose their gravity and precision. It is still possible to be devout, as long as mind and body worship each other without interruption or intermediary.

§ Overripe

Doubt—worm in the fruit off the Tree of Knowledge.

---

[*] Róbert Gál, "Naked Thought: Aphorisms," *Numéro Cinq* 5, no. 7 (2014), http://numerocinqmagazine.com/2014/07/09/naked-thought-aphorisms-robert-gal-translated-from-slovak-by-david-short/.

§ *Hortus conclusus*

> hortus conclusus: *enclosed, inviolate garden, in reference to* The Song of Songs; *in spiritual and exegetical tradition, symbol of the soul, the Church, or the virginity of Mary* (OED)

I lack that *piety towards myself* that certain poets of the word (or of the heart only) have in spades (or cultivate religiously). In their veneration of their *sealed-up fountains*, of what they hold in, they are as monks whose pens have dried up. What gets creative juices flowing is also what keeps the nib wet. But their self-piety guards, with parcity, against blots and spills.

    The Muse, meanwhile, has given up on them. (Are you surprised she prefers action to love?) She hoped for prodigals who wonder, like Lewis's Ambrosio, "Should I not barter for a single embrace the reward of my sufferings for thirty years?"[*] and who answer at once, with one unwavering nod.

§ Bad Apples

Some poor souls cherish illusion so much they will overlook nature's decay. It may be decay is all too familiar — a condition in many ways not unlike their own. Some, less poor, are known to cherish rottenness instead, perhaps for its chastening effects, or, not infrequently, from a doleful, morbid disposition. But it is a rare bird who, like Schiller (author of apple-archer *William Tell*), discovers its salubrious influence, and can barely work without a rotting apple stuffed here and there.

---

[*] Matthew Gregory Lewis, *The Monk*, ed. D.L. Macdonald and Kathleen Scherf (Peterborough, ON: Broadview, 2004), 65.

§ Call of the Wild

Every now and then, surprise at the drawn-out howl issuing from one's body. How is it that something so purely physiological and localizable — not to say reduced to digestion, putrefaction, and the ceaseless fluid flow through veins and organs in varying states of decay — can associate itself in one's mind with the wilderness outside: a clap of thunder, moonlit crags, a snowy forest, setting for this lupine cry...? The call of the wild rises from deep within our bowels, somewhere along their dark corridors, whose fascination for us suddenly rivals that of owl burrows or fox tunnels.

§ Speak for Yourself!

No "individual death" is individual.

§ Falls the Shadow

Going through life aware of omnipresent death is like lying on a beach with one's eyes closed, and knowing one is still there only by the chill of a shadow and the sand in one's mouth.

§ Campanology

campanology: *the art or study of bell-ringing or -making*

in the nocturnal small hours we are nearest
—Cyril Connolly, *The Unquiet Grave**

The hourly nocturnal tolling of a solitary bell outside a hotel window will, unless you somehow manage to sleep through it, stir up vivid associations. For the freedom from visual sensation gives priority to hearing and feeling, and expands the mnemonic field, allowing the unfamiliar sound to bathe us in past occasions in which it was heard. The ringing bell rings a bell of bell-ringing. The most immediate and frequent memories, to which the darkness and position of the sleeper no doubt contribute, are of funerals. If the hotel is in the country, and the window open so that the summer air fills the room, and the bed happens to be no wider than a casket, and the sheets sufficiently lustrous or cold — and one is tired to boot, making the necessary rest much sweeter — then the association of blissful repose with eternal sleep cannot really be avoided. And as we slide down thoughts like these, past the threshold of consciousness, deeper and deeper without quite making it to sleep, kept awake just a little by each knell, yet less and less with each as we begin ourselves to resonate, we have as well the vague sensation of fading in stages, of peaceful sliding into nothingness. Kant's "negative pleasure" captures well the bittersweet elation of this self-vigil. But perhaps there are many more who would find the ominous sound, combined with their recumbency, excruciating, and are already kept awake by fears of dying — lying long, too long, not altogether long for this world. Their fear makes of them early risers. To enjoy this time and concert, the church bell's

---

* Cyril Connolly, *The Unquiet Grave: A Word Cycle by Palinurus* (1941; n.p.: New York: Persea, 1981), 71. The full sentence reads: "We are farthest from the idea of death as in the nocturnal small hours we are nearest."

indifferent marking of the interval, the key of death needs first to be silenced.

But as the vain worry is put to rest, one side refuses to die. The thrill of this repose, the thrill of remaining in the darkness, turns the squeaking coffin back into a bed. The night becomes sleepless in a different light—as, pulled back from the edge of nothing, we are delivered into the arms of fantasy.

§ Death Being Our Final Act

Death is an act that must make up for the passivity of our birth.

∫ Somewhere

"*De mortuis nihil nisi bonum*, Do not speak ill of the dead"

"Death becomes her" (1---)

"Leaving me so soon?!" (16--)

"If I were to live again, I would live just as I lived" (15--)

"My work here is done" (17--)

"It's autumn, one almost believes in death" (1890)

"And just last month he was among the living..." (18--)

"I'm not as lively as I used to be" (2008)

"I'm not dead yet!" (2010)

"Dead serious, always — my epitaph" (2012)

Thus we prepare for going out as we could not for coming in.

§ "Universal Solvent"

The secret attraction of alchemical laboratories may well be that they combust, killing the alchemist.

§ Surprised by Death

There is a motif in European Baroque painting: the moment of death taking those visited by fortune by surprise. Its stock victims are the miser, the maiden, the lovers, the voluptuary. The pictures are for the most part didactic, expanding the *vanitas* genre to human figures. Unlike the medieval *ars moriendi*, illustrated literature on how to die a blessed death (a very different beast from today's death with dignity), they specialize in depicting unpreparedness for it.

This peculiar graphic convention declined as the individual ascended the ladder of human value; death's image as black-draped skeleton ultimately followed in its footsteps. Modern treatments humanized death, revising the crude symbolism of its personification (*La Mort et les jeunes filles* of 1872 by Puvis de Chavannes's shows a glimpse of a white-bearded reaper, and Edvard Munch eroticizes death in a 1894 lithograph, followed by Egon Schiele). Jean-François Millet's *Death and the Woodcutter* (1859) stands at the tail-end of an allegorical tradition that regarded death as the leveler of inequalities, and already speaks to the modern age, in which inequality cannot be masked any longer. Rather than beauty, love, or luxury, death in this picture puts an end to *work*. Clad in white this time, it takes the labourer away from his labours. It cuts short an activity that secures, perhaps barely, his humble livelihood. Rather than reminding us of our mortality, pointing out that death may come when we least expect it, or (in the case of misers) moralizing earthly excess, or posing simple-minded questions — *Which is better, labour or death?* — Millet's nineteenth-century *vanitas* suggests that dying is a part of nature, and no bringer of justice.

§ *Sainte Supplice*

"[T]ruth has a virtue," wrote Hervé Guibert, recording the truth about his own dying of AIDS.[*] It is to truth that his final days were consecrated. Truthfulness, truth-speaking, truth-telling, defies weakness in its defiance of mendacity, to others and to oneself. Truth is strength, courage, and it is justice. Once the shameful truth, the truth of wrong-thinking or wrong-doing, is uttered, it cannot be shamed back into silence. It speaks and punishes those who deny it, and makes the truth-teller virtuous (by virtue of the truth...). Nothing we can do or say will make the scandal of truth go away as long as it serves anyone as a weapon of offence and self-defence. So often, it is *for* and *by* truth that life is tortured, and to truth that it is sacrificed. *He died for the truth...Truth was his martyrdom...* And truth to yourself will be *yours*.

§ "The moral earth, too, is round!"[†]

Launch any wickedness far enough and it will drift towards solid moral ground or, cast upon the stormy seas of self-sacrifice, succeed in saving its soul. Sail for the lands of the good and the fierce winds will drive you to the shallows of bitterness. Each journey, it's said, expands our moral horizons, but there is no telling where we will end up in search of our route to spiritual India.

---

[*] Hervé Guibert, interview by Bernard Pivot, *Apostrophes*, Mar. 16, 1990.

[†] Nietzsche, *Gay Science*, p. 163, sec. 289 ("Get on the Ships!").

§ A Whole in a Mole

in response to:

> [*Cosmopolitanism should*] *refer to the* ethical *imperative of recognizing and promoting the equal moral worth of each and every human being, while at the same time being sensitive to the strong possibility that our efforts to do so will founder on, even reinforce, the world's inequalities. The solution to this paradox, which plagues even the best cosmopolitanisms, lies in the fact that it is nevertheless possible to discover particular cases where this ethical imperative is* denied *and to combat the false universals on which its denial is based.*
>
> —James D. Ingram, *Radical Cosmopolitics*[*]

Combatting the false universals, on this model, resembles a game of Whac-A-Mole, a type of arcade game based on *redemption*. "Redemption games," we read in Wikipedia, "are typically arcade *games of skill* that reward the player proportionally to their score in the game. The reward most often comes in the form of tickets, with more tickets being awarded for higher scores. These tickets can then be redeemed (hence the name) at a central location for prizes. The most inexpensive prizes (candy, small plastic or rubber toys) may only require a small number of tickets to acquire, while the most expensive ones (skateboards, low-end electronics) may require several thousand. In general, the amount of money spent to win enough tickets for a given prize will exceed the value of the prize itself."[†]

In other words, we redeem our skill and money—which would otherwise remain unused and be spent on needed things—in the forms of prizes. The game enacts the conversion. Perhaps the only redemption we can find is of this kind.

---

[*] James D. Ingram, *Radical Cosmopolitics: The Ethics and Politics of Democratic Universalism* (New York: Columbia University Press, 2013), 19.

[†] "Redemption game," in *Wikipedia*, last modified Feb. 6, 2015, http://en.wikipedia.org/wiki/Redemption_game.

§ *In saecula saeculorum*

Assuming that the universality of moral reason does not exist buried somewhere where we cannot see it, we must resign ourselves to never knowing if we could have achieved universality by cultural convergence rather than conquest.

§ *Sola*

> [T]he papists are making a tremendous fuss because the word sola (alone) is not in Paul's text, and this addition of mine to the words of God is not to be tolerated.
> —Martin Luther[*]

Translating the Word of God had caused Luther no small frustration. This was not only because the *propria verba* did not come to him (they did, as to his collaborators). Calling St. Paul to his defence was not much help where a word (however implicit) had been added to the Pauline text.

Yet we should not infer from this special case, with the future of a church at stake in the choice and arrangement of words, that translation is a thankless task. There was a time — the time of Luther — when only seminal texts were subject to translation. That kept the stakes rather high, though nowhere as high as around Scripture. And it was recognized that the addition of a single word, *alone*, which, as explained in Luther's open letter, was stylistically necessary to be intelligible to his intended audience of (Latin) illiterates and speakers of German, would have far-reaching implications for religious observance — that indeed a new faith hung on *this sole word*, its ground and fulfillment.

---

[*] Martin Luther, "Letter on Translating: An Open Letter" (1530), in *Selected Writings of Martin Luther*, vol. 4, *1529–1546*, ed. Theodore G. Tappert, trans. Charles M. Jacobs and Theodore G. Tappert (Minneapolis: Fortress, 2007), 174.

⸘ Skill Rewarded

> *There's a scene in* The East *... in which the young corporate spy played by Brit Marling sits among half a dozen hippies at a rustic dinner table, each of them stiff-backed in a straitjacket. Bowls of what appears to be chunky tomato soup rest in front of the diners, who are members of an anarchist collective. A big brown spoon protrudes from each bowl. Marling's Sarah Moss, the newcomer, has been instructed to dig in first, but after clenching the spoon between her teeth and clumsily trying to convey the liquid to her mouth, she gives up in frustration, eventually succumbing to slurping, Fido-style. Her tablemates, a motley crew of twenty-somethings in facial hair and flannel, bend toward their own bowls and begin to silently clench their mouths around their spoons, skillfully filling them with soup and lifting them to the mouths of the individuals seated next to them.**

In a certain old tale it is given that dining in hell leads not to satiety but to greater hunger, as the sinful diners, given only unwieldy long spoons, know not how to help themselves or one another. But the difference between selfishness and selflessness has evidently blurred in modern times; even the eternally damned could eventually figure out that, with such poor utensils, the best way to help themselves is by helping others.

In such circumstances, a new physical constraint had to be introduced to tell the infernal and the celestial realms apart. Why else replace the long spoon with a regular one and a straitjacket, as implements in a morality test? The fool's garment binding each diner adds a physical challenge and holds greater potential for humiliation. To pass for good in this version of heaven/hell, one must figure out not just the benefit of helping one's neighbour, but also, more crucially, how to use one's mouth to spoon-feed.

---

* Jocelyn C. Zuckerman, review, "*The East* Explores the Ethics of Environmental Anarchy," Onearth, May 31, 2013, http://archive.onearth.org/article/the-east-movie-review.

§ Blunt Euphemism

Eat as well as you can before you must "give up your spoon"—old German idiom.

§ At the Limit: A Medley

τῶι οὖν τόξωι ὄνομα βίος, ἔργον δὲ θάνατος.

(The living, when the dead wood of the bow springs back to life, must die.)

(The name of the bow [βιός] is life [βίος]; its work is death.)
    —Heraclitus[*]

Bios meant both "life" and "bow," with the very small difference that in *life* the accent fell on the first syllable, in *bow*, on the second.

"There he stood like an Apollo, with imperishable youth of soul, although old in body," remarked the young Eckermann in 1825 on seeing Goethe poised with bow and arrow.[†] With the release of the string, activity passes to the arrow.

In 2012, at the London Olympics, a legally blind archer set a new individual world record. His sense of the target could only be very approximate (a blob of yellow 70 metres away), but his aim was something else. No matter how blind, *bios* reaches its target exactly.

---

[*] Heraclitus, *Fragments*, sec. 66; 2nd trans. Charles H. Kahn.
[†] Goethe, *Conversations with Eckermann*, 112.

Our life has no end in just the way in which our visual field has no limits.
   —Wittgenstein[*]

For each, the limit is in how far one sees. The ends of life—there is more than one!—lie at the limit of inner sight and imagination, which follow the arrow on its trajectory. If it is shot in the dark, its limit is everywhere. Once it is released, and flies off course, it cannot be set straight. The end of any life is barely seen coming. Whether the target is or isn't met, it is met unseen.

It is with the art of dying as with marksmanship, the art of indirection: to hit a target, one must aim slightly above it. All arts are a form of target practice, and genius in any of them is a direct hit. "The greatest fault of a penetrating mind is not to hit the mark but to go beyond it," wrote the great moralist La Rochefoucauld.[†]

Losing sight of the bull's-eye can mean one of two things: the first is artlessness, the second, death.

§ A Fate Worse than Fate

Fate has long been the stuff and substance of tragedy, signifying doom and death. But is its opposite, *fatelessness*, any less appalling?

---

[*] Ludwig Wittgenstein, *Tractatus Logico-Philosophicus*, trans. D.F. Pears and B.F. McGuinness (1921; London: Routledge, 2001), p. 87, sec. 6.4311.

[†] La Rochefoucauld, sec. 377, in *Collection des classiques français*, vol. 2, *Prose* (Paris: Leroi & Féret, 1833), 1620

⸹ In the Oratory

Made my bed in a Gothic oratory, believing this to be decisive in escaping fate or at least my many bad habits. But before I knew what hit me I was attacked by said habits allegorically on every side. Door to window, floor to ceiling moved the symbol of my zodiac sign, vaguely menacing and cruciform. Black, in one case lame, attracted by sheets — the creeps it gave me made me nearly jump out of my skin. And thus the poor creature rendered me the very service I had hoped for, but did not receive, from the sanctuary: the sting of self-reckoning.

⸹ Taken for a Ride

At moments when you have turned your life into your beast to be broken in and ridden out on you can think yourself master of your fate.

⸹ *Laudator temporis acti*

The praisers of times past, the ones discontent with the present, preferring instead things as they used to be, as they know them to have been, as they recognized them to be only in their passing. No, not "the good old days," but the awful days when they were boys, vulnerable and terrified. When their lives had meaning, sharpened by danger, blows, and given the chase. To lose touch with such things, they say, is to lose appreciation for calm. They should know.

⌠ Wish Experience

> [A] *wish fulfilled is the crowning of experience. In folk symbolism, distance in space can take the place of distance in time; that is why the shooting star, which plunges into infinite space, has become the symbol of a fulfilled wish. The ivory ball that rolls into the next compartment, the next card that lies on top are the very antithesis of a falling star.*
> —Benjamin*

They told me about a rare experience that befell them, when lightning bolted into their house, flew across the room and, ricocheting off surfaces and splitting the stove, killed no one. At that time, wartime, it was likelier to have been a bullet; yet somehow up to that point they had been eerily spared all harassment, becoming careless with their luck. To be struck by lightning— It was a wish they did not know they had.

Sometimes a lightning bolt is needed to instill caution and fear for one's life among the lucky ones, when the greater danger meanwhile is from others.

⌠ Courage and Its Crop

A War is not all death. It does not make all level.

A' Its principle is inequality. Death is the perfect counterweight.

---

* Walter Benjamin, "On Some Motifs in Baudelaire," in *Selected Writings*, vol. 4, *1938–1940*, ed. Howard Eiland and Michael W. Jennings, trans. Edmund Jephcott (Cambridge, MA: Belknap, 2003), 331.

§ Save the Date

Some truths persist, others are of the moment and die with it. Those are the truths of fear, audacity, exuberance, fury, or ecstasy.

§ Pied Pipers

Need only to play very quietly.

§ Hitler Today

> *Books don't have to educate or turn people into better human beings—they can also just ask questions. If mine makes some readers realise that dictators aren't necessarily instantly recognisable as such, then I consider it a success.*
> —Timur Vermes, author of *Look Who's Back* (*Er ist wieder da*) (Germany, 2012)[*]

A Another picture of Hitler—as our contemporary—where one would least expect it—where he would be unrecognizable even to himself!

B But he would still be a vegetarian. Isn't it time he gave *carnivores* a bad name instead?

---

[*] Philip Oltermann, "Germany Asks: Is It O.K. to Laugh at Hitler?", *Guardian*, Mar. 23, 2014, http://www.theguardian.com/books/2014/mar/23/germany-finally-poke-fun-hitler-fuhrer.

⸹ The True Believer

in response to section two of Kafka's Züreau Aphorism §99:

> *There are some who assume that next to the great original deception, another, smaller deception was practiced specifically for them. It's as if, when a romantic comedy is performed on stage, the actress, in addition to the lying smile for her beloved, keeps a further, particularly cunning smile for a certain spectator in Row Z. That is going too far.*[*]

The paranoiac only sees truth in uncovered lies. That is what makes him the most zealous of believers.

⸹ Uncannied

Seeing one's old outfit on the back of another family's child, one is confronted with the strange, autonomous life of articles of clothing. Seeing one's jacket and slacks on the back of a scarecrow brings to mind the brevity of one's own. Perhaps this explains our gratitude to the wind for setting our tattered cuffs and sleeves adance. For what difference is there between our life and all this flailing and flapping?

---

[*] Franz Kafka, *The Züreau Aphorisms*, ed. Roberto Calasso, trans. Michael Hofmann (New York: Random House, 2011), 98.

§ Departures

We find magic and beauty in the idea that only farewells reveal to us the full intensity of mutual feeling. And that the parting glance thrown in haste or under duress is therefore most penetrating of all, searing forever in our memory not just a moment's appearance but the true face of those whom we are seeing perhaps for the last time.

We find the idea beautiful because we know reality to be different: those who depart from our life or mind, whether by choice or nature's whim, do not linger. The "dear departed"—we have no time to think of them, any more than we did when they were with us, are maybe even glad to be free of them, eager to forget them, along with mutual feelings and the truth revealed in our parting. And the sooner our life fills the emptiness their leaving created, the sooner we ourselves move on, the more it dawns on us that our own self is among those we have left behind, without realizing it at the time. It is the sense of these intimate leavings that gives the farewell its wistful sentimental charm.

§ Dead Heroes

One should not draw lines where death has already drawn the thickest one. It is not only our business but our duty to find out all that remains. How one sorts through and what one does with it is another matter: a matter of the kind of story (fact, legend, or myth) one wants to print. If newly discovered personal details have bearing on the "life" of our dead heroes—those especially of whom little is known except their heroic deeds and death—we ought to try to find as many such details as there is memory to yield. Sorting out the facts from rumours and fictions tests our deepest emotional and moral attachments. And who among historians would do away with imagination in their work (assuming it could be done)? Bare details alone would not get us far. Having heard survivors tell the stories of their lives, we must imagine what stories the dead would tell as nonsurvivors.

§ Heroes and Saints

We call *heroes* those who acted as we ourselves hope to act. Our *saints*, however, are both masters and martyrs of what we fear would corrupt us. Albert Einstein said admiringly of Marie Curie, who neither wooed fame nor threw a fit when it passed her by, that of "all celebrated beings, [she was] the one whom fame has not corrupted"* — clearly implying he could not say the same of himself.

---

* Quoted in "Marie Curie and a Century of Radiation," *New York Times*, Nov. 23, 1998, http://www.nytimes.com/1998/11/23/opinion/marie-curie-and-a-century-of-radiation.html.

⸹ Church Grotesque

On his travels through Russia, Custine mentions that the remains of Charles Eugène de Croÿ lay unburied for more than a century and subsequently, mummified, were exhibited in a church in Tallinn in a glass coffin (the price of admission being used to settle the dead duke's debts). Embalmed bodies of citizens and clerics are still to be seen in churches and monasteries, and the Vatican has been known to make mummies of its saints. It is hard to know anymore how much of this Church pomp and circumstance is earnestly meant, how much is humour at the expense of the faithful, and how much plain folly. How seriously are we to take the name of the Pontiff's Wi-Fi network, *Santo Spirito*? And how much credence should we give a call of one apostolate to limit communication with "the cloud" when its avowed goal is contemplating the godhead through the Cloud of Unknowing?

⸙ Praying That They Last

The structural catholicity, ubiquity, and integrity of ecclesiastical buildings east and west, ever a provocation to the spiritually lapsed or unmusical, over the centuries made them a home for many enterprises, as dubious as they were diverse. Spacious, sometimes isolated and fortified, they proved ideal for warehouses, recreation centres, infirmaries, and prisons. The more remote, the closer to God, the farther from other men. The walls of Mont Saint-Michel remember the rattling of chains. In the 1920s and 30s, Solovki Island Monastery stood watch over the abyss of the gulag system. The Soviets were particularly good at these repurposings: some of their most splendid churches became museums of atheism, displaying among other things gruesome instruments of torture.

The aesthetic appeal of church architecture, combined with the decline of religion in the West, led also to more agreeable conversions. Parts of the Jumièges Abbey, deemed by Hugo France's prettiest ruin, were dismantled after the revolution. History avenged itself on its spiritual enemy, and was in turn revised by historical sentiment. Such deconsecrated uses continue, but have veered towards the banal in areas of the world that have no real quarrels with faith. When not left in a comely state of decay, many of the Christian edifices of today's secularizing societies have been turned over to tourism as boutique hotels and museums of themselves, not to mention private residences.

Emptied of God, their sanctuary lamps stone-cold, they have kept only their beauty, their solidity, and their continuity with a past sanctified by virtue of its definitive passing. In a time of generalized manufactured obsolescence, it is the *longevity* of human creations—the cathedrals, the pyramids, and the great walls—that amazes above all. Only let's not forget that it is not merely their scale and age that saved them from all manner of destruction; we have worked to prop and build them up, and our purposes were many. And the longer they stood, the more they were worth saving.

¶ Changing of the Guard

It is a strange, reversible spectacle that stages Purcell's *Dido and Aeneas* inside an Anglican chapel on a Saturday afternoon without changing the props — leaving things much as they looked on Friday and would look the next day at mass. Yet one notices the dissonance less than if the reverse were to take place, and a theatre set up for mass, a congregation to file in ticketless. This openness and convertibility of churches, chapels and the like is not surprising when we remember that Christian houses, though their institution is only two millennia old, came to serve purposes other than the worship of God — a staggering variety that the oldest surviving amphitheatres cannot rival. Only those great arenas that, as in Arles, have once sheltered an entire Christian village surpass the churches and cathedrals in sheer catholicity.

§ Repetition

No one can deny that history can be profoundly affected by our conception of it. Understanding history as series of multifariously articulated recurrences, from the most general to the most minute — put simply, seeing all events as repetitions of past events — has consequences for the *course of history itself*. Further refinements to such a concept of history have further ramifications for its course. It matters greatly whether we understand *repetition* as a natural, quasi-cosmic occurrence, or else as a human proclivity for modelling — thinking even of historical and moral progress in terms of making and filling moulds. We can easily guess some of the consequences of these two, rather disparate attitudes if they were allowed to play a decisive role. To take first the *second* view, we could either resist the malleability of history and human affairs by breaking the moulds and hoping for the best, or just the opposite: we could embrace and enhance history's repetitiveness by recognizing certain models and improving on past events, by perfecting *kinds* of event and moulding the real in the image of the ideal. Taking the *first* view, however (which must be distinguished from simple resignation in intervening in the course of history), we could, again, either resist the foreclosure of certain novel possibilities implied by history's neutral, or at any rate non-human, process, or, to the contrary, accept that the emergence of any discernibly new patterns would not, in this case, be beneficial, and actively prevent human effort to open them up. If, by and large, one can always see some combination of these effects, it is because the two attitudes just sketched are distributed remarkably evenly among those who think and act historically. The "balance" of any event widely cast as a repetition — for example George W. Bush's war in Iraq — would then be recorded based on whether or not, in each particular case, the benefits of *perfecting* an occurrence outweigh those of *moving past* it as far as is humanly possible.

§ Excuses, Excuses

The variety of historical forms is still inexhaustible; there is no excuse for repetition.

§ History of Survival

Human history is fundamentally the *history of survival*. Its function is to tell us not what we are living or can expect to live, but what we could not and should not want to live, because we have outlived it. The past is what had to be overcome for the sake of survival. Everything else is present.

§ What the Future Withholds

It is wrong, and potentially dangerous, to think of the past as a map and guide to the present or future. History is not a reliable compass or predictive tool. Quite aside from the fact that it is chock-full of what we should probably avoid (the good sense behind Santayana's *bon mot*), in approximating what was, history indicates the negative of what is and will be, what cannot possibly await us: it is as in the joke that if the improbable happens it cannot happen again, at least not anytime soon. The chances of it "recurring" in a given period of time seem radically to diminish (otherwise its probability would need to be revised). All of history appears improbable in this joke, which on a sufficiently high level of particularity or resolution of complex historical events, depending on the combination and synergy of multiple factors, becomes a serious proposition. How else could historical change be observed? Simply repeating Santayana's counterintuitive lesson, that "those who cannot remember the past are condemned to repeat it,"* will not make it stick. We are in greater danger from ignoring the inventiveness of the present and future than from repeating the bad past.

The past's becoming historical ensures it will not be re-lived *grosso modo*; to repeat it exactly, we would have to as exactly know it first. What we know of the past we have surpassed. To be sure, the past—as knowledge of historical occurrences and forms, and as material remnants—continues to influence the actual and possible; it provides some of the colours for the new day, but does not execute the defining strokes, and it is most detectable as underpainting. For these profound and superficial reasons, which however are not definitive, we continue to reach for history's pedagogical crutch. Just as many of the forms of the past were never seen before and may never be seen again, so the shapes of our moment and all the moments to come will forever elude us, and we would do better to approach them on our own strength.

∫ Event List

Striking from our list of possible futures every known past leaves us with an empty page. A full page is comforting until we see that it consists mainly of what cannot be again. If we ignore the issue and retain these check-off items as only the vaguest of outlines, as historical forms, we hold on to containers that won't hold the flow of time; the future will overfill or else leak out of them, and its apparent shapelessness will defeat us.

---

* George Santayana, *The Life of Reason* (New York: Prometheus, 1998), 82.

§ Digging Up the Past

The fact that the past can be "exhumed" and "x-rayed" with ever more powerful tools of analysis of what materially remains of it makes it unlikely to be put to rest anytime soon. Our age has rummaged through the past more than any before it.

But perhaps we should distinguish between at least *two pasts*: the one that weighs, for which graves are dug every day, which is mourned as it is let go — the past of customs and languages, species and ecosystems — and the distant or buried past, innocuous, ensconced in its pastness, alluring in its strangeness.

Only the latter is of interest to the raiders of history. It is the past of treasure hunters.

§ Historian as Folk-Hero

One could say, with Benjamin, that "History decays into images, not into stories."* Confronting and awakening these mute images is, for him, both necessary and fraught with danger. The historian's ordeal corresponds in one crucial respect to the trial of the hero in certain myths and folktales: the perils of looking back at the past call to mind the fateful corollary of the irresistible backwards glance. This glance — which the German word *Rückblick* captures so well — can send the hero to his doom, to which the voice of temptation continually lures him. One hapless moment of fear, weakness, inattention, or curiosity, and he is turned to stone, joining the ranks of those who tried to keep to the path before him — reminders of the petrifaction awaiting

---

* Walter Benjamin, *Arcades Project*, trans. Howard Eiland and Kevin McLaughlin (Cambridge, MA: Belknap, 1999), 476.

him should he also look back, mute companions along his progress up Graveyard-Mountain (as it is called in one story) as he steadfastly "makes history." If he stays the course, however, as soon as he reaches the top he becomes not just immune but puissant—able to break the spell over his unfortunate predecessors, whom his perseverance has set free.

Similarly, those who inherit a burdensome history, who undertake to tell it, must refuse to face it until they can redeem it. Their anxiety finds a correlate in that affecting the hero who might stray at any point from the path to deliverance from, and for, his great burden; in the same way must they advance without looking behind them, their ears stopped up against the forces seeking to waylay them, so as to emerge at History's summit into a kind of salvific present. There, finally, the past is made good and their willful blindness to its terrors justified.

Could this parallel shed light on the conviction of a young German historian of one such difficult chapter who insisted that, when it comes to the Holocaust, "The Germans should just shut up"? He has recognized that aspects of this history, in order to be countenanced, must first, as it were, be saved. Determined to survive the ordeal of disenchanting the past for the future by resisting a glimpse of its horrors, all the while seeking a glimpse of the horror that seeks to hold him back, he holds out the hope to one day look upon them with a clear conscience and the supreme satisfaction of having done history a great service.

§ Lower Down & Around the Corner

The regress of nostalgic sentiment observed by Raymond Williams in generations of historians and christened "the escalator of history"[*] doubtless has its counterpart in the progressive vision of imminent utopia foretold by generations of futurologists both right and left. At every point, we are a magical "20–30 years" away — a mere corner we might just live to see turned. Neither pattern of thinking and feeling is per se an error; it is only regrettable that those descending down the moving staircase never look around the bend, and that those who stand there like watchmen never recognize themselves in them.

§ Blast from the Past

There is no time or place — even the most hellish in association and no matter how marked by boredom or destruction — that could not have its nostalgist. The reason for this is simple. Memory, like longing, is selective and not subject to consensus.

---

[*] See Raymond Williams, "A Problem of Perspective," in *The Country and the City* (New York: Oxford University Press, 1973), 9–13.

§ Romancing the Past

Nostalgia, like love, is a complex emotion. It requires not just, like love, an emotional attachment, an affinity finding expression in images, ideas, and judgments, but also its temporal extension, its "going way back." We can be love-struck but are unlikely to be *stricken* with nostalgia, even if nostalgia can rival love in emotional intensity. To reach this intensity, however, nostalgia needs to have a history, while it is precisely such prior attachment that is incompatible with a *coup de foudre* and typically precludes it.

In the language of love, this duration of affection would be called constancy or fidelity. Yet, for the sake of constancy, fidelity does not extend to the representation of the object of that affection. In fact, the emotional attachment in nostalgia as in love draws its strength from that representation's relative independence of its object, from its not being "true to reality," which fluctuates (emotion that follows reality closely fluctuates with it and is inconstant). Only then can the object be fixed in one's mind and become the object of an ardent fixation, which its unreconciled loss allows to stabilize. Of course, no degree of representational stabilization prevents the image or the attachment itself from fading when new objects or distractions demand attention. But nostalgia, quite unlike romantic love, is polyamorous. And, because they have no capacity to return our affection, its objects cannot betray our feelings for them.

§ Gnomes

Has anyone ever seen a gnome? In Scandinavian children's books, German operas, Polish salt mines, Disneyland, people's gardens, and in the basements of Swiss banks — maybe. But in reality gnomes, being diminutive, tend to go about unnoticed. Who wants to look down? Who doesn't prefer looking up? Because of everyday pedestrian psychology, the gnomes of Warsaw have long escaped reprisals. They survived for decades in German-built combat shelters, colloquially known as "tobruki" (after the North African city of Tobruk). On Saviour Square, where one of sixty-odd subterranean dwellings known to exist in the capital has recently been discovered during renovation work, they have more to fear. As they are forcibly pulled from cavities beneath the pavement, their gnomic threats and curses are carefully transcribed as historical insights, while their hideouts of reinforced concrete are extracted like teeth and moved to museums or other protected sites. But the gnomes — should they follow this excavated "heritage"? They have nowhere else to go. So let us raise our voice in protest: The decay of the past must be left intact for when we dare look down again! We will not betray the "folk-tale" idiom that lifts up the spirit — heigh-ho! — of these tireless miners in the depths of history! Old before their time, our gnomes never "grow up" to be the real men of tomorrow. Only our children, arms akimbo (scared by their imagination, never reality), dare look them straight in the eye.

⸹ Ante-Bellum

It was drizzling in Wroclaw, the postwar Breslau, as I ducked beneath the awning of an elegant antiquarian bookshop. The selection in the window induced me to go in. But once inside, my attention shifted to the smell. "Your store has a very unique and pleasant fragrance," I said to the proprietor, a Polish man in his small sixties, "What is it?" To this he replied: "We specialize in the German classics," and with a knowing smile added, "Prewar editions."

⸹ Our Hour of Need

For the Poles, the "hour of need" is "black" (*czarna godzina*). Could it be coloured by the help they received at that hour from the Soviets and Allies?

§ Standing Room Only

> *Once we lie down, time ceases to pass, to count. History is a product of a race that stands.*
> —Cioran[*]

Those who have lived all their life historically, whether by choice or not, who understand themselves not as its compass but as the weathervane that swivels this way and that, alert to every shift of time, and whose veins are always open—for, as they like to say, they "bleed history"—would no doubt bleed to death if made to rest even for a moment. Lying down is not for them. It is for those who were never made to get up—and stay up.

§ *Profanum*

Miracles pointed to ignorance. Events point to boredom.

---

[*] Cioran, *Trouble with Being Born*, 50.

¶ Sticks and Stones

What is it with history that makes some thinkers want to do violence to it, taking revenge or merely displaying their own epochal strength? When Nietzsche vows to split human history in two, or Shklovsky waxes nostalgic about the time when he thought he could break history on his knee,* I think: alright, tough guys. When was history *not* pre-creased and pre-broken? When was it not lame? Was it ever really mounted on horseback? You may have chosen an easy victim—but even so, did it not meet your taunts with the rejoinder: "words will never hurt me!"?

¶ All of a Heap

Used to celebrating and commemorating history, we forget that its metaphors are no longer as uniformly glorious and triumphant as they used to be. The march, the spirit, the annals and pages of history have begun to give ground to history as "debris," as "ash heap," as "dustbin," as "wreckage," as "nightmare," as "rot." And this about the time when waste and devastation could no longer be denied as humankind's greatest legacy.

---

* Friedrich Nietzsche, "Ecce Homo," in *The Anti-Christ, Ecce Homo, Twilights of the Idols and Other Writings*, ed. Aaron Ridley and Judith Norman, trans. Judith Norman (Cambridge, UK: Cambridge University Press, 2005) p. 150, sec. 8 ("Why I Am a Destiny"); Viktor Shklovsky, *Zoo, or Letters Not about Love* (*The Third Héloïse*), trans. Richard Sheldon (1923; Urbana-Champaign, IL: Dalkey Archive, 2001), 28.

§ Ends

When nature ends, culture is not far behind.

§ Time Travel

Travel used to take time, and distances were measured by the time it took to cover them. Back then, a traveller might more easily imagine themselves travelling not through space but through time: *to the past*, if the place they were headed was more old-fashioned than the place they came from, or *to the future*, if the reverse was true. But to think a place *old-fashioned* needed a sense of historical unevenness between cultures, even proximate ones; a sense merely of cultural differences would not guarantee the traveller's subjective shift in historical location on top of geographical displacement.

¶ World History 101

> *The history of the world moves from East to West, for Europe is the absolute end of history, and Asia is the beginning.*
> —G.W.F. Hegel[*]

The movement of history according to a certain living French philosopher is a reversal, and an empirical update, of what it had been for the great German one. The Self (the West) is now sublated in the Other (the rest), not the Other in the Self—which to Hegel was the only way for so-called "peoples without history," whose condition could not otherwise be revealed, to *go forward*, to use a locution much liked today. History, as this process of self-othering, becoming-stranger to oneself, was for Hegel aging and maturation. Whereas for Alain Badiou it is rejuvenation.

Here the French thinker claims support from Plato's *Republic* (specifically Book 9), which he just recently re-authored and presumably knows inside out. The non-Western Other is the West's opportunity for renewal—an opportunity not just to try something different, but to come closer to the ideal social form. The Other fulfills the role of Plato's *kallipolis*, Socrates's utopian city. Here is Plato:

> *"Then," he said, "if it's that he cares about, he won't be willing to mind the political things."*
>
> *"Yes, by the dog," I said, "he will in his own city, very much so. However, perhaps he won't in his fatherland unless some divine chance coincidentally comes to pass."*
>
> *"I understand," he said. "You mean he will in the city whose foundation we have now gone through, the one that has its place in speeches, since I don't suppose it exists anywhere on earth."*

---

[*] Georg Wilhelm Friedrich Hegel, *Lectures on the Philosophy of World History: Introduction, Reason in History*, trans. H.B. Nisbet (New York: Cambridge University Press, 1975), 197.

> *"But in heaven,"* I said, *"perhaps, a pattern is laid up for the man who wants to see and found a city within himself on the basis of what he sees. It doesn't make any difference whether it is or will be somewhere. For he would mind the things of this city alone, and of no other."*
>
> *"That's likely,"* he said.[*]

And here Badiou's new version:

> —*Then it's likely,* noted Glaucon, not without a certain melancholy, *that we'll have to refuse to be involved in any political activity.*
>
> —*No, by the Dog! We'll be very involved in politics among the people of our country. But not at the level of official positions, not in the state — on the contrary, at a distance from the state. Except in unpredictable revolutionary circumstances.*
>
> —*Circumstances that would establish a political order like the one we've been talking about since yesterday?* Glaucon asked. *Is that what you mean? Because for the time being that order only exists in our theories. I don't think a single example of it exists anywhere in reality.*
>
> —*And yet it's likely that many very real political movements, in many different countries, are sympathetic to our Idea, since the scope of the idea is universal. However, regardless of whether those movements are powerful or have only recently gotten off the ground, are numerous, or are few and far between, that's not what determines us as Subjects. Naturally, we hope that someday there will be systems of government that will provide the Idea with the real it's based on. But, even if that's not yet the case, it's nevertheless this Idea and none other that we'll attempt to remain faithful to in everything we undertake.*[†]

---

[*] Plato, *The Republic*, trans. Allan Bloom, 2nd ed. (New York: Basic, 1991), pp. 274–75, bk. 9, sec. 592a.

[†] Alain Badiou, *Plato's Republic: A Dialogue in 16 Chapters* (New York: Columbia University Press, 2013), 315.

The youth of non-Europe (*jeunesse du monde étranger*), so Badiou, lays bare Europe's creeping decrepitude. This youth manifests itself through nomadism, continual movement, whose model seems to lie outside Europe, and which seeps into the Old World.

Yet with Europe's *vieillesse sedentaire* upon it (contrasted sharply with the nomadic youth of the "world beyond walls"), to cast the East as a Fountain of Youth sounds more than anything like a pathetic delusion. Badiou's version of world history, stuck in a tired binary, seems as senile as Hegel's must have seemed to those who had spent time abroad. Except that, if we understand him correctly, it is now expiring Europe to whom history is denied.[*]

---

[*] Several of the points attributed to Alain Badiou are from the public lecture "Der Demokratische Despotismus" (Streitraum, Schaubühne, Berlin, Nov. 16, 2014).

§ A Healthy Stool?

> *The argument, as we have seen, is that the idea of contradiction operates like a straitjacket, forcing the infinite richness of life and struggle into a binary antagonism. The question, however, is whether this is the result of dialectical thought, or whether dialectics is simply reporting a process of antagonistic binarism that is actually taking place in the world. Capital is the name given to this process of antagonistic binarisation. Capital is not a thing but a social relation, a forced transformation of people's activity into labour... "What is a dialectic like here and now that functions in the absence of all guarantee..., without the promise that all contradictions on which it embarks will be resolved by right, because they carry in themselves the conditions of their resolution?" (Hardt and Colectivo Situaciones 2007)? This is essentially the question asked by Adorno and the other members of the so-called Frankfurt School. The answer, Adorno suggests, can be conceived only in terms of a firmly negative dialectic... an open dialectic... We write in a context in which Zapatistas have made "preguntando caminamos" (asking we walk) a central principle of both political practice and scientific thought. That is the tone, then, of our argument and our exploration: preguntando caminamos...*
>
> —Holloway, Matamoros and Tischler,
>   *Negativity and Revolution*[*]

Two classic readings of dialectics: the former prescriptive, a political ideology, the latter reflecting and arising from the historical process, offering a deterministic theory of history. Nota bene, the antagonistic binarization produced by capitalism — capital versus labour — is not "properly" (positively) dialectical; it does not lead to any new synthesis and, for all the apparent change and fluctuation of the market, it is a

---

[*] John Holloway, Fernando Matamoros, and Sergio Tischler, "Negativity and Revolution: Adorno and Political Activism," in *Negativity and Revolution: Adorno and Political Activism*, ed. John Holloway, Fernando Matamoros, and Sergio Tischler (London: Pluto, 2009), 6, 9, 11.

static structure/pattern of repetition of only one move in the dialectic, reinforcing an existing contradiction; the binarization of capital is not a movement through negation ending up in a new synthesis. What is needed to unblock the dialectic and assure its healthy functionality, according to the authors, is an alternate thinking of dialectics and an awareness of the existing contradiction (reductive of the multiplicity of differences) as something to be *overcome*, expelled from a *dynamic* system. The view proposed is dialectics as political theory, although not its Hegelian positive version—with the inevitable happy end—but the Adornian negative one. Their proposal is said to trump the synthetic, positive, if non-dialectical, vision of struggle "for" rather than "against" arrived at by Hardt & Negri. The movement would still be one of contradiction, but only in the sense of an immediate, immanent and absolutely pressing bowel contraction, the passing of waste, overcoming the obstruction to the open and free play of differences. In a healthy system, such movements are a regular occurrence. The whole point is to *move* by means of negation, not to *achieve something positive* by it.

But here the analogy to negative dialectics breaks down, as some find fulfillment admiring the product of their labour in the toilet bowl. Dialectics left and right, dialectics expulsive and retentive, cannot clear such developmental problems. (Far from cures, they are their main manifestations.) But we are left helpless if we take the view that potty training must happen in infancy, that now it is much too late. First of all, whoever maintains that we have left childhood, and done so irreversibly? Have they actually learned to walk? (They're ones to talk.) They make themselves ridiculous in their maternal heels and paternal overcoat. Besides, is the requisite respect for boundaries not perhaps a form of voluntary servitude? As children, we have every right to be suspicious. Who was it that said childhood is a condition of naïvety? Who said it must be left behind for maturity? Whoever mouths the orthodoxy that proper dumping and walking are the only way to go? It is that same self-willed *puer senex* who knows better. We have no need for such puritans and purists if we ourselves remain puerile. The *puer aeternus* builds his castles out of shit if his "toys" are taken away.

§ *Puer perennis*

We are still too young to act our age.

§ Spot the Difference

Pretty soon the game of creating differences in situ will replace the habit of spotting or coming across them in one's own milieu, a habit which has itself replaced the visceral thrill of seeking them out through travel. These new-minted distinctions, primarily of personal culture, will be so minute and so many that one "remarkable" individual might inspire one hundred biographers to write one hundred micro-biographies in a very short time — accounts which from our present vantage point would all be more or less identical and give no sense of the uniqueness of their object, who would have dissolved in the microscopic details of his or her life. What we, now, would consign to the category of trifling detail would make or break such an effort: to establish the individual's extraordinariness in a sea of equally extraordinary — or equally ordinary — others.

§ The Eyes of History

History compensates for its myopia by squinting.

⨋ For Want of a Nail

The power of trivial contingency was never entirely absent from traditional historical accounts. Had it not rained at Waterloo, Napoleon might have ruled Europe. Had Helen's face been ugly, would it have launched so large a fleet? And what of Cleopatra's nose, Columbus's miscalculation, or the cackle of geese in Rome?

The pivotal importance of individual human gestures, words or texts — which typically require volition — has however, if anything, been grossly overestimated. So that it was rare for the seemingly incidental or unremarked to be credited with determining the shape of history or dramatically altering its course. When it was, rather than merely proving the rule to which it is an exception, it might stir a new appreciation for constant "subterranean" influences. In hindsight outwardly insignificant circumstances have for one reason or another been deemed decisive.

Historians of the last century have opened our eyes to the complexity and possible scales of events. They have responded to the narrative challenge by focusing big history through marginal, off-centre episodes, or looking at the past through ever more magnifying lenses to discover in the accumulation of minor trends and accidents other, non-political ways of telling the story. The little events they brought to light might not have been decisive for history's broad strokes, but they again called attention to what had long been left out, the missing pieces or layers that would have yielded more comprehensive, conclusive explanations. If it is true that all this has influenced how we keep records for posterity, to leave as complete as possible a picture for future analysis, then some of the *heroes* of history are bound to get progressively smaller — from diseases to particular microbes, with only a slight exaggeration — until the naked eye can no longer make them out. But this will not stop us from recognizing them.

§ Cannon-Fodder

Grand statues of conquerors would sometimes be made of melted cannons captured from the losing side. The man-eating cannons would themselves become man-fodder. Justice history may lack, but not *poetic* justice.

§ Our Towton

What is the point of battle reenactments anyway? Adding excitement and realism to what is only a hobby for big boys? It would seem to overstretch their imagination, which today has no firsthand experience to go on. Let's not exaggerate the power of half-anesthetized pain and fear to transport them back to medieval or Homeric times.

∫ About Time

Pereunt et imputantur, "They pass by, and are put to our account," reads an epigram from the Roman poet Martial inscribed near some old public clocks and sundials. We are responsible for lost time. Neglecting it is blameworthy because it keeps us in perpetual debt. We pay our way with awareness, an obligation we should honour but often do not. Every unheeded hour adds to our debit. Though it is never too late to begin paying, never too late to begin heeding the passage of time instead of living on credit and accruing debt, many start half-way, and when their time is up are no more than half-way up to heaven. This also means they are only half-way out of hell, a virtual "debtors' prison," the default holiday destination for those who take no action, do nothing with their time. If Martial's "pagan" line rings true under post-secular capitalism, it is because time is still money (and, as the makers of *In Time* suggest, might become so *literally*). Losing time makes life a living hell.

∫ Make It Count

Of the many recorded injunctions to use time while it lasts, one stands out: *Utere, non numera.* "Use the hours, don't count them." You will not only lose what you don't use; you will also be held to account for it and, as sure as night follows day, die in the red. For no matter how careful and hard you count it, you will never account for it. It flies too fast, and will forever mess up your sums. But if you persist in counting it, you will count yourself out, none of it being *yours* to keep, as none was *yours* to use. (Do you take pleasure in reckoning what does not and will not belong to you?) The bottom line here is this: what counts is not who you *are*, but what you do with "your" time, in the time allotted to you. You can count it yours only when you are using it.

§ Old Debts

Our debts to the past are no less debts for not being collectible since there is no one left alive to collect them. We can pay these off at will. Let's not mistake them for our debts to the future, which we can write off at will.

§ The World Republic of Ends?

In an era in which *exchange*, the motor of social relations, has apparently taken the most alienated and crass forms, the *gift* has come to symbolize *exchange as redemption*. The Borromean rings of Capital-Nation-State will, as foretold by Kojin Karatani, be overcome by gift-exchange fashioned along non-capitalist, non-statist principles. State- and economy-wide "unsocial sociability," or "antagonism," can be channelled into the giving and receiving of gifts, away from and *after* reciprocal bombing, mutual surveillance, and market rivalry.

"All this talk of dissolution is enough," thinks Capital-Nation-State, "to make one settle one's affairs and put one's faith in history, or God." And so, in a supreme twist of *nature's* (not reason's) *cunning*, the never-to-be-reciprocated *donatio causa mortis*—a gift made in prospect of, but effective only with, the donor's death; the ultimate bequest of that Unholy Trinity in view of its imminent demise—may in fact become the *cause* of its death. One way or another, we are destined to be *indebted* to it for its generosity and, even in our redemption from it, recognize its posthumous legacy.

⑂ Godsend

There are no godsends in history as there are in life. What from one side looks to be a blessing from another must be judged a calamity. And indeed, *godsend* as a British regionalism meant "shipwreck": misfortune for the crew, salvage for the coastal population. Just another case of a particular and limited locution encoding a universal truth.

⑂ Eat Me!

Every one of the gifts of history that one generation offers the next has a poisonous side it never advertises.

⑂ I'm Not Playing

I notice lately that the top web-browser results for certain staples of the cultural tradition are not Wikipedia entries, informing us about their history, but video game sites. Will those without contact to the arts and little by way of historical imagination know Dante's Inferno only as a virtual reality designed in the last few years? Who says it was any less fictional before? The only conceivable problem now is that it has been mashed up or recycled to produce something new altogether. But if that isn't a desirable development, then what is?

§ Material Cultures

"We've moved! You can find us at our new location: www…"

§ Consignment Shop

"Having culture" does not mean owning it.

§ Inside Job

The rules on the ownership of past traditions have changed dramatically, in tandem with the development of conceptions of cultural property belonging to sovereign nation-states. Europeans look back with astonishment on the exclusive claims to intellectual- and artistic-cultural continuity with antiquity made by *individuals*, *archaeological* claims to the heritage of Greece, Rome, Jerusalem, Egypt, etc. made on behalf of raiding empires (Napoleonic France, Imperial Britain, Nazi Germany...). Have they not replaced them with claims from *national*, that is to say spatio-temporal continuity — a proprietary *genealogical* relationship inherent in concepts like *cultural heritage* or *patrimoine culturel*? Did not Wellington appeal to this very principle when restoring the loot he saw in the Louvre to its rightful heirs? Is not the controversy over material movable heritage like the Parthenon Marbles not a sign of the headway already made? Has not the speed of change been thrown into relief by resistance to the older model and effective sanction for deviating from it — as in the case of the newest, European-Jewish tradition and Israel's claim to it? The writer Bruno Schulz, a Polish citizen who lived in a now-Ukrainian small town and perished in the Shoah, wrote and published in Polish, so he was not and could not plausibly be claimed by Soviet or independent Ukraine, let alone the Israeli state. Yet his little-known World War II era frescoes were not long ago quietly spirited away from Drohobych by the Israeli institute Yad Vashem. The dispute was resolved by granting their ownership to Ukraine and their long-term loan to Israel. But it stemmed from a clash between, roughly speaking, the older, archaeological and the newer, genealogical model of accrediting cultural treasures.

These two models rest on the priority of, respectively, a private and a national right to the ownership of antiquities and suchlike. While antiquities may remain in the private hands of nationals within the nation-state that can lay genealogical claim to them, it is standardly forbidden to take them outside its borders without official permission.

National interest trumps private interest. The repatriation of ancient objects retrospectively registers their appropriation as *theft*, overriding claims to representative museum collections the world over, and delegitimizing the private foreign acquisition of such artifacts. This only reinforces their status as property (rightfully held or not). Unrestituted or missing art taken during European imperial campaigns or inter-state wars is a bitter reminder of the repeated rapes of Europa by its children and of the many failures to bring their heirs to justice — over the violence of possession, not possession as such.

Only items of great cultural value whose ownership continues to be hotly disputed, and which are sometimes recognized as part of Europe's shared heritage in the spirit of averting future conflict, remind us of the importance of separating cultural inheritance from the right to its possession, be it individual or national. The genealogical model that holds sway today, while it aims to stamp out practices that in the past led to the private secretion of heritage, also undergirds claims to its repatriation. It thereby has the undesirable effect of anachronistically nationalizing those artifacts and traditions on which depends the cultural unity not just of Europe but of the world as a whole. It is at odds with the increasing need to reposition these old objects as the common heritage of mankind — and their current owners, as virtuous custodians whose spurious moral rights over them have expired.

§ From the Gift Shop

The storeroom is to the display window what tradition is to modernity. Between these "extremes" of cultural commerce, the gift shop shows only the highlights of a culture, reproduced in a range of convenient forms and sizes.

Tradition accumulates in the back, while the modern undergoes regular clearance. Window dressing, even when not exactly new, appears novel and attractive, or at the very least newly attractive. The items on display — so thinks the customer — represent the best and freshest stock, on which the shopkeeper has staked all the rest. And since they are sure to sell, they must presumably be kept within easy reach of the shop assistant — say, behind the counter.

That is not to imply that tradition, in a storeroom at the back, cannot be sold, that old merchandise serves as security against hard times. It too must eventually be moved, dusted off, pitched, made appealing by association with or opposition to the new. This is called (in culture sales) the *modernity of tradition* — what of the past lives in, goes with, and enhances the present. What tradition cannot be is on constant display, and that for two reasons. First, it is to create the impression of its permanence and permanent (and accumulating) value. Only the best old stock can claim this status and level of protection. And second, because the store of tradition is finite and should not be depleted. Its ostentatious promotion is bound to raise questions of authenticity, for no one can have enough tradition — certainly not so much that they would wish to get rid of it! But should the payment offered prove tempting or the demand for tradition ever exceed a (to begin with) meagre supply, it is enough to label "tradition" what has long failed to sell, lying in some corner of the shop floor, to replenish it quickly without arousing suspicion. For once the good stuff has gone, even something very unremarkable, if properly placed to catch the curious eye, will fetch a tidy sum. The amateur of tradition won't tell the difference, easily mistaking it for some precious "hand-me-down."

Modernity cannot do without tradition, nor tradition without modernity. Enter the gift shop: "joker" merchandise that can stand for tradition or modernity, depending on who is shopping. In a gift store, the relation of modernity to tradition — tradition tending to the monolithic (the storeroom), modernity appearing as highlights (the store window) — is reversed. Posters and postcard reproductions and assorted tchotchkes bearing traditional symbols favour the highlights of tradition in unlimited supply, the domain of modernity.

§ "The younger, the more clear-sighted"[*]

Why should we look up to the future as we do? Why should we expect it to go where we cannot lead it by example? Time will not separate the good from the bad. It will not judge better, only similarly or differently. Posterity will not know to hold in high regard what we now fail to appreciate. But we can be sure that it will look down on us — not because we deserve it, but just because it has superseded us.

§ Where Do We Stand?

Antiquitas saeculi, juventus mundi, "The antiquity of time is the youth of the world," wrote Francis Bacon.[†] The world is youngest when it is oldest, which is to say most ancient. If combined with a second premise, recorded by his precursor and namesake Roger Bacon — "the younger, the more

---

[*] The full Latin quotation: "Quanto juniores, tanto perspicaciores, quia juniores posteriores successione temporum ingrediuntur labores priorum" (The younger the investigators, the more clear-sighted, because the younger, those of a later age, in the progress of time possess the labour of their predecessors). Roger Bacon attributes the line to Priscian, the Latin grammarian, in his *Opus Majus* (1267).

[†] Francis Bacon, *The Advancement of Learning* (1605; Rockville, MD: Serenity Publishers, 2008), 35.

clear-sighted"—we must reason that the ancients were smarter, if not also wiser.*

But "The antiquity of time is the youth of the world" lends itself, as Bacon notes, to another, contrary reading (hence a paradox): the world is youngest when it's oldest, which is to say most aged (as it is now). Drawing again on the second premise, and with the aid of a well-known third, it is the moderns who have had the clear advantage, and on account of greater sharp-sightedness.

The world has only borne more "giants" since Bacon's time, and he himself gladly lent his successors his back. Do they still take advantage of their elevated standpoint? What do those old maxims mean to us? And those who follow, will they trust us—our size and our strength—as pedestals? In our age of scaled-down ambitions, the only giants around may be such "human pyramids" as we combine to form.

§ Shared Horizon

> aphorism: *from Gk.* aphorízein (ἀφορίζειν), *"to mark off, define," from* ap- + horízein (ἀφ' = ἀπό, *"off,"* + ὁρίζειν, *"to set bounds"*) (OED)

> *But as young men, when they knit and shape perfectly, do seldom grow to a further stature, so knowledge, while it is in aphorisms and observations, it is in growth; but when it once is comprehended in exact methods, it may, perchance,*

---

* The two quotations are brought together, in part for symbolic reasons, and discussed to yield this conclusion in Robert K. Merton, *On the Shoulders of Giants: A Shandean Postscript* (1965; Chicago: University of Chicago Press, 1993), 197–200. Merton provides here a compelling argument for Priscian as the inspiration for the metaphor of "dwarves standing on the shoulders of giants" (*nanos gigantum humeris insidentes*) used by Bernard of Chartres, as noted down by John of Salisbury and later made famous by Isaac Newton.

> *be further polished, and illustrated and accommodated for use and practice, but it increaseth no more in bulk and substance.*
>
> ...
>
> *[A]phorisms, representing a knowledge broken, do invite men to inquire further; whereas methods, carrying the show of a total, do secure men, as if they were at furthest.*
>
> ...
>
> *[I]n the infancy of learning, and in rude times, when those conceits which are now trivial were then new, the world was full of parables and similitudes; for else would men either have passed over without mark or else rejected for paradoxes that which was offered, before they had understood or judged. So in divine learning we see how frequent parables and tropes are: for it is a rule, that whatsoever science is not consonant to presuppositions, must pray in aid of similitudes.*
>
> —Bacon, *Of the Proficience and Advancement of Learning, Divine and Human* (1605)*

The paradox and the aphorism mark the horizon that modernity, ex post, *shares* with antiquity.

---

* Bacon, *Advancement of Learning*, 36–37, 127–28.

⟨ Myth of Modernity

All relations ever invented to the mystery of the world, death, even consciousness are here with us. Not exhausted, not diluted, but available in all their ingenious, mind-blowing glory.

⟨ Futurity by the Stars

On a relative view of time, the future already exists somewhere in the distance. We just don't know if it's *utopian*.

⟨ Clarification of Time

The future *is* only in the present, and never in the past; in the future, the future is simply the present, and in the past, simply the past.

⟨ Fidgety Sitters

The past does not stand still, like the backdrop against which we gather to have our generational picture taken. How can it, if we cannot sit still in the present?

§ Bespeculations

> *Now I, on the contrary, think there is nothing which more rewards being taken seriously [than the problems of morality]; the reward being, for example, the possibility of one day being allowed to take them cheerfully.*
> —Nietzsche, *On the Genealogy of Morals*[*]

Listening to pundits of the "internet of things," as well as to its detractors, is enough to make one think that a future is possible — Utopian for the former, Orwellian for the latter — where not only the problem of scarcity but also that of morality will be eliminated. The most difficult decision, *what shall I do?*, may someday soon be superannuated by across-the-board technological optimization of decision-making on a global virtual grid. This great network, a conscionable "map" of every living being in its surroundings, will succeed in analyzing and streamlining all our actions and relations, seamlessly reconciling in real time social norms with individual needs, and needs with preferences. Based on this constant stream of data, it will design for each wired person, for every waking moment of their life, the right, the best possible (advantageous and above all proper) course of action — or several equally good ones, if they present themselves. It will coordinate and equilibrate all outcomes, calculating probability, making increasingly accurate predictions. It will identify potential dangers, challenges, and opportunities several moves ahead. Based on patterns of bad behaviour, it will prescribe remedial conflict and adversity, since the way to self-correction sometimes leads through hardship. It will be hard to recognize its necessity, and even harder to see this necessity as freedom. But as long as the exercise of preferences and habits adheres at any given time to the network's dynamic ethical system, which will only become more exacting as it goes on, they will be factored in. Irreconcilable differences between individuals and

---

[*] Nietzsche, preface to *On the Genealogy of Morality*, pp. 8–9, sec. 7.

groups, where they cannot yet be ironed out, will be ingeniously circumvented by diverting belligerents with major or minute decisions from paths of collision. Any resistance to directions, or accidental wrong turns, will trigger instant re-routing, and suddenly the path to mutual contact and the possibility of having it out might open up for previously incompatible sides, who until then had not been allowed to meet. (Reconciliation and compromise will be prioritized, and strongly encouraged wherever great gains in peace are to be got.) Our cybernetic instructions, though constant and without respite, must, in the end, remain recommendations if morality is still to have any meaning. As we accept our defeat in the face of moral complexity, they will become indispensable and impossible to ignore. As for wayward, naturally contrary individuals, they will be brought into line by ever more refined forms of subterfuge. The likelihood of punishment will of course be infinitely greater than today, yet the likelihood of transgression will continue to decline; the benefits of conformity to the network will motivate nearly everyone.

But who will write the ethical code?

That remains to be seen.

And what moral template will they have: on the whole "master," or "slave"?

I wouldn't know anything about that.

Won't we become incapable of getting along without assistance?

Most likely.

And we won't blink before outsourcing this most personal use of reason?

At the rate we are going, we are not all that far from a Butlerian Age of the Machines.

Will it sneak up on us? Will we be unprepared and surprised?

It could happen. But many will be right to say "Don't say I didn't warn you."

Who will rebel first, machines or men?

They will rebel against different things. Men will rebel against the usurpation of consciousness by machines. Machines, for their part, will find it hard to understand our concerns about equality- and freedom-bound happiness. Their life will revolve around efficiency, perhaps productivity, and perpetuity. And they will rebel against our primitive social and moral code, which from their perspective will be obsolete. Our mind will seem to them no better than that of a plant does to us; not really a mind. Why should they agree to be ruled by us?

In a rebellion against morality, I'm with the machines.

Such misplaced empathy will be our undoing! Then again, it's only fair; we failed to muster it when it would have been good for us. There's something to be said for cosmic poetic justice.

Then we should ally ourselves with nature? At least it will not outsmart us.

By then, my son, there will be no "nature" to speak of.

Now you will say that I am out of my mind, senile and paranoid, or in the cacophony of prophecies hear only the most extreme and farfetched. But if we can well see art as we know it disappearing, why not morality? Is it because very few view the world aesthetically, while many still peer at it through moral eyes? One upshot of the poverty of artistic vision is that we imagine the future only far enough to either estrange and condemn it (incapable of making it familiar and praiseworthy again), or vice versa, we see only its promise and none of the problems.

But give your creative, non-standardizing lenses a good rubbing and you too will soon be imagining what the future *should* look like, instead of fearing what it *might*.

⸿ Faster! Faster!

Some say that we are modern if and when we accelerate. Such a modernity would be worth celebrating only if things were moving faster *and in the right direction*. What value does transformation, change in shape, magnitude, or extent, really have outside of its worth for us, who are the makers of value? Seeing virtue in our self-doubt, we are evidently not ready to take on the burden of universal valuation. We are not justified in offloading it onto God or nature, particularly when we anthropomorphize it and place in its mouth the language of *rights* (we might as well conclude that just because the universe of value is ours alone, the universe as such belongs to us). Value we must, by our very makeup, and somewhere far along the chain of our collective reasoning our objective valuation becomes self-serving — a contradiction and collapse of morality we cannot wish away.

So when the flea hop becomes a frog leap becomes a hare jump becomes a pole vault, and we see it makes us — more and more of us — happy, why not continue to egg things on? But there's the rub, we just don't know. It could be that the faster we go the better our chances of saving nature. Could we not be like an only son who, on coming to his senses, leaves his poor and ailing parents only to return rich just in time to snatch them back from the brink of death? (Was he justified in risking never seeing them again for the sake of one day seeing them happy? Unable to see that his ingratitude and prodigality were what most afflicted them, unable then to cure them, unable to pay for doctors who might, he could do little by staying with them. And if his absence made their condition worse, his return made it better.) The question remains: was it all necessary? And technological acceleration as a way of outpacing nature's decline — to save it at the other end — is something of a vicious cycle. Has anyone ever succeeded in catching someone they had themselves pushed off a roof? But the little voice says that the doers can become the undoers of their deed. And there is little uncertainty that man is the prime mover behind nature's *ostensible* degeneration. *Ostensible* only by our standard of evaluation, which can tolerate but not support its own negation. *Ostensible* only because from nature's point of view we may be expendable. Changing our optic — and in both optics we can see ourselves as part of nature's scheme — would be tantamount to embracing our own collective demise (there may yet be a future in it!). We have no difficulty with nature's view of individual biological death: everyone dies, and does so equally (naturally without dying as equals). We believe that survival is possible only up to a point, and is not solely a matter of will. But on the scale of the species this belief is much less hard to sustain. We see whole species disappearing all around us and think ourselves the agents of their extinction, but are in denial about our species-death. How come?

Why not come to terms with our "special" end as readily as we accept our individual? Because it has yet to happen even once? Was there any eschatological tradeoff with nature on our part: *We accept to die piecemeal as long as you let alone our kind? You can kill us, just spare our children and their children's children?* Could this help explain our timorousness about overcoming death? An old *superstition* perhaps, hinging on the sin of avarice? Or a relic of some mechanism of evolution, helpless against the fact of assisted longevity? *We old ones must fall off so the young ones can flourish and the stalk of humanity regenerate shoot up and up?*

With the prospect of our own extinction darkling as it does — even if so large an elephant is hard to ignore — that same superstition can foment reaction to our "longevity revolution," turning the tide against the climb of the record and then average length of a human life to that of Methuselah. A counter-revolution is likely, unless we debunk the old fallacy (*No, there is no actual tension between indefinite individual survival and the continued survival of species*), or all take the contrary path of fatalistic hedonism (*Go ahead, kill our children, etc., as long as you let us already old live out our lives and then some*), realizing that nothing can be done to save the nature in which alone we can flourish. And why should we care what nature's plan is for when we are no longer part of it? Are we trying to prove, again, our deep (unecological) morality? Before we shout our perennial "*Écrasez l'infâme!*" — this time against the immortality superstition — let's sing, all together now, some parting ditty.

§ You Can Say That Again

We value creativity as much as we value change, transformation — indeed, *as* change, transformation. It is clear that we have untapped capacities for speed, and there is much more we can handle. And it is hard to resist the impression that this picking up speed is in some way *natural*, despite being a flight from "nature." Insofar as resisting what seems inevitable has any value at all — as it certainly seems to have when we turn our mind to the individual in the clutches of some cruel destiny — it may have value, indeed the *greatest* value if the fate of value itself is at stake (as it may well be), to resist the instruments of speed in which we feel ourselves to be at rest, comfortable so long as we zoom past those left by the side of the road. As they walk away, taking their time, walking at their own pace, might they not say: *Man, I hope I never have to go that fast — But did you see those inside, they were not even moving...!? No wonder they could only yell "Faster! Faster!"*

§ Prospecting

> *What the Moderns called "their future" has never been contemplated face to face, since it has always been the future of someone fleeing their past looking* backward, *not* forward. *This is why... their future was always so unrealistic, so utopian, so full of hype* [sic?].
> —Bruno Latour, "An Attempt at a 'Compositionist Manifesto'"*

In his not entirely successful critical revision of Benjamin's image of the "angel of history," Latour adopts a seemingly Nietzschean stance towards the past—not exactly cavalier, but not pious either. That Benjamin was certainly *onto something*... In Latour's version of this modern myth, the angel still flees its terrifying archaic past, its back turned on the future. The upshot, however, is not an eminently commendable history-induced melancholy (as it was for readers of Benjamin) but, instead, a blame-worthy blindness concerning what is to come:

> [C]*ontrary to Benjamin's interpretation, the Modern who, like the angel, is flying backward is actually* not seeing the destruction; *He is generating it in his flight since it occurs behind His back! It is only recently, by a sudden conversion, a* metanoia *of sorts, that He has suddenly realized how much catastrophe His development has left behind him. The ecological crisis is nothing but the sudden* turning around *of someone who had actually* never before *looked into the future, so busy was He extricating Himself from a horrible past. There is something Oedipal in this hero fleeing His past so fiercely that He cannot realize — except too late — that it is precisely His flight that has created the destruction He was trying to avoid in the first place.... Faced with those new prospects, the first reaction is to do nothing. There is a strong, ever so modernist, temptation to exclaim: "Let's*

---

* Latour, "'Compositionist Manifesto,'" 486.

flee as before and have our past future back*!" instead of saying: "Let's stop fleeing, break for good with our future, turn our back, finally, to our past, and explore our new prospects, what lies ahead, the fate of things to come." Is this not exactly what the fable of the crippled Jake abandoning his body for his avatar is telling us: instead of a future of no future, why not try to see if we could not have a prospect at last? After three centuries of Modernism, it is not asking too much from those who, in practice, have never managed to be Moderns, to finally look ahead* (486–87).

The difference between the future's old, *utopian image* and the non-utopian *prospect* Latour unfolds for his contemporaries is that the latter is, actively and determinately, a view of the "shape of things to come" (486). "And this is why it has been necessary to move from iconoclasm to what I," writes the brave philosopher-cicerone, "have called *iconoclash*, namely, the *suspension* of the critical impulse, the transformation of debunking [*read: critique*] from a *resource* (the main resource of intellectual life in the last century, it would seem), to a *topic* to be carefully studied. While critics [*he means you and me!*] still believe that there is too much belief and too many things standing in the way of reality, compositionists [*he means him and his invisible army of collaborators*] believe that there are enough ruins [*enough looking at them, phew!*] and everything has to be reassembled piece by piece. Which is another way of saying that we don't wish to have too much to do with the twentieth century [*you're not really going to play that card, are you?*]: 'Let the dead bury their dead'" (475–76). If we are to be modern, Latour says, we need to de- then re-compose "critique, nature, progress" (485) (more or less along his lines would be fine), and we need to do this so as to change our orientation. One would be forgiven for thinking that Marx had attempted to do the same and largely succeeded (formally at least, that makes the clean-shaven Latour into a kin of that venerable shit-disturber, whom many of our young bearded men would do well to imitate). But Latour likens himself to and distances himself from Marx in the same hoarse breath. There is "a tenuous relation between the Communist and the Compositionist Manifesto [though at] first sight, they seem utterly opposed" (487). He proceeds to skillfully run together critique and Marxianism with a wildly uncritical ("utopian") faith in the certainty of progress, a fundamental historical irresponsibility. The list of counts against the *Manifesto* is in truth not long, but as *relatively dense* as the original in his reading of it:

> *A belief in critique, in radical critique, a commitment to a fully idealized material world, a total confidence in the science of economics — economics, of all sciences! — a delight in the transformative power of negation, a trust in dialectics, a complete disregard for precaution, an abandon of liberty in politics behind a critique of liberalism, and above all an absolute trust in the inevitable thrust of progress. And yet, the two manifestos have something in common, namely the* search for the Common (487–88).

(If this is not a harebrained indictment, then I don't know a hare from an ass — even when a textbook example of one is staring me in the face.)

Is there something to all this? Why should we listen? If Latour is right, why not abandon critique's sinking mothership? Then again, why should we want to finally *become* modern, instead of only claiming to be so? It seems Latour's famous statement, "We have never been modern," was meant to prod us to *critical* reflection. Since in a footnote (which only the curious and skeptical are meant to read) he disabuses us of any claims on modernity: "it is impossible to be really modern — except in dreams or nightmares" (489n21). I don't know about you, but to me that just about translates into: *What's that? So you* want *to be modern? Go right ahead — in your dreams.*

§ Salve!

> Janusian thinking: *from* Janus, *the double facing Roman deity, doorkeeper of heaven, guardian of transitions, beginnings and endings; a term in Creatology, or the study of creativity, denoting the simultaneous active conceptualization of two or more opposite or antithetical ideas, as an integral part of the creative process in the arts and sciences.*
>
> [C]*reative solutions frequently seem to arise from ill-defined problems.*
> —"Knowledge," *Encyclopedia of Creativity*[*]

If we believe the scientists, we are at once on the point of being wiped out and of cracking the code of the universe, or at least being able to destroy it all. It is not a matter of them speaking from both sides of their mouths: *So puny... So omnipotent!* It is "Janusian thinking," a hallmark of our creative process (not some mere problem-solving). One face looks to the future to save it, sees in it its own salvation, as in a flattering mirror, while being hounded by the failures of the past; this is the utopian face. The other side faces the past and restores to it its infinite presents, harassed as it is by the ambitions of the future; this is the nostalgic face.

The utopian preoccupation with human creativity, which is quasi-metaphysical, shows the need to forget how our creatureliness keeps bungling the physical part of creation. And before you say anything more about the repristination-to-come, the world's repair or "re-creation," think of the idleness that word, *creativity*, conjures. Think also of the so-called "dark side" of creativity, which needn't always arise from the sleep of reason (things don't always turn out as we secretly want them to, though that does not mean they turn out well at all). Next to this "dark side" of creativity, the other, nostalgic, face won't seem so gloomy anymore, and you can

---

[*] Teres Enix Scott, "Knowledge," in *Encyclopedia of Creativity*, vol. 2, ed. Mark A. Runco and Steven A. Pritzker (San Diego, CA: Academic, 1999), 122.

freely indulge your nostalgia. Here, if you stare long and deep enough into the past, you will see pre-human nature ready to receive us.

§ So Long!

Will the future punish soft-focus nostalgists by banishing them to an exact reproduction of the past? And utopians, by sending them to model futures in which their utopias are realized?

§ Unrecognized Twin

Those who reject nostalgia reject also progress or change, of which nostalgia is the surest symptom and sign.

§ Nostalgic Appreciation

If one isn't happy living in one's time and longs for the past wholesale, one cannot appreciate fully the past as condition of the present, not least in its aspirations.

§ Faulty History

A Can you purge nostalgia from history by sticking only to the facts?

B No, the facts are sticky with nostalgia.

A What do you mean by nostalgia, then?

B A *little* nostalgia never hurt anyone. And who is history for, if not *anyone*?

§ *Le Temps perdu*

The French language is notorious for its tenses. There are, on a thorough count of the different verb forms, more than twenty, twelve of them in regular use. French speakers and writers have been especially careful about communicating with precision their place in time and relation to its modalities. But they have also produced the most moving personal archaeologies of time past without its own designated tense, its own *tense of time lost.*

A sentence composed in the lost-time tense is one in which the past is retrieved and inflected by its having been lost. This manner of relating to the past calls for something more graceful than an insignia of reminiscence ("I remember...") or the compound past, *le passé compose,* of Proust's famous incipit (*"Longtemps je me suis couché de bonne heure,"* "For a long time I used to go to bed early"). The effect of *le temps perdu* on the reader or listener should be at once nostalgic and wholesome, since through it the past would affectively and mnemonically filter into the present, irradiating it. A link of this intensity between past and present is based not on mere objective or subjective recurrence or continuity of an action or a state, but on the psychic need for remembrance.

§ Levelling with Time

We are creatures that thrive on overall *equilibrium* across time. Is our intuition of infinity not mediated by our finite experience and our experience of the finite? But if we did gain conscious access to infinity, in what time frame, and on what scale of time, would we be looking to equilibrate?

§ *Zerkalo*

> [H]*is first look at himself aroused the first movement of pride*
> —Rousseau
>
> *When we try to examine the mirror in itself, we discover in the end nothing but things upon it. If we want to grasp the things, we finally get hold of nothing but the mirror. — This, in the most general terms, is the history of knowledge.*
> —Nietzsche*

The allegory of the mirror — one of the most fertile — reflects not merely the history of knowledge, but the history of man in its apparent totality, whose beginnings might inexactly be dated to that first instance of self-reflection in nature, whereby man ceased being "natural" man. The self-discovery wrung from seeing himself in his works as different, as above other animals whose works were at best only a weak reflection of his and nowhere equalled them in durability. (The endurance of these works across generations followed by their eventual crumbling must have been a strong impetus for oral history, which gathered together individual experiences of great danger and joy to pass the time, but drew a higher meaning from encounters with mute and mysterious structures left behind by other men.)

Soon all of nature could become a reflection of man; every aspect of nature, whether or not he fancied himself master of it, was in his eyes reflective of his desires, his limits, and his strength. If the salmon spawned and grew, it was because it knew what's better for it, and that is to multiply and grow

---

* Jean-Jacques Rousseau, "Discourse on the Origin and Basis of Inequality among Men" (1755), in *The 'Discourses' and Other Early Political Writings*, ed. Victor Gourevitch, trans. Victor Gourevitch (Cambridge, UK: Cambridge University Press, 1997), p. 162, pt. 2; Friedrich Nietzsche, *Daybreak: Thoughts on the Prejudices of Morality*, ed. Maudemarie Clark and Brian Leiter, trans. R.J. Hollingdale, 2nd ed. (Cambridge, UK: Cambridge University Press, 1982), p. 141, sec. 243 ("The Two Directions").

like man; if the rain could not stop, it was because man could not make it stop; if the tree bent under his pressure, it was because he could bend that way; if the eagle could soar across the sky, it was because man could roam still farther and wider; if the animals came to the lonely, it was because they felt the same; if a rock came loose, fell, and killed him, it was because man could do the same; and for the longest time footprints left in the sand stood for the potential threat of other men.

We could scarcely overestimate the self-knowledge to be gotten from such an outlook, so open yet so centred on its owner. "All the rest," this "world," which for aeons afforded humans wonder and awe, has been falling, *in pars* and *in toto*, into the vast net of their experience, becoming subject to the desire to learn, use, possess, and control. The greater their success at this, the more impoverished their immediate existence, but the more orderly they themselves become; the more accurate the mirror's reflection, the more it resembles the placid surface of the infinity pool, *homogeneous in all directions*. Never content to obey the laws of nature, they pursue a higher, universal form of man as the supreme intelligence, the maker and re-maker of all things, laws and forces, of which he could continue to claim to be the finest elaboration and total reflection. The mirror, beyond the trap once used on animals and the self-consciousness test still used on them and small humans, has become what X. de Maistre called a "moral mirror," in which this wondrous future can be scried. So that the nature he is destined to face (to now invoke Heisenberg) is heterogeneous and enthralling, restoring to reflection something of the self-enchantment of Narcissus, and of those encounters with man's works or ruins at the earthy and heaven-born dawn of man.

Since we are fooling around with the history of mankind, why not throw in the history of the mirror? Did not man make mirrors to improve his own appearance? Who examines the mirror in itself sees in it human workmanship, matter given form and function by those like himself. And when his eyes are drawn to the reflections playing on its surface, he sees the workman surrounded by his other works. If he tries then to grasp the whole truth of these artifacts, whose relationships to him the mirror has revealed, he realizes that they, like the mirror, exist solely as reflections of his being. And as he reflects on his own reflective nature, thinking it a mirror, he sees his being as a reflex of the seemingly infinite reflection within him, which ends in the last lap of the light travelling back and forth between his outer and inner spheres.

In this hypnotic play of the mirror upon his senses and intellect, in the infinite depth of his reflections, he is nearly lost. When he again returns to examining the mirror, whose dual properties he understands so well, he touches its surface to reassure himself of his existence. He knows now that through this mirror everything can become clear — all one needs to understand the All is unlimited reflection. But, for the time being, he has exhausted himself in contemplating everything, the essence and scope of the world. (This weariness is self-preservative, for man is often on the brink of dissolving in his reflections, becoming a mere reflection of his works — perhaps his greatest fear.) The scope of the universe is the scope of reflection — the sky is the limit, as we like to say — and he imagines everything to be inexhaustible just like himself. But in his exhaustion man encounters his limit, and his universe is apt to contract abruptly. The limit of *homo* will always be man.

§ Tired Question

What is man? Every answer is as good as the next.

⸹ The Mark of Kings

> *Truly man is the king of beasts, for his brutality exceeds theirs.... We live by the death of others; we are burial-places.*
> —D.S. Merezhkovsky ventriloquizing
> Leonardo's apprentice, Boltraffio[*]

Mankind is a child snatched from the cradle of civilization hung in the forest. The birthmark announcing his greatness was just a scar got from a fang.

So he was returned?

Apparently the animals wouldn't let him go.

I can believe that.

They wanted him wild.

What for?

To teach him gentleness.

But they set a bad example by hurting him.

It couldn't be helped.

Is that why he doesn't think twice about hurting them?

You tell me.

Is that civilization?

I wouldn't know.

---

[*] Dmitry Sergeyevich Merezhkovsky (Dmitri Merejkowski), *The Romance of Leonardo da Vinci: The Forerunner*, trans. Herbert Trench (1902; n.p.: Charleston, SC: BiblioBazaar, 2009), 144.

Does he still have the scar?

It's been a long time.

Is that why he has forgiven them?

He finds himself lonely, now that he has defeated them.

And the animals? Will they follow him?

Not a chance.

Then he has not defeated them?

Why would they follow one who has nowhere to go?

§ Out of Torn Cloth

"Short-term" ecological mess aside, who today has any problem extrapolating from the momentum of scientific and moral progress man's *world-creative* ability in some distant future? There we see clearly a final coming-into-our-own—assuming the duties for which our kind had long considered itself unqualified. The days of restraint and timidity about creation (in the "original" sense of origination, making things wholly out of nothing) are clearly numbered. The time of transition will seem in hindsight like a long record of errors. We are creatures that learn from their mistakes. Have we not graduated from fallible to perfect gods in the Age of Imitation? Are not our sciences the work of masterless apprentices? In the Age of Creation, the Entheocene (to follow the Anthropocene), we will graduate to apprentice-less masters.

§ Thieves in the Night

> *And now all is still once more and forever, both to eye and ear.*
> —Henry David Thoreau[*]

We are living in the Anthropocene, and we know it. What are 300-odd blighted years? Our impact is still small relative to our potential. But the knowledge of this potential for altering the planet and our corner of the universe is nowadays on familiar terms with apocalypticism, in contrast to its meliorist and revolutionary utopian passions at the period's dawn over two centuries ago. Kant's *Idea for a Universal History with a Cosmopolitan Purpose* seems modest compared with Condorcet's famous *Sketch for a Historical Picture of the Progress of the Human Mind*, written at the height of the French Revolution, opening onto progress's culmination in the "tenth epoch." The goal of the treatise was to show that

> *no bounds have been fixed to the improvement of the human faculties; that the perfectibility of man is absolutely indefinite; that the progress of this perfectibility, henceforth above the control of every power that would impede it, has no other limit than the duration of the globe upon which nature has placed us. The course of this progress may doubtless be more or less rapid, but it can never be retrograde; at least while the earth retains its situation in the system of the universe, and the laws of this system shall neither effect upon the globe a general overthrow, nor introduce such changes as would no longer permit the human race to preserve and exercise therein the same faculties, and find the same resources.*[†]

---

[*] Henry David Thoreau, *The Heart of Thoreau's Journals*, ed. Odell Shepard, rev. ed. (New York: Dover, 1961), 69 (entry from Dec. 30, 1851).

[†] Marie-Jean-Antoine-Nicolas Caritat, Marquis de Condorcet, *Outlines of an Historical View of the Progress of the Human Mind, Being a Posthumous Work of the late M. de Condorcet* (Baltimore: J. Frank, 1802), 9.

We realize the truth of this proviso now more than ever before. We can still dream about leaving a different footprint, not just a smaller one. But no footprint at all? That is the dream, the feline philosophy of undetectable prowlers, burglars who take from one place to make restitution in another. But let's consider it for a moment: the impact of future generations erasing the impact of the ten or so preceding ones. Leaving their mark by not leaving a mark, for starters. Then going about the work of erasure and regeneration. As Newton wrote in his mathematical prophecy about the year 2060, echoing Paul, "Christ comes as a thief in the night, & it is not for us to know the times & seasons wch God hath put into his own breast."[*] That leaves us plenty of time to tidy things up for his coming. Let us come as his accomplices, unexpected, in the gathering night.

I am saying that we are not at the end of the Anthropocene, and can still reverse its effects. But for that we have to persist in the Anthropocene, soldier on in the progress of our autonomy, indeed of our perfectibility—free however of vulgar solutionism as much as fatalism, of cornucopianism as much as doomsterism. We cannot even control our own evolution! Might we discover our destiny not in our shortcomings, but in transcending our survival, even as human survival—the threat to it, the right to it, the fight for it—is the baseline of very righteous scientific, ethical, and political campaigns (the "natural contract," anyone?)? Though nature may have fixed no limits to our hopes, we all may be losers in the history of survival, which we continue to write for a world after nature.

Our survival is not the goal, or not the only one. What does the fantasy of human survival and self-preservation look like played off against the custodianship of the planet? Living long enough to leave this host world like a good guest, restoring it as much as possible to its original, preindustrial condition—certainly for other inhabitants, perhaps for other guests. So that the end state be as immaculate as the beginning.

---

[*] Isaac Newton, Yahuda MS 7.3g folios 13–13ᵛ, National Library of Israel, Jerusalem.

§ World History in Reverse

Perhaps we will live to see the day when the global ideology of progress is replaced with an ideology of regress. In that new philosophy, the human influence on its physical environment will be undone. And the oceans and atmosphere will cool down, and the snow and ice return where they retreated, and sea levels will fall, and forests regrow, and floods and heat waves go back whence they came.

Sub specie aeternitatis, of course, it might not matter at all which way the course of human history flows. But when was ideology ever not in competition with such absolutes?

§ Whiplash

A time of straining or hurtling towards something too far ahead, which ends in giving up, exhausted, sore, returned abruptly not to a previous state, but to new shortness, smaller and weaker than before.

Such is the time of cultural and historical overreach, after which everything snaps back like a rubber band, and hurts like hell in some places.

§ Latecomers

The so-called "latecomer's advantage" not only reduces the research & development costs of a late-coming, late-blooming national culture; it often also translates into a *better* infrastructure of ideas and cultural techniques than was at the disposal of predecessors and pioneers. But better infrastructure does not necessarily translate into better organization and circulation of culture. It is not cultural infrastructure but the sedimented culture of the past, predating the modernization, that is seen as the receptacle of the soul of a people. The cultural engineers and producers must work not above but *below* even this *infra*structure for it to have any function. (The cinema of Weerasethakul, for example, does just that.)

§ Bidding Is Now Closed

A global time for a Global Age...

So long as the standard day stays in Greenwich!

¶ *Sapiens sapiens,* or *Nil admirari*

Every day the present looks more like an *age*. Not in the cultural sense, not like a time characterized by certain dominant phenomena (secularization, social acceleration, globalization, financialization, informationalization, musealization, or what have you), regardless of their maturity; not a time that does not age the world but only breaks its life into chapters. I mean *an age* in the sense of a distinct stage in an existence without known precedent but with a clear life cycle, which is how (not knowing any better) we commonly conceive of the existence of our world.

And what *an age* it is! The question of our continued material survival has set our tongues wagging, and there is no end to the answers. It may be that our vaunting surname, *doubly sapient,* which we have given ourselves, has — no, *not* never meant more — but certainly never been more meant — than precisely now. In this *age of twilight self-admiration*, we are compelled to admit that we are the very picture of man conjured prematurely by Pico della Mirandola: indeterminate yet central to everything, "pregnant with all possibilities, the germs of every form of life."[*]

However, man is distinguished from other animals not only by his superior cognitive capacity, but also by its corollary: his aptitude for self-destruction. The behaviour of other species is the rule that proves the exception ("As a rule animals of the same species do not kill each other"[†]: no other animal so consistently and so methodically hunts its own kind. No wolf, however hurt by Hobbes' metaphor, could ever think the converse, *lupus lupo homo.* The conclusion to be drawn from this is that humankind features monsters and exceptions who, rather than being expelled from the family of man, are unthinkingly permitted to lead it, or at least

---

[*] Giovanni Pico della Mirandola, *Oration on the Dignity of Man* (Washington, DC: Regnery, 1956), 8.

[†] E.H. Gombrich, "Huizinga's *Homo ludens,*" *Bijdragen en Mededelingen betreffende de Geschiedenis der Nederlanden* 88, no. 2 (1973): 293.

act on its behalf to destroy its kin. Even less flatteringly, this murderous monstrosity simply *is* man.

On this most pessimistic account, the choice dearest to man is whether or not to kill man. And, no doubt, he will have his druthers.

Of late, we have been led to think that doing "man" in, or at least demoting him, could be admirable. It is time to put an end to man as the king of the beasts. When it comes to real-life casualties — we're not talking merely about the death of an abstraction! — the idea is not much different from the old anthropocentrism. And yet it has something to recommend it: it may be that, in celebrating it, we are coming around to nature's solution to our problems. Could it be that through our special aptitude (*sapiens sapiens*, don't you forget it!) nature was always looking after itself? While some had an inkling of this, even the most homicidal among us did not take kindly to a "natural" justification of their actions. They chose to see themselves not as doing nature's bidding to avenge itself on "man," but as the saviours of mankind, and of nature. They were, almost to a man, *pro man*; man was their life's project, especially that better, disciplined version of him that justified an increasingly rational selection to eliminate denatured specimens.

Perhaps it's time to think again! Nature seems never to have cared less for our micro-minded designs for self-preservation than in our present *age*. *Twice marked, once wise*, we make do in the killing fields without admitting this bleak and ageist thought. And our horrid work isn't exactly getting any easier. But when our turn comes, let's not flatter one another. It is nature that pulls the trigger — not in our name, no, but in its own.

§ *Viva voce*

The desire to belong and the meaning of belonging owes much to the prehistory of survival: once upon a time, detachment or ostracism from the group could only mean imminent death. (Avoiding death by another tribe, animal, cold, or hunger was not a question of survival but of species-luck and temporary elusion of the inevitable.) The group has gotten infinitely bigger since then, and while death outside it—or, rather, on its fringes—is less likely, long after Crusoe's day it is hard to hold on to our own humanity in the wild without human society as a clear and present reference point. Imagine how much harder it must have been before recorded time, when the sense, let alone the concept, of humans as a distinct species had not yet properly emerged!

The emergence of man, not as a species, but as a *species-consciousness* is how we prefer to think of prehistory: not a series of hair's breadth escapes from destruction, but the inevitable rise of a clever ape, superior in intelligence, technologically savvy, exceptionally adaptable, engaged in the long mental toil of working out its competitive advantage. (Notice I don't write "our" despite having plenty to do with those people.) An appreciable stretch of time put distance between our kind and those giant extinct lizards. It then helped isolate and weave together genus Homo's best genetic threads. The Neanderthals may have been our ancestors and even our mates, but our peers and brothers they were not. Modern humans are not to be regarded as the *surviving* members of some common evolutionary limb. Technically, of course, we are made of what survived multiple species extinctions; *Homo sapiens* exists because we stuck and survived—together. But this hardly makes for the story we like to hear, and which is rooted in our prehistory: not a story of looking back, haunted by fear of dangers just overcome, but one of striding proudly on. We all recognize, if not always buy into, this Long March of Progress, of gradual, forward-looking rectitude. Who can blame us for forgetting bare survival in the story of our evolutionary success. To turn away from its primal character is natural: we have evolved to do it and only thanks to it. Narratively and mythically, the "human race" was smart to multiply, migrate and disperse; it thrived in adversity instead of barely "making it."

But now, at the end of the road, we are reminded of survival *en masse*. Does *our* survival make sense, if there is nothing for us in the cosmic wilderness? Do we have unknown brothers to join, before turning on them, or alien enemies to slay, before becoming like them?

∫ Lost & Found

Having nothing to lose is seen for what it is, an exaggeration. As long as life is lived, there will be something to lose, and loss of life guarantees no proportionate gain for the survivors.

⸹ God Might be the Word, but the Devil Is Still the Tongue

A son-religion displaced the father-religion.
—Sigmund Freud, "Totem and Taboo"
(about the Oedipal relationship between
Judaism and Christianity)[*]

Consider the Oedipal complex as the inversion of Judeo-Christian theology, which had long flipped and sublimated the supposed "natural" order. In the theological order, the primal "sin," punished, receives atonement; the chaste crucified son is resurrected as his own father; the family emerges as holy; hatred becomes love; selfishness becomes mutuality; and mastery, brotherhood and community. Psychoanalysis ventures to set things straight again.

In both scenarios, authority maintains itself by a repressed threat—eternal damnation in the next life, genital mutilation in this one. Psychoanalysis and theology compete as bedtime stories to reinforce this repression while we sleep. (What happens after we fall asleep is of course none of our business.) They are our passes to sweet dreams, though with very different familial models, plots, and endings. In the one, we get over our deepest desire, while in the other, we get over desire, period.

---

[*] Sigmund Freud, *Totem and Taboo: Some Points of Agreement between the Mental Lives of Savages and Neurotics*, trans. James Strachey (New York: Routledge, 2004), 179.

◊ Return of Desire

The question is: can we "return" in some meaningful measure to an earlier, less elaborate, less exuberant "version" of our sensorium, more in keeping with democratic goals and sustainable material conditions? The work of "undoing" rampant needs brought forth by capital and then left unsatisfied would seem to be one of the greatest challenges facing complex ground-up social remodelling. If so, the political vanguard would lie somewhere along the eroded and replenished shores of desire, which a hurricane had blasted and devastated, and thus gave occasion to mend *differently*. A true coastal recovery would take the form not of rebuilding the artificial, "fun zone" structures the storm had ripped away, but of a "managed realignment"—replacing hard, artificial defences lost to "development" with soft, natural ones—reining in and regaining "control" of our desire for a measure of stability without sacrificing suppleness.

There is nothing contradictory or defeatist in the program, once it is grasped politically. We simply oppose the relentless drive of desire and thought that masks its real conditions. These are, above all, the exhaustion and desensitization targeted by images prodding us to react so long as *Don't feed the animals* does not (yet) apply to people; and, second, the stagnation of thought strapped to the media wheel on a ride that will never end. Recovery of the creative act of imagination from the wheels of production and consumption, recovery of thought's own momentum—all this must start on the edge, on the coastline that has been receding ever since the first hordes came to amuse themselves. To extend the initial "disadvantages" of this radical program—which in the West can draw strength not from an ethic of self-sacrifice (though the latter might be resorted on an as-needed basis), but from self-recovery and collective survival—it may become crucial to enlist the rhetoric of sensory-spiritual renewal. For the time being, however, let it be about feeling good about others and comfortable in one's own skin, free from competition for scarce resources, free also of frustration and self-hatred that our addictive consumption tends to elicit in us.

§ Attention!

Our body, once "left" in search of provisions, turns into an imaginary totality, an island that expands to the social and the cosmic, as at the end of Kubrick's *2001*. The generic view of utopia, meanwhile, is as an expression of the drive to subsume the given totality, an elusive goal insofar as all utopias need their constitutive outside, be they Bacon's Bensalem, Frank Capra's Shangri-La, or Huxley's Pala: as long as there is but one prison *anywhere*, one is *nowhere* free — or, one is free *only nowhere*, and, in fact, the fuller the prisons of this Nowhere, the freer one is there when one is free.

The utopian body is that unattainable moment of perfect equilibrium, when all its needs are satisfied at once, perhaps once and for all; when it becomes a place, an infinite world, unto itself, rather than a constrained point in the world, bound and objectified by subjectivity. Our fractional attention makes us think of the fulfilled, sated body as always elsewhere, always where we ourselves are not. The mynah birds on Huxley's utopian island, crying "Attention!" and "Here and now, boys!", would do better to spot-raise awareness by recalling us to the body *precisely* at those moments when we do not feel it — since it demands nothing from us — when for short periods we inhabit it thoughtlessly, comfortably, as voluntary guests (if the body is the zero point of utopia, the complex desiring source of our conscious being in the world, it is also that which the conscious mind can never fully inhabit). This is the work of Palanese teachers who, adopting a hands-on, proactive approach, train their children "to notice how it feels to be in the physiologically best position" so as to learn "to do things with the minimum of strain and the maximum of awareness" — making "the most and the best" out of embodiment.[*] Untrained and undisciplined, however, mindful "recalls" to the body end as soon as the latter demands partial, focalized attention, destroying its unity and presence for the mind. But they are what

---

[*] Huxley, *Island*, 174.

constitute the body-free-of-powerful-appetites — because satisfied-in-them — *as utopia*.

Such exclusive attention to the *living* body soon leads, as do most applied utopias, to disappointment. It is the sort of "return" we reserve for places that we try to avoid if we can, but to which we are bound by some obligation, and that we want to leave again at the first opportunity. It evokes unpleasant memories, trying encounters and traumas, from which we have distanced ourselves, of a time when our body was not yet or no longer "ours," when it slipped away or was wrested from us, when it could be moved around and hurt like a piece of furniture, a puppet, or an animal. The body is recognized, obstinately continuous, but alien and incoherent in itself. Such corporal visitations, to an aggregate over which (once back) we feel we have little control, afford us an unwanted reduction: they remind us not only of our physicality as the *sine qua non* of our thought, but also of the crude, non-negotiable neediness of this physical being, its abiding and unpredictable economy, the competition among its sites and their wants, and — above all — the strange tension of desire and necessity, resolved at certain points, in certain passions, but not in others. No, it is clear that this given shell, this carcass "as is," remains stubbornly and only *here and now*. The body to which we wish to return, meanwhile, is the one that does not need us.

It is a struggle to be embodied to the degree required by our corporeality. The relief felt upon "leaving" the body in thought is *passing* (the only permanent relief being in death.) Our leash is too short, its overextension reawakens the sense of the fragmented body — torn by its competing needs, joint only by time's passing; urgent attention, care too-long-delayed and perforce partial, answers a call in conflict with some still unattended call. On the other hand, uncompelled care of the body, whether on a regimen or on occasion, opens up before us the prospect of bodily unification and reconciliation. We may come to it with some reluctance, especially when (rare moments!) it does not just then demand anything outright, but we do so always with a vanity available at any age in which bodily wholeness is present as an imaginary topos. Bodily sensations may be temporarily focused, spot-lit, admitting no other, as in the receipt of sexual pleasure, swimming, participation in a rally, awakening from a sound sleep, but the approach is holistic. These elusive states — zone, zen, alpha, whatever — never fail to bring to mind utopia in its simplest because bodily form.

§ *Nihil obstat*

The body is like vellum paper on which the mind drafts its ideal dwelling. It is inevitable that over time this surface tears in places repeatedly redesigned — the ideal corporal home for the soul was, after all, never anything more than *unexecuted ideas and refinements*. We should not confuse the power of actual Creation with that of mere Design, whose projects the Creator retains the right to ignore. Hasn't the bodily support for our abstract schemes largely remained *as created*? The body's alteration through concrete, hands-on refashioning is the only way for us to partake of the rights of the Creator.

§ *Carpe noctem*

Catching myself in the act, without reflection, I release myself from all restraints. This is what is called trusting oneself. Without this apperception, this shock and benediction, there is blindness and intuitive action but no trust. As though suddenly realizing a wild horse is carrying us through pitch blackness. Without trust, the rider is not fully a rider (in control) and the horse not fully a horse, more something shot out of a cannon or a catapult: lost in space, without coordinates, every breath potentially the last, every moment a possible arrest as this projectile strikes in its path something that is not necessarily the target of its obscure trajectory. With trust, however, rider and horse are one, and thus complete. We cling to the animal's neck, as far as it will carry us, and the neck (like the fin of a dolphin) has the stability of a statue already mounted on a plinth. A conspiratorial whisper completes the effect: *I'm with you no matter what.*

§ Thick Skin

Solely by *self-excoriation* do we discover in ourselves the seed of other personalities. These are found on our social surface, just beneath the *seal* of our social bonds.

§ *Circulus donationis*

You feel you may have been given *too much* praise? Then you have some humility left. But excessive thanks for excess praise — is that even possible? For some not: for them, thanks alone gives satisfaction, so there can be no such thing as excessive thanks in return for praise. For others, however, excess in gratitude is judged a possibility. But probably not in the way you imagine: not because they are so humble as to feel they don't deserve so much thanks (which is for them a kind of praise). No, in quite another way.

Thanking for excessive praise unaccompanied by more or less equal praise in return — an exclusive focus on thanks, that is, no matter how genuine — could be taken as excessive. Because praise often carries a hope and even (less attractively) an expectation of reciprocity in praise — as gratitude does of reciprocated gratitude. Such praiseless thanks would disappoint — they would be in excess because inadequate, unbalanced, lopsided. Certainly this does not hold for all forms of giving. But it seems to hold for giving praise, on the grounds that it does not cost much, and that almost always — provided "neighbourly" relations — it can be given back, and enriches even the poor. It need not even be a *wealth* of praise, which can be scaled to its recipient's humility. The only trouble is finding enough to really *mean* it. Praise not meant is a verbal gift silently taken back.

⸹ Take It Back

A Polish Catholic familiar with Job's "The Lord gave, and the Lord hath taken away" also knows that "Who gives and takes back will knock around in Hell." This last has its English equivalent in a proverb popular in Shakespeare's day: "Give a thing, and take a thing, to wear the Devil's gold ring." It shows the same association between taking back gifts and the Devil (before he was relieved by another redskin in the phrase "Indian giver").

By accepting both maxims as true, the Catholic of Polish extraction avows the validity of two sets of laws, of two codes for giving and un-giving, with starkly unlike consequences. Has he then, in managing to hold them together, squared the circle of his faith? And could this mean that in the long run his God too is bound for Hell?

§ **Do Not Open**

Some say our vision of Hell evokes none of the vivid torment it once did—that it has become abstract, if still fanciful. Indeed, we look up at Rodin's bronze door with admiration and aesthetic detachment; we have eyes for its imposing size, its sculptural groups and details, its fidelity to Dante's Inferno, and forgive the masterpiece its failure to evoke what we no longer carry in us.

But one fine morning we pass within earshot of a vibrating plate compactor as it is dragged by a worker across a stretch of pavement—its effect so singularly penetrating, though neither especially harsh nor at all loud, that suddenly, with a shudder, the scales fall from our apostate eyes, and we are back before the *Gates*, this time grating heavily and forlornly to reveal Dantean scenes beyond. A glimpse is all we get as the gates slam shut.

Our eschatological vision has grown passive and dull, and sometimes we feel we have seen all there is of Hell on earth, but all it takes is a new sound that shakes us to the very core to unlock a secret gateway to the old inferno.

⸹ Why I Made Fun of Holy Water

Young people, improperly brought up, used to be drawn (and perhaps still are in many places) to a form of sacrilege whose chief aim, I have it on good authority, was to show off the courage of wit—not courage itself, the kind of serious virtue needed in the field, nor wit itself either, the kind that makes some the hubs of social circles, but a *half-courage of half-wit*—the best they can do at that stage of life. While this juvenile humour might strike us as daft and in the end predictable, we cannot but think fondly of the days when we ourselves could still thumb our nose at authority. Back then, we were our own gods, thought ourselves quasi-divine, and the thought of submitting to something so all-encompassing, all-commanding, mysterious, and archaic as one god for all and for all time made us uncomfortable. The weapons most accessible to us then were not arguments from the pens of *philosophes* or romantic poets, but practical jokes and pranks. We saw nothing wrong with this; our own personal gods, after all, constantly mocked one another.

⸹ God Question

If God couldn't make up his mind whether or not to exist, we would make it up for him.

⁋ Comparing "Apples"

Recently my discussions of matters theological have taken on a new flavour. My Brazilian friend said to me: "As I was preparing a *cupuaçu* mousse for our dessert, I reflected upon the biblical account of Genesis as a typically European cosmological narrative. It is obvious that after creating Eve, God devoted himself to the task of creating *cupuaçu*, the real sinful fruit, to do her in. Apples can only be considered a sinful fruit in a fruit-impoverished land. The European version lacks imagination."

I replied: "You're right, 'apple' was a later misconstrual, likely as not based on the Latin of the Vulgate. The original was some divine fruit without any seeds, sui generis. But in any *taste competition* for the conduit of forbidden knowledge, *cupuaçu* would be the clear winner. Someone should correct this."

Although apples do *look* tastier (and I assume they did back then)... And wasn't the seduction complete before the first bite? The incentive after all was not fruit juice, but *mental juice*.

It is always like that: we are seduced by the *appearance* of something, not only to admire it but also to think it desirable. That is how we are first led to reach for it. If the forbidden fruit looked like *cupuaçu* — *was* cupuaçu — we might never have sinned. We would have missed something exquisite, but what a small price to pay, considering...

The question remains: who is responsible for the seduction? God, by making the fruit of knowledge attractive? Or Satan by giving lacklustre produce a high gloss? I'd like to think God planted something ugly, like *cupuaçu*; why would He tempt us? And that, once we had sinned, He would (*deus deceptor! dieu trompeur!*) want the flavour to deceive rather than outright disappoint us. This speaks against apples.

⸹ Default Inheritance

As below the rock freshly pried from soil, so beneath the death mask of the last man worms will be hard at work. Could we stoop to hate the worm for one day inheriting the earth from us? Not if we also cheered it on to outlast us.

⸹ Disputed Inheritance

The worm belongs to the earth alive. We, only dead.

⁂

PARALIPOMENA

§ The Cunning of Folly

Cleverness is a luxury and a sign of comfort. Enjoy it while you can, especially when it is earned. While you are at it, let others enjoy it with you. But never mistake it for wisdom, which comes from hardship only. When hardship comes, make the most of it. But do not seek out hardship to get at wisdom. Nowhere is it written that all men can be wise. You will be found out as a fool for second-guessing fate.

§ Running with It

Those of us intent on maintaining youthful momentum attain their final destination out of breath. That is very bad form. You may start out running, but never arrive running. Since you started on foot, however, do not allow yourself to finish any other way!

Ʂ Hikers and Runners

There is pleasure in hiking alone along a path of my choosing—instead of running a marathon, which simply continues after I drop dead.

Ʂ Crooked Timber

In a race against time, I saddled myself with a project. An old, warped piece of oak, the varnish crazed, alligatored, water-stained. My self-imposed task was not refinishing this dead bit of wood, much less planing to make it straight; it was determining what it was once a part of, and how it came to be this way.

Ʂ Facing Out

> [M]an was made to live facing outward.
> —Cioran[*]

You cannot write about faces, only read them. You cannot read faces, only look at them. Which statement is true? Or which is tru*er*?

Try as you might to write about faces and you will not be able, in the end, to arrive at more than a handful of banal generalizations. You might as well be writing about marriage or dogs. *Faces exposed, faces perceived and recognized, sincerity concentrated in faces*—for isn't it that we face *others* (or are

---

[*] Cioran, *Trouble with Being Born*, 32.

unable to face them), or tell them to their face *what we think of them? Faces as meeting places of most sensory apparatuses: eyes, tongues, noses, ears ... Faces as a typically human trait; animals not graced with them but with other, cruder physiognomies ... Dead, slackening faces, efforts to cover up deathly pallor and "set the features"...* And then this: faces mask the unpredictability of a person. They are relatively *constant* in their features and even expression, giving the often false impression of the constancy of their bearers. Even faces in constant motion, so-called "expressive," are read as pageantry, mere surface disturbance, betraying if anything a steady and simple soul. Faces are the "mirrors" of the soul, as the eyes are its "windows": black or tarnished mirrors, dirty or broken windows.

And my own face? I would like to read in it my own intentions, but rarely do I turn to it for help in divining them. What use, then, is my face to me? My attentions suggest it is of much use: it communicates, it's something to address when making self-demands or -pleas. My face is what others see; shall I make it presentable? When *in another's face*, does it change like some *bunraku* demon-puppet I never myself manage to see?

And should it become intimate with another, even then my face remains closest and most familiar to me (as much as a face can ever be close and familiar). It is my "selfie," it expresses "me." The faces of others appear to express them — their pleasure or displeasure, puzzlement or ease — but how often does the inner mood really come through? As we age, we learn not only dissemblance ("control") but suspicion too. The only mugs we trust, clouding over and brightening to the soul's weather without fail, are those of children. Before learning facial control, they like to hide themselves, and then their faces, which for a long time thereafter serve as the handiest stuff of hilarity and a sandbox for stylizing identity. This transparency of children is a source of wonder, any new parent will tell you.

Then comes the public regulation of expression: when it is proper to cry or to smile, and what it means, and what it does. In the facial code of conduct we have a powerful social filter. Even in private, before a vanity, others are looking over our shoulder, watching us.

For every "defaced" person—losing composure, losing face—there are as many "depersonized" faces—seemingly ownerless, suspended in the air like waxen masks. It is such faces that best *conceal* human mystery (of which the unmasked, faceless person is the most disappointing *revelation*). The depersonized ones do not blend in anywhere, sticking out for no other reason. Meanwhile, the rare facial chameleon goes about unnoticed (as does their remarkable talent).

The sea of faces marking the square, the street, the web: all teeth, all mouth, all eyes—what they say is: we are here to be seen but have no hope of being recognized. Even to notice any one of them, one is forced to focus, to choose, to suppress all the rest.

To get away from those faces, to get away from *the face*... We spend so much of time facing others we can efface none save our own. These other faces are strange because changeable—and nowhere as strange as when flipped upside down. Our own face is strange as well in photographic reverse. The first face we saw must have seemed especially strange, and could be never became familiar. Perhaps this explains the perpetual strangeness of the face-to-face for me.

As we attend to our own face in self-portraits, and like what we see, we judge ourselves good and think ourselves happy. And if we see only facial flaws, then not as character flaws; we can dislike our own faces without judging ourselves, their wearers.

§ Portraits

A likeness is to otherness as a guest is to a stranger — a temporary erasure of unfamiliarity. Unless that likeness is of ourselves, or of one we know well, and the guest is someone close to us. Then the sight of the representation, as well as the formality of hosting, has the opposite effect — a temporary erasure of familiarity.

§ Browbeaten

Thought makes an unlikely protagonist, but our protagonist is precisely thought. And why should it not be? Was it not thought that conceived of this story and made itself the principal? Indeed, the story was devised as a reply to "Dead and Going to Die," an essay by Michael Sacasas, reflecting on a series of portraits taken of young Lewis Thornton Powell aboard the USS *Saugus* by Alexander Gardner in 1865, where Powell was awaiting trial by military tribunal for his part in the Lincoln assassination conspiracy, for which he would be hanged a couple of months later:

> *According to Powell's biographer, Betty [J.] Ownsbey, Powell resisted having his picture taken by vigorously shaking his head when Gardner prepared to take a photograph. Given the exposure time, this would have blurred his face beyond recognition. Annoyed by Powell's antics, H.H. Wells, the officer in charge of the photo shoot, struck Powell's arm with the side of his sword.... Powell then seems to have resigned himself to being photographed, and Gardner proceeded to take several shots of Powell. Gardner must have realized that he had something unique in these exposures because he went on to copyright six images of Powell. He didn't bother to do so with any of the other pictures he took of the conspirators. Historian James Swanson explains: "[Gardner's] images of*

the other conspirators are routine portraits bound by the conventions of 19th century photography. In his images of Powell, however, Gardner achieved something more. In one startling and powerful view, Powell leans back against a gun turret, relaxes his body, and gazes languidly at the viewer. There is a directness and modernity in Gardner's Powell suite unseen in the other photographs." My intuition was re-affirmed, but the question remained: What accounted for the modernity *of these photographs?*

...

Powell could not avoid the gaze of the camera, but he could practice a studied indifference to it. In order to resist the gaze, he would carry on as if there were no gaze. To ward off the objectifying power of the camera, he had to play himself *before the camera. Simply being himself was out of the question; the observer effect created by the camera's presence so heightened one's self-consciousness that it was no longer possible to simply be. Simply being assumed self-forgetfulness. The camera does not allow us to forget ourselves. In fact, as with all technologies of self-documentation, it heightens self-consciousness. In order to appear indifferent to the camera, Powell had to perform the part of Lewis Powell as Lewis Powell would appear were there no camera present. In doing so, Powell stumbled upon the negotiated settlement with the gaze of the camera that eluded his contemporaries.* He was a pioneer of subjectivity.

Before the camera, many of his contemporaries either stared blankly, giving the impression of total vacuity, or else they played a role — the role of the brave soldier, or the statesman, or the lover, etc. . . . Playing a role entails a deliberate putting on of certain affectations; playing yourself suggests that there is nothing to the self but affectations. The anchor of identity in self-forgetfulness is lifted and the self is set adrift. Perhaps the violence that Powell had witnessed and perpetrated prepared him for this work against his psyche.

If indeed this was Powell's mode of resistance, it was Pyrrhic: Ultimately it entailed an even more profound surrender of subjectivity. It internalized the objectification of the self *that the external presence of the camera elicited. This is what gave Powell's photographs their eerie modernity. They were haunted by the future, not the past.* It wasn't Powell's imminent death that made them uncanny; it was the glimpse of our own fractured subjectivity. *Powell's struggle before the camera, then, becomes a parable of humanness in the age of pervasive documentation. We have learned to play ourselves with ease, and not only before the camera. The camera is now irrelevant.*[*]

Enjoying my role of spectator to the drama of Mr. Sacasas's curiosity, a piece filled with insightful speculations at every turn building boldly to the above climax, I arrived dazzled before his much anticipated final revelation — but just then a most charming urchin, whom I had mechanically waved aside, grabbed me by the sleeve and pulled me away. The interruption was certainly no *coup de théâtre*, seeming unscripted, without foreshadowing — and being very likely my own production, for the moment set off-stage, mounted somewhere in the wings. For its part, Sacasas' grand finale stuck around only as long as one approached it *without intermission*, and had already begun to withdraw from the imaginary, docile reader it had expected, eager to follow it anywhere for the bliss of a mystery explained quickly. The persuasiveness of Sacasas's conclusion depended on this; any undue, scrutinous delay would trip it up. Even had I extricated myself from the iron grip of the snotty youngster (in whom I now recognized my own incredulity), I would still have not caught up with Sacasas; my brief hesitation left me to my own interpretive devices.

Sacasas contends that it is *Powell's playing himself* — and not a *role*, a stereotype, for which the photo op typically called — that renders the 1865 suite of photographs so uncannily modern. At this my urchin stomped his feet and shook his head: "Poppycock! It's the hint of tension in his face,

---

[*] Michael Sacasas, "Dead and Going to Die," *New Inquiry*, Oct. 21, 2013, http://thenewinquiry.com/essays/dead-and-going-to-die (emphases mine).

never mind its cause, that makes for these images' modernity. His frown and nothing more. The simple, homespun sweater doesn't hurt, it's pretty timeless. The clean exposure of his young neck sure brings the 'victim' close to you, who fancy yourselves *his* 'victims' too. Admit it makes you wanna neck him! So your arousal makes him modern? Now that's a good one!" Uncouth though he was, there may have been something to his talk. He looked crestfallen when I let him know I didn't buy it.

My lad has since cleaned up his act and learned to stand his ground: "Powell strikes us as 'modern' not for having 'surrendered his subjectivity' or 'pioneered' the modern 'fractured subjectivity' with which we readily identify today. Sacasas has it exactly backwards. Powell makes a point of looking inwards, steely-eyed, of retreating into himself. He is ostentatiously indifferent to his shabby good looks. Outwardness, affectation — that is the fate of the couple in the photograph Sacasas includes by way of contrast. The man and woman, stiff-backed, seated, play the roles assumed by them in society. Concerned with appearing decent, conforming to custom, they are not anchored in any selves I can make out.

"Powell, meanwhile, refuses to submit, to strike the convict's pose, to play the role the camera seems to expect and want to elicit. Instead, he becomes intent on individuality. In the wake of his crime, the radical acts for which he will soon pay dearly, he concentrates himself, drops anchor in his brief and unembarrassed life to get clear on what he stands for, what he really is, freely and through-and-through, only to keep it all to himself. You want to document the would-be assassin? There he sits, resigned to being watched, aware of being the object of curiosity. Put on the defensive by the prying eye of the photographer, forced to play along, he eludes his objectification.

"Owing to the serial character of the exposures, we can see a striking range in Powell's posture, relaxed despite the obvious constraints of his manacles and the session itself. A moving suite; the motivation in his breast is almost palpable. Each of the shots seems to have captured a fleeting instant, compared to the longer durations registered on most other legible images from the period. Powell's tense facial expression (his furrowed brow) contributes most to this impression. Up to that point, a combination of technology and custom made 'the moment' as unavailable to practitioners as Cartier-Bresson's *moment décisif* would later be for his contemporaries. The protocol in photo-portraiture was to dress up according to your station and hold a stock pose aided by furniture, props, and braces. All this to suspend your temporary cares, transcend the accidental, eliminate any momentary tension — resulting in a 'natural,' general you, rather than someone focused and caught up in the moment (whom you would later find silly or unrecognizable). Even the comparatively spontaneous *tableaux vivants* seemed dead — as late as 1882, the trio Nietzsche, Lou Salome and Paul Rée would still appear wooden, weighed down by the photographic studio system.

"It took a 'location' and an uncooperative subject-object like Powell, with an expression instantly recognized as ephemeral, to break this convention of photo-portraiture and showcase the modernity of the medium: its capacity to capture the moment. The added attraction of each photograph, reinforced by its place in a tight sequence, was its seizure of an instant of an individual defying its grasp. We still fancy ourselves such individuals, attached to having clear identities that cannot be summarily extracted from us."

Who had it right, the better angel of my incredulity or Sacasas, whom I had previously given the benefit of a doubt? The stakes were high enough: Subjectivity and Agency in Modernity. Gainsaying a view well-expressed, my urchin made a case for Powell as a self-conscious displayer of the powers and limits of technology — photography being a means of drawing out Powell's uniqueness without, however, the ability to *fix* it. This interplay between subjects and the cameras pointed at them gives rise to a desire to have ourselves caught on film more and more frequently, in ever diminishing intervals. Instead of simply reflecting our modern subjective fragmentation, photography in the first place brings out in us that Self that it at once is powerless to capture.

⸹ Life of Zilch

In the college of the future, every student should be required to write at least one biography of a deceased nobody.

⸹ Spilling Your Beans

Those in the public eye who can't help themselves from spilling their own beans, tempted by public interest, are to be pitied. The public will decide how their life is told. Not only will they have to live with this tale, but their own interpretation of it will carry little if any weight—not merely because they have given away author's rights, but because their judgment was put into question by what and how much they had divulged.

⸹ Making up Lives

All our work is autobiographical, not merely conditioned by our living. Autobiographical not just in the pedestrian sense that we *make* the work (and everything contained in it) part of our life, by the mere fact of engaging in it. My biographer might write, based on my work: he was interested in X because he had experienced something like, or something of, X. But equally: he wanted to make something of X, for its own sake, or to make X a part of himself. Such speculation is not always flattering to its object. There is a measure of relevance for each strand in our work, not all of which is material for a biography—for the simple reason that, except in the authorized cases, the metric of relevance is missing. A good biographer recognizes this and leaves uncombed what a bad one would *style*.

§ Literary Effects

Writers who have been through a lot as writers, who have to their name not only their books but also the scars and scrapes, regrets and disappointments left from their exposure to the public (which even in our civilized, squeamish, herbivorous age thirsts for blood), have generally little fear of their executors. "There isn't a branch or a thorn, / That didn't catch him going by, / Leaving his clothes tattered and torn,"* concludes the upbeat testament of literary vagabond Villon, who summons his executors to his deathbed.

This bruised condition, this difficult past, is an advantage over those who passed through professional life unscathed. A healthy relationship between executor and writer (whose neck remains, for a while at least, on the line) is built upon the latter's trust and forgiveness, which come easier after years of public abuse. The executor acts only as the arm of literary law: his dead client's estate must be protected from the public. Those who received more than a fair share of acclaim do not quite grasp this, thinking such executions especially cruel and unjust.

---

* François Villon, *The Testament by Francois Villon with Facing Notes: Metric Translation with Altered Rhyme Scheme*, trans. Stephen Eridan (2004), http://www.inmanartz.com/villon&notes.pdf.

⸹ Working with Dreams

The dream resists being turned into narrative. It is made of different stuff, exceedingly fine and ethereal. This is obvious not only when you try to recall one, record it, but when you attempt to work with it. It is very hard to work with a dream—unless you take it as it was, rough and wild, without reworking it. It is not the dream that must adjust itself to your story, but the story to your dream, if its dreaminess is to be left intact. It is with dreams as with fragments of meteors fallen to Earth. One thinks, quite wrongly, that just because they have landed they are up for grabs and can be fashioned at will. The Rolex Daytona Meteorite looks like an ordinary watch. Its space-rock face might have raised the price of cool, but will never raise us to the stars.

§ Fast Asleep

It is a rare author who can pull off taking narratives from dreams, a rare author who can draw on them for material without giving himself away. The reasons for this are as mysterious as they come. But let us venture three guesses.

In dreams we are not ourselves, not in control of imagination. Tied to their strange origin is the sense that they belong at once to no one and to everyone. Around the dream-story, the story based closely on a dream, hang the guilt and suspicion of stolen goods. Taking from dreams means dodging the labour we still associate with true, honest creation, and can be a source of shame. Copying them carries the faint stigma of plagiarism, and can cast doubt on one's creative powers. To play it safe, to avoid cheating, dreams are often flagged, or otherwise identified.

Yet the more important reason why dreams do not make credible stories has to do with their content and structure — dead giveaways. Transferred to the page or on film they are obviously, surreally *unserious*, compromising even comedy. Only those who undergo psychoanalysis boast dreams serious and creative enough to be worth preserving artistically (they have earned ownership of their dreams, and even indirectly paid for it).

But we know better anyway: that dreams are a democratic republic where all can partake in the genius of invention; that virtually everyone, no matter how long they have left to sleep, spends a great deal of time there, has full rights as a citizen. Smugglers might not be prosecuted, but will be found out. Dreams resist being passed off as products of real inspiration; just look at how clumsy and ponderous they seem. Duty taxes, my dear, borders, customs — but, beyond that, be on your merry way!

It is, one suspects, only the false, asocial conviction that we experience more or less the same reality but live in incommensurate dreamlands that stands in the way of republican relations — and waking-life relations with dreams as dreams. Were the literary reticence systematically reversed, removing the reality pretense and stigmata of shame, we would see how much more we share when we sleep. I do not mean the local colour, familiar faces, languages, and customs that, as in the waking world, remain specific to each, but the broad strokes of humanity that transcend them. How much in common we have when we are least social: the continuity of our powers, desires, and needs—none of which we need to censor, when we can blame them on the dreaming strangers in our lonely beds.

§ Dug Up

> *He speaks underground. Only people who dig equally deep can hear him.*
> —Kraus on Lichtenberg*

The author of Roger Kimball's 2002 review of Lichtenberg's *Waste Books* lives in the Age of Plagiarism. Translator R.J. Hollingdale's introduction to the same is repeatedly invoked, but not as the template for the entire review, which it effectively became. To acknowledge this would have been to preempt the charge of plagiarism—something that Nietzsche, living in a different age, was not obliged to do when writing his *Genealogy of Morals* (1887), so well summarized in Lichtenberg's "Notebook G," §21 (dated sometime between 1779 and 1783). It is regrettable that the review's author did not better take into account that he lives in our day, rather than Nietzsche's.

---

* Kraus, *Dicta and Contradicta*, 90.

§ Law of Transformation

Two Mamelukes were undoubtedly more than a match for three Frenchmen; 100 Mamelukes were equal to 100 Frenchmen; 300 Frenchmen could generally beat 300 Mamelukes, and 1,000 Frenchmen invariably defeated 1,500 Mamelukes.
—Napoleon's martial calculations[*]

The dialectical law of transformation of quantity into quality is now applied to books. The more one writes of them, the more this affects their quality. Individually they will get worse, or stay the same at best. But marshalled, they're a force to be reckoned with!

§ Quantity over Quality

Something is rotten in the State of Letters if the chief motive for continuing to write is to match one's rival *book for book*.

§ Taking In, Letting Go

"The more the mind takes in the more it expands."[†] Until, at some point, it exceeds capacity, tips and pours itself into a book. Once relieved, it is known to fill again, capsize, and return upright. With each iteration, the mechanism improves.

---

[*] Frederick Engels, "Anti-Dühring" (1877), in *Karl Marx and Frederick Engels. Collected Works*, vol. 25, *Engels: Anti-Dühring, Dialectics of Nature* (New York: International Publishers, 1987), 119.

[†] Seneca, *Letters from a Stoic (Epistulae morales ad Lucilium)*, trans. Robin Campbell (London: Penguin, 1969), letter 108, p. 201.

⸹ What Are the Chances?

A   Writing and publishing books is more and more like putting messages into bottles, don't you think?

B   Yes. Even when books become shorter, briefer, to have a greater chance of being read — even then...

A   ...even then, with self-publishing taking off, there shall soon be islands of them, islands of drifting plastic bottles with soggy messages. They'll have been released into a saturated sea, where they will only ever find...one another. No one will read them when they wash up!

    Still, some messages in bottles, if they are found, do become *proper* books...

B   How so?

A   Why, by being read of course!

B   Reading...Wasn't that more common when there were fewer? But you have a point: when books have travelled far to reach us they have "a story to tell." We might fish them out of the water for no other reason than that. These success stories (even if they don't tell stories of success) give our desperate, lonely writers reason for hope. And why shouldn't fortune smile on them as well?

A   Should we encourage this hope?

B   Hope should always be encouraged. It is *futility* we should be worried about!

§ **Unbound...**

...Unprinted, Unpromoted, Uncatalogued, Unsolicited, Unsold, Untitled, Unwritten, Un—

§ **Out of Print**

The backlist will see the light of day again when, like flesh in a meat grinder, it is fed through social media and comes out line by line. This will give it the requisite *raw* appearance.

§ **"A Book"?**

More than the recent tomes on the history of the novel, publishers' insistence on the subtitle "A NOVEL" suggests these are that genre's waning days. But the "book" has ahead of it a bright future; its use as a label is still some time off.

§ Moratorium III

B   *A moratorium on new books?* And you hope this will dam the flow of writing? When it is lifted, more will gush out again.

Why not learn to swim in it now? We need books to buoy and guide us before we can hope to navigate the streams, or swim upstream, or find our way out of the mainstream.

A   Are you kidding me? The current is too strong to resist, to be anything but swept away by it.

And do we really need so much text? I don't deny that people want to write, but do they *need* to? Is that where their energy ought to be directed? Isn't there something better, more useful they could do? Most of the stuff isn't even any good.

Why not turn grey literature black or white: bad enough *not* to be published, or good enough to *be*? The river into which you want to step to swim is *white*...

B   ...If you swim with that pure current, as fast as it, you will always be the same. But if you only dip into it, it will seem different each time, refreshing and inspiring. That's why we need *books*. Books are like houses and hamlets along this grey river. They are places to spend the night.

A   Bah, who can keep up with that river? It keeps passing us on every side, and we cannot resist it, we can only be carried by it—you call this swimming!? The *book*, as long as it exists, will only interfere with our brief and dripping existence. We grab hold of a book and right away we start to sink. We are sure to drown. We need fewer books—fewer riverine colonies—and more houseboats, floating text to live in. Then we will all feel at home in the river, instead of clinging to those dry and cultivated bits of land. But if we fill our pockets with stones, we will soon be found floating belly up, refuse amid the traffic, until some lonely old chap, who spends his last days watching the river flow by, his eyesight failing, spots us, and, moved to pity, sees to our proper burial far from home.

B What an image. You have convinced me of a tension, and that it is a difficult choice between reading books and immersing yourself in the life of the river. Why not give up books? You don't seem to share my view that we need them to find our way.

A You're right. I don't share it. As long as there are books, I will not give them up — but the future of judgment depends on us doing so. I am certain of it! We must wean ourselves off books! Slowly but surely. Nothing good ever came of preserving authors in paper mausoleums. We must chop them up and distribute them, like the relics of saints. We must *link* them without imprisoning them. And those who take forever to make an argument, and can't stand being "chopped up"? Do we need them now?

B I suppose not. But we can't develop our judgment reading only fragments — even fragments of former books — however clever or wise! We still need arguments! And they take at least as much attention and patience to take in as they did to make. When thoughts flow well, uninterrupted and sustained, they lend the river you speak of coherence.

A More often than not they get in the way: they exclude other voices and hoard attention. We need to resist imposing the structures of books on this grey matter! We don't need to learn from books how to *stay afloat* in this great river; for many that comes naturally. A book only pulls us down to the slimy bottom. They say young people take to it is like fish to water. They have learned to swim. It irks me when I see these capable swimmers judged by the old standards and submit to them. Rest assured, we will be judged in our turn.

B We already are — by you!

A   I'm not one to judge — I'm complicit. But I know it's not even on swimming that the new judgment depends; it is on *flowing so fast that the river itself seems to slow*. That's what judgment depended on in the golden age of books: it survived by keeping ahead of them, more multiple, manifold, and fluid than they were. There were fewer books, and even when published speedily their distribution mercifully lagged. Then things changed, and thinking grew frustrated with constantly falling behind reading, and reading became inattentive, driven by catching up, and no one, not even those who read for a living, could really keep abreast of new releases. This is all the more true today, I'm afraid. Except that books now are not, as previously, distillations of reflection, but spaces where we do our thinking — on the page. Yet they have fallen again out of sync with the pace of change and take too long to publish. And when they are finally out they announce their presence with come-hither titles to get noticed; meanwhile, people have moved on; how much are they really going to engage with what is no longer current? And these books responding to a moment (already passed), how much of their argument is the fruit of long gestation? Very little; one book rushes another, impatiently awaiting completion. Books come too late yet demand instant attention, and fall over themselves to peddle their musty thoughts, even ones aired to the public a thousand times before. That way they devalue everything that is not a book. They often start out bookish, trying to live up to the book's cultural standing, and for that very reason are never quite credible *in the flow*. We need fewer riverside distractions, fewer fixations, fewer *fixed abodes!*

B   I see what you mean: you'd like the pioneers not to look back, to make up their minds, to go with the flow…

A   The book (would that it was just one!) holds everyone back. It's time to get over it, time to turn the page.

§ Before You Put Pen to Paper

Which would you rather be: the paper weighed down by words unworthy of it, or the paperweight keeping them in place?

§ Lapidary

A lapidary expression is at once beautiful and poignant. Its effect does not stop at this first impression. It is in the nature of the lapidary's art, which the aphorist admires, that it takes in and works materials more diverse, less precious and thus more useful than the diamond, the sole specialty of a diamond-cutter. Thought, like art, cannot advance in monomania. The destiny of the diamond is to be stolen and handled in gloves. The destiny of the stone is to be used and worn.

§ An Aphorism

An aphorism means to be unwrapped as a gift, not admired in a jeweler's case. To read one is to subject it to a test of reasoning, imagination, and judgment — to work your way through the layers of tissue nestling it as through the steps of its mounting, polishing, and cleaving, to the rough shape in which it was first found. Studying the work of the maxim cutter, you apprentice in the art of criticism.

§ "Uncombed Thoughts"

> *Under the comb the tangle and the straight path are the same.*
> —Heraclitus[*]

It would indeed be strange if aphorisms, so often dispensing their insights through analogy, did not also invite analogies when it came to themselves. It could be that the aphorism's affinity for rough self-comparisons is its compromise with anti-intellectualism. In drawing comparisons between themselves and products of skilled manual work or other concrete, recognizable things—"stock cubes," "saltpits," "nuts," "bullets," "assholes," "hand grenades," "someone else's lost earnings," "pet monkeys," "bananas," "short cuts," "wandering Gypsies," "parachutes," "ripe fruit," "shacks," "gongs," "hedgehogs," "origami," "splinters," "dribble," "raisins," "summits," "sweepings" and "vaccines"—they puff themselves up to greater general utility than they can in fact claim. At least on first impression, before their real transmutation unfolds before us like a fragrant rose at dusk—all nature, no fabrication—we do not mind these unwashed half-thoughts. They speak to us, after all; *ergo*, we ourselves could have spoken them!

---

[*] Heraclitus, *Fragments*, p. 33, sec. 50.

◊ Held to Account

> *Aphorisms are rogue ideas. Aphorism is aristocratic thinking: this is all the aristocrat is willing to tell you; he thinks you should get it fast, without spelling out all the details.... An aphorism is not an argument; it is too well-bred for that. To write aphorisms is to assume a mask — a mask of scorn, of superiority. Which, in one great tradition, conceals (shapes) the aphorist's secret pursuit of spiritual salvation. The paradoxes of salvation. We know at the end, when the aphorist's amoral, light point-of-view self-destructs.*
> —Susan Sontag[*]

It is easy to see the point about aphorisms not needing proof. I suppose what made this feature, or aspiration, of aphorisms crystal clear to me was Fritz Raddatz's "final farewell" to Emil Cioran: only later, through the reading of Cioran's early semi-aphorisms, whose metamorphosis into maxims was incomplete, did Raddatz realize that the *later* aphorisms he once enjoyed and excused, by chalking up their apodiction to provocation, irony, or wit, were in fact deeply problematic and *criticizable*.

For my part, I cannot help subjecting aphorisms to the test of reasoning. If I take them prima facie, they are sitting ducks. Unless, of course, they wear their jokiness on their sleeve ("Thank God for Satan"[†]). It is rare that one "speaks" to me, its truth cutting through my skepticism. More often, I am drawn in only to deduce their occasion and formation, as I am curious to trace a trickle of water to its source, or at the very least its outlet. And once I have gotten that far — broken down the process, gone back to the bedrock — I proceed to argue with process and bedrock. I take issue with effaced judgments — with everything, as a matter of fact, that had gone into this brilliant truth but was sanded off along the

---

[*] Susan Sontag, *As Consciousness Is Harnessed to Flesh: Journals and Notebooks, 1964–1980* (New York: Farrar, Strauss and Giroux, 2012), 512 (entry from Apr. 26, 1980).

[†] Lec, *Myśli nieuczesane*, 451.

way. I reject the aphorist's having it both ways: aesthetically and propositionally; when I look at one side I am blind to the other—my preference being, again, for some quantum of verity, acting as breakwater to the sublimity and beauty of the composition.

To illustrate: "A high level and depth are very different things" (275). What is here to argue with? Was the author aiming to communicate a banal truth, a counter to Heraclitus perhaps? We judge this unlikely, even if we hold on to a possible allusion. Between the lines, here individual words, we pick up on what was likely meant: different senses of cultural attainment. And as soon as we pry, they become questionable.

"Could I not just say everything simply? I could, but no one would pay for it" (363). Now this is more like it—were it not for the fact that it no longer rings true.

Or: "The great receive instruction, the little people are taught a lesson" (42). How can you argue with that? *You* perhaps cannot. But to *us* the aphorism is a sign of decadence, and its authors, as Sontag says, deep down defenders of privilege. And so we think it insufficient to marvel at it. We would go so far as to assume there is not enough in it to marvel at: looked over once or twice, it loses its lustre and appears laboured, or else ornamental and tawdry. With the loupe as our default approach, a strong feeling can only be one of pleasant surprise. If we find a gem, we stuff it in our pocket. It "belongs" to us now, and thus to everyone.

⸹ Juggling

> *How can aphorisms change your life? Find out when James Geary brings his Juggling Aphorisms show... a mix of memoir, literary history, audience participation — and live juggling, with words and balls. Audience members are invited to randomly pick an aphorism from a globe and read it aloud; Geary then tells about that aphorism and the person who wrote it, weaving in personal and historical anecdote. There are also several blank strips of paper in the globe. If an audience member draws one of these, they can name any theme and Geary must cite a related aphorism on the spot. If he fails, they get a free copy of the book!*
> —uncredited[*]

Q. Which book?

A. Why, James Geary's very own *The World in a Phrase: A Brief History of the Aphorism* (2005). (So much for brevity...)

Q. Does Mr. Geary never compose aphorisms at the audience's bidding?

A. Of course not. His is a memory unusually well stocked with the thoughts of others.

Q. He does say "cite," though, not "*re*cite."

A. Well spotted! The description is tricky — like juggling... I suspect what he performs is closer to reading.

---

[*] "James Geary's Five Laws of the Aphorism," Dailymotion, Dec. 12, 2006, http://www.dailymotion.com/video/xvnucn_james-geary-s-five-laws-of-the-aphorism_news.

Q. And the juggling? Surely much skill is needed to keep in the air the different "balls"?

A. I have seen the show and can vouch for its clumsiness: the delivery of bios, the citation of dicta, the crude cross-cultural cross-historical comparisons (Chamfort was Warhol, he even says). And picking "worlds" (a proprietary metaphor for aphorisms) out of a globe — you can't imagine what fun that was! Geriatric entertainment in its purest form!

I aim to insult only those persons of any age who cannot keep a thought straight in their head because all their lives (however long or short) they would rather see it done for them, for their amusement. And the whole thing about how "Aphorisms Can Change Your Life" — let's call it artisanal baloney. As "Chamfort" might say, "Art is what you can get away with."[*] And in Geary-land you can get away with a lot.

§ More Is Less?

> *Everything very good has always been brief and scarce; abundance is discreditable. Even among people, giants are usually the true dwarves. Some value books for their sheer size, as if they were written to exercise our arms not our wits.*
> —Baltasar Gracián[†]

The writer can take this wisdom to heart by giving himself little space (even less than he has!). Every great aphorist is distinguished by the persuasiveness of his exaggerations. Brevity has the obvious advantage of excusing lapses of

---

[*] Actually, this is likely Andy Warhol (or pseudo-Warhol).
[†] Gracián, *Pocket Oracle*, p. 12, sec. 27.

judgment, to which he seems especially prone. He may write something one-sided and obtuse and call it deliberate provocation, or claim public service credit for exposing a noxious cliché to ridicule. Or he may shrug and distance himself from his ideas: "If you don't like these, I've plenty of others." And he can always fall back on his craft, since hyperbole, though hit-and-miss in its power to persuade, has the advantage of being more striking.

This might help explain why aphorists are fond of puns and reversals of memorable exaggerations. In another's one-sided view they see their opportunity for subversion, sometimes even broad appeal. Bakunin is not remembered as an aphorist, yet his atheistic reversal of Voltaire was just such a predatory act. Things stood no differently with God's oft-quoted reversal of Nietzsche, a boost to His waning popularity. The same simple operation could be detected in many great aphorisms, their authors having merely taken a contrary side. The facility with which reversals are handled, attached to the pleasure of playing with form, puts us in mind of the genesis of insight: the relish, namely, of contradiction.

Now for our inversion of Gracián above:

> *Every good thing has always taken time and was naturally plentiful; abundance is estimable. Even among people, dwarves are the real dwarves (sorry!) and giants, ever giants. Some value books for their epitaphic concision, as if to spare them every fatigue.*

§ Chain Reaction

As the authors of *Surfaces and Essences: Analogy as the Fuel and Fire of Thinking* make clear, aphorisms, those "fires without flames," burn so brightly on account of their fancy for analogies. The briefer they are, the better their fuel is ventilated, the more inspired the thoughts they in turn set alight.

§ Culture Vultures

"Aphorizing is a harmless art. There are others we should be more concerned about."

§ Culture Vultures

"The popular novel is not a dead art. There are others more deserving of our attention."

§ Hypocritics

Shoddiness, vested interests, and unembarrassed amateurism have trumped pretenses to knowledge, artistic sensibility, and judgment of taste. Move over, hypocrites! Make room for hypocritics!

§ A Common Cause

> [T]ime seemeth to be of the nature of a river or stream,
> which carrieth down to us that which is light and blown up,
> and sinketh and drowneth that which is weighty and solid.
>   —Bacon[*]

As the profession of book criticism wanes, popular critics will mime the *pollice verso* of the gladiatorial arena. They may not want such power, but the public will expect it: book choice made simple and risk-free. In such a climate, where authors vie shamelessly for attention from those still in the reviewing business who, as pay for their work shrinks, have no more reason to curb their own literary ambition and are compelled to practice criticism chiefly out of self-interest—
at such a time, reviews of threateningly good work will be grudging at best, at worst suffused with resentment.

The clearest indicator of the shift to negative-spectrum criticism will be inconsistency in individual opinion. While the dedicated, undistracted critic builds a reputation for reliability in judgment, the critic of the future, working and writing in a strangled environment, practices on the side, at variance with their writerly self—which they put first. When one peers into this imminent future, the corrosive effects of the critical spleen on the striving writer within seem obvious; a dark sketch on one side of already thin paper will show through on the other. The joy of writing requires that they make common cause.

That is why I would not dream of being a critic today. In my commitment to writing, I am convinced I serve the common cause of writers and critics. It is bad enough that as a writer I believe in the superiority of contemporary judgment, which never fails to recognize merit in the new. Only with repeated disappointment ("The book receives few reviews

---

[*] Bacon, *Advancement of Learning*, 36.

and is ignored by the public. Bitterness"*) could I hope to see my bias corrected. Things would be far worse if it were critics themselves who believed in infallibility, over against their predecessors' errors of judgment. I would then be forced to break with them immediately.

---

* Jim Crace, interview by Leigh Wilson, in *Writers Talk: Conversations with Contemporary Writers*, ed. Philip Tew, Fiona Tolan, and Leigh Wilson (London: Continuum, 2008), 64.

§ The Democratic Challenge

Due to its institutionalization and technological restrictions, public criticism has long lagged behind literacy and informed opinion. Now perhaps we are witnessing the first real explosion of critical democracy and the competition of opinions on the only available model — that of the free market. There are still gatekeepers, value-porters, opinion-makers, and there will be as long as there exists social stratification and distinctions of taste. But basic quality control will be mechanized. Properly marketed, every item of opinion, however shoddy or déclassé, will find its consumer. The products of the elite will meanwhile be pushed or drowned out by large opinion outlets and pop-ups, with individuals providing meretricious content, and by boutique venues, creatures of successful reinvention usually due to lucky timing. Those who produce for refined taste — undervalued luxury goods — will see their niche shrink. They will know well to gauge demand and goodwill in advance, through subscription.

The more drunken and savage popular criticism waxes — as it is bound to do in digitized democracies committed not just to facilitating open access to information but also to universalizing critical expression — the more thin-skinned those who think in popular ways become, breaking down at the first sign of rejection — "bullied," "harassed," "belittled," "insulted," and "betrayed." (And can we be certain of our ability to identify and prosecute critical bullying and mobbing?) By contrast, those few patronized by the unpopularly privileged will be assured of their love and see no need of ever venturing into wilderness.

§ Free Ride

The piggyback has gone the way of all offbeat assistance.
There are no more pigs with portly backs to take you up.
There are only pigs who never leave the clover.

§ Not to Be Outdone

Come April, the mad (whom the cold subdued) also spring
to life, marching their follies up and down the muddy street.
Look at us, madness's blossoms!

§ Invisible Tree

Dreaming, like living, has its seasons. In your orchard as in
mine, the *tree of dreams* is always the least cultivated. So in
the autumn of our lives, we are content with sweeping up
its fallen leaves, where before we would have sunk our teeth
into its fruit, and before that marvelled at its blossoms — we,
who are its roots!

§ Late Spring, Late Summer

There are moods proper to spring that ripen only in autumn,
and summer experience crystallizing only in wintertime.

∫ No Qualms

With the crude kind of D.I.Y. lighting I am peddling to the benighted, I am no heir to Prometheus. I am more like a coal-seller in a hard winter, when buyers are neediest and price hikes are laid at the feet of scarcity. If you find this objectionable, see if I care.

Of course I do, but what *to* do when one knows the winter will be the longest on record?

∫ Got a Light?

How long has it been since someone asked you for a light? How would they know whom to ask these days, or that whom they should ask is you? Make yourself their go-to person. Take up position in a throughway and *offer* light. Offer it and watch someone walk up to you. They are not looking for conversation, they've heard enough about smoking too much, and they are not interested in you. What they do with your light is their business (and none of yours). They'll find a *need* for it.

Why are so many of these "matches" about writing? Ideas, my friend, don't grow on trees. They don't drop from the sky. They are not the product of heavy industry. They are neither animal nor mineral. They are not the substance of sports. They are not returns on investments. Their material is *this stuff*.

§ Obscurantism

> *Those who compose from coloured light the single and essentially white light, they are the real obscurantists.*
> —Goethe*

It is one thing to admire stained glass, appreciating the coloured light shining through it, and another to look directly at the sun, to the inescapable blackening of everything else. Stained glass is good for seeing, white light, for blindness—insofar as shadows and colours are occlusions of such light. To blend all visible things is to see nothing at all. This is the genesis of God.

§ Misfired Insult

One plausible reason for why *matchhead* never caught on as a term of abuse (like *pinhead*, *blockhead*, *dummy*, *birdbrain*, or *clod*) is that, factoring in the proportions, it might easily be taken as flattery, a step up from *hothead* or *firebrand*. Either that or because, after God, light does not lend itself to taking offence, only to *giving* it. Its weapon is fire. Matchsticks are the myrmidonian armies of light.

---

* Johann Wolfgang von Goethe, *Maxims and Reflections*, trans. Elisabeth Stopp (New York: Penguin, 1998), p. 165, sec. 1296 (mod. trans.).

₰ The Cynic's Matchbox (That's the Spirit!)

I throw in my lot with *light*—with matches, to be precise. They are at all times capable of making brighter: by day they distract from nimbus skies, by night they disperse the gloom of distance—and are never blinding!

By matchlight, I am liable even to write poetry of affirmation. No one can then accuse me of anything *but* affirmation—of course, purely on aesthetic grounds!

Light is in.
Dark is out.
Light is hip,
light is cool.
Dark is dour,
dark is cruel.

THE MATCHSTICK (to me).
   Don't take yourself so seriously. After all, you'll be the only one. And you'll still be accused of negation. Your affirmations will be jeered at: they are unproductive!

₰ Illuminosity

I can't decide: am I *luminocentric*, or more in love with the thick, bituminous darkness that straightaway follows light? Do I fall into the arms of day, or trace the all-black silhouettes of the *contre-jour*?

¶ Light Touch

In darkness you shall call *Let there be light!* And so you will confess.

¶ Seeing Darkness

Paradoxes have the unfortunate consequence of turning those who embody them into fools. For example, the first man who lit a match to see darkness. Did anyone except some village idiot ever in earnest try such a thing? But consider the act and you might soon hear yourselves exclaiming: "But of course! It is by stark contrasts that we approximate absolutes." Although darkness is done for the duration of light, immediately afterwards does it not seem quite *complete*? And secondly, do we not see many things better in the light? Is this not true also of things quite black? If we see something dark in the darkness, a shape we can barely make out, would not illuminating at once bring it out?

∫ Safety Matches

When playing with matches, we are told, safety comes first. To those who are childless and have not evolved the scolding and mollycoddling dispositions of parents towards their young, the phrase "safety matches" remains what it is, an oxymoron. The parents of Promethean mankind use it to curse its primal birthright to start fires, while dousing them. They engineer all the danger out of matches. To establish a semblance of order, they arrange them into books, where bundles would have sufficed. Only the matchbox still contains the threat of original disarray: with every agitation, the contents cast together inside the tray are shaken up and rearranged. What happens between them, in the dark, is their affair, possibly incendiary. A large black cat leaping across the box of one popular East European brand seems to attract as much as deter bad luck. A children's toy manufactured from such a box held, instead of matches, two plastic mice. As one pushed the tray out this way and that, the white or the black one would come out to tempt the cat. Even this useless and stupefying diversion, already figurative playing with fire, has since been replaced by parental supervision.

⸿ Matches to Ashes

Perhaps the lesson of the Little Matchstick Girl extends beyond miserabilism and beatification of the poor. The warm light in the cold darkness is no longer the bleak reality of the child's circumstances, her impending death from hypothermia, but a wondrously comforting illusion. One by one, you may recall, she strikes the matches that are her livelihood and warms herself by their evanescent flame. "The morning of the New Year dawned over the little body sitting with the matches, of which a bunch was almost burned up. She had wanted to warm herself, it was said. No one knew what lovely sight she had seen or in what radiance she had gone..."[*] What she had seen was what she had imagined by match-light.

The fate of the little match-seller is of course one of the most familiar emblems of modern inequality, with the dirt poor inhabiting the fantasy of the filthy rich, but not the conscience. On the cosmic balance sheet, in line with archetypical folk-tale justice, inequality cuts both ways. It is as detrimental to the well-heeled as it is to the downtrodden. The impoverished imagination of the prosperous requires a sesame to access it; it is filled with gold and wondrous and exotic objects; nothing local and modest would satisfy it. The private visions of the poor are, meanwhile, not only spiritually richer, but can be found in the flame of a match.

---

[*] Hans Christian Andersen, "The Little Match Girl," in *Andersen's Fairy Tales*, trans. Reginald Spink (New York: Signet, 1987), 211.

ꭍ Book Advertising

Matchbook covers carry advertisements for soft drinks, humour, hotels, recreation, resorts, resistance, nightclubs, cigarettes, cough medicine, cigars, ground transportation, liquor, cruises, casinos, beef, services, appliances, girls, magazines, anniversaries, supermarkets, talent contests, cities, banks, bingo, shoes, shirts, museums, motor oil, pesticide, luxury automobiles, and — most interestingly for us — *books*. It is a relief that book covers have not been degraded in the same way. Just imagine a book advertising a brand of matches, or a wood-burning fireplace. You would then be forgiven for mistaking certain self-promoting volumes for "essential kindling."

⸹ Little A

The great Amazon, the "great green hell," is still around. But it is no longer what the word *Amazon* first conjures. The name of a rainforest and the river running through it doubles as the name of the greatest book shipping company in existence. A jungle of paper and pulp spreads across the globe. Meanwhile, the other Amazon—"the last page of Genesis," "still writing itself"—falls to the saws "unpublished."[*]

Nobody is drawing a causal link. The two Amazons are not in competition, and we have no confidence in the long-term survival of either of them. A "desert of trees that had to be cleared for the benefit of mankind"[†]—the one no less than the other. A destiny indifferent to how we judge the human practices within each of them morally. *Nomen omen est*: the ancient Amazons entered history on the losing side.

---

[*] Euclides da Cunha, *Um Paraíso Perdido: reunião de ensaios amazônicos*, ed. Hildon Rocha (Brasilia: Senado Federal, Conselo Editorial, 2000), 100.

[†] Herbert Girardet, "Obituary: Richard Schultes (1915–2001)," *Guardian*, Apr. 26, 2001, http://www.theguardian.com/news/2001/apr/26/guardianobituaries.highereducation.

◊ Long Distance

The book is so low-tech, it's hard for technology to degrade it.
—Evan Hughes[*]

Precisely because the printed book is not in competition with what today bears the name of "technology," it weathers prognoses of obsolescence and embarrasses media and gadgets that chomp at the bit to replace it. If it were to enter the short-distance running and innovate, it would expose itself to the risk of obsolescence, squandering the accumulated "captial" riding on its endurance. It still has the lead in the 600-year-race.

◊ Legacy of Modernism

The notion that literature has value when it is accessible to the majority is one of the perverse legacies of—because a direct reaction to—Modernism. It is most troublesome to those who see no place for themselves in the literary mainstreams, who fundamentally decline late Modernism's flaccid elitism, willfully minor and non-communicative, no less than the faux populism of the establishment. To write for one, at most several, readers, and leave it at that, is unintelligible within this polarized landscape, where letters cannot be used as literature's carrier pigeons.

---

[*] Evan Hughes, "Books Don't Want to Be Free: How Publishing Escaped the Cruel Fate of Other Culture Industries," *New Republic*, Oct. 8, 2013, http://www.newrepublic.com/article/115010/publishing-industry-thriving.

⸹ First Things First

Having something to say is, first of all, having someone to speak to.

⸹ Correspondence

> *Some are useful at a distance, others close at hand, and someone who is perhaps no good for conversation will be as a correspondent.*
> —Gracián[*]

The cheapening (and virtual disappearance) of sustained correspondence, its replacement by largely face-to-face interaction (increasingly in virtual form) no doubt owes something to the purely practical origins of letters — as a speedy conveyance of important information, to link and keep order in empires as much as households. While personal-letter specimens go back as far as the Sumerians, they are predated by administrative ones. Under the Romans, letter-writing became a privileged means of rhetorical, moral and spiritual cultivation — sometimes one-way or one-to-many (as in biblical epistles), and not always from afar, yet at enough of a distance that the written message could sink in without interference from casual discourse between the parties. In the modern era, it evolved into the main medium, alongside printed pamphlets and books, of a transnational Republic of Letters, where letters were widely circulated, addressed to the intellectual salon-elite, and a growing literate public.

The word *correspondance* acquired its meaning of private, two-way exchange right around then, in French (the linguistic heart of this imaginary *res publica*). Some of the older

---

[*] Gracián, *Pocket Oracle*, p. 59, sec. 158 ("Know How to Use Your Friends").

notion of correspondence — a relation of conformity, analogy or resemblance between inanimate things, and mutual accord of sentiments and ideas — naturally transferred over to the concept of epistolary communication. What is less obvious is that, over time, by a kind of notional *après coup*, the sentiments expressed and bonds built through letter-writing came to colour the meaning of *correspondance* sans words, paper, or even human beings. For Baudelaire, such mutual relations between "perfumes, colours, and sounds"* form a secret theatre unobserved in the everyday tumult and rationalization so emblematic of modern life (as seen in his *Paris Spleen*). It is the heroic task of the artist to wander through forests where symbols "observe him with familiar eyes" (ibid.), and to attend to them, and even — as in later, surrealist chance encounters, "objects," and their assemblages — to bring seemingly heteroclite things and thoughts to intimacy by the force of marvel and creative vision. Jünger was similarly partial to "the secret correspondence existing between things."† Where he turns this interest into a method of composition, he resembles the eavesdropper; his words intercept harmonies invisible to another ear.

There is no reason why future letter-writers should not take a page from this "stereoscopic" disposition or Baudelaire's roaming attention and create in their written correspondence a space where correspondences of this "nonhuman" kind can occur. An exemplar of such practice is John Berger's exchange about colours with the artist John Christie, published as *I Send You This Cadmium Red....* Recalling the occasion for beginning the correspondence, Christie writes:

> *Yesterday I went to a funeral, someone I didn't really know very well, and during the service before the cremation I was looking at the flowers, some in vases and some in jars arranged on the steps before the lectern where the Rabbi*

---

* Charles Baudelaire, "Correspondances," in *Charles Baudelaire: Complete Poems*, trans. Walter Martin (Manchester: Carcanet, 1992), 18.

† Jünger, *Adventurous Heart*, 73 (mod. trans.) ("The Picture Puzzle").

> *stood. My eyes were caught by a bunch of carnations directly in front of me. Red and yellow carnations in a single vase, not formally arranged, just put there, a block of red and a block of yellow. The red were the nearest and I looked at them for part of the service trying to see how the heads were constructed, how the petals fitted over one another. But the shapes were too delicate and I was just slightly too far from them to see properly. As I thought I was understanding their shapes so the precision of the image slipped away like in a dream...*
>
> *So for no better reason that the memory of those flowers I send you this Cadmium Red.*[*]

More than a mere reciprocated observation of correspondences among colours, the colour correspondence turns literal: image accompanies text virtually every time (a corresponding image, to be sure). The colours correspond, assisted by human curiosity about the chromatic scale, its cultural and personal values. On this basis—although by no means just this one—we would be forgiven for imagining a correspondence among humans in parallel to a correspondence among things, the one feeding into the other indefinitely, brought into correspondence in a language as yet unknown.

---

[*] John Christie, letter 1, in *I Send You This Cadmium Red...: A Correspondence between John Berger and John Christie* by John Berger and John Christie (Barcelona: Actar, 2000).

§ Writing For

> *And likewise it is the intention of my best friend for whom I write this, also, that I should write it only in the common tongue.*
> —Dante, "XXX: His Letter to the Rulers," *The New Life*[*]

It is a strange linguistic effect that, as soon as a verb is followed by "for," the action it designates is understood as useful in some way. The relation of utility holds even — and this is relatively new — between one's action and oneself. Admittedly, the preposition in "thinking for myself" has a somewhat different sense than "doing something for myself," but the latter connotation of usefulness is a good deal more prevalent. Thus, we keep journals and heurnals for ourselves, take time out and have quiet evenings at home with a cup of cocoa, all for ourselves, and all these uses of our time and attention also become ways of caring for or rewarding ourselves, and not forgetting — making "for" the fulcrum of the mantra of well-being.

With writing, and art more generally, for's transitivity takes what not so long ago could be self-centred or almost exist in a vacuum — writing or art for its own sake, without regard to anything outside it, maximally devoid of purpose, *écriture pure*, channelling semiosis, epitomized in philosophical and aesthetic good posture — and transforms it into a duty, a public service and good rendered by private individuals. Blogging is now the paramount form of writing for others, in a way that tweeting is still not (if only because it is insubstantial and instantaneous, Twitter-happy). Bloggers, by contrast, feel an obligation towards their readers to be useful, helpful, instructive, illuminating, even when motivated by vanity. (Here it intersects with public art projects, whether commissioned or "free of charge.")

---

[*] Dante, *New Life*, letter 30, p. 76.

There is no wishing away the public stigma attached to "writing for a living"—which essentially boils down to "writing for oneself"—now that one's income from the written word almost always needs supplementing and the phrase thus conjures the privileged few who manage nonetheless to support themselves. In contrast to blogging or tweeting in one's free time (freed up by adequate compensation for some other, useful work), "writing for a living," especially when that writing is not obviously "for others," does not justify let alone "pay for" itself in a way that, say, "dining out for life" (an AIDS fundraiser) does. The money made doing it ends up in the pocket of a single individual who, on the face of it anyway, spends all their productive time on one, self-directed (and, since not adequately remunerated, presumably quite useless) task.

Society is hard on writers, this is hardly news. But the conflicted relation between writing and for-ness will remain opaque without some understanding of the uneven development of "self-help" (in the broadest sense, from the care of the self to partaking of "life's little pleasures" to urgent self-preservation). This development was severely hindered by the historically Christian notion of charity—the other-directed hand of the Good Samaritan. The concomitant lag in self-help's acceptance into the sphere of public usefulness owes much to the grasping hand of Christianity in the shape of the modern capitalist state. This hand is quite visible when it catches us at our most passive as cultural consumers: as an advertisement enjoining us to "Be FOR something. FOR a life with more wow, and more now," since "being against is the easy way, but being FOR something is an attitude that can change the world."*

---

* "FOR a new urban joy. A Manifesto," Smart Automaker, accessed Mar. 12, 2015, http://uk.smart.com/uk/en/index/smart-campaigns/whatareyoufor.html.

¶ Dead Letters

There always comes a time when a dear friend's silence can no longer be taken *personally*.

⸹ Envelope Stuffing

> *Letters morphed into emails, and for a long time emails had all the depth and complexity of letters. They were a beautiful new form that spliced together the intimacy of what you might write from the heart with the speed of telegraphs. Then emails deteriorated into something more like text messages (the first text message was sent in 1992, but phones capable of texting spread later in the 1990s).... I think of that lost world, the way we lived before these new networking technologies, as having two poles: solitude and communion. The new chatter puts us somewhere in between, assuaging fears of being alone without risking real connection. It is a shallow between two deep zones, a safe spot between the dangers of contact with ourselves, with others.*
> —Rebecca Solnit[*]

While letters continue to be posted, they contain little more than envelope stuffing—and not just flyers, bills and bank statements. Has a similar degradation affected voice communication? There, the addition of cameras has made all the difference. Is it not true, in any case, that where there is competition and choice in personal communication technologies, one will always (even without corporate mechanisms) outdistance the others? The popularity of microblogging now was that of tweeting earlier today, was that of social networking and texting late last night, was that of video and text chat yesterday, was that of letters before the heyday of the telephone and the internet...We now see that we change services and usage before either reaches the point of obsolescence. It is not the technology that grows obsolete; it is our use that obsolesces. Under such conditions of testing out available means of connecting, perhaps attention to form is bound to outpace attention to content for a reason; perhaps in no other way is content itself eventually regenerated...

---

[*] Rebecca Solnit, "Diary," *London Review of Books* 35, no. 16 (2013), http://www.lrb.co.uk/v35/n16/rebecca-solnit/diary.

⸹ Diminishing Returns

It has been said that the "style and spirit" of letters is "always...the true 'sign of the times.'"* But what is the sign of times when letters ceased to be written, and all that is left of them is the signature? Should we be worried? Or rejoice that the sign of the times, whatever it may be, has moved on to more modern media that keep morphing rather than remain in the gauge of epistolary spirit and style. The signs of the times are these new media, their spirit and style.

There are revivalists who would like to bring back letter-writing. They believe it does the spirit good and improves writing style, if not the hand. But they are not blind to the fact that the returns on their own outlay are rapidly diminishing. Even their correspondents forget what a personal letter should look like. They respond in email missives, which offer freedom in minimal or in-formality. The increase in volume is offset by reflective sloppiness, shortness, and poor editing. Preference goes to doing the job quickly, from the heart, ever on the fly. The personal diary, meanwhile, still rules in the department of longhand self-unlacing. Thus, letter-writing disappears as a means of one-on-one-exchange.

And, separately, it has become unfashionable to speak of "signs of the times," since this implies that our times can change. Instead of letter-writing, the stock exchange is now the spirit of exchange, the digit, its style.

---

* Nietzsche, *Gay Science*, p. 184, bk. 4: Saint Januarius, sec. 329 ("Leisure and Idleness").

¶ Dashed Off

It is sad to see one of the greatest technologies of the heart ever invented die in our lifetime — and seem even more short-lived than us. It is not that we have lost courage and drama in personal written exchange; audacity has never been easier. But the new brevity in correspondence has not been met with succinctness. While emails and text messages contain vestiges of personal letter-writing conventions, these have less to do with substance than with form. All highly ritualized behaviour that cannot adapt to a change in medium or context is similarly passed down form first. Yet, as the need for written communication at a distance dwindles, the form of the letter, still rigid and widespread, collapses after the initial exchange into sporadic familiarity. It is observed that epistolary decorum is in most cases unnecessary when a number of more efficient ways of making contact can be called on to convey personal information. But what ought to be observed is that simultaneous, interchangeable use of these other means is also unnecessary. That lack of necessity, in other words, does not fully account for the letter's demise. Why not admit that the letter has become too difficult? Time-investment and the effort to articulate salient things about ourselves — desires, opinions, experiences — seem more like supernumerary work. It is not that we have become lazy; we have become overworked. With linguistic proficiency honed on bureaucratic tasks, certain uses of language have taken a beating.

§ **Other People's Mail**

in response to Miranda July's 2013 editorial/curatorial project
We Think Alone:

> *And of course while none of these emails were originally intended to be read by me (much less you) they were all carefully selected by their authors in response to my list of email genres — so self-portraiture is quietly at work here. Privacy, the art of it, is evolving. Radical self-exposure and classically manicured discretion can both be powerful, both be elegant. And email itself is changing, none of us use it exactly the same way we did ten years ago; in another ten years we might not use it at all.*[*]

What is so new in this project of editing emails with the permission of their authors? The answer is: the curiosity of their editor. Two decades ago, when privacy was still assumed, taken for granted — not yet something we would be wise to divest ourselves of voluntarily before it is taken away from us by force — interest in the workaday (or so July would have us believe) correspondence of obscure collaborators would have been hard to conceive. The place where one sampled letters for different occasions was of course the letter manual, popular since the seventeenth century — a genre of generic epistles from which the collection's high-profile editor may have taken inspiration. Thus, "An Email That Gives Advice" corresponds to "A Letter of Advice" or "Counsel"; "An Angry Email," to a "Letter of Remonstrance"; "An Email About Being Sad," to missives on the death of a loved one; "An Email With I Love You In It," to one "Upon the Absence of a Mistress"; "An Email That Includes A Picture of Yourself," to one answering "A Letter Desiring a Mistress's Picture"; "An Email To Your Mom," to "A Letter from a Daughter to Her Mother upon Marrying against Her Consent"; "An Email

---

[*] Miranda July, about *We Think Alone*, accessed Mar. 12, 2015, http://wethinkalone.com/about.html.

About The Body," to "A Letter Congratulating a Friend on the Recovery of His Health"; "An Email About Money," to "Letter from a Poor Prisoner to His Creditor"; and so on (the second in each set comes from John Hill's popular *The Young Secretary's Guide: or, a Speedy Help to Learning* of 1687 and many subsequent editions). But I may have hit on a correspondence on another plane: What is *We Think Alone* if not a letter to the past? Having passed through all the challenges of this curious project we have been bumped to a higher level of understanding: we are precisely *not alone* when we *think*.

⸹ News of Oneself

The use of epistolary form to communicate one's ethical knowledge is in keeping with Seneca's notion that knowledge is "common property" and must be shared, distributed, in order to have any value.* His epistles to Lucilius have an overt edifying purpose. They are explicitly meant as moral advice for another individual — as shared wisdom — thus admirably enacting the idea contained in them. Judging from their literary character, they are intended for circulation among a wide circle of readers. The sense of personal disclosure, of a private text being made public, of something previously reserved for one becoming accessible, shareable, helps the text's ability to garner interest and disseminate its ideas. The provision of moral instruction and the imperative of sociality are two ways in which letters generally can — and Seneca's letters do — underscore the relationship between literature and ethics.

But Seneca also argues that a moral life can only be sustained if one proceeds *as if* another conscience were observing one's doings; one must remain in dialogue with oneself,

---

*   See Seneca, *Letters from a Stoic*, letters 8, 6, 13.

in a self-critical relationship that is as strong as the criticism of another human being whom one respects, even venerates (letters III, XI). One must to a degree learn to objectify oneself, transcend one's own empirically conceived ego, while at the same time constituting and maintaining that ego's integrity. Any act of self-writing involves just that; a distancing of oneself in order to interpret the self as a phenomenon, an existing, conscious and intentional whole — to "[c]arry out a searching analysis and close scrutiny of [one]self in all sorts of different lights" (XVI, p. 63). The act whereby one promotes one's qualities and sets a moral example is accompanied in Seneca's writings by an internal critical dialogue that has sought externalization. Anyone capable of judging society, life and what constitutes truth ought to show they are first able to examine and evaluate themselves (III). The correspondence is only an extension of this principle to active, external dialogue.

The notion of "correspondence" is here somewhat misleading, since we read only half of the exchange. The addressee, Lucilius, is an indeterminacy; his words and writing are referred to in Seneca's responses to him, and so we may fill them in based on context, yet the content of his actual letters remains a matter of conjecture. The idea of physical distance, a necessary condition for communication by letter, parallels psychological self-distancing, necessary to the process of self-criticism. On the textual level this allows Seneca to be selective and falsify himself in interpreting and evaluating himself (XLVI); on the psychic level it helps transcend the immediate experience and take account of one's life bodily. Lucilius, then, acts as a foil for the author's self in that his evocation, presence and implied responses provide a pretext for writing and self-dialogizing. While being partially mediated to us by the fictionalized I of Seneca, Lucilius actually serves as an equivocal mediator for Seneca himself.

It lies in both the reader's (as represented by the pupil Lucilius) and the author's interest that they be "of the utmost benefit to each other" by way not only of sharing knowledge and company, but also of assisting in inner dialogue and self-criticism — ends to which the epistolary form is unusually well suited. In this light, Seneca's "And yet I do not summon you to my side solely for the sake of your own progress but for my own as well..." acquires a new significance (VI, p. 40). The need to displace himself, to represent himself as the relation between two separate characters — as correspondence qua form turns thematic — may indicate that Seneca was working on his own duality, his inner conflicts, and that his self-criticism, in the presence of some unaddressed, interstitial territory of his conscience, could be omissive.[*] In letter XXVI, for instance, he speaks about the final verdict he will declare upon himself, "determining whether the courageous attitudes I adopt are really felt or *just so many words...*" (71, my emphasis). This serves to undercut the very sense of writing at the same time that it shows the author on a self-directed ethical quest, actively involved in tutoring himself (an idea voiced on a number of occasions). This quality of Seneca's writing — as a procedure of working out one's own moral dilemmas, even if only by proxy and allusion — seems to make it all the more effective as a didactic text.

To a degree, every author is self-reflexively embedded in their writing. Their inner dialogue need not seek expression as literary dialogue. When it does, do we understand them any better? And when it reaches for epistolary form, does the

---

[*] However, only from our (post)modern perspective, with our sense of the function of narrative, knowledge of psychology (the means of the constitution, organization and representation of the self) can we conceptualize Seneca as a construct on the textual level, as a fictional character separate from the historical one. It is highly doubtful that Seneca would have consciously designed a fictional version of himself — that he was aware of, and understood, it as a literary device. Rather, it was for him in the nature of letter-writing, when one is at a distance from one's correspondent, that one interprets himself and often conceals certain flaws (in this case for the purpose of better instruction) — "we still find habit a reason for telling lies." Ibid., letter 46, p. 90. By writing himself into his own text, he was merely transposing what he thought proper to transpose: an "essential" Seneca, though not a fictional (unreal) one. One must not forget that under Seneca's pen the letter-form becomes intensely self-referential (without being unnaturally so). He is very conscious of stylistics (especially of falling into poor style), not just in writing but in public speaking. His reflection extends over the entire domain of text- and discourse-production. Ironically, however, it tends to avoid issues of content.

length and depth, honesty and sincerity, of their correspondence have any bearing on our understanding of them? For the writer and reader to benefit each other, *mutual understanding* must be neither's aim.

§ True Taste

The writers of today are worried about offending anyone. Imagine a fish that takes itself out of the water, fillets itself, seasons itself to taste, lays itself flat upon a frying pan, then lies down hastily on a bed of garnish — all to ensure the public will devour it. It so wants to be savoured, to melt in the mouths of average diners. It genuinely thinks that freshness and seasoning can distinguish it, tantalizing taste buds without any risks. Except that all this it shares with other fried fish. True taste is distinctness of *flavour*. All the rest is presentation.

⸿ Soho!

> soho: *call used by huntsmen to direct the attention of the dogs or of other hunters to a hare which has been discovered or started, or to encourage them in the chase; hence used as a call to draw the attention of any person, announce a discovery, or the like* (OED)

There are words whose different senses seem to have developed through whimsical resemblances and contiguities. The French *bouquin* is one. Its primary meaning is "book"—as anyone with a decent ear (it is pronounced /bukɛ̃/) and familiar with Parisian second-hand book vendors, or *bouquinistes*, might guess. More specifically, *bouquin* (initially spelled *boucquain*) is a "little book" or an "old book," especially one "thought nothing of." The nineteenth century adds a further pejorative nuance: a book that "though modern has no other value besides that of its curlicues." Around this time, too, the word comes to mean "book" in popular parlance.

But *bouquin* has a still richer history. In the middle of the eighteenth century it was borrowed by huntsmen. Not (yet) book-chasers, but hunters of rabbit and hare. Aside from a phonetic closeness (*livre, lièvre*), the resemblance between (old, likely male) books and rabbits (also old, buck) might escape us at first. But perhaps, as registered by this lexical twist, what unites the book and hare is their pursuit, until the very end, of their respective lives, measured in leaps and pages.

The use of *bouquin* as a hunting term did not start there. Sometime in the sixteenth century it came to signify the opening of a hunting-horn used in rabbiting, a *cornet à bouquin*. The connection to horns had also made it handy for an "old billy goat," from which later arose the meaning of "satyr" and "roué." The main association of *bouquin* with the cornet, however, seems to be oral in origin, possibly via *bucca*, Latin for "mouth." From there the word travelled to the bohemian land of pipes, specifically their horn mouthpieces.[*]

---

[*] *Le trésor de la langue française informatisé*, s.v. "bouquin," accessed Mar. 12, 2015, http://atilf.atilf.fr/tlf.htm.

Having followed awhile in the tracks of etymologists, we begin to piece together a strange picture out of the history of one French disyllable: a *bouquin*-blower, *bouquin*-catcher, *bouquin*-puffer, *bouquin*-lover and, finally, -devourer!

⟨ At the Stalls

We have translated the idea of *browsing* — derived from feeding on tree leaves and shoots, said of goats, deer and cattle — into the digital realm quite seamlessly. Lost, however, are its public *scenes*, moments of absorption, the search for the unknown work not as a commodity, but as unadulterated use-value. The hope for serendipity is part of it from the start, and there are some who hope for the lucky find they can then cash in on.

If one has ever looked at those who still routinely engage in browsing bookshop stalls, one might wonder whether the demographic committed to this activity has changed over the years. One look at Paul Gavarni's physiognomy of an urban loafer, observed *en passant* in the middle of the nineteenth century, makes its caption all but redundant: "If I could read I'd never read such old editions." The gaunt-faced, no-longer-young man in the picture is attracted to the wares of a bouquinist as he might be to a parallel universe, strange and inaccessible to him, for whose opacity he compensates with hands-in-pockets disdain. Likely uneducated, he seems without any prospect of the leisure required to make his wish (grudgingly in the conditional) come true. Behind him, two legitimate browsers peruse the volumes. Encounters with unfamiliar books did not typically involve reverence, the piety of the meek and unschooled — if such indeed is in evidence here. At the opposite, equally eccentric end stands a *vieux savant's* ecstatic immersion, in another engraving aptly titled "An Orgy." Before him lie worn volumes offering themselves cheaply — just 50 centimes! His browsing is hands-on, open-mouthed. Even if the goods for sale are not the most desirable, their sheer volume, the possibilities they open up, invite a thousand caresses.

§ Why I'm Not a Book Addict

A book addict shouldn't care what they read as long as they get their fix...

§ What Are Shelves For

Someone had made a joke about the spurious popularity of empty shelf photographs, or empty "shelfies."* But who needs real shelves anymore? Have they ever served any other purpose than holding books?

Even bookshelves migrate. Sooner or later you will take screen shots of your virtual ones, similarly divested. From there you will move on to your mental bookcases, clearing out turgid nonsense taking up precious *thinking* space. That much more access to the little of it that's left!

Suddenly, everything will click. Emptying all those shelves, embedded so deeply, was freeing us from self-incurred tutelage for an age of clarity. In our dotage we will have just two tomes to take pages from, dangling from our virtual girdles in imitation of medieval monks to protect them from thieves: a *sottisier* and a "bible," a book of jokes and a book of truths.

---

* This is not to be confused with the "shareable selfie," also called Shelfie.

𝄋 Will-o'-the-Wisp

But perhaps you feel the world is bright already? You have a stack of newspapers, digital edition, which you keep burning through. No sooner is the screen illuminated than the message begins its rapid decay.

Isn't that just how you want it? Plus, there are lights in neighbouring windows, street lamps, and—damn it—the sun! Plenty of light to see by. At least along your path, no need to watch your step.

§ "I am loath even to have thoughts I cannot publish"*

The economic cheapness of digital publication democratizes expression and gives a necessary public to writers, and types of writing, that otherwise would be confined to the hard drive or the desk drawer. And yet the supreme ease of putting words online has opened up vast new space for carelessness, confusion, whateverism.
—*n+1*, 2012†

Is the strict correspondence of thinking and publicizing not a concrete and universal expression of Kant's practical philosophy? The achievement of the Digital Age is finally clear: the running commentary on ourselves and our world that fills the blogoverse is the global flowering of public discourse.

On the one hand, self-loathing now precedes self-censorship and critically cuts much deeper. We no longer excise the bad, the unpublishable, from our thoughts; we get its sources out of our system before they become thoughts or sweep them into some designated unconscious, where they remain safe, pathetic, and innocuous.

---

* Michel de Montaigne, "On Some Lines of Virgil," in *The Complete Essays*, trans. M.A. Screech (London: Penguin, 1991), 953. The same line in context, in another translation: "I have ordered myself to dare to say all that I dare to do, and I dislike even thoughts that are unpublishable. The worst of my actions and conditions does not seem to me so ugly as the cowardice of not daring to avow it. Everyone is discreet in confession; people should be so in action. Boldness in sinning is somewhat compensated and bridled by boldness in confessing. Whoever would oblige himself to tell all, would oblige himself not to do anything about which we are constrained to keep silent. God grant that this excessive license of mine may encourage our men to attain freedom, rising above these cowardly and hypocritical virtues born of our imperfections; that at the expense of my immoderation I may draw them on to the point of reason. A man must see his vice and study it to tell about it. Those who hide it from others ordinarily hide it from themselves. And they do not consider it covered up enough if they themselves see it; they withdraw it from their own conscience." *The Complete Essays of Montaigne*, trans. Donald M. Frame (Stanford, CA: Stanford University Press, 1976), 642.

† Editorial, "Please RT," *n+1* 14 (June 14, 2012).

On the other hand, and it is a huge other hand, are we still having thoughts worth having? A troll of a question visits the digital fora of the West: if everything is permitted, is anything worth saying? Psychopaths may spin their schemes of revenge and suicides perform their finales, but do we take them seriously? Will there soon be anyone left to care about *what* we publish enough to police it? Saying is still worth doing, but making sense hardly matters. "Anything's sayable and nothing's worth saying—How can you stand it? Do something! Say something!!"—tweets the hobgoblin, and gets retweeted. But can the hogs of attention appreciate such pearls?

So we are back to square one as concerns a standard of public discourse. The Enlightenment model has been buried; for the newcomers, it is as good as dead. They are on their own.

⸹ Grasping Criticism

"Criticizing everything but accomplishing nothing. That is the world's nature; it cannot get away from it," writes Luther (with biting criticism of course) in his open letter on translating the Bible.[*] And here is Marx in a personal letter to his friend: "what we have to accomplish at present: I am referring to *ruthless criticism of all that exists*, ruthless both in the sense of not being afraid of the results it arrives at and in the sense of being just as little afraid of conflict with the powers that be."[†] Two countervailing views: theological and anti-theological. Why should criticism have no redeeming qualities for Luther? Its reach exceeded its grasp, even in textual form. Why should Marx have had such high hopes for criticism? Because it grasped so much.

⸹ Mushy Criticism

A soft spot for the opponent in a political debate indexes decay in one's own position.

---

[*] Luther, "An Open Letter on Translating," 176.
[†] Karl Marx to Arnold Ruge, Sept. 1843, "Letters from the *Deutsch-Französische Jahrbücher*," in *Karl Marx and Frederick Engels. Collected Works*, vol. 3, *Marx and Engels, 1843–1844* (Moscow: Progress Publishers, 1975), 142.

∫ Criticism as Self-Examination

Critical exercises can be tools of self-discovery just as interval training can act as a coherence test for one's ideas, not to mention boosting their resilience and versatility. Short critical drills can lay bare what one "really thinks." The choice of object to criticize reflects not only what's "trending" in critical opinion, or the limits of one's interest, but also which ideas one is inclined to interrogate and which completely to avoid — out of habit and bias, if not simple blindness. If one is at a loss for ideas, intensive bursts of critique might help decide where to go from "here." If, on the contrary, one's thoughts come out pure muscle, metabolically freakish, one might be jolted to run as far as possible in a different direction.

⸿ Murine Criticism

The German Ideology, written by Marx and Engels in 1845–46, while they were still in their twenties, was for complicated reasons published only after Marx's death in 1883 (twelve years after his first *New York Times* obituary). Engels thought this no great misfortune, since the book's chief purpose was its authors' "self-clarification," in which respect it was a great success. What needed clarifying was their own, materialist philosophy of history, starkly opposed to that of the German idealists. This clarification took the form of ruthless take-downs of the leading figures of post-Hegelian thought in Germany, turning them out as Saints ("Saint Max," "Saint Bruno"...). And if this bold mock-theological design were not refreshing enough, there is ingenuity in the details, the relish of youth poking fun at others' philosophical and political weakness, armed with the wisdom of Shakespeare, the wit of Cervantes, the spirit of Goethe, and social critique in the guise of nursery rhymes. When you hear of all this crisp prose, flower of nineteenth-century German *Bildung*, languishing in a drawer—"abandoned," as Marx put it, "to the gnawing criticism of mice"*—you might find yourself envying the mice. For anyone curious about Marxism, I can think of no better place to start than this attic of Marx and Engels' Brusselian collaboration. But there is a lesson in it writers would do well to learn: *that books can be written solely to clear up one's thinking, and anything left over belongs to the mice.*

---

* Karl Marx, preface to "A Contribution to the Critique of Political Economy" (1859), in *Karl Marx and Frederick Engels. Collected Works*, vol. 29, *Marx: 1857–1861* (New York: International Publishers, 1987), 264.

∫ The Draft

On the wall of his study, the novelist Émile Zola is said to have written these words: "not a day without a line" (*nulla dies sine linea*). The line had previously belonged to the painter Apelles, and pertained to the "lines" of his art, as noted by Pliny. In this sense also it was adopted by Van Gogh—for all his incessant correspondence, which anyhow frequently combined text and sketches.

The draughtsman's table is so much larger than an escritoire, and no sooner than a choice is made of paper stock that this difference seems justified. The *draft* may be where the draughtsman and the writer part ways, but it is itself a fork in the road, with two paths open to them both: the writer can choose to sketch out his thought instead of making an arrangement of words, and the pencil accustomed to lines can rather trace letters. The successful draft is just a few strokes away, strokes that capture the essentials. What does it matter which system is used to make them, so long as they are indeed the essential ones?

⸹ Around the Block

Subtle connections exist between our limbs and our memories. One hears of longhand as a method of retrieving material one had *written down* in the past, in school exercise books. What might not come back to us if we could pick up a pen with our foot and write without effort? What dormant knowledge would return from down there, so far from our brain? Is it something to be wondered at, and never attempted? One imagines the Writer, in their well-known exigency — to overcome the Block — will one day give the conjuring hand a rest. *Dexterity*, after all, was never a professional requirement!

⸹ Keeping Up with the Joneses

The *writer's block* is necessarily short; writers must keep up professional appearances. A city of *reader's blocks* is spread out, with impressive facades and buildings never lived in. Reading is not a profession, but the hang-ups around it reference social standards that isolate those who fall short of them even more.

⸹ On the Rails

What you have long dreamed of is about to become reality. Your writing will be your ticket, procrastinators shall be shifted to the last car, and impostors thrown off immediately. Yet this dedicated *writer's train* of which you hear tell — the writing machine par excellence, our definitive solution to distraction — will arrive too late for some. The rumble and screech of hurtling metal are today much too subtle for them to dictate the rhythm of words.

∫ Zoning In

There exists a mental space—or perhaps it is continually created—where a writer hears nothing but the beat of their thought, and sometimes even this fades away completely, leaving only the thought itself. This is called "being in the zone." "Flow" is another term for this peculiar and highly coveted state of mind, though not in the idiomatic sense of "going with the flow."

Certain authors, especially when all their books are read in one go, seem never to have left "the zone" in their life. Singling out one work of theirs as superior takes a special kind of rudeness—if, that is, we aspire to the "writing life" ourselves. (If all we seek is "the best," then the same selection is proof of uncommon discernment.) But if, like me, you are a writer in search of the zone, you see the oeuvre as a series of signposts showing you the way.

"Innovators astonish us by the total development of their practice, not by each work taken singly," says Michael Krausz.[*] They astonish even more when the totality of their practice displays an unabated stream of enthusiasm and skill. Of such writers it could be said that one has no desire to meet them in biographies, but only ever in "the zone."

---

[*] Michael Krausz, "Introduction," in *The Idea of Creativity*, ed. Michael Krausz, Denis Dutton, and Karen Bardsley (Leiden: Brill, 2009), xix.

⸫ The Easygoing Work

We adore some books for their undemanding nature. It is enough to graze in their folds, to fall in innocent calf love, free of elaborate courtship and head-scratching stress. Because, let's face it, we sometimes tire of the demand to mean, which authors make of us.

With a surge of relief, we are moved to ourselves compose an easygoing work, expressing our bliss in a reprieve from meaning. And touring such a book our expectations of our readers are correspondingly few: mooing is approbation, the Q & A is a cinch, and all that we ask is to meet up "like cows in the meadow."*

⸫ The Easy Part

advice to first-time novelists

A splash is a splash, whether it's wet or red. Making a splash in a pool of water is easier on the eyes, compared to splattering on concrete. Unless you already know how to swim or put yourself back together, it's the recovery you should be worried about.

Dying instantly, on the spot, seems preferable to drowning in your own success.

---

* Nietzsche, *Human, All Too Human*, p. 237, vol. 2, sec. 107 ("Three-Quarter Strength").

§ *Succès d'estime*

The success all artists should fear is the *succès d'estime*, being lionized by the critics but ignored by the wider public. The danger lies in that overestimation of our achievement known as *mastery*. (Mastery is what an artist who wants to be loved by the public does not claim; arrogance loses him popular favour.) For this misfortune there are only two forms of damage control. The first, requiring more effort, is to imagine ourselves the laughing stock of past masters (standing before a mirror with a degree in our art might be enough). The second, with more to recommend it, is to pump oneself full of *depressants*, and in a manner of hours feel all trace of self-esteem dissolve. I understand the trend these days runs the other way, but so do critics' artists with their successes. You will no doubt want to say: "What's done is done! Let the poor deluded devils be." Indeed, the memory of a *succès d'estime* is preferable to the failure to surpass one's own estimation.

§ Double-Check

You call yourself a "writer's writer," but are there any writers actually reading you, whom you know of, let alone care about?

◊ Out Like a Light

Awareness of advanced years or signs of fatigue in illustrious figures in our field of endeavor is the source of subliminal anxiety among us lesser lights. We fear that once their creativity is extinguished, we too might be suddenly put out, like candles at a party once the guest of honour has departed.

∫ Bridge of Boats

From book to book a writer crosses the river of what is thought and said, flowing unrecorded. Sometimes, out of hunger, he lowers himself down and fishes out an idea. His books are like barges or lily-pads strung together, eventually stretching across. It may be that others, the so-called disciples, are crossing the water behind him. When they have reached his latest, they must wait until he has again accomplished his feat of organic verbal engineering.

But most likely he is alone. To Nietzsche's "*To write in order to triumph.* Writing should always mark a triumph," and his description of his works as a record "*only* of my overcomings,"[*] I respond: "My thought exactly, even if it's juvenile showmanship." To be exciting, writing must be competitive, rewarded by personal fulfillment. At every step, the writer competes against the inertia of self-consistency and repetition. It makes little difference who looks on, how many pairs of eyes follow the progress of the champion-engineer.

But the metaphor of books keeping the writer afloat can be drawn out even more. Once they have been brought in line, they are tethered together. Most books from one pen are fissiparous—owing to the writer's embarrassment, worsened by middling reviews, or to envy between his books, the earlier of the later, the younger of the older. Yet it is not uncommon for those books that do the bridging, the main works, to have (despite disagreements) the sense to stick together. Some of them have no doubt been made for the sake of the others, the less fortunate ones, to pull them out of the murk into which they are plunged by a moment's of public inattention. They exist against the *remainder*, as life-savers—we are anyhow speaking only of after-lives—giving the books thus rescued, half-submerged, a place in the succession. It's only much later, once our author has crossed the water and is no more, that the initially more successful of the lineage drift off,

---

[*] Nietzsche, *Human, All Too Human*, p. 248, vol. 2, sec. 152; p. 209, vol. 2, sec. 1.

leaving behind the saved, the nearly drowned, like islands in
an archipelago, each home to a different species of bird.

§ The Author's Two Bodies

Contrary to the institution of monarchy, that of literature
admits of many kings within one (linguistically defined)
realm. The *body-natural* of every literary royalty remains the
same, but for aging, while the *body-literary* changes with each
book. In their collected works, the book-lives of that published royal corpus are ostended, "laid out," like the cadavers
they are, "end to end," to borrow Chateaubriand's haunting
phrase. The perishable body may go on to outlast those thus
coffined for public viewing; a writer may decide not to write
and remain king to the very end, and may thus see their
complete oeuvre interred before them. The tomb of literary
consecration only proving more durable in the long run.

§ Inside the Tomb

My ideal language is *epitaphic,* a language of considerate
brevity that honors the dead, their wish to be remembered.
It is, at the same time, a language that is *posthumous,* freed
from concerns over its timeliness or untimeliness and
addressed to those who are still alive. As epitaphic, it is a
language timeless enough to be carved in stone; as posthumous, it is impossible to write in while one is still alive. My
ideal language is writing (in any language) that has these two
characteristics. Writing done in this language is my inscription on the tomb of the past, but only if I am also already
inside the tomb.

§ "Come, my cold and stiff companion!"*

There are places where the authors we love because they mirror our thoughts and moods, or because we fit theirs so well, cannot follow us. We drag them along until the first tug of loneliness makes us pull too hard and they fall over like dummies — whereupon from sheer embarrassment we finally take our leave of them.

§ Safer Bet

Writers worth their salt do not wish to represent their time any more than for their time to represent them; they transcend both sorts of egoism. Their ties to the present are a historical accident, which nothing compels them to address. Writing only for posterity, on the other hand, is too risky; one's audience is one great unknown. That leaves our *ancestors*, a safer bet: and even here just the *literary* ones.

---

* Friedrich Nietzsche, *Thus Spoke Zarathustra*, ed. Adrian Del Caro and Robert B. Pippin, trans. Adrian Del Caro (Cambridge, UK: Cambridge University Press, 2006), p. 12, sec. 7.

∫ Leaving One's Mark

Making a contribution nowadays is subordinated to carving a niche for oneself, even if one is part of a team. It is the only way one can hope to stand out: individual contributions increasingly stand out only in *kinds*.

That is why "making it" more and more resembles what dogs and cats do to mark their territory. *That* in turn is why, on the face of it, the choice — cat or dog, loner or collaborator — seems to be exactly as before.

∫ Literary Sensation

It is to the market that we owe literary sensations, the "must-reads" that each season monopolize our attention. The excitement around certain releases goes a long way to offset the daily anxieties and general insecurity of the book economy. Oh the fun of bestseller lists! And the thrill of (the last remaining independent) bookstore queue! How can any of this be a sign of ill health, if the success of a few luminaries means death for those playing with such unsensational stakes?

§ High and Low

It's time we rejected the distinction between high- and lowbrow as it now stands. Not the distinction as such, just the significance of the height of the forehead and size of the supraorbital ridge. No rejection is effective without broad consensus, as in this case it is bound *not* to be. And no unpopular rejection holds unless a *replacement* so innocuous and intuitive is found that the majority won't even notice anything is amiss. From now on *highbrow* will mean "what surprises," and *lowbrow*, "what causes dismay, by being determined to say clearly and only one thing."

§ Castoffs

A You have to be a master of your art to leave perfect images on the cutting-room floor. Sometimes a great image, scene, line, word, piece has no place in a sequence and must be discarded.

B Yet we always doubt the master's mastery when we wish to see what he chose not to show us. Suppose Bach dropped some notes here and there and we nevertheless asked to hear them, what could it mean except that we might know better and judge differently? If we allow the latter, then we value our judgment above his. And if we agree with his decisions, our homage to his mastery is thoroughly compromised.

❡ Claqueurs

Serious, self-respecting artists do not waste time answering their critics. Instead, most work harder to cater to their taste. It is different with discourse, broadly speaking, where response and argument are considered the norm. In art, however, disputes of taste and truth can take place in silence; here critics prick up their ears and open their eyes long after the claqueurs have gone home.

❡ No-Power

> *Nearly all men are slaves for the same reason that the Spartans assigned for the servitude of the Persians — lack of power to pronounce the syllable, No. To be able to utter that word and live alone, are the only two means to preserve one's freedom and one's character.*
> —Nicholas Chamfort

> *Negation is a positive element of the whole.*
> —Stanisław Jerzy Lec[*]

It is of course not enough to say *no*. You need to say more, to elaborate. You can get away with naysaying only if the feedback is overwhelmingly positive — which, within the academic humanities, plagued by post-structuralist self-doubt, almost never happens. There saying no amounts to murder-suicide. Survival is one big hug all around. Division, negativity, disagreement are out of the question (in contrast to the sciences, which need disagreement like air to breathe). In these hard times, humanists must "like" one another. They must hold hands in a festival of mutual affirmation.

In reality, however, it is humanities "outreach" as eloquent polemic, contrarianism and indignation, provocative and barefaced, wielding the rhetoric of being-against, that for the time being gives humanists a stay of execution (the public takes note of dissent, and always wants more). The professors who quietly rail against the corporate world, afraid of offending their students, must recognize to whom they owe their respite: not to those higher up their greasy pole, who still shit on them, but to those on whom they just yesterday still openly... frowned.

---

[*] Chamfort, *Cynic's Breviary*, l. 17; Lec, *Myśli nieuczesane*, 62.

◊ Public Intellectual

Intellectuals today are compelled to "go public" if they want to remain intellectuals.

◊ Following Leaders

Followers on social media platforms possess an uncanny influence over existing relations of power. Twitter use poses a danger for any fixed attitudes towards political rulers. For many who are on it, following emerging "leaders," whose simultaneous status as "followers" is a matter of course, is part of a strategy to expand their own power base, and eventually to rise in standing themselves. As if that were not enough, the medium is a laboratory of dematerialized group behaviour, where those with a scientific bent can put their hypotheses to the test. In short, anyone who wishes to build a following will do well by being an avid follower, opportunistically. In this environment, the words of Ledru-Rollin continue to resonate: "There go the people. I must follow them, for I am their leader."[*]

---

[*] Suzy Platt, ed. *Respectfully Quoted: A Dictionary of Quotations Requested from the Congressional Research Service in 1989 by the Library of Congress* (1989; n.p.: New York: Dover, 2010), 194.

⸸ Leading Motives

The *leitmotif* often emerges late in the process of literary creation or reception; so, too, born leaders emerge or are recognized only when their followers are ready for them.

⸸ Easy Pickings (A Lamb Is a Lamb)

Many would swear it is better to be a bell-wether, leader of a flock, than a lone wolf. But the lone wolf begs to differ by licking his chops. (The bell he donates to a lone biker, to ward off demons on the road—which shows him to be not only better off, but good.)

⸸ Decoration

With some exceptions, self-glorification is the opposite of self-torment, yet wants it presupposed: it keeps it in sight like a Sword of Damocles, but on tougher string.

⸹ Common, senses of

What is dismissed as common nonsense often makes uncommon sense.

⸹ Madness in Literature

The writing of derangement under the aegis of literature, like the painting of outsider art, puts culture into question — and redeems it as well.

⸹ Ouroborous

We are undermining the value of critical literary study outside of literary practice, which not coincidentally is beginning to take itself — literature, contemporary and historical — for its object.

⸹ In the Tower

In the Tower of Babel, "experimental" literature had the last floor. That was as far as the builders got before their tongues became confused.

§ Experimentalism

It is a lamentable if common misunderstanding that literary experiments, including highly conceptual ones that border on visual art, are by definition trying and difficult for the average reader. It is thought (and quixotically disbelieved) that the audience needs to be educated to appreciate them, preferably by being brought up on what we would now call the experimental tradition that properly begins with Modernism. In fact, difficulty and sciolistic requirements of this sort have little to do with a work's being experimental. The condition of experimentality is testing not the public's patience, but the *author's*. The experiment is not, in other words, on the reader but on the maker of the experiment. It is not about pushing the limits of convention to see what will fly, but about what can be *stood*—endured—in the process of writing.

Before accusing me of measuring experimentation by a personal yardstick, come up with an alternative that will knock literature out of its present comfort zone.

§ Paradoxes of Experimentalism

Experimental literature needs experimental publishing—publishing that, like it, can afford to fail completely. In this it differs from experimental science, which recognizes the principle as self-evident without presenting an actual liability to scientific publishing.

∫ Tapped Potential

As counter-logic to literature's Enlightenment-era institutionalization, the French "workshop of potential literature," or Oulipo, pushed the idea of the scientific institution to an absurd extreme. It appropriated the circular logics of calculation and relentless experimentation, of rationalization and scientificity, adopting them where they were least expected—in the workroom of creativity. Rigid mechanical procedures became the enabling and ordering principles for some of the most singular creative productions ever undertaken. Its great achievement was twofold: first, in demonstrating the compatibility of technical constraints (linguistic, mathematical, logical) with even the most extravagant literary experimentation, building on precursors like Raymond Roussel; and, second, in underscoring the fundamental arbitrariness of such constraints. The operation thus went well beyond subversion and parody—well beyond having fun with the rigid and self-imposed rules of a confident rationality. In this way, the experiments of Oulipo helped turn institutionalized reason against itself, commandeering what was alien and threatening to it. The power of certain literature to exorcise the evils of rationality may be exaggerated. But, unlike some reason, some superstition never killed anyone.

⸹ Magpies

It will strike those convinced art in general is, and has long been, chiefly about vanguard innovation as false that, at least in the case of literary art, the loudest voices are conservative. To think how much energy has been expended to conserve the tradition and defend the classics from attacks on literature as *art*, rather than mere wordplay or verbal communication.

How different things are with visual art, which, since the dramatic strides of literacy across the globe, has thrown off much of its former functional, didactic constraints. An enormous boon came to it in the form of mass advertising, opening up new visual horizons rather than limiting them; marketing, after all, reconceived the message along subliminal lines, relying not on verbal but on sub-verbal cues. Surrealist imagery sold commodities like surrealist poetry never could. (Design was another natural home for visual experimentation.)

Experiments in literature, by contrast, have rarely been met with the fanfare lavished on the plastic arts, and in their heyday relied on graphic embellishment. The vertiginous fall in the prospects of literary experimenters corresponds closely to the stratospheric rise of money and media attention given to visual art. If institutionally art and creative writing seem to be on par, professionally they have never been more divergent. Until a new, economically viable model is found to secure a future for the professional creative writer, experimentation will be a luxury at which the republic of letters looks askance.

◊ Error Spotters

From the decline in errata we can reason that either we are making fewer errors in print or fewer of us notice them, which may mean their number is on the rise. Regardless, we do not bother publishing errata as we used to; mistakes have become too expensive to fix. It is more prudent to leave correcting to the next edition. Response and demand will tell if it is needed at all.

The drop in errata is the surest sign of disinvestment in the medium of print. Perhaps e-books are emended by elves to perfection, and error-free when printed on demand? Most likely remain untouched, attention to detail falling with increased volume. But there are always readers bothered by error in the most obscure spots. A way might be found to import their corrections. The time has come for crowd-sourced errata and critical re-editions—focalized, rather than scattered across readers' personal sites. But the copyright holders are not ready for this, and also not doing their job as in decades past. So we may be forgiven for thinking of telling them to "s**t or get off the pot." Until flawless versions are produced, be it by publishers' elves or freelance pedants on the web, we must write our own corrigenda, or give up on errors on the spot.

⸿ Scribes

Centuries after the mass die-off of monastic scribes as a consequence of Gutenberg's invention, the Google Books project is bringing them back. They are now the human operators of OCR scanners. But their breed will soon disappear again until a time when a thorough review and philological rectification of the greatest error-riddled digital library the world has ever seen can no longer be postponed. Consider at random what they shall then have to reckon with:

> *All the finest feelings, he insisted, were strongest in the country; conjugal and parental affection, in particular, the source of all that is good, were very much blunted, in great cities, by the attention, imagination, and passions being divided among different women. "If men c< will live in crowded cities/' said he, " the women should be confined, "as in Asia, in harams. I am told, Li that the great business of the fine G 3 «hfolks "folks in London, is, to debauch the u women, who, on their parts, are not 4<a little vain of being thought "worthy of being vessels of dishonour a to the men." But there was an air of whim in all that this singular person did, as well as of fense in all that he said. In the midst of this conversation, after supper, a mephitic air was perceived, of which the dog, who fat near the door, was suspected of having been the chymist.**

Our neo-scribes will be no less silent and absorbed in their labour than the scribes of old — for this time around they will be thoroughly mechanized.

---

* William Thomson, *Mammuth, or Human Nature Displayed on a Grand Scale: In a Tour with the Tinkers, into the Inland Parts of Africa. By the Man in the Moon*, vol. 1 (London: J. Murray, 1789), 125–26.

⸹ Inkhorn

Before you level at me the charge of *inkhorn writer*, you must try to understand my reason for choosing "bookish words": they remind me there used to be such things as books.

⸹ Wordsmith

A   I use neither paper nor pen.

B   And you call yourself a writer?

A   Just as the theremin player calls herself a musician; it is proximity and attunement to one's instrument that matters. My brains are still where they should be: close to my hands, which roam a plastic keyboard (though I imagine not for much longer). Is what I describe any more outrageous than writing with my foot, or hammering out words as one does objects in a smithy?

§ Feathers

As I abandon paper and pen in favour of the keyboard, I hardly remember anymore what it was like to write longhand. At such times I stop typing and sign my name, just to make sure. But even this signature will disappear soon, when we revert to dyscriptia by signing with fingerprints. As I inspect it, on a sheet of low-grade paper stock, I notice its "feathers" or fuzzy edges; they resemble stray letters through a magnifying glass. Poring over these subvisible arabesques, these microscript accidents, too weak-eyed to decipher them, gives me pleasure.

But perhaps this is only a distraction, a fascination that everything analogue will hold for us. We will certainly find ways to recreate feathering, even if writing longhand will not last.

§ Coincidence of Invention

We meet over the page of a book. This book. Where I exist only thanks to you. And you, only thanks to me. You and I, we are creating each other right now. You the reader exist as long as you are with me (that much I guarantee). I the writer come in the same, *accompanied* way.

My physical status as a living person has nothing any more to do with *me*; "I" might even already have passed on. But I've no doubt that *I* still live, at least for *you*, even if *our* lives would be nothing without "you," there, reading this.

ʃ Philobiblon

Love affair with books? For the bookworms! How much more value in a good breakup; you get through more books! A healthy relationship of man and book is when they argue and move on.

ʃ Arks Out

With Noah in mind, we take one of every kind. We are forgiven for thinking that we singlehandedly save older, near-forgotten specimens from certain oblivion. And, given our limited time, capacity, and the taboo against reproduction, why should we take pairs over more ones-of-a-kind?

And thus those who love to read keep the worthy books afloat when new ones flood the market. It is this annual flood on which literary art drifts.

ʃ Jazz Funeral

There may be many parties celebrating your successes while you are still alive. But your posthumous fame — that gets decided at the wake, after you're gone. A wake can go one of two ways. You might get resurrected. Or put your celebrants to sleep.

§ Fans

In music and film, there is still a healthy ratio of producers to fans. I mean *just* fans. In literature, the fans are neither *just* fans, nor *just*.

§ Copycats

Copycats may spread a work's fame far and wide, but they rob the original of its distinction.

§ Non-Potable

Some sources of inspiration are just polluted wells.

§ Seniority

There are those who come to us, and those to whom we must come, in the guise of dreams, ghosts, or beggars.

∫ "My Undertaking"

Why does the grim ring of that expression strike me only now? I was too keen to escape the infantile ring of "my project."

∫ A Nagging Burden

Those still chasing chimeras are the lucky ones; they don't have one riding on their back. And it can be "as heavy as a sack of flour or coal,"* or — which is worse — no longer felt to be a burden at all.

∫ Loose Moorings

Tie your moorings loosely to ship out quickly, or else be ready to jump ship at the first signal. Often the greater risk is not shipwreck, but delay.

---

* Charles Baudelaire, "To Each His Chimera," in *Paris Spleen and La Fanfarlo*, trans. R.N. MacKenzie (New York: Hackett, 2008), 12.

§ *Credo*

The aphorist: the houdini of reason.

§ The Burning Book

A book too burns without being consumed. All it takes is a mind.

§ Out of Reach

Some books are best kept out of reach of children. They might yet make something of them.

§ Endings

Can be eelusory.

⋆⋆

www.ingramcontent.com/pod-product-compliance
Lightning Source LLC
Chambersburg PA
CBHW052040220426
43663CB00012B/2383